T0390169

Advances in African Economic, Social and Political Development

Series editors

Diery Seck, CREPOL—Center for Research on Political Economy, Dakar, Senegal
Juliet U. Elu, Morehouse College, Atlanta, USA
Yaw Nyarko, New York University, New York, USA

Africa is emerging as a rapidly growing region, still facing major challenges, but with a potential for significant progress—a transformation that necessitates vigorous efforts in research and policy thinking. This book series focuses on three intricately related key aspects of modern-day Africa: economic, social and political development. Making use of recent theoretical and empirical advances, the series aims to provide fresh answers to Africa's development challenges. All the socio-political dimensions of today's Africa are incorporated as they unfold and new policy options are presented. The series aims to provide a broad and interactive forum of science at work for policymaking and to bring together African and international researchers and experts. The series welcomes monographs and contributed volumes for an academic and professional audience, as well as tightly edited conference proceedings. Relevant topics include, but are not limited to, economic policy and trade, regional integration, labor market policies, demographic development, social issues, political economy and political systems, and environmental and energy issues.

More information about this series at http://www.springer.com/series/11885

Sam Moyo · Praveen Jha
Paris Yeros

Editors

Reclaiming Africa

Scramble and Resistance in the 21st Century

 Springer

Editors
Sam Moyo
African Institute for Agrarian Studies
Harare, Zimbabwe

Paris Yeros
Federal University of ABC
São Bernardo do Campo, São Paulo, Brazil

Praveen Jha
Centre for Economic Studies
  and Planning
Jawaharlal Nehru University
New Delhi, India

ISSN 2198-7262   ISSN 2198-7270   (electronic)
Advances in African Economic, Social and Political Development
ISBN 978-981-10-5839-4   ISBN 978-981-10-5840-0   (eBook)
https://doi.org/10.1007/978-981-10-5840-0

Library of Congress Control Number: 2018950205

This Springer imprint is published by the registered company Springer Nature Singapore Pte Ltd.
The registered company address is: 152 Beach Road, #21-01/04 Gateway East, Singapore 189721, Singapore

To Sam,
Teacher, comrade, brother, friend.
A luta continua!

Preface

Reclaiming Africa is the result of a tri-continental research project launched in 2011 by the Agrarian South Network (ASN), by the initiative of Sam Moyo. This is the third work in a series which began with *Reclaiming the Land* (2005) and *Reclaiming the Nation* (2011), thus bringing to fruition a trilogy which has given shape to the tri-continental trajectory of what has become ASN. This effort has evolved together with the principal activities of the network, namely the annual Agrarian Summer School, begun in 2009 at the African Institute for Agrarian Studies, in Harare, and the *Agrarian South: Journal of Political Economy*, founded in 2012, both also tri-continental in character.

The focus of this book on land grabs and the scramble for natural resources has been debated over several summer schools. It was made the main theme of the 2011 Summer School and continues to be discussed in the subsequent sessions in relation to diverse themes, such as land and agrarian reform, the peasantry, social movements, gender and labour. This, therefore, has been one of the most basic concerns in the intellectual evolution of ASN. And it could not be otherwise, given the intensity of land grabbing on the continent today, as well as the history of the scramble for Africa, which saw major land appropriations by European settlers.

The project has had a long gestation period. Delays such as this have often to do with inadequate funding, but unfortunately, this was not the real cause. In November 2015, we lost Sam in a tragic traffic accident in New Delhi, during a conference held at Jawaharlal Nehru University. Sam had always been the vital force of ASN, having conceived it and toiled under difficult circumstances to bring us all together and put us on the right track. He has now bequeathed this great treasure to us, for which we must show our gratitude by continuing the cause and taking it to a new level. After a period of mourning, we relaunched the book and have now brought it to a close. We are especially pleased to be publishing two chapters which Sam had drafted as lead author, Chap. 1, the Introduction, and Chap. 11 on the experience of Zimbabwe.

The book is composed of two parts. Part I focuses on the new competitors for Africa's land and natural resources, the so-called emerging countries, including China, South Africa, India and Brazil, whose role has been subject to much debate and controversy. Part II is devoted to national experiences of land grabbing, including by the weightier and more established scramblers of the North, as well as of experiences of resistance. Two countries are represented from each of the three regions, namely West, East and Southern Africa, including Mali, Senegal, Tanzania, Uganda, Zambia and Zimbabwe. The book includes an introduction by the editors and a conclusion by Issa Shivji.

We are grateful to the (renamed) Sam Moyo African Institute for Agrarian Studies for the moral and material support provided throughout this trying endeavour. We also express our gratitude to the Open Society Initiative for Southern Africa for the financial support provided to the 2011 Summer School; to our publisher, Springer, and its entire team for their kind patience; and to the contributing authors for their solidarity and perseverance.

Overview of the Chapters

The introductory chapter by Sam Moyo, Praveen Jha and Paris Yeros, entitled 'The Scramble for Land and Natural Resources in Africa', explores the historical and systemic dynamics of the new scramble for Africa and the current land grabbing patterns and agents. It is argued that, despite the emergence of new competitors from the South, the key drivers of the scramble remain the Western monopolies and their state patrons, in the course of the systemic crisis. It is also argued that the scramble has set off new structural tendencies on the continent which are transforming Africa's trajectory in the twenty-first century. The tendencies point towards a convergence of economic and social characteristics among the regions, within the overall trend of intensified marginalization and subordinate integration of the continent into the world economy. Nonetheless, new forms of resistance have also emerged, from the local to the national and regional levels, which have made concrete and substantial advances, especially in Southern Africa.

Chapter 2, by Valéria Lopes Ribeiro, entitled 'Chinese Expansion in Africa in the 21st Century: Characteristics and Impacts', argues that China's new position in the international economy, and especially the rise of Sino-African commercial and financial relations, has contributed to the improvement of macroeconomic conditions in Africa. Export volumes and export profits have increased, while investments and aid have created new opportunities. However, the new relationship has raised once again the fundamental question regarding African countries' dependence on primary goods exports. Ribeiro analyses the general features of Chinese expansion in Africa in the first decade of the twenty-first century, focusing on China's new commercial and financial relations with Africa and their impact on socio-economic trends and structural change on the continent.

Chapter 3, by William G. Martin, entitled 'South Africa and the New Scramble: The Demise of Sub-imperialism and the Rise of the East', argues that South Africa today cannot be considered a sub-imperialist state, despite its economic weight in Africa, and Southern Africa in particular. The question, Martin argues, is how

South Africa's relationship with Northern states and its African neighbours is changing in its reorientation to the East. The chapter discusses the different theoretical conceptions applied to South Africa before assessing South Africa's historical and current power across the region and the continent, empirically and historically. It is argued that South Africa has undergone transformations that are distinct from other semi-peripheral states. Furthermore, it is argued that the declining importance of the North and the creation of new networks of accumulation orienting the region and South Africa towards the East present new tendencies and conceptual anomalies.

Chapter 4, by Praveen Jha, Archana Prasad, Santosh Verma and Nilachala Acharya, entitled 'The Scramble for Africa's Agricultural Land: A Note on India's Excursus', maps the scope and extent of transnational land acquisitions and investments in Africa by Indian entities. It also establishes the links between such investments and state policy, for both the host and the destination countries. In order to bring out the broader implications associated with the ongoing scramble, the authors refer to the experiences of three nations with a high concentration of Indian investments, namely Ethiopia, Mozambique and Tanzania. The authors discuss the impacts of land investments on the livelihoods on smallholders and the accelerated process of marginalization of the peasantry.

Chapter 5, by Paris Yeros, Vitor E. Schincariol and Thiago Lima da Silva, entitled 'Brazil's Re-encounter with Africa: The Externalization of Domestic Contradictions', traces Brazil's Africa policy as a function of its changing position in the world economy and the trajectory of its internal contradictions. It is argued that the country's policy towards Africa is an expression of the evolution of its own settler capitalism and its articulation with monopoly capital and finance. Brazil's post-war transition, marked by conservative agrarian modernization, dependent industrialization and recent de-industrialization, saw the rapid, systematic and violent expulsion of the Black majority from the countryside, with universal suffrage only being established as late as the 1980s. This set the stage for a new set of contradictions that have left their mark in domestic and foreign policies alike. In its recent re-encounter with Africa, Brazil has been externalizing a set of domestic contradictions that are most clearly manifested in its conflicted approach to agricultural cooperation. The chapter outlines the main instruments and policies of cooperation in agriculture, as well as the general trends in economic relations.

Chapter 6, by Mamadou Goïta, entitled 'Land Grabbing, a Virus in the Fruit of Food Sovereignty in West Africa: A Case Study from "Office du Niger" Zone in Mali', presents the major challenges that have emerged in recent years in Mali, related to land governance, access to and securing of land for smallholder farmers and, most significantly, the appropriation of land by private national and international companies in areas with high agricultural potential. These challenges are related, more generally, to the current trends in the privatization of agricultural land in Mali. Land legislation has been under reform in Mali for diverse purposes, aiming to promote land registration, do away with public estate land, recognize customary rights in their diversity, as well as to promote the decentralization of land management through the creation of local land institution. Yet, in the context of the appropriation of large tracts of land, particularly in irrigated and irrigable areas, by private international and local players, the more progressive aspects of the legislative reforms may be marginalized under the weight of land grabs and land speculation. The chapter begins with some conceptual issues related to sustainable natural resource management before focusing on the land question in Mali and the specific case of land appropriation in the Office du Niger (ON) zone.

Chapter 7, by Abdourahmane Ndiaye, entitled 'The Scramble for Agricultural Land in Senegal: Land Privatization and Inclusion?', considers whether land grabbing, as a set of principles and a system of actors, has the capacity to operate as a lever for development. The first aim is to bring forward and discuss the foundations and challenges of the land question. Second, taking as the point of departure the contradictions linked to the plurality of legal systems governing land and the conflicts they generate, Ndiaye questions the role of public policies and land policies in the scramble for agricultural land in Senegal. Third, the details of land acquisitions in Senegal are presented. The analysis makes it possible to assess land utilization between 2006 and 2010, map out a typology of investment projects and evaluate tentatively their early impacts on economic, social and environmental developments in Senegal.

Chapter 8, by Godfrey Eliseus Massay and Telemu Kassile, entitled 'Land-Based Investments in Tanzania: Legal Framework and Realities on the Ground', focuses on the socio-economic crisis that Tanzania experienced in the 1970s and 1980s. It is argued that, in an attempt to turn things around and accelerate economic growth, the government embarked on a broad range of policies, legislations and institutional reforms, which opened the doors for foreign direct investment. Further initiatives have been taken to create a more open environment for investments to flourish in the country. This chapter provides highlights and an analysis of the legal framework governing investment in Tanzania, discusses the context of investment within the existing legal framework, provides an overview of land acquisition procedures and gives an analysis of some land deals. The findings show that mixed procedures, some of which are not guided by laws, are currently used to acquire land for investment in Tanzania. Moreover, land acquisition and compensation practices are poor and have flaws in the way community consultations are carried out.

Chapter 9, by Giuliano Martiniello, entitled 'Accumulation by Dispossession and Resistance in Uganda', explores the dynamics of escalating large-scale land acquisitions in Uganda, their impact on the agrarian social structure and their underlying political and social struggles. In doing so, Martiniello sheds light on the drivers, agents and implications of large-scale land enclosures, as well as the related social struggles, which have all been amplified by neoliberalism. The chapter enquires into why and how land enclosures are occurring in Uganda, as well as the ways in which everyday struggles are shaped by, and are shaping, the mechanisms for uneven capitalist development. Framing land struggles at the core of social analysis, Martiniello argues, serves to illuminate the relational character of accumulation, dispossession and resistance.

Chapter 10, by Horman Chitonge, entitled 'Customary Land in Zambia: The New Scramble and the Evolving Socio-political Relations', argues that the demand for land has increased over the last two decades in Zambia, due to various reasons including population growth, the growing global interest in farmland and also the government development strategy of 'opening up the countryside' for development. The conversion of customary land, which is part of the broader land grabbing trend supported by the government, is creating many challenges. A close analysis suggests a deep-seated struggle for the control of resources between the state and the traditional authorities, resulting in tension and conflicts in rural and peri-urban communities, which is compromising the current and future livelihoods of the rural poor and promotes social segregation in the countryside. Conversion of customary land into leasehold tenure is broadly analysed in the context of large-scale land acquisitions.

Chapter 11, by Sam Moyo, Walter Chambati and Paris Yeros, entitled 'Land and Natural Resources in Zimbabwe: Scramble and Resistance', examines the contemporary scramble by capital for the control of Zimbabwe's land, natural resources and minerals, in the light of three policies that have been elaborated and put into practice, especially since 2000: the Fast-Track Land Reform Programme, the Indigenisation Policy and the Look East Policy. The authors analyse the state-led restructuring of capital and the diversification of foreign investments under the weight of Western sanctions and political destabilization, as well as the promotion of accumulation strategies from below and by domestic capital. The authors highlight the contradictions of these processes and their impact on the evolution of national policy and strategy. The various forms of resistance are also brought to the fore, including at the local level and at the levels of regional and larger foreign policy.

Chapter 12, by Issa G. Shivji, entitled 'Whither Africa in the Global South? Lessons of Bandung and Pan-Africanism', traces the trajectories of the Bandung and Pan-Africanist projects to assess the present conjuncture. It is argued that Bandung and Pan-Africanism were, first and foremost, political projects, not subservient to economics. They were ideological rallying points providing vision, hope and dignity to the struggling peoples at the periphery. They were also anti-imperialist in their conception and development, seeking to provide an alternative to imperialist integration. Yet, they were led by bourgeois forces which failed to install an auto-centric development path, and this proved to be their failure as peoples' projects. The bourgeoisies in Asia and the proto-bourgeoisies in Africa were eventually compradorised, thus yielding BRICS and NEPAD projects of today, both integrationist and both subject to the logic of primitive accumulation.

Overall, the book offers fresh perspectives on the systemic, continental, regional, national and local processes entailed in the new scramble for land and natural resources in Africa. Having matured over several years within ASN, the book provides substantial coherence in its approach to the debate, highlighting the adverse, immediate and long-term effects of the scramble on the national and regional trajectories of the continent. Yet, the book also does not fall into the trap of postulating an analytical equivalence with regard to the systemic conditions and modes of engagement of the established Northern and 'emerging' Southern competitors. On the contrary, it seeks to move the debate towards a more conceptually rigorous and empirically grounded consideration of the contradictions underway.

New Delhi, India   Praveen Jha
São Bernardo do Campo, Brazil   Paris Yeros

Contents

About the Editors

Sam Moyo (1954–2015) was Executive Director of the African Institute for Agrarian Studies (AIAS, 2002–2015), Harare, Zimbabwe; President of the Council for the Development of Social Science Research in Africa (CODESRIA, 2009–2011); and Founding Editor-in-Chief of *Agrarian South: Journal of Political Economy* (2012–2015). An eminent scholar of land and agrarian studies, he published widely in academic journals and authored several books, the most recent being *The Agrarian Question in the Neoliberal Era* (Pambazuka, 2011), *Land and Agrarian Reform in Zimbabwe: Beyond White-Settler Capitalism* (CODESRIA, 2013) and *Land in the Struggles for Citizenship in Africa* (CODESRIA, 2015).

Praveen Jha is Professor of economics at the Centre for Economic Studies and Planning (CESP) and Adjunct Professor at the Centre for Informal Sector and Labour Studies (CISLS), School of Social Sciences, Jawaharlal Nehru University (JNU), New Delhi, India. He has been a visiting fellow at a number of universities and institutions in Germany, China, Switzerland, South Africa and Zimbabwe and has collaborated in research programmes with UN agencies, including ILO, UNICEF, UNDP and FAO. He has published widely on labour and agrarian relations, the economics of education and public finance. He is Co-editor of *Agrarian South: Journal of Political Economy.*

Paris Yeros is Professor of international economics at the Federal University of ABC (UFABC), São Paulo, Brazil, and Coordinator of the Post-graduate Programme in World Political Economy. He has been a visiting fellow at universities and institutes in Brazil, South Africa and Zimbabwe. He has published widely on labour and agrarian relations, social movements and nationalism. He is Co-editor of *Agrarian South: Journal of Political Economy.*

Part I
Introduction

The Scramble for Land and Natural Resources in Africa

Sam Moyo, Praveen Jha and Paris Yeros

Introduction

The transnational competition for the control of Africa's land and natural resources has been escalating since the early 2000s. Increased land grabbing drew the attention of key media, policy and academic circles around 2008, when world food deficits and food prices spiked and popular protests grew (Moyo 2008). This recent wave of primitive accumulation is shifting the land ownership and property relations significantly, reconfiguring the social character of the utilization of natural resources and restructuring the continent's accumulation trajectory. Furthermore, it is deepening the integration of Africa's agriculture and natural resources into world markets, leading to the intensification of labour exploitation and depletion of natural

Sam Moyo (1954–2015)

This paper was first presented by Sam Moyo at the Round Table Dialogue on 'Land Reform, Land Grabbing and Agricultural Development in Africa in the Twenty-first Century', 17–18 June 2013, Addis Ababa, Ethiopia. The authors are grateful to Ndabezinhle Nyoni, Steve Mberi and Tatenda Matengu of the Sam Moyo African Institute for Agrarian Studies (AIAS) for their research assistance.

S. Moyo
African Institute for Agrarian Studies, Harare, Zimbabwe

P. Jha (✉)
Centre for Economic Studies and Planning, Jawaharlal Nehru University,
New Delhi, India
e-mail: praveenjha2005@gmail.com

P. Yeros
Federal University of ABC (UFABC), CECS, sala D337, Alameda da Universidade,
s/n°, Bairro Anchieta, 09606-045, São Bernardo do Campo, São Paulo, Brazil
e-mail: parisyeros@gmail.com

Table 1 Sectors affected by land deals in Africa (2000–2012)

Sector	No. of deals	%	Hectares (millions)	%
Agriculture	323	72	12,317,372	73
Forestry	37	8	1,008,437	6
Livestock only	45	10	304,545	2
Mining	7	2	53,040	0
Tourism	10	2	1,844,019	11
Industry	4	1	30,000	0
Conservation	4	1		0
No information	18	4	1,345,096	8
Total	448	100	16,902,509	100

Source Compiled by authors from Land Matrix (2012)

resources. The net impact of these processes is the expanded marginalization of rural communities and expulsion from the countryside, without resolving chronic problems of food insecurity, unemployment, low agricultural productivity and poverty.

The extent of the area being acquired by over 130 foreign investor firms, originating from over 30 countries, ranges from a high of over 50 million ha of large-scale landholdings to around 17 million ha, and entails about 500 'commercial' land deals (Land Matrix Data 2012). This amounts to the alienation of between 8% and 15% of Africa's cultivable land, at an annual rate ranging from 4 to 10.7 million ha. This surpasses by far the annual rate of colonial land grabs that occurred in Southern African settler colonies at the end of the nineteenth century, although the proportion of land alienated still remains much lower.

This trend is alarming for a continent in which peasant agriculture remains the main economic activity and location of social reproduction and in which biodiversity directly provides a range of raw materials for households, including wood fuel, bush meat and various medicinal products for the majority of the population (FAO 2001a; UNEP 2002). Indeed, although Africa holds 20% of the world's land mass, only 21% of it is considered suitable for cultivation (FAO 2001b).[1]

Around 75% of the land grabs are targeting the agricultural and livestock sectors, putatively to produce a variety of agricultural commodities (Table 1). Forestry and tourism account for 17% of the land being grabbed (also called a 'green grab'), with ecological services dominating the acquisition or concessioning of woodlands, wildlife sanctuaries and nature conservancies under the pretext of mitigating climate change and other adverse ecological processes. At the same time, two percent of such land is used for mining purposes, given its concentration in a few site-specific endowments, and a lesser amount for urban-based activities related to industry and other real-estate purposes.

---

[1]By the turn of the century, about 200 million ha (32% of the suitable area) were being cultivated and 30% of the total land area (892 million ha) was under permanent pasture (FAOSTAT 2001).

There has been a systematic effort to justify these land acquisitions by proposing that they are developmentally benign and will compensate for the finance and technology gaps facing Africa, so as to enhance productivity, utilize 'underutilised' land, and obtain food security through a new 'green' revolution (Moyo 2008). Externally derived examples of 'successful' agricultural development, such as Brazil's idealized bi-modal agrarian experience, have been touted as the solution, despite the evidence that Africa's 'food crisis' reflects land-use shifts and productivity declines occasioned by the promotion of cash crops at the expense of food corps initiated under colonial rule, and the more recent neoliberal retreat of the state from promoting domestic food supplies, accompanied by the growing reliance on food imports to achieve 'food security'. Indeed, key multilateral financial institutions and Western think-tanks have sought to posit land alienation and markets as presenting 'opportunities' for investments in Africa (World Bank 2008; Cotula et al. 2009).

This land grab constitutes a 'scramble' in the classic sense of the term, involving primitive accumulation by monopolistic firms and escalating 'geopolitical' competition by major states, in a context of a generalized systemic crisis, compounded by energy and ecological crises (Moyo et al. 2012). Yet, the land grab debate has generally eschewed analyses of the systemic roots of the scramble, reproducing Eurocentric distortions regarding, especially, the rise of Asian influence on the continent. In particular, the debate has served to reinforce the narrow perspective which holds that external investment under the control of Western monopoly-finance capital remains the key driver of a new African growth path.

In the following sections, we will explore the historical and systemic dynamics of the scramble, the current land grabbing patterns and their agents and the overall structural tendencies that are transforming Africa's trajectory in the twenty-first century.

Historical and Systemic Dynamics of the Scramble for Africa

Systemic Crisis and Transition

The current scramble for Africa is shaped by important historical specificities associated with the continent's pre-colonial integration into the world economy as a slave reserve, its relatively recent history of colonial subjugation, which on the most part came to an end in the 1960s, and its settler-colonial experience in Southern Africa, which ended as recently as the mid-1990s. The opening up of the continent in the 1980s by means of neoliberal structural adjustment programmes removed a significant level of protection which had hitherto been established, leading to the intensified penetration of monopoly capital and the deepening of the continent's dependence on the West, not least through an externally coordinated system of debt management. This turn of events consolidated the West's neo-colonial strategy, denounced by Kwame Nkrumah already in the mid-1960s (Nkrumah 1965). In all, the above sequence of historical events has enabled an intense and continuous process of primitive accumulation on the continent, which has been fortified ideologically by the racialised global culture woven over centuries of European expansion, yielding an enduring 'hierarchy' of peoples and exuding special contempt for, and paternalism towards, Africa.

Primitive accumulation under capitalism is not a one-off event to establish the historical conditions for expanded reproduction (the pure form of exploitation by capital over labour). Imperialism has systematically deployed extra-economic and violent force to commodify both labour and land and to offload the costs of social reproduction onto the working peoples themselves, especially women. To this day, super-exploitation continues to be the norm, that is, the exploitation of labour through the appropriation of labour power far beyond the labour time necessary for the social reproduction of the workforce. While the first wave of monopoly competition, militarism and colonial expansion in the late nineteenth century set the stage for the 'classic' scramble for Africa, it is now clear that the requirement of primitive accumulation and scramble remains the fundamental pillar of monopoly competition, in its perennial search to overcome recurrent crises of accumulation at the centre and re-create the necessary relationship between primitive accumulation and expanded reproduction for the reproduction of capital on a world scale.

This historical necessity constitutes an enduring centre–periphery contradiction, draining surpluses systematically from the periphery to the centre. The intrinsic economic mechanics of this relationship have been conceptualized and elaborated especially over the last half-century: they consist in an arsenal of mechanisms from unequal exchange, to profit repatriation, payments of interest, dividends and royalties, and generally the imposition of monopoly rents (Marini 1969, 2000; Patnaik 1972; Rodney 1973; Amin 1976, 2010; Dos Santos 1978; Patnaik 1999; Patnaik and Patnaik 2017). The cumulative historical weight of unequal development has resulted, especially in the postwar period, in a massive and accelerating rural–urban exodus in the peripheries and the creation of a global reserve army of labour of monumental proportions. This, in turn, has created permanently semi-proletarianized social formations, reproducing themselves in highly oppressive, violent, migrant and degraded conditions (Moyo and Yeros 2005; Shivji 2009; Moyo et al. 2012; Tsikata 2016; Prasad 2016; Jha et al. 2017; Schincariol et al. 2017).

Imperialism evolved significantly in the postwar period. On the one hand, it entered a phase marked by a vicious cycle of social, energy, and climate crises, which monopoly capitalism is patently unable to overcome. On the other, it is a phase deprived of colonies and constrained by the globalization of the states-system, even despite the neo-colonial transition. For the systemic rivalry of the early postwar period which subjected monopoly capitalism to unprecedented contestations by socialist revolutions and national liberation movements established a new room for maneuver across the South and experimentation with new development strategies. In this sense, the same neo-colonial situation that has given second life to monopoly capital, especially by the shift towards internationalized production and a collective form of imperialism (Amin 2003; Foster et al. 2011), has also established the possibility of new regionalisms, new tri-continental alliances, and new visions of a post-imperialist world led by the peoples of the South.

If the above has been a basic systemic shift under imperialism, as we have argued (Moyo et al. 2012), its second important feature has been the dollarization and subsequent financialization of monopoly capitalism as a means of systematically dislocating the crisis of accumulation, spatially and temporally. Indeed, the reincarnation of finance capital anchored in the dollar has been an intrinsic aspect of collective imperialism. If finance capital in the 'classical' period of imperialism was strongly linked to industrial expansion and secondarily to speculative activities—even if the latter had profound effects on colonial expansion—the centre of gravity today has shifted much more resolutely from production to finance. Not only has finance gained a life of its own, industrial enterprises have themselves become 'financialised', in the sense of drawing an ever-greater part of their profits from financial instruments, including aggressive speculation on the energy, mineral and food commodities on which the South so intensely depends. As such, beyond the process of accumulation conducted by adding to the stock of capital, financialized accumulation gives priority to adding to the stock of financial assets, to the point where speculative asset-pricing has transformed asset-price bubbles into the engine of global growth (Foster 2010a, b). This has established monopoly-finance capital as the principal agent of imperialism today.

A third systemic shift, which has created a new series of controversies, concerns the rise of semi-peripheral states to global prominence, as these have sought to gain their own footing within the system of monopoly-finance capital. On one level, this is a concrete result of the systemic rivalry of the postwar period, noted above, by the fact that diverse development paths advanced to the point of obtaining substantial monopolies, both private and state-owned, with roots in the semi-peripheries themselves. Yet, this has been a profoundly contradictory rise among states with very diverse economic structures, trajectories, and politics. The key question remains as to the systemic function of these semi-peripheries: are they reproducing monopoly capitalism, giving it a 'third' life? Or are they breaking it up into a 'multipolar' world? Are they reproducing the logic of the centre–periphery contradiction via a systemic 'sub-imperialism'? Or are they overcoming this logic, creating new room for maneuver for the South as a whole?

What is certain is that much of this debate has not adequately penetrated the systemic logic of monopoly capitalism, leading to moralistic condemnations or celebrations of the phenomenon in question. There has also been significant dissonance and confusion regarding the conceptual terms employed (including 'multipolarity' and 'sub-imperialism'), such that opportunistic conceptual conflations have flourished, not least by the reduction of imperialism to 'sub-imperialism'. Indeed, the theory of sub-imperialism, irrespective of its strengths or weaknesses, has given play to serial emerging-power bashing. For our purposes, two points should be stressed. First, we are dealing with a system in deep crisis, which renders the rise of the semi-peripheries unstable and unviable as an historical phenomenon. Indeed, it has strongly been argued deflarionary pressures on the South are the heart of imperialism (Patnaik and Patnaik 2017) and also that the emergence of just one of these semi-peripheries, China, spells the demise of the capitalist system as a whole in the twenty-first century (Li 2009), despite the pronouncements or intentions of the country's leadership.

Second, monopoly capitalism, by its very logic, bucks any sharing of its extraordinary profits with aspiring newcomers to the club, such that emerging semi-peripheries must be resubordinated by the instruments of the dollarized-financialized system, or otherwise crushed by military means—even the use of nuclear weapons. The primordial menace for the super-exploited working peoples of the South, therefore, including those of the semi-peripheries, remains the collective imperialism of the US-led alliance and its genocidal reflexes. This is precisely the systemic context in which the scramble for Africa is playing out, and which should leave no doubt as to which alliances should be prioritized and what kind of counter-strategy should be developed. What is required is neither a moralistic condemnation of the contradictions of the semi-peripheries in question, nor a celebration of their participation in the scramble, but the rekindling of the spirit of Non-Alignment and the elaboration of a new Positive Non-alignment strategy relevant to the systemic transition underway (Moyo and Yeros 2013).

Antecedents of the Current Scramble

Land alienation in Africa has a longer, almost uninterrupted history, although variegated among the different regions of Africa based upon different modes of colonial capitalist penetration. The first major wave of land and mineral grabs accompanied settler colonial expansion, mainly in the Africa of the 'labour reserves' (Algeria, South Africa, Rhodesia, Namibia, and Kenya). This was paralleled by resource grabs in the 'concessionary' economies of Central Africa, via the establishment of mining and agricultural enclaves, but also, to a much lesser extent, in the colonial trade economies of West Africa (Amin 1972). While in the settler colonies, the dispossession of peasant lands was not complete, it substantially undermined the peasantry, indeed, almost completely in South Africa.

Land alienation, displacement of the peasantry, and extra-economic coercion of labour epitomized the first wave of capitalist penetration in the settler colonies, until the mid-1900s (Arrighi 1973). Monopolistic control over national water resources and public infrastructural investments enabled the expansion of white-owned large-scale commercial farms based on private property rights, while spatially segregating black Communal Areas and establishing the conditions for the super-exploitation of cheap migrant labor. The extent of land alienation varied (Table 2), yet the whole region was drawn into the settler dynamic. After World War II, the accumulation trajectory was adjusted through state promotion of new 'enclaves' of agro-industrial estates in the settler colonies, and, on a smaller scale, in the neighboring territories, alongside renewed extra-economic compulsion of migrant labor. Overall, this resulted not in the creation of 'enclaves' as such, but a

Table 2 Settler alienation of land in Southern Africa

Country	Land alienated by settlers (percent)		White settlers (percent of population)	
	1958	2000	1960	2000
Angola	6.0	5.4	1.0	0.2
Botswana	0.0	5.0	0.3	0.5
Lesotho	5.0	5.0	0.3	0.8
Malawi	43.0	4.3	8.0	0.4
Namibia	43.0	44.0	19.4	11.1
South Africa	89.0	83.0	2.8	13.7
Swaziland	49.0	40.0	0.2	–
Zambia	3.0	3.1	3.0	0.1
Zimbabwe	49.0	41.0	7.1	0.8

Sources Hendricks (2000), figures for 1958 and 1960; CIA (2001), figures for 2000

'functional dualism' which subjugated labor and repressed peasant farming through discriminatory commodity markets, shifting production from peasant foods towards commodities dominated by large farmers, with the support of state marketing boards and European merchants.[2]

In 'non-settler Africa', two broad land alienation histories prevailed under colonial rule (Amin 1972). In the concessionary economies, largely in Central Africa, land alienation by European trading and mining companies led to the creation of a few significant enclaves formed around agricultural plantations, with rudimentary agro-processing facilities, as well as mining enclaves. The mode of primitive accumulation entailed raw material plunder and limited infrastructural investments. Meanwhile, in the colonial trade economies, which evolved from two centuries of European mercantilism, there was widespread African resistance to Lord Lugard's attempts to alienate land in the British colonies (Mamdani 1996). This led to the pervasive growth of small cultivators (Mafeje 2003). Crucially, this mode of colonization also entailed the institutionalization of labour migration, including the incorporation of migrant farmers from the northern territories of West Africa into the economies of the coastal and forest regions. This led to the creation of diverse peasantries, including independent lineage producers, farming labour tenancies and various forms of sharecropping arrangements. Smaller scale agricultural estate enclaves (for palm oil production) also emerged in various colonies.

The belated decolonization of the continent in the 1960s left little room for nation-building, compared to other continents and regions in the South. Indeed, between decolonization and neoliberal restructuring, less than two decades transpired, truncating the tentative drive towards autonomous development. Moreover, in the former settler Africa specifically, where historical land grabs peaked by 1960, decolonisation was effectively conditioned upon economic liberalization, as the

---

[2]For an elaboration of the concept of 'functional dualism', see de Janvry (1981).

Cold War came to an end, and acceptance of the colonial legacy of racially unequal property rights, starting with Zimbabwe in 1980 (Moyo and Yeros 2013).

In the 1960s, colonial dispossession gave way to the developmentalist policies of the newly independent states, although some land alienation occurred via state-led 'modernisation' projects (Moyo 2008). The latter sought to promote expanded reproduction among the peasantries, through improved productivity and access to markets, albeit enabling the extraction of surplus value through marketing monopolies (Shivji 2009). Exploitative labor regimes were also moderated by rescinding rural taxes and rationalizing institutionalized labor migration. Nonetheless, surplus extraction and an increasingly extroverted orientation of African agriculture persisted within the developmentalist strategy, which was promoted as a means to finance the expansion of Import Substitution Industrialization (ISI), including piecemeal attempts to nurture larger-scale capitalist farmers and some state farms (Mafeje 2003; Mkandawire 2011). These experiments lasted for a relatively short time, before the whole continent was resubordinated to intensified primitive accumulation.

At this juncture, the 1980s, the distorted agrarian transitions in Africa came to be blamed by the Bretton Woods institutions on the 'inefficiencies' of state interventions, such as in trade and domestic markets, and state farming (Mkandawire and Saludo 1999). By the imposition of conditionalities for the refinancing of debt, African states were compelled via structural adjustment programmes to cease subsidies to agriculture, at the neglect of peasant farmers, while state-owned agricultural estates began to be gradually privatized.

The immediate precursor of the current scramble for Africa is what we have called the 'second phase' of land alienation, which took off in the 1990s, precisely under structural adjustment, when land tenure reforms were set in motion to enable the commodification of land held under customary tenure and its conversion into private property (Moyo 2008; Moyo et al. 2012). This wave of land alienation was led by aspiring domestic bourgeoisies under the wing of foreign capital and World Bank advice, shifting land use to 'non-traditional' crops, such as cut flowers, horticulture and tourism (Moyo 2000). Thus, the neoliberal prying open and financialization of African economies reinforced a 'silent' and 'scattered', smaller-scale process of land alienation by domestic and foreign capital, at this time. The combined process of liberalization and renewed land alienation extended the disarticulation of African economies and increased their dependence on food aid and imports. Rather than enhancing the participation of the majority of small African producers, agrarian reforms under neoliberalism mainly sought commodity marketing and land tenure reforms, which led to the deeper integration into the world food system and prepared the ground for the current land grabbing.

Indeed, the current scramble cannot be understood without reference to neoliberal economic and land tenure reforms, which consolidated the position of local and foreign capitalists during the 1990s.

The 'Third Wave' of Land Alienation

The current process of land alienation in Africa is widely experienced as the 'third wave' of primitive accumulation and is combined with a wider scramble for mineral energy and biogenetic resources, amounting to a comprehensive scramble under neo-colonial conditions. Much of the new land grabbing is associated with the acquisition of previously privatised large estates, which the newly independent states had already alienated, although peasant 'communal' lands have increasingly come under the hammer. A renewed interest in land appropriation for the production of food and biofuels has widened the scope of primitive accumulation and the geographic origin of the investors. The land grabs include private investors and capital funds from as far afield as the United States, Europe, China, South Korea, the Gulf States and Brazil (GRAIN 2008).

To be sure, the more complex interlocking investments made by monopoly-finance capital, including the Western agro-industrial complex, energy firms and capital funds, are the key drivers of the land and resource grabs. The overall strategy is to broaden the scope of speculation in agricultural and energy commodities in various regions of the world. Africa is regarded as the 'last frontier', with putatively extensive 'underutilised' and 'unowned' land. The interest is to hold diverse land and resource assets in order to spread risk and enhance security, while realizing extraordinary profits through the acquisition of cheap land and tapping into the growing labour reserves (Moyo et al. 2013). Even so, the speculative drive has only fed upon an established historical structure of demand compression and super-exploitation in the South, which has undermined the capacity of the world's peasantries to produce food crops and defend national sovereignty (Patnaik 2008; Patnaik and Patnaik 2017).

The third wave of land alienation, which intensified during the food-price crisis from 2005, has been wrongly explained via a supposed increase in grain consumption, above own production, in India and China. Initially, the causes highlighted were the growth of demand for feedstock to supply the rising middle-class demands for high protein meats in these regions and the search for stable supplies by food deficit countries of the Middle East. Others pointed to the reduction of Western grain stocks due to weather-induced harvest failure, especially in Australia; or the restriction of rice and wheat, albeit after the fact, by countries such as Thailand, Vietnam, India, Russia and Argentina (Mitchell 2008; IFPRI 2010).

Eventually, these explanations gave way to considerations regarding the effects of the surge in the price of oil and, hence, of farm input prices, with the diversion of grain to biofuel production being identified as the key problem. It has now been convincingly shown that, while the diversion of food production to agro-fuels and the oil-related price increases accounted for 85% of the food price increases, this process is itself closely tied to the financial crisis and the ensuing asset-price bubbles targeting agricultural commodities (Ghosh 2008; Tabb 2008).

The scramble is the natural result of overall systemic pressures, combined with regional dynamics and some conjunctural events. It is thus important to note that, alongside recurrent financial bubbles, the prospect of prolonged instability in Western Asia following the 9/11 attacks on the United States triggered a new US strategy for the control of oil production in Africa—as detailed in the Cheney Report on energy (NEPDG 2001)—as well as China's upgrading of its own Africa strategy in response to the US invasion of Afghanistan and Iraq and the threat of exclusion from this region which the invasion presented for China (GoC 2006). The aggressive, post-Cold War re-militarization of NATO strategy in Africa, by the creation of the US Africa Command (AFRICOM) is intimately related to this renewed interest in establishing monopoly control over Africa's energy resources.

Overall Patterns of Land and Resource Grabs in Africa

The national incidence of the foreign land grabs suggests that the phenomenon thus far has mainly targeted about 20 African countries to any significant scale. The bulk of the area targeted (87.3%) is concentrated in about 11 countries, while another 6 countries account for 8.5% of the targeted land (Table 3). Indeed, only 6 countries account for almost 77% of the total land area being grabbed, in the following order: Sudan (18.5%), Ethiopia (14.3%), Madagascar (12.9%), Mozambique (11.9%), Sierra Leone (6.4%) and Benin (6.2%).

The countries targeted are also unevenly distributed within each region, with three West African countries (Mali, Sierra Leone and Benin) accounting for about 15.4% of the continental land grabs; four East African countries (Sudan, Ethiopia, Tanzania and Kenya) accounting for 42.2%; two Southern African countries (Madagascar and Mozambique) accounting for about 25% of the land; and three Central African countries (Cameroun, DRC, and Congo) accounting for only 5.2% of the land grabbed. Regionally, Southern Africa accounts for 29% of the area concerned, while East and West Africa jointly account for 47%, and Central and North Africa jointly account for 10% (Table 4).

It is evident that the recent land grabs are occurring mainly in non-settler countries where no significant amount of land alienation, and land privatization, had occurred historically. However, some privately owned lands in the former settler colonies have been subject to the recent land grabs. Where the colonial land alienation process was most extensive, namely in South Africa, Namibia and Zimbabwe, the area submitted to the recent land grabs has been proportionately lower. Indeed, the former settler colonies of Southern Africa account for only 4.5% of the area targeted in the region, largely due to the fact that, historically, most of the high-value agricultural land had already been grabbed by 1960, when decolo-nization began; most of these new foreign deals have involved transfers of white-owned freehold land. This tendency has affected Kenya as well.

Moreover, it is notable that the countries which have limited lands with high agro-ecological potential, given their lower rainfall and extensive desert lands, such

Table 3 Top 30 African countries targeted for land grabs (2000–2012)

Country	Size		Deals	
	ha	%	No.	%
Sudan	3,123,430	18.5	17	4.2
Ethiopia	2,412,562	14.3	56	13.7
Madagascar	2,176,241	12.9	36	8.8
Mozambique	2,017,912	11.9	96	23.5
Tanzania	1,115,179	6.6	41	10.0
Sierra Leone	1,085,742	6.4	21	5.1
Benin	1,040,900	6.2	9	2.2
Liberia	662,000	3.9	5	1.2
Kenya	480,000	2.8	8	2.0
Mali	471,891	2.8	25	6.1
Congo	338,000	2.0	3	0.7
Cameroon	300,340	1.8	14	3.4
Zambia	273,413	1.6	8	2.0
Ghana	259,900	1.5	7	1.7
DRC	243,870	1.4	6	1.5
Zimbabwe	201,171	1.2	2	0.5
Angola	183,000	1.1	4	1.0
Nigeria	142,532	0.8	18	4.4
Ivory Coast	100,200	0.6	2	0.5
Uganda	91,012	0.5	6	1.5
Senegal	34,800	0.2	7	1.7
Malawi	30,147	0.2	4	1.0
Niger	29,969	0.2	3	0.7
South Africa	27,124	0.2	3	0.7
Somalia	21,500	0.1	2	0.5
South Sudan	20,450	0.1	1	0.2
Swaziland	15,124	0.1	2	0.5
Rwanda	3,100	0.0	1	0.2
Burkina Faso	1,000	0.0	1	0.2
Total	16,902,509	100	408	100

Source Compiled by authors from Land Matrix (2012)

Table 4 Land deals by sub-region in Africa (2000–2012)

Region	Hectares	%	Deals	%
Eastern Africa	4,123,353	24.4	114	27.9
Western Africa	3,828,934	22.7	98	24.0
Northern Africa	3,143,880	18.6	18	4.4
Central Africa	882,210	5.2	23	5.6
Southern Africa	4,924,132	29.1	155	38.0
Total	16,902,509	100	408	100

Source Compiled by authors from Land Matrix (2012)

as Namibia and South Africa, have much less land available for this new wave of land grabs, such that the new foreign land buyers are acquiring this mainly from white landowners. This also applies to most of the North African countries, where land grabbing for agricultural purposes has been low due to the extensive desert formations there. It is also notable that, in the case of Zimbabwe, the bulk of the historically grabbed land had already been redistributed by 2010, leaving a few privately and state-owned agro-industrial estates involving existing and new foreign investors, principally in sugar, tea and wildlife conservancies; even so, most of these private foreign-owned estates have come under pressure to 'indigenize' by transferring 51% of their shareholdings.

Furthermore, in non-settler countries, where migrant farmers had historically been allocated significant amounts of high potential land (such as Ivory Coast, Ghana, Nigeria), the land questions there have also been politically charged, to the extent of generating civil conflict (Ivory Coast), while significant social movements have emerged which have the tradition of resisting land alienation through customary tenure arrangements.

Nonetheless, over 80% of the overall land grabs in Africa have entailed 'fresh' alienation of customary lands (estimated at over 70% of targeted lands), which is facilitated by the state and/or the transfer of land which had previously been alienated by the state, such as for agricultural estates, forests and conservancies, amounting possibly to about 10% of the overall area grabbed. The latter situation affected mainly countries, such as Tanzania, Malawi, Zambia. Indeed, the recent foreign land grabs amount to a significant trend of land alienation by and through the vesting of land ownership in the state, which, in turn, has transferred such land through leaseholds. This has led to the intensification of land markets, accompanied by significant use of extra-economic force by the state apparatus to shape the evolution of these land markets.

The above patterns of land grabbing in Africa have critical implications for the associated concentration of the control, ownership and use of water resources, given that the continent is well endowed with big rivers, large lakes and vast wetlands, as well as widespread but limited groundwater. These water resources, mainly in the Central African region and island countries, include 17 rivers with catchment areas of over 100,000 km^2, and over 160 lakes larger than 27 km^2, especially around the equatorial region and sub-humid East African Highlands within the Rift Valley (such as Lake Tanganyika). Groundwater represents 15% of Africa's water resources, with the major aquifers located in arid zones of northern Sahara, Nubia, Sahel, Chad Basins and Kalahari (Lake and Souré 1997). These water resources are very unevenly distributed among the different regions of the continent, as well as within each country, while their availability is also variable in time and space (Table 5).

However, at the moment Africa only utilizes 3.8% of these water resources for agricultural, industrial and human consumption. Indeed, a rather small proportion of Africa's irrigation potential (estimated at below 10%) is being tapped, while below five percent of the cropped land is irrigated. Yet, much of the land that is being grabbed is reportedly of high agro-potential and biogenetic value, largely in relation

Table 5 Water use, renewable water resources and water availability by sub-region in Africa

Sub regions	Available water resources (km³/year)			Water use (km3/year)			Water use in relation to water resources (%)		Per capita water availability 103 (m³/year)	
	Local	Inflow	Total	1950	1995	2025	1995	2025	1995	2025
Northern	41	140	181	43.0	110	144	61	80	0.62	0.32
				34.6	78.0	94	43	52		
Western	1088	30	1120	2.3	26.0	52	2.3	4.6	0.62	2.1
				1.7	20.1	32	1.8	2.8		
Central	1770	80	1850	0.5	2.5	14	0.14	0.76	4.9	12.0
				0.18	1.4	9.0	0.08	0.49		
Eastern	749	29	778	3.7	50.4	83	6.5	10.7	27.2	1.5
				2.8	41.0	59	5.3	7.6		
Southern	399	86	485	6.5	26.4	43	5.4	8.9	3.6	2.8
				5.0	19.1	28	3.9	5.8		
Continent	4050	–	–	56.0	215	331	5.3	8.2	5.3	2.4
				45.0	160	216	4.0	5.3		

Source Economic Commission for Africa (ECA 2003)

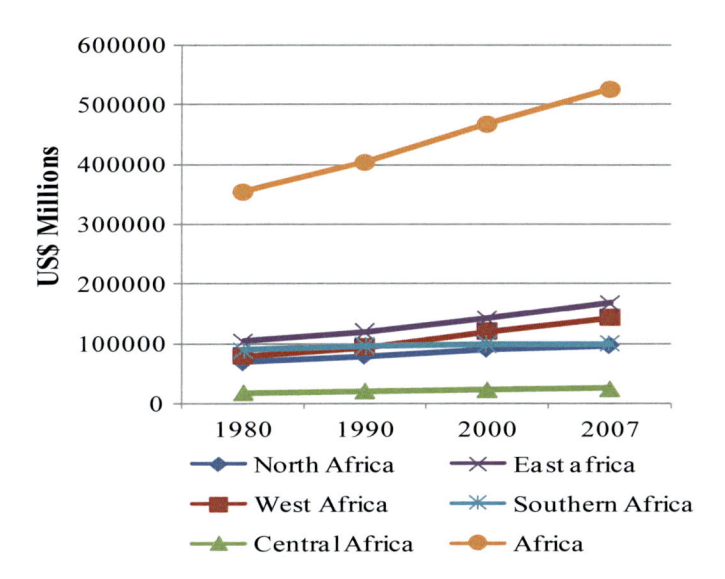

Fig. 1 Capital and investment in agriculture: agricultural capital stock (constant 2005 prices). *Source* Food and Agriculture Organisation (FAO 2013)

to its water endowments. As such, the degree of foreign control over African water resources is also on the rise.

On the face of it, the growth of capital stock and investments into African agriculture has been on the rise, albeit at a rate below 70% over 27 years (Fig. 1).

This rate of investment is extremely low compared to investments in other regions of the South. Moreover, since 2000, the level of recorded growth in agricultural capital stock only rose by eight percent over 7 years of escalating land grabs. This suggests that a substantial degree of the land grabs may be speculative, as the actual production has yet to commence.

The External Agents of the Scramble and the Compradors

Western Investors in the New Scramble for Africa

Contrary to popular perceptions driven by a poorly informed media, which suggests that China and India are the main land grabbers in Africa, a large proportion (47%) of the large-scale land acquisitions in Africa directly involves investors from the key Western nations (Tables 6 and 7). Indeed, investors from a variety of semi-peripheral states, including marginal European countries, some of the oil-rich countries, and the so-called emerging powers, account for 39 percent of the land targeted, as we will see below. Similarly, the current pattern of land grabbing is not driven by rich oil-producing countries, such as in the Gulf, which in any case is mainly seeking to improve their food supply. Moreover, various African investors, comprising mainly state corporations and domestic capitalists, mostly in partnership with foreign capital, are at the bottom of the ladder of land grabbers. This indicates the largely external orientation of the scramble for African land.

When we examine the country origins of the investors from the West, it is evident that seven countries—United Kingdom, United States, Italy, Germany, Portugal, Canada and Norway—jointly account for about 37% of the land being grabbed. The Anglo-Saxon countries alone account for about 21% of the land being grabbed, which reflects their historical influence in Africa, as well as the shift of focus towards countries which are not former settler colonies.

Over 132 investor firms located in Western countries are directly involved in the grabbing of about 44% (6.6 million ha) of the total land of 14.4 million ha that is verified as having been acquired. It is important to note, however, that when we remove the land deals involving 'Africa investors' (which amounts to

Table 6 Land grabbers by major foreign regions (2000–2012)

	Investor Regions	No of countries	No. firms	Hectares	%
1	Western Countries	17	132	6,625,119	46.6
2	Emerging Power Countries	5	43	3,319,108	23.3
3	Others semi-periphery	9	21	2,257,217	15.9
4	African countries	22	85	2,024,928	14.2
	Total			14,226,372	100

Source Compiled by authors from Land Matrix (2012)

Table 7 Investors from Western countries by area of land (ha) (2000–2012)

	Investor country	No. firms	Hectares	%	% of total	Target countries	Range
1	United Kingdom	28	1,523,584	23	10.6	Tanzania, Mozambique, Sudan, South Sudan, Malawi, Zambia, Liberia, Madagascar, Ghana, Angola, Uganda, Sierra Leone, Ethiopia, Nigeria	15
2	United States of America	18	1,438,858	21.7	10	Ethiopia, Tanzania, Sierra Leone, Sudan, Mali, Cameroon, Madagascar	8
3	Italy	11	564,792	8.5	3.9	Mozambique, Congo, Nigeria, Ethiopia, Benin, Senegal, Madagascar	7
4	Germany	10	475,012	7.2	3.3	Ethiopia, Mozambique, Tanzania, Zambia, Madagascar, Uganda, Kenya	7
5	Portugal	12	358,734	5.4	2.5	Mozambique, Angola, Sierra Leone	4
6	Canada	7	339,138	5.1	2.3	Kenya, Sudan, Madagascar, Ghana, Congo, Mali, Sierra Leone	8
7	Norway	6	325,450	4.9	2.3	Ghana, Tanzania, Sudan, Uganda, Mozambique	5
8	Sweden	5	267,791	4.0	1.9	Mozambique, Tanzania	2
9	Israel	5	248,000	3.7	1.7	Madagascar, Ghana, Ethiopia	3
10	Switzerland	4	182,800	2.8	1.3	Sierra Leone, Kenya, Mozambique	4
11	France	12	136,485	2.1	0.9	Mali, Madagascar, Senegal, Cameroon	4
12	Australia	2	123,000	1.9	0.9	DRC, Madagascar	2
13	Belgium	5	84,475	1.3	0.6	Tanzania, Cameroon, Kenya, Nigeria, Sierra Leone	5
14	Japan	3	71,000	1.1	0.5	Kenya, South Africa, Madagascar	4
15	Liechtenstein	1	60,000	0.9	0.4	Ethiopia	1
16	Cyprus	1	50,000	0.8	0.3	Ethiopia	1
17	Denmark	2	16,000	0.2	0.1	Ethiopia, Mali	2
	Total	132	6,625,119	100	43.5		

Source Compiled by authors from Land Matrix (2012)

2.2 million ha of the verified land), the investors from Western countries are involved in the grabbing of about 52% of the land targeted by foreign investors. Furthermore, it we consider that most of the foreign firms which are partnering with domestic land grabbers are from the West, we may surmise that the latter accounts for at least 60% of the African land grab, directly or indirectly.

The general trend shows a concentration of the phenomenon of land grabbing in a few foreign countries, alongside a few other Western countries which have been involved in a spattering of large-scale land deals. Thus, the Western investors are key actors within the top 20 African countries which have opened up their lands to foreign investors. This further suggests that while investors from the East, South and the Gulf region, or from the semi-peripheries and so-called emerging powers, are active in Africa, they face stiff competition from the investors from the West. Yet, Western media and scholarly sources have led the charge that the African land grab is predominantly led by countries from the East.

Semi-peripheral and African Investors

Nonetheless, a range of semi-peripheral countries are also involved in the scramble for African land, including the so-called emerging powers. Their modes of engagement in land grabbing in Africa are more diverse in scope. However, it must not be forgotten that they are part of a process rooted in the world crisis and its systemic causes and that, insofar as they are beneficiaries, they have ridden the wave of the neoliberal prying open of African economies that began in the 1980s, under the aegis of the West.

About 14 semi-peripheral countries constitute the main source of non-Western land grabbing in Africa (Tables 8 and 9). Of these, four have come to be known as 'emerging powers' (China, India and Brazil, as well as Turkey), while South Africa, as a 'pretender' to power, is mainly a symbolic representative of Africa within the BRICS arrangement. Together, their investor firms control about 39% of land areas being grabbed so far. However, only three countries, led by the United Arab Emirates, India and South Africa, account for over 90% of the land grabbed by semi-peripheral countries. China is one of the larger land grabbers, but the scale of its landholdings is far below that of investors from the top three semi-peripheral countries, and this is also well below the scale of grabbing by the top seven Western countries. On the other hand, countries such as Turkey, Iran, Indonesia, Syria and Vietnam are rather minor landholders in Africa.

Even so, the investors from these semi-peripheral countries have focused their land grabbing on the same 16 African countries on which Western investors are focused. Moreover, it is mainly five African countries (Sudan, Ethiopia, Mozambique, Madagascar and Tanzania) which account for the bulk of land acquisitions by the main foreign investors from both the semi-peripheral and the Western nations.

Table 8 Emerging semi-peripheral investor countries: deals and size (ha) (2000–2012)

	Investor country	No. firms	Hectares	%	% of total	Target countries	Range
1	India	21	1,784,820	53.8	12.4	Cameroon, Ethiopia, Mozambique, Madagascar, Sudan	5
2	South Africa	13	1,340,617	40.4	9.3	Benin, Mozambique, Ethiopia, Angola, Congo, Zambia, South Africa, Madagascar, Zimbabwe	9
3	China	6	162,171	4.9	1.2	Zimbabwe, Mali, Sierra Leone, Benin, Ethiopia, Cameroon	
4	Brazil	2	28,000	0.8	0.2	Ethiopia, Mozambique	2
5	Turkey	1	3,500	0.1	0.02	Tanzania	1
	Total	43	3,319,108	100	23.1		14

Source Compiled by authors from Land Matrix (2012)

Table 9 Other semi-peripheral investor countries: deals and size (ha) (2000–2012)

	Investor country	No. firms	Hectares	%	% of total	Target countries	Range
1	United Arab Emirates	2	1,880,000	83.3	13.0	Zambia, Sudan	2
2	Lebanon	2	110,000	4.9	0.8	Madagascar, Ethiopia	2
3	Republic of Korea	1	100,000	4.4	0.7	Tanzania	1
4	Saudi Arabia	3	65,000	2.9	0.5	Mali, Ethiopia	2
5	Viet Nam	1	50,000	2.2	0.3	Sierra Leone	1
6	Maldives	2	21,500	1.0	0.1	Somalia	1
7	Syrian Arab Republic	1	12,600	0.6	0.1	Sudan	1
8	Iran (Islamic Republic of)	2	10,117	0.4	0.07	Sierra Leone	1
9	Indonesia	1	8,000	0.4	0.06	Tanzania	1
	Total	*15*	*2,257,217*	*100*	*15.6*		*9*
	Grand Total[a]	58	5,576,325		38.7		16

[a]Comprises emerging power countries and other semi-periphery investor countries
Source Compiled by authors from Land Matrix (2012)

There are about eight African countries (excluding South Africa, classified here as semi-peripheral) with domestic capitalists reportedly found to have acquired large-scale quantities of land (Table 10). These deals range from 14,000 to 464,500 ha in size, and the land is dedicated to various 'commercial' uses. A few

Table 10 African investor countries by area and country targeted (exc. South Africa) (2000–2012)

	Investor country	No. firms	Hectares	%	% of total	Target countries	Range
1	Sudan	5	464,500	22.9	3.2	Sudan	1
2	Ethiopia	9	367,550	18.2	2.6	Ethiopia	1
3	Sierra Leone	2	273,400	13.6	1.9	Sierra Leone	1
4	Egypt	3	141,800	7.0	1.0	Sudan, Ethiopia	2
5	Libya	4	136,100	6.7	0.9	Benin, Mali, Mali, Mozambique	4
6	Tanzania	6	128,226	6.3	0.9	Tanzania	1
7	Ivory Coast	4	110,200	5.4	0.8	Ivory Coast, Mali	3
8	Mali	4	99,100	4.9	0.7	Mali	1
9	Mozambique	6	84,800	4.2	0.6	Mozambique	1
10	Cameroon	3	42,400	2.1	0.3	Cameroon	1
11	Senegal	2	29,000	1.4	0.2	Senegal	1
12	Malawi	3	27,647	1.4	0.2	Malawi	1
13	Uganda	3	23,100	1.1	0.2	Rwanda, Uganda	2
14	Niger	2	22,100	1.1	0.2	Niger	1
15	Madagascar	6	20,730	1.0	0.1	Madagascar	1
16	Kenya	3	15,560	0.8	0.1	Tanzania, Sudan, Kenya	3
17	Nigeria	2	14,500	0.7	0.1	Benin, Nigeria	2
18	Ghana	1	14,000	0.7	0.1	Ghana	1
19	Djibouti	1	7,000	0.3	0.05	Ethiopia	1
20	Zambia	1	1,215	0.1	0.01	Zambia	1
21	Burkina Faso	1	1,000	0.05	0.01	Mali	1
22	Mauritius	1	1,000	0.05	0.01	Madagascar	1
	Total	85	2,024,928	100	14.2		

Source Compiled by authors from Land Matrix (2012)

African investors have acquired land in other African countries. The evidence available suggests that there are two to nine domestic firms which invest in each country, and that such domestic land investments mainly comprise state-owned entities involved with foreign partners. Furthermore, the data shows that only eight African countries account for the (African) investors who acquire land in countries other than those from which they originate. Indeed, five African countries (Libya, Egypt, Ivory Coast, Madagascar, and Kenya) have been notable providers of African investors in other countries. Most of those countries (besides Libya) that have acquired large-scale lands outside their own country do so mainly in neighbouring countries.

Structural Transformations Towards Accumulation 'from Above'

The main effects of the scramble for land and natural resources include a creeping structural transformation of Africa's largely agrarian economies, based upon the rising concentration of land ownership, the expansion of land markets, and the increased concentration of agricultural production targeting external food and biofuel markets. Furthermore, foreign land grabbing is significant in terms of the extraction of value surpluses. In general, this amounts to an intensification of the continents' subordinate integration into the world economy and the marginalisation of the peasantry and other food insecure people.

Renewed Extroversion of the Agrarian Economy

The tendencies and contradictions of this evolving agrarian structure is the persistent dominance of agricultural exports in terms of value of outputs, as well as the associated inputs utilised, such as water and irrigation resources, agro-chemicals, machinery and transportation infrastructure. This is occasioned by the greater insertion of finance capital into the continent, through markets, credit and contracts.

Thus, of the 12.6 million ha targeting agricultural land, 12.3 million ha are focused on the farming of various crops, while over 300,000 ha are targeted at livestock ranching. Crop farming is targeted at about 10 groups of commodities, which are mostly destined for external markets rather than local 'subsistence' (Table 11). Moreover, eight planted crops, including biofuel feedstock crops, dominate the crops pursued by foreign land grabbers, with food grains accounting for only 17% of the uses to which the land is put. In area terms, biofuel feedstocks are followed mainly by oilseed and tubers, both of which can also be used as biofuel (feedstocks), and these are followed by forestry. Other minor crops include flowers, medicinal plants and fruits.

The largest area under food grains is devoted to maize (64 percent), followed by rice and sorghum (Table 12). This trend suggests that the allegation that the recent land grabbing may be due to food grain shortages and/or the food grain price hikes are overstated, as the investors seek control of a wider portfolio of agricultural commodities, including the world food grain and feedstock markets.

The primary effect of the primitive accumulation process is a reduction of autonomous food production, despite the fact that net agricultural production per capita has been rising since 2003. Indeed, the estimated net growth of production per capita of 22% over 21 years, which amounts to about a one-percent growth rate per annum, was below half the annual rate of population growth. Nonetheless, there was a 12% leap in the production index in 2000–11, which is largely accounted for by 10 African countries, including Kenya, Malawi, Zambia and a few West and East African countries (Fig. 2).

Table 11 Land deals by crop category in Africa (2000–2012)

Food no.	Category	Area involved		Number of deals	
		Ha	%	No.	%
1	Food grain	1,640,725	16.7	58	17.3
2	Food vegetable	10,500	0.1	7	2.1
3	Food tubers	1,224,094	12.4	82	24.5
4	Flowers	21,000	0.2	3	0.9
5	Oilseed	2,468,794	25.1	62	18.5
6	Forest	853,597	8.7	20	6
7	Fruits	137,731	1.4	9	2.7
8	Medicinal	400	0.0	2	0.6
9	Food beverage	4,024	0.0	3	0.9
10	Biofuel	3,488,388	35.4	89	26.6
Grand Total		9,849,253	100	335	100

Source Compiled by authors from Land Matrix (2012)

Table 12 Land deals by crop: food grain in Africa (2000–2012)

No.	Food grain	Projects		Deals	
		Ha	%	No.	%
1	Rice	276,118	16.8	22	37.9
2	Corn (Maize);	1,007,407	61.4	24	41.4
3	Wheat	7,000	0.4	1	1.7
4	Barley	5,000	0.3	1	1.7
5	Sorghum	88,200	5.4	4	6.9
6	Other Cereals grains	257,000	15.7	5	8.6
	Total	1,640,725	100	58	100

Source Compiled by authors from Land Matrix (2012)

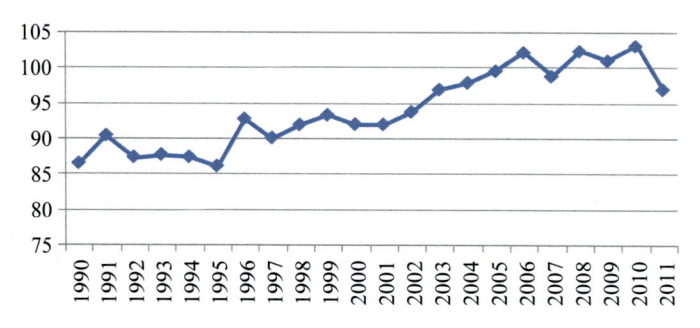

Fig. 2 Net agricultural production per capita index (2004 = 100). *Source* FAOSTAT (2013)

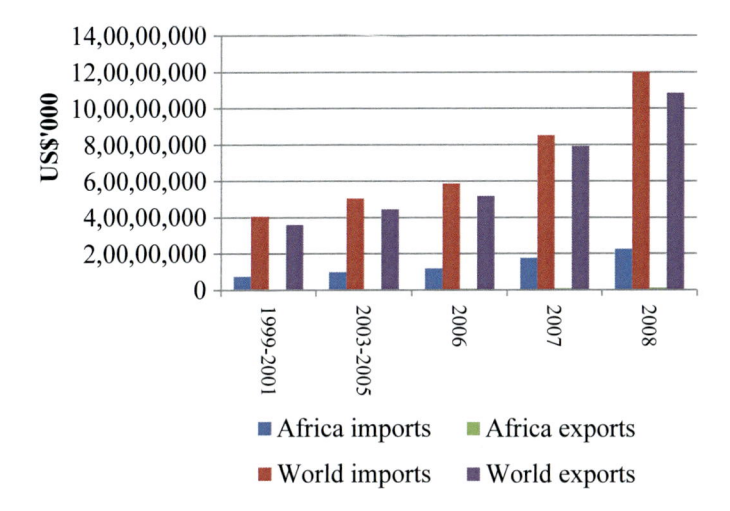

Fig. 3 Value of imports and exports of cereals: World versus Africa (USD'000). *Source* FAO (2010)

The data on cereal imports and exports also reveals the tendency of Africa's negative integration into world agricultural markets. While Africa's cereal imports tripled between 1999/2001 and 2008, Africa's cereal imports only doubled, and this at a very low starting level. Compared to world imports and exports of cereals in 2008, Africa's imports accounted for 19% of world imports, while its exports represented barely one percent of world exports (Fig. 3).

Competing Modes of Agrarian Accumulation

The key structural outcome of these land grabs is the creation of competing trajectories of accumulation, within a new 'tri-modal' agrarian structure being formed, based upon different types of producers vying for different types of labour and state policy interventions (Moyo 2011a, b, c). Specifically, the new tri-modal structure consists of marginalised peasants, new domestic small-scale capitalists, and large-scale foreign-owned estates, and is leading towards an accumulation trajectory that is rapidly evolving beyond the structures inherited at independence in the 1960s.

This is to say that there has now been an expansion of large-scale commercial farming across the continent against peasant production, which, as we have seen, was spread in the colonial period across the continent but was most prevalent in the 'economies of trade' and most suppressed in the 'labour reserves' of the settler colonies. This is consequent upon the third wave of land grabs, and extends far beyond the settler colonies to regions that have had little colonial and post-independence experience with large-scale estates. As noted, the latter are

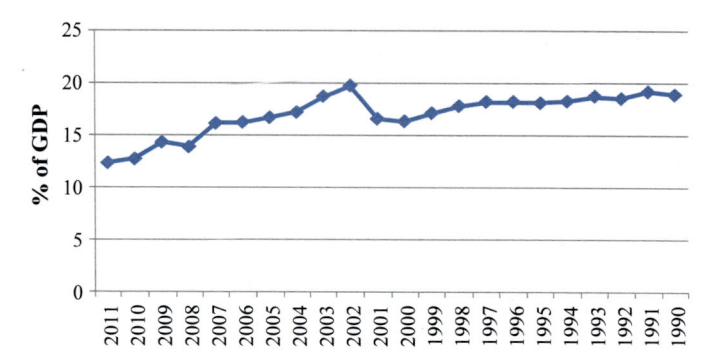

Fig. 4 Agriculture value added (% of GDP) in sub-Saharan Africa. *Source* UN Data, http://data. un.org/Data.aspx?d=WDI&f=Indicator_Code%3ANV.AGR.TOTL.ZS, access 9 July 2018

intrinsically integrated into Western monopoly-finance capital and extroverted in their market orientation. Thus, the third wave of land grabs is installing a new type of 'junker path'[3] in non-settler Africa, which maintains an aggressive posture towards peasant accumulation 'from below', domestic food security, employment and agro-industrial growth.

Meanwhile, there has also been an expansion of a middle 'merchant path',[4] building especially upon the second wave of land grabs and feeding into the third wave, even if this middle stratum has not been clearly articulated in state policies, except, most recently, in countries such as Zambia, Tanzania, Namibia and Ghana (as well as in Zimbabwe, post-land reform). Such middle-scale capitalist farms now compete for domestic resources, such as labour, credit and water, with the growing number of large-scale highly mechanised foreign-owned estates, at the same time as they compete and tend to prevail over the demands of marginalized peasant farmers.

Nonetheless, it is also notable that the organization of production in terms of the use of fertilisers and pesticides appears to have changed very little during the era of land grabs. The rate of value addition in agriculture as a percent of GDP has hardly grown since 2000, and in fact it declined (Fig. 4).

While a few countries record increases in the use of such inputs, the majority experienced a decline in their use (Table 13). This is not surprising, because the relative cost of such inputs, which are mostly imported into Africa, rose sharply from the onset of the energy crisis in 2001, and again since the 2005 food price crisis.

---

[3]The junker path, generally of landlords turned capitalists, has its variants in the white-settler societies of Southern Africa and today operates in tandem with transnational capital (Moyo and Yeros 2005).

[4]A merchant path consists of non-rural capital, including merchant capital, petty bourgeois elements, bureaucrats, military personnel and professionals who gain access to land. They farm on a smaller scale than capitalist farms but are integrated into export markets and global agro-industry (Moyo and Yeros 2005).

Table 13 Utilization of inputs in selected African countries

Country	Fertiliser consumption/ha of arable land (kg/ha)		% change	Pesticide consumption/ha of arable land ('000 kg)		% change
	2000–04	2005–09		2000–04	2005–09	
Morocco	49.0	20.8	−57.6	28,042	25,437	−9.3
Tunisia	32.5	42.3	30.2		2,136	–
Burkina Faso	11.9	9.1	−23.5	26	1,044	3915.4
Gambia	7.5	6.8	−9.3	559	597	6.8
Ghana	13.2	11.9	−9.8	8,729	14,702	68.4
Niger	0.2	0.1	−50.0	62	15	−75.8
Cameroon	11.1	7.4	−33.3	6,728	6,248	−7.1
Burundi	1.1	0.9	−18.2	1,017	610	−40.0
Kenya	27.7	32.4	17.0	3,156	–	–
Ethiopia	5.6	7.9	41.1	1,260	–	–
Madagascar	2.2	2.6	18.2	43	36	−16.3
Malawi	34.4	26.6	−22.7	1,264	–	0.0
Mauritius	287.8	209.4	−27.2	2,072	2,435	17.5
South Africa	54.5	49.2	−9.7	53,714	–	–

Source FAO (2013)

Table 14 African crop yields (kg/ha), 1961–2011

Crop	1961	1970	1980	1990	2000	2009	2010[a]	2011[b]	1961–2000 (%)	2000–11 (%)
Cereals	810	907	1,131	1,176	1,270	1,479	1,300	1,546	36	19
Pulses	499	452	565	553	550	593	600	626	9	12
Roots/tubers	5,779	6,235	6,873	7,858	8,161	9,280	9,400	10,134	29	19
Fibers	264	327	347	368	374	369	345	312	29	−20
Oil crops	237	214	239	270	264	317	300	327	10	19
Fruit	5,526	7,205	8,264	8,817	9,585	10,514	7,794	7,836	42	−22
Vegetables	6,835	6,071	6,005	6,245	6,624	6,885	10,056	9,963	−3	34
Tree nuts	552	543	564	517	742	769	760	887	26	16

Source Dietz (2011); [a]FAO (2013); [b]FAOSTAT (2013)

Relatedly, between 2000 and 2011, the yields per hectare for eight of Africa's main crops only grew at a limited rate of between 12 and 19%, with the exception of vegetables which grew at 34% and fibres and fruits which actually declined substantially (Table 14). Compared with the prior 40-year period, 1961–2000, when the yields of these crops grew at rates between 26 and 42%, with the exception of pulses and oil crops which grew at 9–10%, and vegetables which experienced decline, it is clear that the recent decade of land grabbing has not significantly altered the low agricultural productivity trap facing the continent.

It is no surprise that Africa's agrarian question is increasingly reappearing as a social question of exclusion, inequality, food insecurity and poverty, as a direct result of growing land dispossession and the super-exploitation of labour (Moyo et al. 2015). Consequently, demands for popular sovereignty focused on the control over land, minerals, oil and other natural resources, are assuming once again the form of 'resource nationalism', and emphatically place the political dimension of land rights ahead of the so-called 'classical' agrarian question focusing on reversing 'backwardness' through industrial development (Moyo et al. 2013).

Structural Transition and the Challenges of Pan-Africanism

There is a clear prospect that the twenty-first-century political economy of Africa will be driven by foreign-sponsored rentierism based in large-scale agricultural land, minerals and energy resources, escalating the expulsion of rural populations, land degradation and immiserization. Indeed, the overall tendency points towards a certain convergence of the underlying economic structures that had previously differentiated the three macro-regions of Africa. The tri-modal agrarian structure described above, which is now spreading across the continent, is accompanied by the longer post-independence expansion of the mineral and oil sectors in regions which, outside of the concessionary economies of Central Africa and the labour reserves of the settler colonies, also had little colonial experience of integration into the world economy on this basis. This, therefore, compounds the tendency towards a general structural convergence among the regions.

If we take further into account the escalating expulsion of Africa's rural population and the rapid rates of urbanization, without absorption into urban industrial employment, we are also witnessing the creation of a 'labour reserve' writ large, in tandem with the more general tendencies across the South (Jha et al. 2017). The mechanisms of this labour reserve are evidently different from those operating in the original settler colonies, yet the result is that of an expanded process of super-exploitation, including the intensification of the productive and reproductive labour performed by women (Tsikata 2016; Doss et al. 2014). This goes far to explain why the politics of land has become explosive across the continent, especially where inequalities fuse class with race or ethnic difference, as well as with the pervasive patriarchal relations.

Resistance to the land grabs has taken various forms, from the more diffuse protests at local level to the more organized among social movements, as well as to national and regional initiatives. The latter have been most pronounced in Southern Africa, instigated by the re-radicalization of nationalism in Zimbabwe. In this case, the radicalization has led to the implementation of a fast-track land reform programme, which has rowed against the tide of land grabs, and has been reinforced by the policy of 'indigenisation' of mineral resources and a 'Look East' foreign policy, within a new Positive Non-Alignment strategy (Moyo and Yeros 2013). The region as a whole has been challenged to respond, to the point of incrementally adopting a mutual defense pact against the West's military maneuvers in the region generally, and the political destabilization strategy against Zimbabwe, in particular. Indeed, this has been a unique experience of re-radicalization of nationalism with substantial regional ripple effects, precisely at a time of an escalating scramble for Africa and AFRICOM interventions in North, West, East and Central Africa.

The experience has demonstrated that the alternative to the scramble must be found, in the first instance, in collective resistance to military and political interference. This must be combined with the systematic advance towards regional and continental coordination for the purpose of promoting inward-looking agro-industrial development to stabilize the countryside, alongside policies to absorb migrant semi-proletarian populations in decent employment and to reorganize priorities in defense of gender-sensitive social reproduction. In the specific conditions of peripheral social formations marked by endemic semi-proletarianisation, the immediate strategy must involve the strengthening of peasant farming and women's land rights, and the advance towards new forms of cooperative production.

Such are the challenges posed for Pan-Africanism in the twenty-first century, as well as for a New Bandung project. Both will stand or fall in the coming decades on their ability to respond to the systemic transition underway.

Conclusion

The current systemic transition is unprecedented in the challenges that it presents. It is inconceivable that monopoly capitalism will overcome its deep and advanced contradictions to launch a new era of accumulation and prosperity, and respond to the social, energy, and ecological crises that are unfolding. The current tendency is indeed to the contrary: the escalation of NATO-led plunder, pillage and war. This requires a clear understanding of the systemic determinants of the transition and a new solidarity and vision capable of providing answers to the crisis of our times.

Africa has once again become a key terrain of competition, conflict and struggle. The new scramble is clearly led by Western monopolies and the hyper-speculative logic that has taken hold, and which has now turned its sights on agricultural land and other natural resources in Africa, as elsewhere. While oil and minerals may continue to command higher rents and be much more closely tied to AFRICOM strategies, the grabbing of agricultural land takes a heavy toll on whole populations that are stripped of their means of production and reproduction and forced *en masse* into perpetual misery and migration.

The fact that monopolies reared in other countries of the South have also emerged to compete globally, and over Africa's land and natural resources in particular, should not lead us to conclude that the centre–periphery contradiction has been overcome. Rather, the contradiction is at its systemic limits; it is, in fact, insuperable, lest the transition begins towards a post-imperialist, truly multipolar system that enables new and autonomous development paths and solidarities to flourish in the South.

Under the circumstances, it should also be no surprise that some of the most important processes of nationalist radicalization and resistance in the contemporary world have occurred in Africa, particularly in Southern Africa, despite the routine media and academic distortions of such events. Whatever their shortcomings, or even despite them, the recent re-radicalization of nationalism has concretely shown that reclaiming Africa is within the reach of the present generation.

References

Amin, S. (1972). Underdevelopment and dependence in black Africa: Origins and contemporary forms. *Journal of Modern African Studies, 10*(4), 503–524.

Amin, S. (1976). *Unequal Development* (B. Pearce, Trans.). New York, NY & London: Monthly Review Press.

Amin, S. (2003). *Obsolescent capitalism: Contemporary capitalism and global disorder*. London & New York, NY: Zed Books.

Amin, S. (2010). *The law of worldwide value*. New York, NY: Monthly Review.

Arrighi, G. (1973). International corporations, labour aristocracies, and economic development in tropical Africa. In G. Arrighi & J. Saul (Eds.), *Essays on the political economy of Africa*. New York: Monthly Review Press.

CIA [Central Intelligence Agency] (2001). The World Factbook. http://www.odi.gov/cia/publications/factbook/geos/, accessed in July 2001.

Cotula, L., Vermeulen, S., Leonard, R., & Keeley, J. (2009). *Land grab or development opportunity?* London & Rome: IIED, FAO & IFAD.

de Janvry, A. (1981). *The agrarian question and reformism in latin America*. Baltimore, MD: The Johns Hopkins University Press.

Dietz, T. (2011). Silverlining Africa: from images of doom and gloom to glimmers of hope; from places to avoid to places to enjoy. Inaugural address, Leiden University and African Studies Centre, January 14. Available at http://www.padev.nl/other_output/Dietz_2011_Silverling_Africa.pdf.

Dos Santos, T. (1978), *Imperialismo y dependencia*. México: Era.

Doss, C., Summerfield, G., & Tsikata, D. (2014). Land, gender and food security. *Feminist Economics, 20*(1), 1–23.

ECA [United Nations Economic Commission for Africa] (2003). Land tenure systems and sustainable development in Southern Africa. Document No. ECA/SA/EGM.Land/2003/2, (pp. 2–3).

FAO. (2001a). *Gender and food security fact files*. Available on http://www.fao.org/Gender/en/agri-e.htm.

FAO. (2001b). *Forest resources assessment 2000*. Rome: FAO.

FAO (2010). The state of food insecurity in the World: Addressing food insecurity in protracted crises. Rome: Food and Agriculture Organization of the United Nations.

FAO (2013). Towards successful family farming in Africa. Position paper from Cape Town Dialogue. Rome: United Nations Food and Agriculture Organization.

FAOSTAT. (2001). *Statistics database of the united nations food and agriculture organization*. Rome: FAO.

FAOSTAT. (2013). FAOSTAT database. Available at http://www.fao.org/faostat/en/#data.

Foster, J. B. (2010a). The age of monopoly-finance capital. *Monthly Review, 61*(9), 1–13.

Foster, J. B. (2010b). The financialization of accumulation. *Monthly Review, 62*(5), 1–17.

Foster, J. B., McChesney, R. W., & Jamil Jonna, R. (2011). The internationalization of monopoly capital. *Monthly Review, 63*(2), 1–23.

Ghosh, J. (2008). '*The Global Food Crisis*', Public Lecture delivered at the University of Turin, Italy, May, http://www.networkideas.org.

GoC [Government of China]. (2006). *China's Africa policy*. www.gov.cn/misc/2006–01/12/content_156509.htm.

GRAIN. (2008). *Seized: The 2008 land grab for food and financial security*. http://www.grain.org/briefings/?id=212.

Hendricks, F. (2000). Questioning the land question: Agrarian transition, land tenure, rural development in the former settler colonies of southern Africa. In Kwesi Kwaa Prah & Abel Ghaffar Mohammed Ahmed (Eds.), *Africa in Transformation: Political and Economic Issues*, Vol. 1 (pp. 33–64). Addis Ababa: Organisation for Social Science Research in Eastern and Southern Africa (OSSREA).

IFPRI. (2010). *Food security and economic development in the Middle East and North Africa*. IFPRI Discussion Paper 00985.Current State and Future Perspectives.

Jha, P., Moyo, S., & Yeros, P. (2017). Capitalism and 'Labour Reserves': A note. In C. P. Chandrasekhar & J. Ghosh (Eds.), *Interpreting the world to change it: Essays for Prabhat Patnaik* (pp. 205–37). New Delhi: Tulika.

Land Matrix. (2012). *The online public database on land deals*. http://landmatrix.org/en/. Retrieved December 2012.

Lake, W. B., & Souré, M. (1997). *Water and development in Africa*. Ottawa: International Development Information Centre, CIDA.

Li, M. (2009). *The rise of China and the demise of the capitalist world economy*. New York, NY: Monthly Review.

Mafeje, A. (2003). *The agrarian question, access to land and peasant responses in sub-Sahara Africa*. UNRID Programme papers on Civil Society and Social Movements.

Mamdani, M. (1996). *Citizen and subject: Contemporary Africa and the legacy of late colonialism*. Princeton, NJ: Princeton University Press.

Marini, R. M. (1969). *Subdesarrollo y Revolución*. Mexico: Siglo Veintiuno.

Marini, R. M. (2000). *A Dialética da Dependência*, ed. E. Sader. Petrópolis: Editora Vozes.

Mitchell, D. (2008). *A note on rising food prices*. Policy Research Working Paper No. 4682. The World Bank. Development Prospects Group. July 2008.

Mkandawire, T. (2011). Rethinking pan-Africanism, nationalism and the new regionalism. In S. Moyo & P. Yeros (Eds.), *Reclaiming the nation: The return of the national question in Africa, Asia and Latin America* (pp. 31–53). London & New York, NY: Pluto Press.

Mkandawire, T., & Soludo, C. (1999). *Our continent, our future: African perspectives on structural adjustment*. Dakar, Ottawa and Asmara: CODESRIA, IDRC and AWP.

Moyo, S. (2000). *Land reform under structural adjustment in Zimbabwe: Land use change in the Mashonaland Provinces*. Uppsala: Nordiska Afrikainstitutet.

Moyo, Sam. (2008). *African land questions, agrarian transitions and the state: Contradictions of neoliberal land reforms*. Dakar: CODESRIA.

Moyo, S. (2011a). Three decades of agrarian reform in Zimbabwe. *Journal of Peasant Studies, 38* (3), 493–531.

Moyo, S. (2011b). Land Concentration and accumulation after redistributive reform in post-settler Zimbabwe. *Review of African Political Economy, 38*(128), 257–276.

Moyo, S. (2011c). Changing Agrarian relations after redistributive land reform in Zimbabwe. *Journal of Peasant Studies, 38*(5), 939–966.

Moyo, S., Jha, P., & Yeros, P. (2013). The classical agrarian question: Myth, reality and relevance today. *Agrarian South: Journal of Political Economy, 2*(1), 93–199.

Moyo, S., Tsikata, D., & Diop, Y. (Eds.). (2015). *Land in the struggles for citizenship in Africa*. Dakar: CODESRIA.

Moyo, S., & Yeros, P. (2005). The resurgence of rural movements under neoliberalism. In S. Moyo & P. Yeros (Eds.), *Reclaiming the land: The resurgence of rural movements in Africa, Asia and Latin America*. London & Cape Town: Zed Books & David Philip.

Moyo, S., & Yeros, P. (2013). The Zimbabwe model: Radicalisation, reform and resistance. In S. Moyo & W. Chambati (Eds.), *Land and agrarian reform Zimbabwe: Beyond white-settler capitalism* (pp. 331–357). Dakar: CODESRIA.

Moyo, S., Yeros, P., & Jha, P. (2012). Imperialism and primitive accumulation: Notes on the new scramble for Africa. *Agrarian South: Journal of Political Economy., 1*(2), 181–203.

NEPDG [National Energy Policy Development Group]. (2001). *National energy policy*, May. http://www.whitehouse.gov.

Nkrumah, K. (1965). *Neo-colonialism: The last stage of imperialism*. London: Thomas Nelson & Sons Ltd.

Patnaik, P. (1972). On the political economy of development. In *Economic and political weekly*, Annual Number (pp. 197 − 212).

Patnaik, U. (1999). Export-oriented agriculture and food security in developing countries and in India. In Utsa Patnaik (Ed.), *The long transition* (pp. 351–416). New Delhi: Tulika.

Patnaik, P. (2008). *The Accumulation process in the period of globalization.* http://www.networkideas.org/feathm/may2008/ft28_Globalization.htm.

Patnaik, U., & Patnaik, P. (2017). *A theory of imperialism*. New York, NY: Columbia University Press.

Prasad, A. (2016). Adivasi women agrarian change and forms of labour in Neoliberal India. *Agrarian South: Journal of Political Economy, 5*(1), 20–49.

Rodney, Walter. (1973). *How Europe underdeveloped Africa*. Dar es Salaam: Tanzania Publishing House.

Schincariol, V. E., Barbosa, M. S., & Yeros, Paris. (2017). Labour trends in Latin America and the Caribbean in the current crisis (2008–2016). *Agriarian South: Journal of Political Economy, 6*(1), 113–141.

Shivji, I. G. (2009). *Accumulation in an African periphery*. Dar es Salaam: Mkuki na Nyota Publishers Ltd.

Tabb, W. K. (2008). The global food crisis and what has capitalism to do with it. www.networkideas.org/focus/Jul2008/fo28_Global_Food_Crisis.htm.

Tsikata, D. (2016). Gender land tenure and agrarian production systems in Africa. *Agrarian South: Journal of Political Economy, 5*(1), 1–19.

UNEP. (2002). Africa Environment outlook—Past, present and future perspectives. Available on http://www.unep.org/dewa/africa/publications/aeo-1/171.htm. Retrieved on April 5, 2013.

World Bank. (2008). *World development report 2008: Agriculture for development*. Washington, DC: The World Bank.

Part II
New Competitors for Africa's Land and Natural Resources

Chinese Expansion in Africa in the Twenty-First Century: Characteristics and Impacts

Valéria Lopes Ribeiro

Introduction

After a trajectory of continuous economic expansion that has already lasted for 30 years, China is currently the biggest economy in the world, with a GDP reaching USD 19.6 trillion, in 2015.[1] Although it presents the typical contradictions of developing economies, such as income inequality, China occupies today a key position on the global stage, especially with regards to its participation in international trade and economic relations generally.

One fundamental feature of the Chinese expansion is its strongly state and investment-led accumulation pattern, especially in the industrial sector (Medeiros 1999). Contrary to liberal claims, the determinant factors of Chinese growth since the 1980s have not been associated with policies of 'free market capitalism', but to the political decisions (taken then) of achieving a gradual shift of its socialist economy, while maintaining the state as the central element in regulation and planning, as well as major investor.

Thus, following an already vast expansion of investment in heavy industry during the Maoist era, a period of reform and opening began from 1978 onwards, with Deng Xiaoping at the helm, which would prove fundamental to the redirection of the Chinese economy towards large-scale growth. The economic opening had begun in the 1970s with the resumption of relations with the United States and other countries, which had opened up a fundamental channel for expansion via direct

---

[1]In the same year, the United States registered a GDP of USD 18,036,650, both in terms of Purchasing Power Parity (IMF 2013).

V. L. Ribeiro (✉)
Center of Engineering, Modeling and Applied Social Sciences,
Federal University of ABC, Rua Arcturus, 03, CECS, sala D339,
São Bernardo do Campo 09606-070, São Paulo, Brazil
e-mail: val_ribeiro@yahoo.com.br

investment and exports. Two decades later, in the 1990s, China became the receiver of enormous amounts of Foreign Direct Investments (FDIs), which were directed towards Special Economic Zones (SEZ) in search of tax and exchange incentives: the objective was to produce in China and export worldwide.

The way through which the Chinese government managed to articulate these FDIs for the benefit of its own national industry is one of the key aspects to the understanding of Chinese expansion. By means of various technology transfer policies and the expansion and protection of the national industry, besides investment in infrastructure and an autonomous foreign exchange policy, the government achieved that gradually the national enterprises could secure their place in the market and fight their foreign counterparts for space, be it in the considerable Chinese consumer market or worldwide.

As early as the beginning of the twenty-first century, China entered a new cycle of growth marked by expansion in infrastructure and heavy industry investment, which presupposes the enlargement of the use of primary inputs—from raw materials for industry, such as iron and copper, to essential energy resources, such as oil. From this moment onwards, the maintenance of high growth rates and the legitimacy of the Communist Party would depend on access to primary inputs.[2] Such an imperative has continually shaped the expansion process abroad, with the government and state companies promoting diverse approaches in regions that are rich in natural resources, such as Latin America and Africa. The interest in primary inputs and energy resources has been driving imports from, and the expansion of FDIs in, these regions. This has had important consequences for both the international economy and peripheral countries, such as in Africa.

From the beginning of the 2000s to at least 2011, African countries saw their exports rise substantially with the increase in Chinese demand. Besides the growth in export volumes, there was an increase in the prices of primary goods, which improved the terms of trade and further favored exports, while Chinese enterprises also expanded towards African countries, to widen financial flows and external assistance. In this period, African countries experienced significant improvements in macroeconomic conditions, with an average growth rate of almost five percent of GDP for the continent as a whole and 5.5% for sub-Saharan Africa. The expansion of exports, especially, allowed for a reduction in external vulnerability.

---

[2]This trend began to show signs of exhaustion after the 2008 crisis, mainly due to the plunge in external demand in the United States and the European Union. China presented much less impressive growth rates after 2009, and responded with an anticyclical policy to sustain domestic demand by means of state investments in heavy industry, construction, and urbanization (Wei 2016; Ocampo and Erten 2013). More recently, the country has been searching for a more sustainable growth regime, less capital-and energy-intensive, less dependent on state investments, and more articulated to a widening domestic income and consumption base (Cintra et al. 2015). But despite these changes, the external expansion of the country does not seem to have been interrupted, at least for now, due to the already established strong linkages to the external market, including reliance on energy and mineral resources, consumer markets for Chinese goods, the expansion of financial flows, and the creation of the Asian Infrastructure Investment Bank to finance infrastructure mainly in Asia.

China's position on the global stage, and especially the increase in Sino-African commercial and financial relations, contributed strongly to this improvement, although it has raised once again the fundamental question regarding African countries' dependence on primary goods exports, the associated adverse impacts on structural change, and the nature of the improvements in economic and social conditions. Thus, the objective of this chapter is to analyze the general features of Chinese expansion in Africa in the first decade of the twenty-first century. The chapters that follow discuss China's foreign policy towards Africa, map out the new commercial and financial relations, and assess their impact, before offering some final considerations.

Chinese Foreign Policy Towards Africa

China's approaching developing countries is not a recent fact and takes one back to the Popular Republic period, in the 1950s. The modern history of China–Africa relations begins in the 1950s, in the Popular Republic period, in the context of the Bandung Conference of 1955, which defined the first foreign policy directives. The conference brought together Asian and African countries motivated by the common search for instruments of support and cooperation to confront colonialism and imperialism and the movements of the superpowers, the United States and the USSR. On the occasion, China defended the 'Five Principles of Peaceful Coexistence', which would come to shape its diplomatic posture towards the rest of world, including Africa, not only in that period but to this day. The five principles are: mutual respect to territorial sovereignty and integrity; mutual non-aggression; non-interference in internal affairs; equality and mutual benefit; and peaceful coexistence (Oliveira 2007; Quiang 2008; Youfa 2011; Aremu 2009).

Thereafter, Sino-African relations would be marked by the support given by the Chinese government to several national liberation movements, through weapons donations and guerilla training, as well as financial aid to create infrastructure in countries embroiled in conflict. Liberation movements in Zimbabwe (then Rhodesia), Angola and Mozambique received moral and material support in their struggles (Quiang 2008), while the distinctive mark with regards to infrastructure was the construction of Tanzam highway, to connect landlocked Zambia to Tanzania and the Indian Ocean and free Zambia from its dependence on infrastructure controlled by apartheid South Africa (Youfa 2010; Kaplinksy and Morriss 2009)—a project which the United States had earlier refused to finance. In the 1970s, African countries also reciprocated by supporting China on Resolution 2758 of the United Nations (1972), which led to the recognition of China in all instances of the institution, in detriment of Taiwan. Of the 76 countries that voted favorably, 26 were African (Youfa 2011).

Along the 1990s, Africa established itself as the main focus of Chinese foreign policy, especially after the economic structural reform programmes implemented in several countries. In the bosom of the open door and 'Going Out' policy, relations with Africa were strengthened and efforts were made to stimulate commercial cooperation and the expansion of investments (Quiang 2008). At that moment, China saw in African countries significant possibilities for the commercial expansion of manufactured products.

The current phase of Chinese foreign policy towards Africa began in the 2000s. Thereafter, the institutional spheres created to consolidate Sino-African relations were strengthened, especially through the creation of the Forum on China-Africa Cooperation (FOCAC). Created in 2000, FOCAC is a platform for consultation and dialogue, which takes place every 3 years and alternates between China and Africa. This forum would seek to formalize a relationship that already existed for over 50 years (Taylor 2011).

The first Ministerial Conference of FOCAC, in October 2000, was attended by representees of 54 African countries. This first encounter had three objectives: to make a revision of the global order and affirm China's position; to discuss strategies for Chinese foreign policy; and to improve the position of developing countries on the global stage. According to Taylor (2009), there was the intention by part of the Chinese government to make clear its position towards the debate on human rights and affirm China's posture of mutual respect and non-conditionality with the African elite. Besides, China announced several measures, such as the reduction or cancelation of African countries' debt and financial aid and support for Chinese companies in Africa.

In the second Conference, in Ethiopia, in 2003, China proposed the increase of aid to Africa, the promotion of cooperation in the sphere of human resources, and the concession of zero taxes to several products exported by African countries to China (White Paper 2010). In trade and the services sector, several African countries signed treaties of cooperation in support of tourism in Africa, with policies of promotion of infrastructure adopted by the Chinese government. In the agriculture area, the Chinese government announced investments through the Addis Ababa Action Plan (2004–06), according to which China would support agricultural infrastructure, food security and agricultural manufacturing sectors. The Exim Bank of Chinese would give support to companies willing to undertake agricultural development projects in cooperation with African governments. Besides, China financed the building of highways and railways in several African countries and created joint ventures to facilitate such investments (Cissé 2012).

In the third FOCAC meeting, in Beijing, in 2006, China announced eight points which would be the base for the strengthening of commercial relations and development of African countries, including: the concession of US$3 billion in preferential loans; US$2 billion in buyers credits; the opening of the Chinese market by raising from 190 to 440 the number of tax-free items exported from Africa; US$1.4 billion in cancelled debt; the training of 15,000 African professionals; the doubling of African students in Chinese universities; the dispatch of 100 agriculture professionals and 300 volunteers for technical support to Africa; and the building of three hospitals and 100 rural schools. Moreover, a development fund was created to increase the amount of investments of Chinese companies in Africa. The Chinese government declared its support to the African Union and proposed to create Export Processing Zones in African countries and agricultural technology centres (Taylor 2009; White Paper 2010).

The year in which the third FOCAC conference took place coincided with the publishing of the *China White Paper*. This document formalizes the Sino-African engagement and establishes the general terms and contours of the official policy towards Africa. Accordingly, the general principles and objectives are: sincerity, friendship and equality, following the five principles of peaceful coexistence; and support of African development through several forms of economic, cultural, and social cooperation. The Chinese government committed itself to adopt more affective measures to facilitate the entry of tax-free African products in the Chinese market; to support investments, loans, and financial and agricultural cooperation, as well as infrastructure, education, culture, research and technology[3] (White Paper 2006). As a result of decisions taken at the third FOCAC, an important co-operational tool was established in 2007, the China-Africa Development Fund (CADFund).

In 2009, at the fourth FOCAC conference, in Cairo, the Chinese government presented eight extra points to be added to the Fund's program. On that occasion, new areas and sectors were considered, such as the cooperation on environmental issues. China proposed a partnership with Africa in the development of projects linked to the use of new energy sources and desertification prevention and control. The Chinese government has shown a greater preoccupation with support in agricultural projects which contemplate sustainable growth.

In 2010, the Chinese government published the White Paper on *China-Africa Economic and Trade Cooperation*. In this document, the government presented the actions of economic cooperation implemented, among those proposed during the four previous Forums. It presented the results of the increase in Sino-African trade via the tax-reducing measures and in Chinese investment. The document emphasizes the investment made in infrastructure and the maintenance of the volume of loans conceded, as well as the cancelation of the debt of African states. Some highlights include the maintenance of cooperation programmes in the education[4] and technical training programs undertaken by the Chinese in several areas, such as agriculture (the sending of 104 technicians to 33 African countries in 2009, to boost

---

[3]The Fund would begin with roughly US$5 billion, financed by the China Development Bank, and would be used to boost and support Chinese companies investing in Africa. The fund operates on certain market rules and not as a government aid organ, and invests in projects alongside Chinese companies to promote the expansion of resources available to companies, as well as investments of capital and in management support and consultancy. It targets companies in agrigulture, manufacturing and infrastructure, as well as natural resources, such as oil and minerals (China Development Bank 2013).

[4]By the end of 2009, 107 schools were built in Africa with Chinese assistance and 29,465 African students were received in Chinese schools, while China had also sent 312 young volunteers to Africa, who offered courses on Chinese language, medicine and public health, physical education and computer science. By 2010, the Chinese government had conceded 5,000 scholarships per year to African students.

development and administer courses[5]), construction (assistance in projects of low-cost rehabilitation, digging of wells, and sewage treatment), health (construction of hospitals, sending of doctors), and humanitarian aid (China-Africa Economic and Trade Cooperation 2010). One could still highlight Sino-African cooperation projects in new areas, such as banking, tourism, civil aviation and environmental protection.

According to Taylor (2009), despite all the institutional efforts and the several cooperation projects undertaken, it is difficult to affirm that there is one single Chinese foreign policy towards Africa, as it is practically impossible to speak of China as a monolithic entity. China's foreign policy in Africa is put in practice not by one unitarian entity, but by a growing group of agents who pursue their own diverse interests and objectives. The foreign policy is articulated by Beijing, from the central government of the Chinese Communist Party (CCP), in the sense of tending to the objectives of economic growth and increase in cooperation following the Five Principles of mutual respect. But, nowadays, not all policy in China is exerted and conducted by one and the same interest. There are currently a whole series of interests that come from groups inside the CCP, provincial bureaucracies and counties, and also state companies that have diverse objectives when it comes to relations with African. Even if the central government does have one policy for Africa, such a policy is mediated and fragmented by economic interests of state and private corporations, as well as by those from political localities that do not necessarily share the same vision as Beijing.

Trade, Investments and Financial Flows

China–Africa Trade

Trade between all of Africa and China (imports and exports added) has grown substantially in the last years (Fig. 1). China is already Africa's largest commercial partner, overcoming the United States and France, with a total trade reaching US $135 billion in 2015—almost 15% of the whole of African trade. In 2000, Sino-African trade represented only US$10.6 billion (UNCTAD 2016).

The data shows the continuous expansion of African trade with the world and also with China, since the 2000s. The picture remained the same until 2011, when a drop occurred in African trade with the world (Fig. 2), marked mainly by the decline of exports associated with the downturn of the commodity boom cycle after the 2008 crisis. Yet, China's share in the total of Africa's trade does not decline,

---

[5]According to this document, China has cooperated with the United Nations Food and Agriculture Organization (FAO) and signed a treaty (the South–South Tripartite Agreement) with Mauritania, Gana, Ethiopia, Gabon, Serra Leoa, Mali and Nigeria, sending to these countries more than 600 agricultural experts and technicians.

Fig. 1 Africa's total trade with the world (left axis, billions of dollars) and with China (right axis, percentage of total) 2000–15. *Source* UnctadStat (2016)

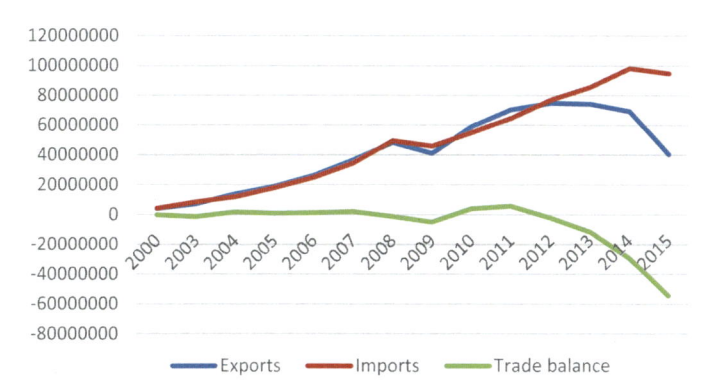

Fig. 2 Africa's exports, imports and trade balance with China (billions of dollars) 2000–15. *Source* UnctadStat (2016)

even if one considers the larger size of Chinese exports to Africa, which shows a clear deficit for Africa.[6] The increase in Sino-African trade still reflects a process of substitution of the traditional African trade partners, such as Europe, for developing countries, such as China, but also India and Brazil. In the 1990s, African exports to Europe reached 40% of total exports, while in 2009 they declined to 31% (UNCTAD 2016).

Trade between China and Africa is marked by a focus on a few countries, especially in imports from Africa. In this case, the largest partners from which China imports are Angola (36%), South Africa (21%), Congo (6%), Democratic

---

[6]While Chinese imports from Africa dropped after 2011, following the deceleration of the Chinese economy and the drop in the price of commodities, Chinese exports to Africa continued to grow.

Republic of Congo (6%), Zambia (4%) and Mozambique (4%), which add up to nearly 80% of Chinese imports from the continent (Atlas of Economic Complexity 2016). The high concentration of Chinese imports in a few countries is related to the type of products imported: mainly primary goods and energy and mineral resources.

In 2010, the category of 'mineral fuels, lubricants and related materials', which includes coal, oil and natural gas, accounted for 61.9% of total imports by China from all of Africa (UNComtrade 2011). Moreover, 'raw/brute materials' accounted for 17.8% of total Chinese imports from Africa. This includes different articles used as raw material for industry, including cotton, wood, leather, furs, seed oils, rubber, paper and cellulose, textile fibers, fertilizer and ferrous and non-ferrous minerals. One can, therefore, perceive that approximately 80% of all Chinese imports from Africa are primary goods, mainly mineral fuels. Manufactured goods represent only 12% of these imports, while, in fact, most of these pertain to only slightly processed primary goods (textile fibers, for example), very much inferior to the more elaborate manufactured goods.

Regarding Chinese exports to Africa, one observes that there is greater diversification, especially in relation to the greater number of countries involved. China gradually became a large supplier of manufactured goods to Africa, occupying the place that traditionally belonged to the central powers. From light consumer goods, such as textiles, parts and components, and transport equipment, to durable goods, such as machines, cars, vans and trucks, these are all currently common in several African countries. Nonetheless, Chinese exports to Africa also reveal a degree of concentration, even if less intensely, in countries such as South Africa, Nigeria and Egypt. In 2011, of the total of Chinese exports (about US$70 billion), 18.8% corresponded to South Africa, 13% to Nigeria, and 10% to Egypt, while Algeria and Liberia each accounted for about 7% (UNComtrade 2010). The data further reveals the predominance of the machine and manufactured products. In 2010, the total amount exported by China to Africa, 42.16% correspondent to machines, equipment, and transport material, 19.16% to diverse manufactured articles, and 5.86% to chemicals and related goods (UNComtrade 2010).

According to Ncube et al. (2010), a significant part of the above Chinese exports of manufactured goods to Africa relates to light consumption goods such as electronic toys and textiles, which contribute to raising the level of consumption of African countries due to the low price of Chinese goods. In the case of the substantial amount of exports of machines, equipment and transport materials, the authors highlight that there is a strong relation to the increase of Chinese companies in the infrastructure sector (especially in telecommunications), railway building, and construction.

Investments

Over the last three decades, China has been receiving a growing amount of external investments, absorbing a total of more than US$1 trillion dollars in FDIs between

1979 and 2010. The trends have now been reversed, as the Chinese have expanded their own investments abroad, supported by a substantial volume of accumulated reserves (about US\$3.2 trillion) and government aid (Shambaugh 2013). This is the result of the consolidated gains of economic growth, as well as the articulation of the 'Going Out' policy, articulated by Jiang Zemin in 1996, inciting Chinese companies to expand abroad. This followed an earlier affirmation at the 14th CCP Congress that the Party would grantee the country's companies favorable conditions for external operations (ibid 2013). Thus, big companies and conglomerates began to expand, with China National Chemical Import and Export (SINOCHEM) being among the first to receive approval from the State Council to venture abroad. Thereafter, not only commercial, but also manufacturing companies, such as Capital Steel and Iron Corporation, followed suit.

In 1992, the outflow of Chinese FDI added up to a total of 913 million; in 1994 this had already surpassed US4 billion. The outflow reached US\$12.6 billion in 2006 and US\$68 billion in 2010, while the accumulated stock was US \$317.2 billion. About 12 national companies established themselves in 177 countries (MOFCOM). Despite China's low share in world FDI, the expansion of Chinese investments is very relevant to the world economy, especially because the FDI flows to developing countries have grown over the years.[7] Africa and Latin America have been important destinations for Chinese investments. Chinese FDI to Africa, despite remaining small in relation to the total (9.8% in 2008), has been growing especially since the 2000s. From 2003 to 2009, the Chinese FDI flow to Africa totaled US\$55 billion; in 2015, it totaled US\$123 billion (National Bureau of Statistics of China 2016).

The analysis of Chinese investments in Africa in the 2000s allows one to identify the process through which an articulated Chinese policy has directed the growing Sino-African relations, uniting three elements: government, financial institutions (mainly Exim Bank), and Chinese companies (state-owned mostly, but not only). The policy has followed a certain logic: the government, supported by an enormous financial capacity, approaches African countries offering vast amounts of resources, through credit and loans. Financial institutions, and especially Exim Bank, have played a definitive role, conceding voluminous loans with low interests and distant maturities, often without conditionalities. Having secured the financial deals, Chinese companies enter the fray and invest in primary goods exploration projects, mainly oil and mining. Others invest in construction, taking control of the infrastructure projects they finance, while manufacturing and telecommunication companies, aiming at the local consumer market, build subsidiaries and sell manufactured products and services.

Chinese FDI is fairly different from that originating in the West. US and European companies are mostly private and their investments in Africa tend to have

---

[7]Among the main receivers of Chinese investments is Hong Kong (which received US \$38.5 billion in 2010), followed by the Virgin Islands (US\$6 billion) and the Cayman Islands (US \$3 billion), which in fact are tax havens through which investments are channeled to many other places (Shambaugh 2013).

short-term profitability interests, whereas Chinese FDIs tend to be state enterprises with a profile founded foremost in long-term objectives, supported by a credit and financing structure that allows them to work with wider investment horizons and with non-immediate profitability interests. Moreover, Chinese investments (even those concentrated upon natural resource exploration projects) have also been directed towards larger infrastructure projects.

FDI flows to Africa, as in the case of trade flows, are fairly concentrated upon a small number of countries. Although China is present in all of the 53 African countries, the data shows that between 2003 and 2009 a few countries received most of the investments. These were South Africa (48.9%), Nigeria (9.2%), Zambia (5.2%), and Algeria (6.7%) (NBSC 2016). Such investments are directed to mining, manufacture, construction, infrastructure and hunting and fishing sectors.[8]

According to the UNCTAD report (2007), between 1979 and 2000, Chinese investments in Africa were mainly linked to manufacturing sectors, resource extractions, construction and services. According to the official document of the Chinese government (White Paper 2010), mining, manufacture and construction appear among the leading sectors in Chinese FDI in Africa (totalling about 67%), while the financial sector is also significant (White Paper 2011).

Blankendal (2008) affirms that Chinese FDIs in Africa encompass investments in oil, minerals and manufacturing, with companies expanding to Africa in search of consumer markets for low-cost Chinese products, alongside the big companies in construction, infrastructure, agriculture and military equipment. Examples of such investments in oil and minerals include big state companies such as China National Petroleum Corporation (CNPC), but also many other companies in the production of oil and its derivatives in countries such as Angola and Nigeria, in addition to the smaller producers such as Chad, Mauritania, Niger, and Equatorial Guinea (ERA 2009).

The mineral sector, including iron, copper and bauxite, among others, is the one in which China, in fact, has fundamental power, given that it is one of the biggest importers on the planet and, therefore, can dictate prices and influence the export volumes of many countries. The Central and Southern African regions have vast mineral reserves of copper, gold and manganese, among others, in countries such as South Africa, Tanzania and Mozambique. In the Democratic Republic of Congo (DRC), the flow of Chinese investment led to one of the largest deals ever signed between China and an African country in the mineral sector. Called the 'contract of the century', the deal had worldwide repercussion over China's role in Africa.[9]

---

[8]The FGI statistics provided by the Chinese Ministry of Commerce do not present the investments by sector. The data used here is drawn from secondary sources and documents provided by the Chinese government.

[9]In 2007, China announced a loan of US$5 billion to the DRC, aimed at the development of infrastructure. This was followed in 2008 by another loan of 3,5 billion for mining projects. In all, China conceded credit of approximately US$9 billion to the DRC, aimed at infrastructure, construction, and mining projects. These loans occurred in exchange for concessions to exploit copper and cobalt mines over 15 years, and included some conditionalities aiming to limit Chinese

Investments also take place in the manufacturing and telecommunications sectors, where Chinese companies position themselves in consumer markets for the sale of Chinese goods, as well as in the supply of parts and components to other companies in Africa. Companies such as Huawei, Alcatel Shangai, China Mobile and ZTE have been expanding their activities in Africa as suppliers of final products (cell phones, for example) as well as suppliers of parts and components. The largest African markets for the Chinese companies of the telecommunications sector are Algeria, Egypt, Tunisia, Morrocco and South Africa, which represent 60% of the total of assets in the sector. Nigeria and Angola are also rising in importance. The location of all these countries in the coastal region of Africa represents, for some, the Chinese strategy conscious of security and geopolitics (ERA 2009).

Agriculture also presents an important area for Chinese involvement, Chinese FDI has been growing in recent years. Many projects and farms have been created in the last decades in many African countries involving Chinese firms, African producers and African governments. The Chinese Ministries of Foreign Commerce and Economic Cooperation, Foreign Relations and Agriculture began to promote a series of activities with a view to encourage involvement in Africa's agriculture and emphasize the willingness of the government to support the expansion of companies. This support takes place through the facilitation of loans and technical assistance.[10]

By 2013, the stock of Chinese investment in cultivation projects in Africa totaled US$540 million (Brautigam 2015). Between 1987 and 2014, the Chinese agricultural investments in Africa corresponded to approximately six million hectares (ha) of land, but according to the author, only 239,000 ha have actually been acquired by the Chinese. These lands cover 21 African countries, with Cameroon, Mozambique and Madagascar as the top of receivers. Cameroon alone accounts for 43% of all accumulated lands actually acquired by the Chinese, most of which are used for rubber.

---

workers in the mines to one in five, to sub-contract 10% of the work to Congolese companies, allocate half of the investments to technology transfer and personnel training of Congolese, and devote a percentage to social and environmental expenditures (ERA 2009). The deal caused controversy in the West, especially through the IMF, and also in the DRC itself. The IMF was contrary, claiming that the risks of such a large loan were too great, while sectors of the Congolese society and Member of Parliament complained of the consequences for present and future generations (Lee 2009).

[10]For example, Chinese investors have entered joint ventures in the proccessing of fish in Gabon and Namibia, and have leased land in countries such as Zambia, Tanzania and Zimbabwe (Blakendal 2008: 52). In 2006, the China Development Bank and the Ministry of Agriculture announced a deal to cooperate and promote projects that utilized land and water resources in other countries. China Exim Bank also promised financial support to agricultural projects in Africa. At the same time, China has promoted a series of support, formation and technical aid programs. In 2003–08, for example FOCAC trained about 4,000 African students in agricultural courses in China, apart from the investing in the the construction of research centres in African countries (Brautigam and Xiaoyang 2009).

According to Brautigam (2015), despite the many projects and land acquisitions by the Chinese, Western theories and media reports regarding Chinese expansion in Africa's agriculture do not represent the reality of the situation. According to the author, few of the Chinese investments headlined in media stories have actually taken place, and no one has yet to identify Chinese farmers anywhere on the continent, adding that 'a careful review of Chinese policy shifts shows steadily rising support for outward investment of all kinds but no pattern of sponsoring the migration of Chinese peasants, funding large-scale land acquisitions in Africa, or investing "immense sums" in African agriculture' (ibid.: 3). In a similar argument, Nakatani et al. (2014) indicated that, in recent years, China has constituted itself not as a buyer but actually as a platform for acquiring land by the world, whereby various institutional funds and foreign companies, such as BioPalm Energy (Singapore), AmirgaGroup (India), Adeagro (USA) and Bunge (USA), among others, use China as a platform for buying lands all over the world.

Finally, another strong sector of Chinese investment is infrastructure. Projects such as the construction of airports, hospitals, government buildings, schools, and hydroelectric plants and dams are common in Africa. A great portion of these investments was made viable with the financial support of Exim Bank, and most of the infrastructure projects are made in the energy (hydroelectric plants) and transportation (railways) sectors (Foster et al. 2008).[11]

Impacts on African Growth

The first decade of the twenty-first century is marked by a shift in the trajectory of most African economies after almost three decades of endebtening and recession in the late twentieth century.[12] From the 2000s, a large part of the continent showed signs of progress in the GDP and GDP per capita growth, expansion of international trade, and improvement in poverty indexes. In 2000–10, the continent grew at an average annual rate of 5.12%, compared to 1.59% for the developed economies and 2.76% of the world, in the same period (UNCTAD 2012). In all, Africa grew by 8% and doubled its GDP, which stood at US$1.71 trillion in 2010, while also registering some improvements in GDP per capita, although it remained very low. After

---

[11]Besides these sectors, and among the various financial flows to Africa, it is important to note that foreign aid, which is not FDI, includes credit lines specifically directed to projects linked to development, infrastructure, and humanitarian areas, in addition to those linked to cooperation or technical assistance, and also the cancelation of debt. A large portion of these flows, especially the loans, comes from China Development Bank and from Emix Bank (Exim Bank Anual Report 2011).

[12]In the 1980s and 1990s, Africa presented a low GDP growth rate and an even lower GDP per capita growth rate. In sub-Saharan Africa, the growth rate was of only 2.1%, while the GDP per capita growth rate was negative. Inflation remained hihg and reached 27.36% in the 1990s, while external debt constituted 61.7% of GDP (IMF 2013).

the 2008 crisis, there was a worsening trend, but also a recovery by 2010, when the growth rate for the continent was of 4%.

Given the high dependence of primary goods exports, the improvement of foreign trade and the rise in export profits have been fundamental for the establishment of a macroeconomic framework more favorable for growth and the expansion of government expenditures and investments. As discussed above, a great part of this shift corresponds to the improvement in the terms of trade for primary goods and the rise of China as a consumer of natural resources. According to the World Bank (2012a, b), the better African performance was accompanied by a reduction in poverty levels. Despite the great challenges still faced by the continent, for the first time since 1981, less than half of the African population (47%) lives with less than U$1.25 a day. In 1981, this rate was 51%. In sub-Saharan Africa, the portion of the population that lived in this condition dropped about 10% since 1999. The data regarding mortality shows that, in 1990–2009, maternal mortality declined by 26%, accompanied by a decline in child mortality. Improvements in income per capita were accompanied by an increase in the rate of urbanization, from 28 to 40% since the 1980s, improved levels of schooling, and access to a wider array of consumption goods, such as cell phones and TVs.

Yet, despite the improvements, mostly linked to socioeconomic indices, there have been strong limitations to structural change.[13] While there has been an improvement in the macroeconomic framework and a greater capacity to fund investments and social programs, Africa has not undergone a process of structural change, with the enlargement of industry or an expressive internal income rise. In 2000, the share of industry in the total earned value of Africa as a whole was 33%; in 2014, this share was 32%. The portion of services and agriculture also remained practically the same, at 51 and 15%, respectively (UnctadStat 2016). Moreover, the data on exports presented above reveals that primary goods still prevail, as in the case of Angola in 2014, where oil exports accounted for 96% of the total exports, or Nigeria, one of the biggest economies in the continent, in which oil constitutes 91% of its exports. Even a more diversified economy such as South Africa remains dependent on primary goods, at nearly 50% of total exports (Atlas da Complexidade 2016).

Two cases, Angola and South Africa, may serve to elucidate this issue. In the case of South Africa, primary goods exports have increased, mostly directed to China, which has been accompanied by an increase of external investments to the country, in both mining and manufacturing. The growth spurred of the last decade has allowed a certain improvement in the government's power to intervene, mainly from 2005 onwards, when investments in infrastructure, public expenditures, and consumption were enlarged. This did result in some improvement in employment and reduction of poverty, but both unemployment and poverty rates remain at a

---

[13]According to Prebisch (1949), for example structural change is linked to a country's ability to incorporate technical progress through industrialization, reduce structural heterogeneity and increase domestic income levels.

high level. Surely, the most alarming fact is the persistence of an extremely serious income concentration that makes the country one of the most unequal in the world.

Angola made a promising transition from civil war to the conjuncture of the 2000s, marked by the flow of Chinese financial assistance and investments. The expansion of oil exports, the increase in export profits, and the expansion of Chinese investments in large infrastructure projects sustained an accelerated rate of economic growth. Here, too, the expansion of government expenditures, consumption and investments further boosted growth. Poverty and inequality rates showed some improvement, even though poverty conditions have persisted for most of the population. And, as in other cases, larger structural changes were not observed in the country during the decade. Many criticisms have been directed to Chinese construction companies for not using Angolan workers, as well as to the Angolan government and elite for being the primary beneficiaries of Chinese investments. Even with the expansion of the infrastructure projects and the relative improvement of the socioeconomic indices, the government has not created mechanisms for the social development of the general population (Alves 2012; Power and Alves 2012).

Conclusions

Chinese expansion from the 2000s onwards has promoted fundamental transformations in the international economy. After a long trajectory of expansion, founded first and foremost upon an industrialization project based on state planning and investment, China entered the new millennium in a new growth cycle, featured mainly by heavy industrial investments. This new cycle has made China an important center of manufacturing, but also as a large importer of primary resources. Even though the country does possess large reserves of natural resources, including oil and minerals, the internal demand for such goods has been expanding at an accelerated pace, making China a global center of demand for raw materials. The transformation promoted in the international economy has reverberated among peripheral countries. The improvement in the terms of trade for primary goods has occurred alongside expanding Chinese investments and financial flows directed to peripheral economies which possess the natural resources that China needs. African countries have thus been establishing themselves as important destinations for Chinese investment and financial flows.

The resumption of growth in this period is linked to an important reduction of the external economic vulnerability of African countries. The expansion primary goods exports have allowed the expansion of internal expenditure, both by governments and consumers, and also a greater capacity for investments. This improvement in the external position and exports volumes is strongly linked to the expansion of Chinese demand for primary goods. China has thus also been establishing itself as an important destination for African exports, a position traditionally occupied by Western countries, mainly the United States and Europe.

Chinese investments in the African continent have also increased substantially during the decade. A significant portion was directed to sectors related to natural resources, such as oil exploration and mineral extraction. Chinese companies expanded towards several African countries, opening branches and new companies associated with African companies and aiming at the production of primary goods. Investments have also been directed to several other sectors, such as manufacturing and telecommunications, in search of new consumer markets for their products and services. Chinese investments in infrastructure have been an important element of the country's approach to Africa. Big projects of construction and rehabilitation of highways, railways, harbors, bridges, airports, hydroelectric plants, dams and several projects of construction of schools, hospitals, houses, and public buildings have been undertaken.

To African countries, China seems to be an ally. As Grimm (2011) has argued, the country must not be seen as an agent capable of saving Africa, since its approach to the continent generates adverse effects: China pursues, first and foremost, internal goals. The sale of consumer goods, such as textiles, for example, has had negative effects on local industry in South Africa and Zambia. It is important, therefore, to be cautious when defending the positive effects of China's expansion into Africa. Not only because some aspects of this Chinese expansion, such as the competition in manufacturing, reverberates negatively, but also because African countries face great internal limitations to structural change. The limitations are diverse, linked to weak infrastructure, strong specialization, income concentration, and extreme poverty. Even countries with a more diversified economy, such as South Africa, remain extremely unequal and poor, while others which have experienced expressive growth, such as Angola, have failed to promote structural changes.

In this sense, even with the improved macroeconomic conditions associated with Chinese growth and investments, the transformations observed by African countries seem timid when compared to the enormous challenges still faced.

References

Alves, A. C. (2012). Taming the dragon: China's oil interests in Angola. In Power and Alves (2012), 'China and Angola—A marriage of convenience?'. Pambazuka Press.

Aremu, F. A. (2009) *A comparative study of Japan and China's African diplomacy in contemporary historical context*. Ritsumeikan Asia Pacific University, http://r-cube.ritsumei. ac.jp/bitstream/10367/225/1/RJAPS23_A%20Comparative%20Study%20of%20Japan%20and %20China's%20African%20Diplomacy%20.pdf. Retrieved June 22, 2017.

Beijing Action Plan. (2007–09). Forum on China-Africa Cooperation, http://www.fmprc.gov.cn/ zflt/eng/zyzl/hywj/t280369.htm. Retrieved June 22, 2017.

Blankendal, N. (2008). *China's energy supply security: The quest for African oil*. M.Sc. thesis, International School for Humanities and Social Sciences, University of Amsterdam.

Brautigam, D. (2015). *Will Africa feed China?* (p. 2015). Oxford: Oxford University Press.

Brautigam, D., & Xiaoyang, T. (2009). China's engagement in African agriculture: Down to the Countryside. *Foreign Affairs, The China Quarterly, 199*(September), 686–706.

China-Africa Economic and Trade Cooperation. (2010). *Information office of the state council.* Beijing: PRC.

Cintra, M. A., Pinto, E. C., & Silva Filho, E. B. da. (Eds.). (2015). *China em transformação: dimensões econômicas e geopolíticas do desenvolvimento.* Rio de Janeiro: IPEA.

Cissé, D. (2012). *FOCAC: Trade, investments and aid in China–Africa relations.* Policy Briefing, Centre of Chinese Studies, Stellenbosch University.

ERA [Executive Research Associates]. (2009). *China in Africa: Strategic overview,* http://www.ide.go.jp/English/Data/Africa_file/Manualreport/pdf/china_all.pdf. Retrieved June 22, 2017.

EXIMBANK. (various years). Annual Reports, http://english.eximbank.gov.cn/. Retrieved June 22, 2017.

Foster, V., Butterfield, W., Chen, C., & Pushak, N. (2008). *Building bridges—China's growing role as infrastructure financier for Africa, trends and policy options,* no. 5. The World Bank.

IMF [International Monetary Fund]. (various years). *World economic outlook database,* http://www.imf.org/external/pubs/ft/weo/2013/01/weodata/index.aspx. Retrieved June 22, 2017.

Kaplinksy, R., & Morris, M. (2009). Chinese FDI in Sub-Saharan Africa: Engaging with large dragons. *European Journal of Development Research, 24*(1).

Lee, P. (2009). *China's copper deal back in the melt, Asia Times,* http://www.atimes.com/atimes/China_Business/KF12Cb02.html. Retrieved June 22, 2017.

Medeiros, C. A. de. (1999). Economia e Política do Desenvolvimento recente na China. *Revista de Economia Política, 19*(3), 75.

MOFCOM [Ministry of Commerce of the PRC]. (various years). *Statistical bulletin of China's outward foreign direct investment,* http://english.mofcom.gov.cn/. Retrieved June 22, 2017.

Nakatani, P., Falerios, R. N., Vargas, N. C., Felipe, P. C., Nabuco, G., Helder, T., et al. (2014). A expansão internacional da China através da compra de terras no Brasil e no mundo [The international expansion of China through the acquisition of lands in Brazil and the world]. *Revista Textos & Contextos (Porto Alegre), 13*(1), 58–73.

NBSC [National Bureau of Statistics of China]. (various years). *China statistical yearbook,* http://www.stats.gov.cn/english/. Retrieved June 22, 2017.

Ncube, M., Lufumpa, C. L., & Ndikumana, L. (2010). Chinese trade and investment activities in Africa. *Policy Brief, 1*(4). (The African Development Bank Group Chief Economist Complex).

Ocampo, J. A., & Erten, B. (2013). The global implications of falling commodity prices, http://www.project-syndicate.org/commentary/china-s-growth-slowdown-and-the-end-of-the-commodity-price-super-cyle-by-jose-antonio-ocampo-and-bilge-erten#iRdPGvyaBZhv1xRW. 99. Retrieved June 22, 2017.

OECD. (various years). StatExtracts database, http://stats.oecd.org. Retrieved June 22, 2017.

Oliveira, A. P. (2007). *A política africana da China,* www.casadasafricas.org.br/site/img/upload/674760.pdf. Retrieved June 22, 2017.

Prebisch, R. (2000). [1949] O desenvolvimento econômico da América Latina e alguns de seus principais problemas. In R. Bielshowsky (Ed.) *Cinquenta anos de pensamento da CEPAL.*

Quiang, Z. (2008). *Mapping Chinese development assistance in Africa: A synthesis analysis of Angola.* Mozambique e Zimbabwe, AFRODAD, http://www.afrodad.org. Retrieved June 22, 2017.

Shambaugh, D. (2013). *China goes global: A partial power.* Oxford: Oxford University Press.

Taylor, I. (2009). *China's new role in Africa.* Lynne Rienner.

Taylor, I. (2011). *The Forum on China-Africa Cooperation (FOCAC).* New York, NY: Routledge.

UNComtrade. (various years). Database, http://comtrade.un.org/db. Retrieved June 22, 2017.

UNCTAD. (various years). UnctadStats database, http://unctadstat.unctad.org. Retrieved June 22, 2017.

Wei, S.-J. (2016). *'China's Slowdown and Asia's Economy',* https://www.project-syndicate.org/commentary/china-slowdown-asian-economy-by-shang-jin-wei-2016-01. Retrieved June 22, 2017.

White Paper. (2010). *China-Africa economic and trade cooperation.* Beijing: The Information Office of the State Council, http://www.gov.cn/englisFh/official/2010-12/23/content_1771603.htm. Retrieved June 22, 2017.

White Paper. (2006). *China's African Policy.* Beijing: Information Office of the State Council.

World Bank. (2012a). *African regional briefing.*

World Bank. (2012b). *Annual report.*

Youfa, L. (2011). '*Chinese expert on China-Africa relations over past 55 years*', interview of Vice President of China Institute of International Studies, www.focac.org/eng/zfgx/t805423.htm. Retrieved June 22, 2017.

South Africa and the New Scramble: The Demise of Sub-imperialism and the Rise of the East

William G. Martin

Introduction

As apartheid's last days ran out, expectations blossomed of a more equitable and prosperous era for the people of South and Southern Africa. Certainly, the defeat of apartheid had come at a high cost: according to United Nations (UN) estimates, in the 1980s over a million persons died across the region in the wars that accompanied the death throes of apartheid. It was widely accepted that democratic rule would bring plentiful dividends, from the end of the South African state's costly domestic repression and foreign military operations, to a democratic South African state that would be a peaceful developmental partner across the region.

A generation later, frustration, poverty and perplexity abound. South African economic growth has been much slower than expected, inequality has increased, and well-being has stagnated. South Africa's regional and transcontinental relationships have been equally disappointing and puzzling, particularly after the early Mandela glow faded away. For many radical analysts, the lack of regional amity and progress may be traced to an increasingly corrupt African National Congress (ANC) and the South African state's willing role as a direct agent of Europe and the United States. As the most prolific chronicler of the ANC's move to the right put it over 10 years ago, for those interested in equality and social justice 'Pretoria appears to be merely sub-imperialist' (Bond 2004: 599). From this perspective, the formation of the BRICS group (Brazil, Russia, India, China, South Africa) simply extends the cast of sub-imperial states acting in support of neoliberalism generally and of monopoly/corporate capital and the United States in particular. It is non-

W. G. Martin (✉)
Department of Sociology, Binghamton University, PO Box 6000
Binghamton, NY 13902-6000, USA
e-mail: wgmartin1@gmail.com

W. G. Martin
University of New York, New York, USA

© Springer Nature Singapore Pte Ltd. 2019
S. Moyo et al. (eds.), *Reclaiming Africa*, Advances in African Economic,
Social and Political Development, https://doi.org/10.1007/978-981-10-5840-0_3

sense, Bond argues (Bond 2014, 2015: 15), to argue that South Africa and the BRICS are becoming 'anti-imperialist'.[1]

Yet, others lend more agency to the South African state and especially its powerful corporations that now operate across the continent, casting both as imperialist powers in their own right. As Lesufi (2004: 810, 2006) puts it, 'the global and South African multinational corporations are the social actors orchestrating the opening up of the continent'. Charges of South African imperialism and hegemony are, however, equally contested: 'South Africa's ability to [...] exercise "imperialism" is less significant than many think or fear', given its demonstrated inability to lead a regional, much less continental project (Taylor 2011: 1233; Alden and Le Pere 2009). South Africa also undeniably suffers from other African states the harsh, under developing winds blowing from the North.

These conflicting assessments reveal more than a debate among scholars: they signal fundamental and growing anomalies in our understanding of the relations that bind together the North and South. Regional powers, such as South Africa, that are caught between the rich North and poor South amplify incongruities to traditional models of capitalist development and imperial relations. On the one hand, despite claims of a sub/imperialist role, Pretoria is, for example increasingly viewed as an unreliable ally by the West, being unwilling to oust President Mugabe, lead on AFRICOM, or project capable military power on behalf of the United States and Europe. On the other hand, distrust and resentment of South African expansionism by other African elites, firms and states are widely evident. Thus, while there is no denying South Africa's economic weight, how this relates both economically and politically to the region, the continent and Northern powers is unclear.

In this chapter, I unpack this conundrum in three steps. First, I draw out and specify the different theoretical conceptions behind the varying answers to the question of whether South Africa is imperialist in its own right, sub-imperialist on behalf of the North (the United States, Europe, and International Financial Institutions (IFIs), or, like neighbouring African states, is an object of new imperialist pressures emanating from the North. Second, South Africa's historical and current power across the region and continent is assessed empirically and historically against these models of capital accumulation and imperial relationships. The South Africa state, it is argued, was not a subservient sub-imperialist state in the interwar period, but became one at considerable cost in the apartheid period. Finally, I argue that contemporary anomalies to past models point toward the end of

---

[1]It is not clear who makes the argument that the BRICS are 'anti-imperialist'. Bond names five authors, including this author, but they seem a phantom target: as far as can be ascertained, none of the five authors use the term as cited by Bond (2015: 15). What is common is the argument, as Escobar (2013) notes in the article by him that Bond cites, is that the BRICS are unexpectedly powerful ('for the first time in 150 years, the combined output of the developing world's three leading economies—Brazil, China and India—is about equal to the combined GDP of the long-standing industrial powers of the North') and this is leading the BRICS to 'not only deploy their economic clout but also take concrete steps leading towards a multipolar world'. None of this means they are 'anti-capitalist' or 'anti-imperialist', and to ignore these shifts leads to analytical and political missteps, as we argue below.

this role for the South African state, given the declining importance of the North and the creation of new networks of accumulation orienting the region and South Africa towards the East. If there is a sub-imperial role for South Africa in the future, it would need to be in relation to Asian powers—and there is little sign of this prospect, as yet.

Framing Imperialism, Africa and South Africa

There can be no denying the compelling forces that have led so many to revisit theories of imperialism. As in the late nineteenth and early twentieth centuries, we are living in a conjuncture marked by economic crisis, the expanding power of capital, increasing rivalry among great and emerging powers, the forcible opening up of closed markets, and a new scramble for raw materials, foodstuffs, and land. Ballooning discussions of land grabs, commodity and financial booms, and, more generally, a 'new scramble for Africa', certainly pose close parallels to the classic imperialist epoch of the late nineteenth and early twentieth centuries.

Lenin's *Imperialism* remains, of course, a touchstone guide. In its most common reading, imperialism took on a specific form, whereby monopolies replaced free competition in the late nineteenth century, only to be superseded by the domination of finance over productive capital in the early twentieth century. This, moreover, was a global process, producing increasing global inequality and aggressive competition among states—including powerful new contenders from outside Europe and North America. In Lenin's words in 1917 (1970: 744): '[c]apitalism is growing with the greatest rapidity in the colonies and in the overseas countries. Among the latter, new imperialist powers are emerging (e.g., Japan)'. The relevance to South Africa and other powerful members of the Global South—today's 'emerging powers' and especially the so-called BRICS—is immediate. One may easily draw the conclusion, as does Lesufi (2006: 33), for example that 'South African capital has all the essential features of imperialism as conceptualized by Lenin'.

Such conclusions are, however, difficult to sustain. As Giovanni Arrighi pointed out in his definitive conclusion to the 1970s debates over imperialism, if nothing else, Lenin was consistently, insistently, historically determinate in his analysis of imperialism (Arrighi 1983: 12). And historical facts, as Lenin paraphrasing British empiricists emphasized at the time, are stubborn things. Contemporary capitalist development and underdevelopment are not, quite simply, being driven by financial cartels that have absorbed productive capital. In the late nineteenth and early twentieth century, finance capital, married to state power, expanded during periods of economic crisis through colonial conquest. Competition among capitalist firms had turned into a competition among states. Indeed, the strength of Lenin's argument rested upon careful historical analysis of the transition from competitive to monopoly forms and their linkage to inter-state rivalries. It was powerfully predictive: the scramble for Africa would indeed be followed by thirty years of war among the great powers.[2]

Between this period and today little but distant analogies hold. Surplus capital does now reside in large financial firms, yet these are quite divorced from the productive capital and show no taste for territorial conquest and direct, colonial rule. Today's largest Western banks—JP Morgan Chase, Barclays, Deutsche Bank, PNB Paribas, and the like—bear little resemblance to the merger of the state and capital that drove late nineteenth-century imperialisms. Indeed, the most innovative and profitable US corporations, from Apple to Google to Microsoft, often employ few and own few, if any, factories. And while US militarism is accelerating today, this is more a testimony to how a declining world power increasingly relies on brutal force rather than legitimacy and consent.

Analogies to early twentieth-century theories of imperialism are on firmer ground when they call up the concept of 'primitive accumulation' as a central component of the neoliberal era. As during previous global great depressions, core states and capitalist firms have sought, since the 1970s, to solve economic and political crises at home via expansion abroad. Since the 1980s, this has been developed under the term 'accumulation by dispossession', whereby a crisis of overaccumulation in the North is resolved by the exploitation of untapped resources in the South. Central here are neoliberal policies of commodification and privatisation, brutally imposed on peripheral, formally non-capitalist zones (Harvey 2003). South Africa is fitted into this framework as a transmission belt for neoliberal imperialism as devised and deployed by Europe, the United States, the IMF, and the World Bank. As Bond puts it (2006: 113), 'modern imperialism necessarily combines neoliberalism and accumulation by dispossession in peripheral sites like Africa along with increasing subservience to the USA's indirect, neocolonial rule'. As Bond says, '[t]his is 1885 all over again' (cited in Fabricious 2013).

In a recent review of the debate over South Africa as sub-imperial power, Melanie Samson (2009: 96) argues that Bond and other proponents of the sub-imperialism thesis fail to provide 'an adequate theorization of subimperialism', leaving us with an 'ahistorical, unchanging conceptualization of sub-imperialism'. This overstates the case,[3] but it does point to a major difficulty for current models of imperialism (and its derivative sub-imperialism): the concept inevitably traces downward from crises of accumulation in advanced capitalist states (via overproduction, underconsumption, falling rate of profit, etc.), to their resolution by a new

---

[2]'Imperialist wars are absolutely inevitable' (Lenin 1970: 674); and '[t]he struggle among the world imperialisms is becoming more acute [...] what means other than war could there be *under capitalism* to overcome the disparity between the development of the productive forces and the accumulation of capital on the one side, and the division of colonies and spheres of influence for finance capital on the other?' (ibid: 744–745, *emphasis in original*).

[3]In more recent work Bond (2012) has more carefully constructed the historical growth of South African financial institutions and speculative excesses.

burst of forcing open and exploiting poorer, so-called 'pre-' or 'non-' capitalist areas, states and peoples (Harvey 2003).

This is, quite simply, a reductive, Euro–American conception. As I have argued at greater length elsewhere (Martin 2013a; see also Moyo et al. 2012), contemporary discussions of imperialism via 'accumulation by dispossession' construct a relatively homogeneous, residual and objectified Global South that is operated upon from above. In these formulations, the South and its peoples play little role, if any, in the crisis and its resolution other than offering a new, non-capitalist area to exploit. In this sense, 'primitive' or 'ongoing' accumulation too easily becomes to 'capitalist' accumulation what 'traditional' is to 'modern': a residual construct that relegates the majority of the world's population to lives outside capitalist modernity proper.[4]

This is a particularly problematic concept for eminently capitalist areas like South Africa, where land and labour have long been commodified and integrated into global capital accumulation. Even in Lenin's day, this posed difficulties for theories of imperialism, as illustrated by Lenin's short, ambiguous references to 'semi-colonies' and 'semi-independent countries'. In the post-World War II period, the term 'subimperialism' emerged to address these problems, most notably in the work of Ruy Mauro Marini, which focused on how class actors across Brazil and the United States changed Brazil's class configuration and its position in the world economy (Marini 1965, 1972; see also Evans 1979). More recent studies have updated the argument (Flynn 2007), noting that Brazilian elites in the early 1990s (like South Africa) followed neoliberal precepts flowing from the North. Even under President Lula (2003–10), who was elected with strong support from trade unions (as was, of course, the ANC), the Brazilian government remained committed to the basic tenets of neoliberalism as accepted by dominant classes, including debt payments, large primary surpluses, high interest rates and free investment flows. Flynn draws the conclusion that 'theories of global capitalism are not incompatible with Marini's theory of sub-imperialism. The case of Brazil, a key nation in the semi-periphery, suggests that the two views are complementary' (Flynn 2007: 24).

---

[4]While capital accumulation can be carefully delineated following Marx's M-C-M sequences, it is often very hard to define what constitutes primitive accumulation. 'Accumulation by dispossession', as Harvey coins it, covers an exceedingly wide range of phenomena outside of the processes of capital accumulation proper. As Harvey (2003: 153) says: 'A close look at Marx's description of primitive accumulation reveals a wide range of processes: the commoditization and privatization of land and the forceful expulsion of peasant populations; the conversion of various forms of property rights (common, collective, state, etc.) into exclusive private property rights; the suppression of rights to the commons; the commodification of labour power and the suppression of alternative (indigenous) forms of production and consumption; colonial, neo-colonial and imperial processes of appropriation of assets (including natural resources); the monetization of exchange and taxation, particularly of land; the slave trade; and usury, the national debt, and ultimately the credit system as radical means of primitive accumulation'. To these, one then adds today's myriad forms associated with structural adjustment, land grabs, commodity booms, and neoliberalism generally.

This conclusion rests in large part on the growing transnational activities of Brazilian firms, transnational class alliances and the regional projects of a relatively autonomous Brazilian state.

There are sharp comparisons to be made with South Africa. Like South Africa, Brazil is far more indebted now than in 1990, has privatized many state-owned enterprises, and has witnessed a decimation of a manufacturing sector built up under preceding authoritarian and neoliberal governments. It has also, like South Africa, sought to create regional alliances and a regional market, with mixed success, again like South Africa. Unlike South Africa, however, foreign direct investment (FDI) into Brazil accelerated in the last generation, even as Brazilian firms, particularly since 2000, expanded abroad. Despite liberalization, continuing state support in forms of financing, R&D support, and protection against foreign takeovers has been critical to the success of Brazilian firms, like the oil giant Petrobras, the commercial jet exporter Embraer and the mining giant Vale.

As these conclusions and comparisons indicate, while reframing the debate over sub-imperialism in comparative and class terms does not resolve it, it does move us away from purely core-centric theories of accumulation and state power, and toward a narrower and more focused investigation. South African and Brazilian patterns press us to assess, over global booms and busts, whether and to what degree state action has engaged and been shaped by relations with local and foreign capital as well as neighbouring states. If sub-imperialism is a project, it should be evident in measures of regional domination and subordination to international partners. But what does the South African case show?

Positioning South Africa in the World Economy

For many analysts, South African sub-imperialism is easily and explicitly evident in every major store in the region and increasingly the continent: to shop for cell phones, foodstuffs or banking services is often to confront a wall of South African products and firms. On the regional terrain, South Africa clearly stands out as an economic elephant, whether measured in terms of the types of good and services produced, the level and depth of its labour and consumer markets, the size and weight of local firms, or the strength of physical, technological and financial infrastructures.

Just how great the gap is and its direction can be traced in long-term trends in national income per capita. For while this reveals little regarding levels of inequality and well-being, it does indicate the relative world economic and geopolitical weight of states and their dominant classes. And here the evidence is quite clear (see Fig. 1): South Africa has, for over 60 years, stood well above the states of the region and the continent—and has done surprisingly better in the last thirty neoliberal years than all but the few states that possess new and disproportionately large mineral and oil discoveries (e.g. Angola and Botswana).

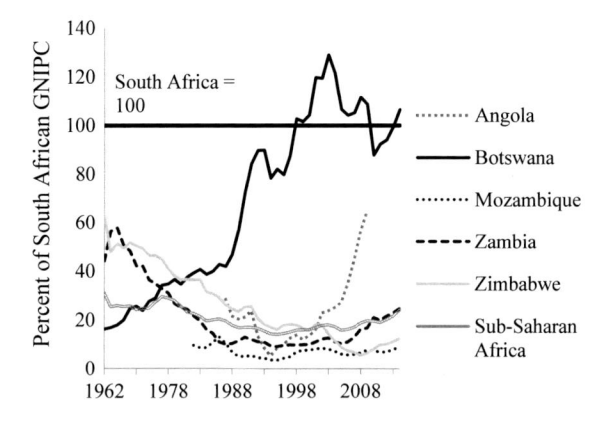

Fig. 1 South Africa versus Region 1962–2014. *Source* World Development Indicators, available at http://data.worldbank.org/, accessed 23 April 2016

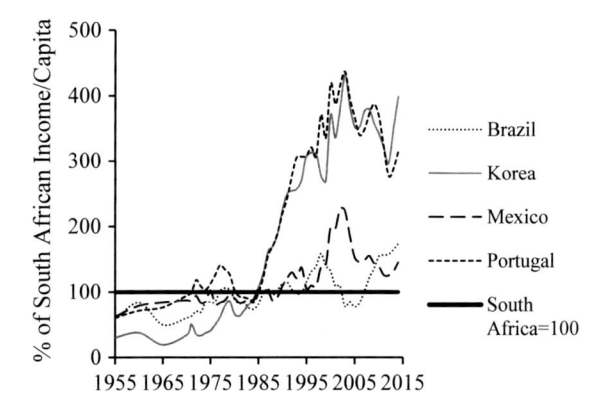

Fig. 2 Overtaking South Africa: Semiperiphery, 1955–2014. *Source* United Nations, Statistical Yearbook (1948); World Bank, World Tables (1994) and *World Development Indicators*, available at http://data.worldbank.org/, accessed 23 April 2016

At the same time, it must be pointed out that in the post-World War II period, South Africa did not fare well by comparison to Brazil and other semi-peripheral or the 'newly industrializing states' (NICs) of the period, as Fig. 2 indicates.

The hesitancy with which South Africa is included or excluded from the category of 'emerging' states and the BRICS group thus has real foundations: South Africa's economy has been stagnant for at least 20 years, a pitiful record by comparison to the NICs and its partners in the BRICS group (see, for example, Andreasson 2011; Shaw et al. 2009; and Fig. 4).

How far back this comparative decline may be traced is suggested by relating South Africa's performance to Europe and the United States. As Fig. 3 suggests South Africa closed the gap with core states in the interwar, imperialist epoch. This success turned into stagnation in the apartheid decades and a real decline in the post-apartheid epoch—the recent commodity and gold boom notwithstanding.

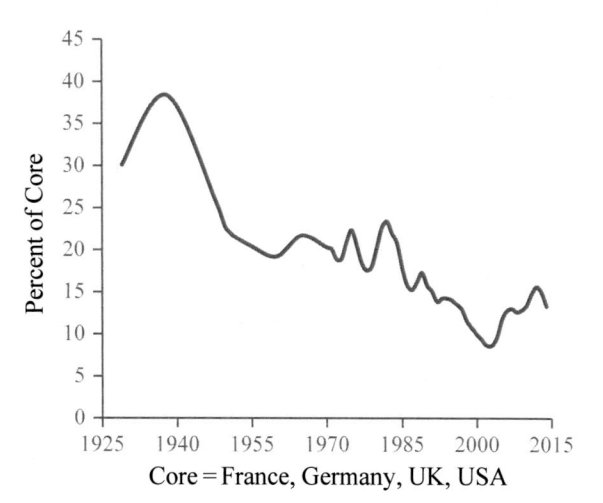

Fig. 3 South Africa versus Core Zone. *Source* United Nations, Statistical Yearbook (1948); World Bank, World Tables (1994) and *World Development Indicators*, available at http://data.worldbank.org/, accessed 23 April 2016

Core = France, Germany, UK, USA

In short: if South Africa was a newly industrializing country in the 1920s, in the short period of American hegemony it became not a NIC but a NUC, a newly under developing country. This finding reverses the common depiction of the post-1948 apartheid period as the era when South Africa first industrialized, entered into a long boom, and came to dominate surrounding states (Martin 2013b).

While these data mark out the rank and direction of South Africa's position in the world economy, they tell us only of outcomes and not the processes and relationships by which South Africa's position was attained or sustained. What did the relation of the South African state and firms with foreign states and firms have to do with this track record? Did imperialism or sub-imperialism, as sketched and predicted in such various ways by such different theories, have much to do with it? And what might the future bring?

South Africa's Record

If South Africa today dominates the region and large parts of the continent, it was not always so. As suggested by Mamdani (1996) trenchant argument that apartheid was the generic form of colonialism, South Africa through most of its early history stood in a colonial relation to Europe like its neighbours: racially colonized, exporting primary products and importing European manufactures. As the data in Fig. 3 suggest, it was in the interwar period that this pattern was broken. Under a new anti-British, Afrikaner government, South Africa after 1925 industrialized and become not just richer than its neighbours, but a producer of much more advanced goods. Protecting the home market through high tariffs and related measures not only fostered the expansion of local firms but also permitted the creation of state industries in leading sectors, where no local or foreign firms would invest—such as the giant Iron and Steel Corporation (ISCOR). At the same time, US multinationals leapfrogged colonial and settler tariff walls and began to build branch plants in South Africa (from auto producers Ford and General Motors, to consumer-goods manufacturers like Kellogg's). By the end of World War II, South Africa was not only richer than other African territories, Korea, Brazil and most of southern Europe, but was one of the very few industrial powers outside Europe and North America.

Was this the result of a new 'sub-imperial' strategy? It clearly was not a path or role directed by core powers: South Africa's advance was made possible by an aggressive rupture with the British state and British firms which opposed South African industrialisation. Nor were capital flows along the lines suggested by Lenin (or later theories of monopoly capital) fundamental to this process. US firms, it is true, began to locate in South Africa in this period, but this was largely driven by new tariff controls and not excessive US exports of capital—indeed, the major new advancements in higher wage, industrial production were propelled by the South African state.

Nor did the South African state or firms expand into the region. Far from it: barriers were constructed to the imports, both material and human, from neighbouring states. South Africa in the interwar period might, for example still import some Rhodesian tobacco, but it returned to Rhodesia in the form of South African cigarettes. South African mines might similarly expand production, particularly after the gold price leaped upward in the early 1930s, but the state assured that far fewer Mozambicans were employed and far greater numbers of black South Africans were hired and spent their earnings inside South Africa.

In relation to theories of sub-imperialism, it is notable that this strategic move took place not by replicating models of imperial powers or foreign capital—as suggested by some sub-imperial analogies—but rather by nationalist and relatively autonomous state seizing opportunities created by a colonial world in chaotic disarray. This required reconfiguring relations with both core states overseas and surrounding colonial territories (Martin 2013b). In short, this was very much the creation of an aggressive semi-peripheral state, engaging both core and peripheral elites and firms. The South African state emerged as the modern Janus: facing and fighting both the rich North and surrounding colonial and white-settler states.

During the postwar period, these conditions accelerated the increasing reliance of neighbours upon South Africa. Based on interwar advances, South Africa came to export industrial manufactures to the region and import cheap African labour for its mines and farms. Apartheid's secret was not just racial segregation and repression at home, but the differentiation of cheap, territorially differentiated labour forces and markets across the region. This was uneven development personified, forging for the first time a 'region' defined by interdependence, and divergent patterns of social reproduction by race and gender—all to the design and advantage of white South Africa and domestic and foreign firms alike.

At the same time, warm relations with the new hegemon, the United States, resulted in adherence to the new rules and institutions behind the US world order.

This meant above all commitments to new international agencies, from the United Nations to new international financial institutions, and, especially, an open to door US multinationals. This marked a significant change from the British world order and reliance upon equity versus fixed capital and commercially oriented, competitive capital. Significant Foreign Direct Investment (FDI) did occur, while South African conglomerates grew as well, particularly in mining, engineering and finance.

As Fig. 3 suggests the stability and prosperity made possible by this set of relations with the North and the region failed to survive the mid-1970s, marking a substantive break in South Africa's developmental fortunes. In part, this may be traced to the outbreak of the global economic crisis and rebellious new trade union, student and black power movements in South Africa—and also in the North. Yet, as suggested again by Fig. 2, South Africa suffered a far greater decline than competing semi-peripheral states and especially the NICs—many of which faced similar protest waves in the wake of 1968 (e.g. Brazil, Korea, Portugal). What the South African state proved unable to do throughout this whole period, in striking contrast to many other semi-peripheral states, was develop new state and state-supported enterprises and attract significant manufacturing investment as unruly manufacturing capital fled the North for cheaper, less regulated semi-peripheral locations. This was the cost of its adherence to the US world order. There would be no South African equivalent to Brazil's jet exporter Embraer, Korea's auto producer Hyundai or Taiwan's computer hardware giant Acer.

As sanctions advanced internationally and national liberation movements came to power in 1975 and 1980, the regional spaces open to South African and foreign firms contracted. By any measure—trade, investment or migration—relationships between South Africa and all her neighbours plummeted. By the mid-1980s, Pretoria was forced to concede all but the military domination of the region. This was, as we know, a failing strategy at home and abroad. Regional relationships, so central to accumulation under apartheid and white-settler colonialism in the region, were withering away.

Post-apartheid South Africa: Scrambler or Scrambled?

The negotiated settlement that led to majority rule is widely held to have been a moment of 'elite transition', entrenching neoliberalism and a new black elite (Bond 2000). Facing Europe and the United States, the new ANC government continued the late apartheid state's commitment to neoliberal trade, investment, and finance policies. At the same time, sanctions fell and states across the continent rapidly opened their doors to trade, investment and finance. Opening economic doors were followed by political ones. After hesitation under President Mandela, the South African government aggressively moved to lead new continental programs and institutions (e.g. the formation of the African Union, NEPAD, the African Parliament, etc.). Given the neoliberal foundations of South Africa's domestic, regional, and continental policies, it is easy to depict the current South African government as little more than a willing transmission belt for neoliberal programs promoted by the United States, United Kingdom and Europe in general. It is clearly a failed developmental strategy.

This interpretation produces, however, a severely limited understanding of South Africa's transnational relations, and certainly fails to account for many anomalies of what might be called the 'subimperialism subservience' model. This is due not only to the lack of research on South African firms, foreign multinationals, and transnational alliances—although this is very much the case to our collective detriment (for exceptions, see Miller 2004, 2006; Verhoef 2011). More central to the problem is the lack of historical and theoretical precision. The late nineteenth-century 'scramble' was carried out by states and increasingly large capitalist firms seeking enclosed markets spaces demarcated by formal colonial territories. Post-World War II expansionism took place, by contrast, under the new forms promulgated under US hegemony. Multinational corporations led the way, facilitated by free investment policies. But do today's phenomena replicate postwar accumulation and spatial patterns in service of US imperialism?

To track investment flows and vehicles from South Africa to the region and the rich North indicates something quite different is afoot in the 'new scramble for Africa'. Postwar monopoly capital in its classic form (Baran and Sweezy 1966), and multinationals more broadly, were large, self-managing and self-financing firms that set prices and managed demand versus earlier forms of competitive capitalism. They expanded worldwide by investing in branch plants that allowed them to leapfrog the tariff walls raised during the interwar great depression. But are South Africa's current relationships with the North and region understandable in terms of these historic processes?

The short answer is no.[5] As all observers and data agree, the coming of majority rule did not lead to the expected revival of direct investment by foreign multinationals. To be sure, the struggle against apartheid can account for the flight of capital during the 1970s and 1980s, when other semi-peripheral states drew in manufacturing from the de-industrializing North. Since 1994, however, FDI flows have been volatile and meagre, particularly by comparison to similarly situated states. As the *Financial Times* summarized for its international business readers in 2008, 'between 1994 and 2002, average net annual inflows of FDI were 1.5% of gross domestic product compared with 3% for South Africa's international rivals' (Hawk 2008: 3). While the subsequent commodity boom led to higher levels of FDI, these peaked in 2008 and fell by 80% in the next two years, to a point where South Africa's FDI inflows as a proportion of GDP ranked 128th in the world, right behind Burkina Faso (UNCTAD 2011: Web Table 28). And while the collapse of the commodity super-cycle impacted all natural resource investment in Africa, South Africa has recently suffered more than the rest: in 2015, FDI to South Africa fell by 74%, far more than elsewhere in the region or Africa (UNCTAD 2016: 5). If

---

[5]For the counter case, see Foster (2002).

South Africa is being scrambled, in the sense of being the target of significant new direct investments, there is little evidence of it. The one case where significant direct investment and exports in manufacturing took place after apartheid, automotive production and parts, is telling: it is the one sector where the state imposed trade and investment regulations and incentives. This leads to a parallel observation: if foreign multinationals in the neoliberal, post-apartheid era are using South Africa as a sub-imperial springboard to the region and continent, there are few signs of it.

Might one make a better case for South Africa's own firms? Within the borders of the apartheid state, large conglomerates grew apace, paralleling trends in core states. In the more advanced manufacturing sectors, they also became heavily dependent on the region for exports. After World War II, South Africa's relations with its neighbours increasingly took the form of the historic relations holding between core states and their colonies: South Africa exported manufactured goods and services and received in return primary products and cheap labour. And while South Africa was the major trading partner of most regional states, no regional state provided a significant proportion of South Africa's imports. This was, as Hirschman (1980) emphasized long ago, a classic case of unequal power.

As the doors closed on the apartheid era, it was expected that the re-opening of the region and the continent would enhance the presence and power of South Africa's own multinational conglomerates across the region and farther north. In relation to the North, what took place was something quite different: as soon as capital controls were relaxed, the richest and biggest South African firms, internationalized themselves—by fleeing the country. This was a capital flight with a vengeance, as some of the country's largest firms in the mining, financial, and energy sectors (e.g. Anglo-American, De Beers, Old Mutual, South African Breweries, Liberty, Sasol and Billiton) moved their primary exchange listings and headquarters to London. Decisions, henceforth, were made in London, while dividends and other payments could now be legally moved out of South Africa as well.[6]

Illegal capital flight accelerated as well after 1994. Estimated at 5.4% of GDP a year in the late apartheid years (1980–93), it rose to an estimated 9.2% between 1994 and 2001, and accelerated to 27% in 2007 (Ashman et al. 2011: 9). Despite all the language of non-racialism and the rainbow nation, capital movements are highly racialized: historically white firms have fled North with the wealth built up under apartheid, while locally a small black capitalist stratum was pump-primed into existence by the state and local firms seeking post-apartheid legitimacy.

South African firms did expand northward into the rest of Africa. The path here was paved by the North's imposition of structural adjustment, which served to shrink African state power and open doors to unfettered trade and investment.

---

[6]International agencies and South African government reports often lag considerably in catching the transition of multinational firms from South African to British or US (e.g. Anglo-American to AAC, South African Breweries to SAB), rendering data surveys questionable. See the data and comments in Verhoef (2011).

Mandela and Mbeki's acceptance and application of neoliberal policies facilitated this process mightily: in the first 5 years after majority rule exports from the South African Custom Union (overwhelmingly South African) to regional Southern African Development Community (SADC) partners tripled (from Rand 5 billion in 1993 to Rand 16 billion in 1998). Imports doubled (from Rand 1.3 billion to Rand 2.6 billion (Davies 2001, 51)). South African imports from Africa also grew over this period, largely due to oil imports from Nigeria and Angola, while exports also moved steadily upward. By 2005, South Africa was exporting goods worth Rand 47 billion to the rest of Africa, around 15% of its total exports, while importing only Rand 16 billion of goods (or less than four percent of South Africa's imports).

This fostered unequal exchange along two dimensions. First, South Africa continued to import raw materials and simple manufactures from other African states, while finding in Africa its best market for up to 50% of its advanced manufacturing exports (Cassim et al. 2002; see also Buthelezi 2003). Second, South Africa imported little from SADC or Africa as a percentage of its total imports, yet for many countries, South Africa became the key, overwhelming import partner. Ten years after apartheid ended, South African imports accounted for 45% of Mozambique's imports, 44% of Zambia's, 33% of Malawi's, 32% of Zimbabwe's and 10–15% of the total imports of Angola, Mauritius, the Democratic Republic of Congo (DRC), and Tanzania (South Africa, Department of Trade and Industry 2010). Even in distant Kenya, these patterns held, where exports to South Africa in the 5 years up to 2007 moved up to only Shilling 1.3 billion, while imports from South Africa ballooned from Sh12 to Sh35 billion in 2007 (*Business Daily*, Nairobi, 10 July 2008).

These inequalities were replicated in both equity and direct investment flows. By some estimates, South Africa was Southern Africa's largest foreign direct investor ten years after the end of apartheid (Wolfgang 2006: ix). By 2003, South Africa was, for example the largest foreign investor in Botswana, the DRC, Lesotho, Malawi, Mozambique, Swaziland and Zambia. By the end of 2004, South Africa's FDI in Africa amounted to Rand 24 billion (US$3.7 billion) (South African Reserve Bank 2006, S101–S103).[7] By 2008, direct investment in Africa was over US$100 billion, almost 25% of total FDI, and three times the amount in North America (South African Reserve Bank 2010, S92–S95). As with trade, expansion has been particularly strong across the continent and not just the surrounding member-states of SADC: after 2000, the annual growth of South African FDI in Africa was 29%, compared to an annual rate of investment in SADC of only six percent (Gelb 2006).

---

[7]Estimates of South Africa's FDI in the rest of Africa vary quite widely among those who use project-based data versus those who rely on official capital flow data, e.g. between researchers (the Human Science Research Council, Business Map, South African Institute of International Affairs) and the South African Reserve Bank and international agencies such as UNCTAD. For the range of data, see Wolfgang (2006: 17–19), and for related problems with Chinese FDI, Kaplinsky and Morris (2009).

These investments were spread right across the financial, retail, mining, telecom and energy sectors. South African banks have moved beyond the region to open branches across the continent, absorbing in the process of local banking and insurance companies, from Nigeria to Kenya to Togo. Retail forms a special case of success, with Shoprite as the leader. Shoprite opened its first foreign stores in Namibia in 1990, the first central African store opened its doors in Zambia in 1995 and there were 187 corporate and 43 franchise stores in 15 African countries outside South Africa by 2012 (Angola, Botswana, Ghana, Lesotho, Madagascar, Malawi, Mauritius, Mozambique, Namibia, Nigeria, Swaziland, Tanzania, Uganda, Zambia and Zimbabwe) (Shoprite 2012). Cell phone operator MTN, incorporated only in 1994, has had equally remarkable success, spreading through Africa to the Middle East. By 2010 it was the largest listing on the Johannesburg Stock Exchange (MTN 2012), and by 2015 had 241 million subscribers in 21 countries (MTN 2015).

More broadly considered, South African firms operate breweries, run airports, build roads and bridges, and manage hotel chains all across the continent. Given South Africa's long-standing mineral and energy complex, large investments have also been made in zinc, coal, gas, gold, platinum and diamond mining. The South African state has itself financed projects in over 20 countries through its Industrial Development Corporation, which has, for example a 24% share in the US$2 billion Mozal aluminium smelter project in Mozambique. South Africa's lack of oil or natural gas reserves has propelled similar investments in the region, particularly in Namibian and Mozambican gas; Eskom, the state-owned utility, is engaged in building a regional power grid and has projects in seventeen African countries.

These initiatives must be set against, as noted above, the actual flight from South Africa of some of its largest private mining and energy firms, which now operate their global operations from London and not Johannesburg. South Africa is also not a major consumer of key industrial minerals—the new consumers and price-setters of copper, zinc, aluminium, and iron ore are to be found in the East. South African firms do not integrate the exploitation of new resources into an expanding South African manufacturing sector; indeed, they export raw materials elsewhere. And South African mining and energy companies are increasingly being out-flanked by Asian states and firms that can draw on new models of financing, pricing, and higher levels of state support.

These developments are hard to derive from classic models of imperialism. The introduction of notions of 'primitive accumulation' or 'accumulation by dispossession' provides little additional explanatory power. Much has been written on the 'new scramble for Africa' in general and on 'land grabs' in particular. But while there has been a much alarming discussion, there has until recently been little depth of observation. As Hall (2011: 205) survey of land dispossession in Southern Africa concludes, the media-driven depictions of a massive new wave of land grabbing in Southern Africa need to be moderated, given the failure of proposed deals and investment, particularly in relation to Western corporations, China, and Korea. In part, this reflects successful resistance on the ground, the complex and incomplete state of land reforms and land titling, and the uncertain blurring of foreign and domestic investors and lessees. Studies of land grabs illustrate, moreover, little connection between financial agents in Europe and North America, the home of neoliberal solutions to the economic crisis, and agents on the ground—particularly from Asia, the Gulf, and local states.

South Africa is, in any case, hardly a target for large 'land grabs'. Far from being the target for 'primitive accumulation', South Africa suffers from the excessive dispossession of land and labour under apartheid, as the cheap labour thesis postulated long ago. This has not only stifled the possibility of innovation and growth at home, but also put South Africa very much at a disadvantage in relation to other states that have long been investing in, rather than dispossessing, social and human capital (Arrighi et al. 2010). Older forms of dispossession do continue into the region, however, driven by the changing economic and political situation for commercial farmers in South Africa; after majority rule, their numbers fell from over 60,000 in 1996, to 45,000 in 2002, to below 40,000 in 2007 (South Africa 2012: 6). This has generated a new trek by white farmers into Zambia and Mozambique, among other locations. Whether the relatively small numbers of white farmers involved turns into a flood remains, however, very much to be seen (Hall 2012).

One might make the case for a land grab movement north by South African agribusiness, most notably in the sugar sector, where the two major firms, Illovo and Tongaat Hulett, rapidly expanded their estates, outgrower operations, and processing plants across Mozambique, Tanzania, Zambia, and Zimbabwe (see Richardson 2010). This reflected, as in the case of white commercial farmers, as much an exodus from South Africa as an expansion from a strong South African base. Illovo, now Africa's largest sugar producer, expanded outside South Africa in the 1990s by taking over privatized operations in Malawi, Swaziland, and Zambia. This led to British Sugar buying a controlling share in Illovo in 2005. By 2012, only 7% of Illovo's operating profit came for its South African operations (Illovo Sugar Ltd. 2012: 11), and, in early 2016, Illovo was wholly taken over by Associated British Foods (which had seen its European sugar operations collapse). Tongaat Hulett's post-apartheid expansion is similar: it began with the acquisitions in Mozambique in 1998 and in Zimbabwe in 2006, and by 2015 was operating in six regional states. In 2012, its South Africa operations contributed but a scant eight percent of the profits derived from its sugar operations (Tongaat Hulett Sugar 2012: 65). Subsequent revival of profits from South African sugar production could not forestall, however, the effects of the halving of real-world sugar prices since 2011 (OECD 2015: 119). The case of the jatropha boom-and-bust land grabs in the region, from Tanzania to Mozambique, is even more telling as project after project has collapsed due to falling yields and prices.

Looking East and the BRICS

Simply stated, South Africa's current role in world accumulation and geopolitical relationships cannot be fitted into twentieth-century models of how relations were regulated between rich and poor, core and peripheral, areas of the world. Since at the least the 1920s, the South African state and its dominant classes have struggled to maintain and advance its 'semi-peripheral' position—with more success when it sought to resist the winds and agents of underdevelopment from the North. Indeed, its greatest advances came during the opportunities afforded by the transition from British to US hegemony, and from free trade to free enterprise forms of regulating and organizing North/South relationships.

Yet, the anomalies presented today do not fit the global accumulation or semi-peripheral patterns we have known for over a century. In part, this marks the end of apartheid, in larger part, it signals the end of a century of Anglo-American hegemony and corresponding models of imperialism. In this interregnum, the semi-peripheral post-apartheid state had floundered. On the one hand, the continuation of the developmental alliance with the North led the ANC to embrace the late apartheid's regime adoption of neoliberal and non-racial principles without realizing the long-term underdevelopment these entailed. On the other hand, these ideological and policy commitments to the past hegemon undercut the state's attempt to lead continental states.

Neo-Gramscian and left analyses that stress the failure of South Africa's bid for continental hegemony are quite correct on this score. Mbeki's deployment of the notion of Ubuntu was not simply 'hypocrisy' or the sign of a 'revolution betrayed': it expressed a real attempt to maintain an alliance with the North and yet find a way to forge legitimacy with other African states. It should not surprise us, then, that mutually exclusive policies to the North and the region emerge; they reflect and reproduce unequal exchange and the highly racialized nature of transnational relationships in the post-apartheid epoch. Looking North, the proclamation of non-racialism and the celebration of formal racial equality serves to protect long-standing, highly racialized forms of wealth and accumulation. Looking South, the promotion of a black elite, Ubuntu, and remembrances of the colonial and apartheid eras conversely aims to forge allegiances in a common African condition. In summary: the semi-peripheral position constructed under apartheid and continued since inextricably involves contradictory stances toward richer, core states and institutions and underdeveloping relations with fellow Africans and states.

If past North/South forms of accumulation had continued, the post-apartheid state and South African capital might have indeed benefited more directly from an alliance with the North and its exploitative relations with neighbouring states. Yet a very different situation holds as South Africa and surrounding states face a future that is increasingly dependent far more upon accumulation and state formation processes spreading outward from Asia than those that emanate from Europe or the United States. The empirical evidence on the importance of these developments for Africa is quite clear, accelerating, and unsettling for the North and theories of sub/

imperialism. For most African states, Asia is now by far the more important partner, and one that is disrupting past North–South colonial relationships. In 2000, China, for example received 14% of Africa's exports; by 2007, a World Bank study noted the figure has risen to 27%, on par with exports to the United States and the European Union (EU), with the EU share being halved over 2000–05 (Broadman 2007: 2). By 2008, China alone was the continent's largest source of Africa's imports and second only to the United States in its share of exports.

The impact has been even more direct and disruptive for rich South Africa. By 2009, China was South Africa's largest trading import and export partner; by 2014, South Africa was importing twice as much from China as from the United States. Figures for investment are less reliable, but are rising rapidly as well. While concentrated originally in mining, investment has extended to construction, energy, and some electronic goods assembly. The largest gold producer in China, the Zijin Mining Group Company, is engaged in a mining project worth Rand 1 billion, while Sinosteel is involved in two chromium mines, and state-owned firms have majority states in platinum projects. In 2010, Jidong, the largest cement producer in northern China, announced an investment of Rand 800 million in a 1.65 billion Rand (US$221 million) cement manufacturing project, building on past activity by the Chinese construction firms Citic and Covec. In October 2007, the world's largest bank, the Industrial Commercial Bank of China, purchased 20% of Africa's and South Africa's largest bank, Standard Bank, for US$5.5 billion. The attraction for China of the Standard Bank deal, like others before and after it, was to gain access not only to South Africa's market but also to the African market through Standard Bank's extensive banking and commercial network in 18 countries across the continent. By 2012, China's Public Investment Corporation has started to loan funds directly to South Africa's state investment agency, the Industrial Development Corporation.

Such interventions mark a sharply disruptive intervention in South Africa's relations with the North and continental Africa. The centuries-old orientation to Europe and the United States is slowly being eclipsed. Despite the highly racialized rhetoric from the West surrounding the 'new imperialists' (e.g. Economist 2006, 2008; Walt 2006), Chinese, Indian, and, to a lesser extent, Brazilian and Korean, engagements simply do not follow the twentieth-century patterns associated with Western states, banks and multinationals. Asian firms and entrepreneurial diaspora networks rely upon very different financing, organizational, and state linkages than their northern counterparts. Chinese trade, investment and aid is, for example much more tightly targeted and bundled, and legitimated by a common experience with Western colonialism. This often makes Chinese firms more competitive than South African companies across the region, particularly in sectors such as construction and infrastructure (Burke and Corkin 2006). The operations of China's state-owned enterprises (SOEs) are particularly distinctive, driven as they are by both political party and profit drivers. As Kaplinksy and Morris' (2009: 562) survey of Chinese investments notes, 'with access to cheap (and often subsidized) long-term capital, Chinese SOEs firms operate with distinctive long-term time-horizons and are less risk-averse than their northern counterparts'.

This does *not* mean that such relationships are not exploitative of African land, labour or natural resources. It *does* mean that vectors of accumulation, development and underdevelopment are now being driven along new lines, with new political actors, new forms of capital and new geostrategic imperatives. Analogies to late nineteenth-century colonialism and imperialism serve us poorly as do claims that South Africa and BRICS remain in subservient roles to the United States. If we are not blinded by this old vision, we are able to ask more relevant questions. As South Africa's sub-imperial role for the North continues to decline, can or will the South African state seek a sub-imperial position for Asia in relation to Africa? To be sure, the evidence to date suggests not. Might one imagine not leaning to the East but learning from it, by seeking more sovereign economic policies suited to the new world economy centred around the Indian and Pacific Oceans?

These kinds of possibilities pose new challenges for the South African state, firms, and elites. The South African state's reaction to these developments from the East, wedded as it is to its historic partners in the North, has come very belatedly and met with harsh responses from those committed to the old North/South networks. When the government finally announced in June 2012 a new 'Look East' trade and industry policy, European officials could only express anger (Africa-Asia Confidential 2012); parliamentary opposition figures called for a focus on Africa instead, as a replacement for declining trade with the North; and the white liberal establishment demanded more attention to historical alliances with Europe and the United States. China's response has been stronger despite a slowing economy at home, leading to a 4-day visit by Chinese President Xi Jinping in December 2015, during which $6.5 billion worth of deals were announced. These ranged from a $2.5 billion credit line to South African rail and transport operator Transnet, through a $500 million China Development Bank loan to electricity utility Eskom for badly needed power plant construction, to plans for the country's largest automobile plant. South Africa has yet to see gains, however, from the movement of low-wage, low-cost manufacturing out of China, with textile production moving instead to more densely populated and infrastructure-rich locations in southeast Asia.

These mixed economic signals are enhanced by China's 2010 nomination of South Africa to membership in the BRICS group, which bolstered South Africa's flagging bid to act as a spokesperson for the continent. South Africa is the Lilliputian member of the BRICS group, accounting for barely two percent of the group's population and two percent of its economic output (total gross national income). South Africa's wealth and long industrial history are also being rapidly surpassed by members of the group, most notably by China (but not by India) as suggested by Fig. 4, which compares South Africa's gross national income per capita to other members of the group.

These data serve to situate South Africa's BRICS membership: South Africa signifies not the growing economic power of the South, but rather the representation of Africa—as in the country's membership in the G20 and nearly successive terms

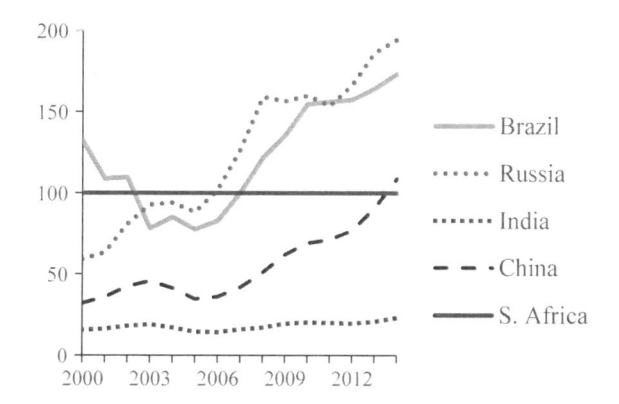

Fig. 4 BRICS per capita income South Africa = 100. *Source* World Development Indicators, available at http://data.worldbank.org/, accessed 23 April 2016

in the UN Security Council. For some, this is only 'symbol representation', marking the continuing failure of South Africa to dominate the region despite the Ubuntu, NEPAD and African Union political initiatives (Alden and Schoeman 2015). As the history of South Africa's faltering economic relations with both North and the region attest, there is substance to this assessment.

What this assessment and other like it miss, however, is the future towards which South Africa's BRICS membership points, for the BRICS initiative, signals not just a geopolitical shift but a world economic one. As hard data presented above on trade, investment, and aid indicate, a reorientation from the North to Asia, and, especially China, is taking place. China, and the BRICS more generally, are not, of course, an anti-capitalist initiative. But neither are they handmaidens of US neoliberalism: they portend a far more competitive world economic order, and one in which Asian forms of capitalist development do not follow Western developmental lines. One might recall here that in the past century, Asian imperialism operated through forms of state power and capital quite different from those that drove western imperialism—and resulted, in the Japanese case, in a colonial division of labour quite distinct from European–African forms.

Looking forward the question is, thus, not whether South Africa can continue as a sub-imperial agent of Europe or America. The question that needs investigation is whether and to what degree South Africa may find alternatives to this role as Africa and the world pivots toward Asia. In moments of global crisis, past dependencies have been broken and new and potentially more prosperous relationships have been forged. There should be no lamenting the passing of classic, Euro-American imperialism; there should be much attention to constructing something new from the possibilities in front of us.

References

Africa-Asia Confidential. (2012). South Africa looks East. https://www.africa-asia-confidential. com/article/id/763/South_Africa_looks_east.

Alden, C., & Le Pere, G. (2009). South Africa in Africa: Bound to lead? *Politikon, 36*(1), 145–169. https://doi.org/10.1080/02589340903155443.

Alden, C., & Schoeman, M. (2015). South Africa's symbolic hegemony in Africa. *International Politics, 52*(2), 239–254. https://doi.org/10.1057/ip.2014.47.

Andreasson, S. (2011). Africa's prospects and South Africa's leadership potential in the emerging markets century. *Third World Quarterly, 32*(6), 1165–1181. https://doi.org/10.1080/01436597. 2011.584725.

Arrighi, G. (1983). *The geometry of imperialism: The limits of Hobson's paradigm.* London: Verso Books.

Arrighi, G., Aschoff, N., & Scully, B. (2010). Accumulation by dispossession and its limits: The Southern Africa paradigm revisited. *Studies in Comparative International Development (SCID), 45*(4), 410–438.

Ashman, S., Fine, B., & Newman, S. (2011). Amnesty international? The nature, scale and impact of capital flight from South Africa. *Journal of Southern African Studies, 37*(1), 7–25. https://doi.org/10.1080/03057070.2011.555155.

Baran, P. A., & Sweezy, P. M. (1966). *Monopoly capital: An essay on the American economic and social order.* New York: Monthly Review.

Bond, P. (2000). *Elite transition: From apartheid to neoliberalism in South Africa.* London: Pluto Press.

Bond, P. (2004). The ANC's 'Left Turn' & South African sub-imperialism. *Review of African Political Economy, 31*(102), 599–616. https://doi.org/10.1080/0305624042000327778.

Bond, P. (2006). *Looting Africa: The economics of exploitation.* New York: Zed Books.

Bond, P. (2012). Financialization, corporate power, and South African subimperialism. In R. Cox (Ed.), *Corporate power and globalization in US Foreign policy* (pp. 114–132). London: Routledge.

Bond, P. (2014). BRICS and the tendency to sub-imperialism. *Pambazuka News, 10.* http://www. pambazuka.org/governance/brics-and-tendency-sub-imperialism.

Bond, P. (2015). BRICS and the sub-imperial location. In P. Bond & A. Garcia (Eds.), *BRICS an anti-capitalist critique* (pp. 15–26). Chicago: Haymarket.

Broadman, H. G. (2007). *Africa's silk road: China and India's new economic frontier.* Washington, DC: World Bank.

Burke, C., & Corkin, L. (2006). *China's interest and activity in Africa's construction and infrastructure sectors.* Stellenbosch, South Africa: Centre for Chinese Studies, University of Stellenbosch.

Buthelezi, S. (2003). S.A.'s Role in Africa's economic recovery. *New Agenda, 9.*

Cassim, R., Onyango, D., & Van Seventer, D. E. (2002). *The state of trade policy in South Africa.* TIPS. www.tips.org.za/research/papers/getpaper.asp?id=501.

Davies, R. (2001). Regional integration. In *Regional integration in Southern Africa: Comparative international perspectives* (pp 51–53). Johannesburg: SAIIA.

Economist. (2006). *China in Africa never too late to scramble.* http://www.economist.com/world/ mideast-africa/displaystory.cfm?story_id=E1_RDRJSTJ.

Economist. (2008). *A ravenous dragon: A special report on China's quest for resources.*

Escobar, P. (2013). Brazil, Russia, India, China and South Africa: BRICS go over the Wall. *Asia Times.* http://www.globalresearch.ca/brics-go-over-the-wall/5328662.

Evans, P. B. (1979). *Dependent development: The alliance of multinational, state, and local capital in Brazil.* Princeton, N.J.: Princeton University Press.

Fabricious, P. (2013). Will SA's new pals be so different from the West? *The Star,* 8 March, https://www.iol.co.za/the-star/will-sa-s-new-pals-be-so-different-from-the-west-1.1483040#. UVRTwTfJJSk.

Flynn, M. (2007). Between subimperialism and globalization: A case study in the internationalization of Brazilian capital. *Latin American Perspectives, 34*(6), 9–27. https://doi.org/10.1177/0094582X07308113.

Foster, J. B. (2002). Monopoly capital and the new globalization. *Monthly Review, 53*(8), 1–16.

Gelb, S. (2006). *Business Day*. www.businessday.co.za/articles/topstories.aspx?ID=BD4A213580.

Hall, R. (2011). Land grabbing in Southern Africa: The many faces of the investor rush. *Review of African Political Economy, 38*(128), 193–214. https://doi.org/10.1080/03056244.2011.582753.

Hall, R. (2012). The next Great Trek? South African commercial farmers move North. *Journal of Peasant Studies, 39*(3–4), 823–843. https://doi.org/10.1080/03066150.2012.677037.

Harvey, D. (2003). *The new imperialism*. New York: Oxford University Press.

Hawk, T. (2008). The wrong kinds of inflows. *Financial Times, 3*.

Hirschman, A. O. (1980). *National power and the structure of foreign trade*. Berkeley [usw.]: University of California Press.

Illovo Sugar Ltd. (2012). *Integrated Annual Report 2012*. Illovo Sugar Ltd.

Kaplinsky, R., & Morris, M. (2009). Chinese FDI in Sub-Saharan Africa: Engaging with large dragons. *European Journal of Development Research, 21*(4), 551–569. https://doi.org/10.1057/ejdr.2009.24.

Lenin, V. I. (1970). Imperialism: The highest stage of capitalism. In *Selected works in three volumes* (Vol. 1, pp. 666–768). Moscow: Progress Publishers.

Lesufi, I. (2004). South Africa and the rest of the continent: Towards a critique of the political economy of NEPAD. *Current Sociology, 52*(5), 809–829. https://doi.org/10.1177/0011392104045372.

Lesufi, I. (2006). *Nepad and South African imperialism*. Johannesburg: Jubilee South Africa.

Mamdani, M. (1996). *Citizen and subject: Contemporary Africa and the legacy of late colonialism*. Princeton, N.J.: Princeton University Press.

Marini, R. M. (1965). Brazilian 'interdependence' and imperialist integration. *Monthly Review, 17*(7), 10–29.

Marini, R. M. (1972). Brazilian sub-imperialism. *Monthly Review, 23*(9), 14–24.

Martin, W. G. (2013a). Living in a theoretical interregnum: Capital lessons from Southern African rural history. In F. Hendricks (Ed.), *The promise of land: Undoing a century of dispossession in South Africa* (pp. 159–184). Auckland Park, South Africa: Jacana.

Martin, W. G. (2013b). *South Africa and the world-economy: Remaking race, state, region*. Rochester, NY: Rochester University Press.

Miller, D. (2004). South African multinational corporations, NEPAD, and competing regional cliaims in post-apartheid Southern Africa. *African Sociological Review, 8*(1), 176.

Miller, D. (2006). 'Spaces of resistance'—African Workers at Shoprite in Mauto and Lusaka. *Africa Development, 31*(1), 27–49.

Moyo, S., Yeros, P., & Jha, P. (2012). Imperialism and primitive accumulation: Notes on the new scramble for Africa. *Agrarian South: Journal of Political Economy, 1*(2), 181–203. https://doi.org/10.1177/227797601200100203.

MTN. (2012). *MTN global footprint*. www.mtn.com/MTNGROUP/Pages/CompanyProfile.aspx.

MTN. (2015). *MTN Group Limited. Company Profile 2015*. https://www.mtn.com/MTNGROUP/Documents/Profile2015/index.html.

OECD. (2015). Sugar. In *OECD-FAO agricultural outlook 2015*, by OECD and FAO. OECD Publishing. http://www.oecd-ilibrary.org/agriculture-and-food/oecd-fao-agricultural-outlook-2015/sugar_agr_outlook-2015-9-en.

Richardson, B. (2010). Big sugar in Southern Africa: Rural development and the perverted potential of sugar/ethanol exports. *Journal of Peasant Studies, 37*(4), 917–938. https://doi.org/10.1080/03066150.2010.512464.

Samson, M. (2009). (Sub)imperial South Africa? Reframing the Debate1. *Review of African Political Economy, 36*(119), 93–103. https://doi.org/10.1080/03056240902888774.

Shaw, T., Cooper, A., & Chin, G. (2009). Emerging powers and africa: Implications for/from global governance? *Politikon, 36*(1), 27–44. https://doi.org/10.1080/02589340903155385.

Shoprite. (2012). *Corporate holdings*. www.shopriteholdings.co.za/pages/1019812640/about-our-company/history.asp.

South Africa. Department of Agriculture, Forestry, and Fisheries. (2012). *Abstract of agricultural statistics 2012*. Pretoria: Department of Agriculture, Forestry and Fisheries.

South Africa. Department of Trade and Industry. (2010). South African trade statistics. www.thedti.gov.za/econdb/raportt/rapmenu1.html#13.

South African Reserve Bank. (2006). *Quarterly bulletin*. www.resbank.co.za/Publications/QuarterlyBulletins/Pages/QuarterlyBulletins-Home.aspx.

South African Reserve Bank. (2010). *Quarterly bulletin*. www.resbank.co.za/Publications/QuarterlyBulletins/Pages/QuarterlyBulletins-Home.aspx.

Taylor, I. (2011). South African 'imperialism' in a region lacking regionalism: A critique. *Third World Quarterly, 32*(7), 1233–1253. https://doi.org/10.1080/01436597.2011.596743.

Tongaat Hulett Sugar. (2012). *Integrated annual report 2012*. Tongaat (South Africa): Tongaat Hulett Sugar.

United Nations (1948). *Statistical Yearbook*. Lake Success, NY: United Nations.

UNCTAD (United Nations Conference on Trade and Development). (2011). Web Table 28. Inward FDI performance and potential index rankings. In *World investment report 2011. Non-equity modes of international production and development*. New York: United Nations. http://unctad.org/Sections/dite_dir/docs/WIR11_web%20tab%2028.pdf.

UNCTAD (United Nations Conference on Trade and Development). (2016). *Global investment trends monitor*. United Nations. http://unctad.org/en/PublicationsLibrary/webdiaeia2016d1_en.pdf.

Verhoef, G. (2011). The globalisation of South African conglomerates, 1990–2009. *Economic History of Developing Regions, 26*(2), 83–106. https://doi.org/10.1080/20780389.2011.625242.

Walt, V. (2006). China's Africa Safari. *Fortune*. http://money.cnn.com/magazines/fortune/fortune_archive/2006/02/20/8369164/index.htm.

Wolfgang, T. (2006). *South Africa's foreign direct investment in Africa: Catalytic kingpin in the NEPAD process*. Pretoria: Africa Institute of South Africa.

World Bank. (1994). *World Tables*. Baltimore, MD: Johns Hopkins University Press.

World Bank. *World Development Indicators*. https://data.worldbank.org/.

The Scramble for Africa's Agricultural Land: A Note on India's Excursus

Praveen Jha, Archana Prasad, Santosh Verma and Nilachala Acharya

Introduction

It is common knowledge that the scramble for land and all that goes with it has a very long history, a large part of which has been coterminous with human history itself. Furthermore, it is also generally, well acknowledged that transition from pre-capitalism to capitalism and uneven capitalist trajectory on a global scale has been characterized by land grabs and control on natural resources, not only during the high tide of hoary colonialism but all through this journey. What have kept changing, of course, are the particular combinations of impulses and the hues associated with such scrambles. At the current juncture the obvious question, then, is what are the forces driving the heightened interest in land and other natural resource acquisitions, which have acquired extraordinary dimensions (in terms of pace, scale, etc.) in several regions of the world.

This chapter attempts to provide an analysis of the recent land acquisitions and investments in Africa by Indian entities. It does this through a discussion of the policy context and the global framework for agricultural investments in the first section. Thereafter, the extent and nature of Indian investments in African

P. Jha (✉) · N. Acharya
Centre for Economic Studies and Planning, Jawaharlal Nehru University,
New Delhi 110067, India
e-mail: praveenjha2005@gmail.com

A. Prasad
Centre for Informal Sector and Labour Studies, Jawaharlal Nehru University,
New Delhi 110067, India

S. Verma
Tata Institute of Social Sciences, Hyderabad, India

N. Acharya
Centre for Budget and Governance Accountability, Jawaharlal Nehru University,
New Delhi, India

© Springer Nature Singapore Pte Ltd. 2019
S. Moyo et al. (eds.), *Reclaiming Africa*, Advances in African Economic,
Social and Political Development, https://doi.org/10.1007/978-981-10-5840-0_4

Agriculture are explored in the second section. The third section is a further elaboration of the land acquisition by Indian actors with particular reference to three countries, namely, Ethiopia, Mozambique and Tanzania. The final section makes some observations about the impact of Indian investments on livelihood insecurity and the accelerated process of semi-proletarianisation of the peasantry. Overall, the chapter explores the mechanisms by which Indian companies are helped by the States and ruling classes of host and destination countries in their quest for super-profits from natural resources particularly land.

Contextualising Indian Acquisitions in Africa: The Global Picture

Burgeoning evidence over the last several years (approximately last couple of decades) shows a remarkable increase in the transnational hunt for land, by economically powerful international and national players like multinational corporations (both agribusiness as well as others), national governments, equity funds, banks, etc. Such a hunt also includes relatively less powerful entities like the associations of farmers, who are getting active support from their domestic governments. In the recent times, several transnational companies, mostly agribusinesses with headquarters in the United States and Europe, are acquiring prime agricultural land in developing countries, for a variety of purposes including cultivation of biofuels and a range of cash crops. Subsequently, the race has picked up with a handful of land abundant as well as land scarce 'emerging' economic powerhouses entering the competition. Thus, companies and governments from China, India, Brazil, South Korea, Kuwait, United Arab Emirates, Saudi Arabia, Qatar, Japan, Vietnam, Bahrain, South Africa, Saudi Arabia and also countries like Egypt and Libya facing political turmoil, had emerged, during the last couple of decades, as significant players in the global land rush. A majority of agricultural land has been acquired in sub-Saharan Africa, including countries such as Sudan, Ethiopia, Ghana, Nigeria, Kenya, Tanzania, Mali, Madagascar, Democratic Republic of Congo, Malawi and Zambia. The process of this acquisition has been accelerated by significant policy initiatives by African governments, who have expressed their own inability to make investments for agricultural development and food security, particularly after the global economic crisis of 2008. This inter-regional and sectoral patterns of land acquisition are illustrated in Table 1.

The table above shows that agricultural investments in Africa are mainly undertaken for growing agro-fuels and food crops. As far as Indian companies are concerned, many of them make land investments for mass production of agro-fuels and cereals, both of which can be cultivated simultaneously on the same farms. It is not surprising that this trend in land investments by transnational supply chains has picked up pace after the global food crises in 2008. Owing to surging prices of rice, wheat and vegetable oils, the food import bills of the least developed countries (LDCs) increased by 37% between 2007 and 2008, from USD17.9 to

Table 1 Region-wise land acquisition for different purposes, 2000–2016 (in percentage of total area)

Area/region	Agro fuels	Food crops	Livestock	Non-food /HypSlash> crops	Multiple use (Several crops in different categories)
All Continents	21	38	8	9	23
Africa	32	39	3	9	17
America	29	50	16	1	4
Asia	16	21	1	29	33
Europe	1	45	17	1	37
Oceania	16	30	11	3	40

Source Nolte et al. (2016, p. 11). This paper and its data is downloadable from www.landmatrix.org

USD24.6 million, in comparison with the previous year where the increase was only by 30%. These developments reportedly added 75 million people to the ranks of the hungry and drove an estimated 125 million people in developing countries into extreme poverty (FAO 2008). In this situation, global finance appears to have sensed an opportunity due to the spike in food prices for investments in land acquisitions in the developing countries, partly in order avoid the losses from the bond market. Some of the TNCs have got into agricultural production to grow food and non-food commodities and cater to the basic requirements of the masses both in the home and the host country, as also to fulfil the conspicuous consumption of the elites in the developed countries.

The recent rush for land in the Global South has been well acknowledged by the studies of several agencies such as International Land Coalition (2012), OXFAM (2011), the World Bank (2010) and GRAIN (2011). Though credible data is hard to come by, many of the land databases compiled by these agencies give us some idea of the scale and scope of the investment. One such massive and important database is the Land Matrix, which reveals the following regional patterns in the scale of recent land acquisitions (Table 2).

Table 2 Region wise investments in land deals for agriculture, 2002–2016

Region	Area under all deals (ha)	Percentage of all deals	Percentage of total deals		Percentage of concluded deals	
	Total		Transnational	Domestic	Transnational	Domestic
Africa	32,681,344	48.58	87.43	12.57	83.98	16.02
America	7,873,645	11.71	70.38	29.62	69.56	30.45
Asia	13,786,451	20.50	70.99	29.01	60.24	39.76
Europe	10,406,704	15.47	58.58	41.42	58.34	41.66
Oceania	2,518,516	3.74	93.04	6.96	93.04	6.96
Total	67,266,660	100	77.81	22.19	72.63	27.37

Source Calculated from Land Matrix downloaded from www.landmatrix.org on 31 July 2016

Table 3 Regional comparisons of land investments in agriculture, 2002–2016

Target region	Total number of deals	Percentage of total deals in agriculture
Caribbean	2	0.18
Central Africa	40	3.61
Central America	9	0.81
Central Asia	4	0.36
Eastern Africa	232	20.96
Eastern Asia	7	0.63
Eastern Europe	97	8.76
Melanesia	36	3.25
Middle East	1	0.09
Northern Africa	42	3.79
Northern Europe	3	0.27
South America	191	17.25
South Asia	8	0.72
South-East Asia	286	25.84
Southern Africa	7	0.63
Southern Europe	3	0.27
Western Africa	139	12.56
Total deals in Africa	460	41.55
Total	1107	100.00

Source Calculated from Land Matrix April 2017

As seen above, nearly half the investments from 2002 onwards have taken place in Africa. Of these, about 1326 are deals that have already been executed through written and oral agreements. If sorted out by the intention of investment, the Land Matrix data shows that about 1107 (83.4%) are dealt with the intent to invest in agriculture including food crops, biofuels, flex crops, commercial crops and unspecified agricultural aims (Nolte et al. 2016). About 41.55% of these deals are in different regions of Africa. The number of deals in different regions can be compared in Table 3.

This regional distribution of land deals in agriculture makes it amply clear that Eastern and Western regions have the highest number of land deals within Africa. It also illustrates that Africa is an attractive destination for investors compared to other continents/broad regions.

A pertinent question to ask is: why is Africa's land so attractive to investors? Several answers are given to this question from different protagonists in the debate. For example, a report of World Bank entitled *Rising Global Interest in Farmland: Can it Yield Sustainable and Equitable Benefits* (2011) argued that a 'broad review of experience with expansion of cultivated area illustrates not only that land expansion has happened in the past, but also that buoyant demand for agricultural produce provides opportunities that relatively land abundant countries can use to foster social and economic development' (Deininger and Byerlee 2011, p. 41).

Yet another thesis sees increasing demographic pressure and the rapid commercialisation of land through the process of urbanisation as the primary drivers for land grabs (Knapman et al. 2017).

It is worth noting that simplistic 'supply–demand analysis' ignores the changing character of the States and transforming class structures within Africa's agrarian transformation. This gap is filled by the relevant political economy literature which shares a lot of evidence about the role of the African states and their policies for attracting investments. Studies like Hall et al. (2015), show that African states work through alliances between foreign investors and local elites. Case studies from multiple countries clearly indicate that there is an African ruling class which mediates and benefits from the process of foreign direct investments. Hence, the institutional mechanisms for land acquisitions required some collaboration with traditional elites, most of whom pushed the interests of large-scale farming (Hall et al. 2015, p. 11). This is also evident from the Land Matrix data which shows that as compared to other continents like Latin America, the small farmers are the biggest land losers in Africa and Asia (Nolte et al. 2016, p. 37). Furthermore, such outcomes need to be contextualised in broader trajectories of transformations shared by global South in general, where the linkages between dispossession and proletarianisation are quite complex and often messy. As Moyo and others have argued, the dispossessed small farm holders/peasantry, in general, were entrapped in a process of semi-proletarianisation through the web of transnational corporations, global finance and various other entities through their investments. (Moyo et al. 2013). In this sense, the new land grab in Africa, is firmly located within the neo-liberal structural adjustment programme and monopoly-finance capitalism (Moyo et al. 2012). It is also driven by the growth of agricultural value chains which use different models to lure small producers into their financial web. Thus, 'the self-exploitation of the semi-proletariat is a key dimension of super-exploitation, and is itself an extra-economic contribution to capital, in the sense of not being accounted for by the market' (Moyo et al. 2012).

India and Foreign Investments in African Agriculture

Extent of India Investments in a Global Context

The recent growth of foreign investments for land acquisitions in Africa by Indian companies goes back to a couple of decades since the turn of the twentieth century. Between 2000 and 2011 such investments are relatively higher according to the Land Matrix. India figured in the top ten investors in Africa. Between 2012 and 2016, this pace of investment seems to have decreased and India's position slipped below the top 10 investing countries. However, in terms of total investments, the country still remains one of the ten top investors in Africa as shown in Table 4.

Table 4 Top 10 investor countries for between 2000 and 2016 (Million Hectares)

Investor countries 2000–2016	Area	Investor countries 2000–2011	Area	Investor countries 2012–2016	Area
Malaysia	37.7	USA	31.12	Malaysia	9.34
USA	33.4	Malaysia	28.03	Singapore	7.12
UK	18.38	UK	14.61	Cyprus	4.45
Singapore	16.79	Saudi Arabia	14.14	UK	4.22
Saudi Arabia	14.38	India	11.40	China	2.96
Netherlands	12.63	Hong Kong	10.82	Netherlands	2.64
India	12.45	Netherlands	10.00	Virgin Islands	2.04
Hong Kong	10.82	Singapore	9.67	USA	2.03
China	10.06	China	7.09	France	1.95
Argentina	7.44	Argentina	6.02	South Africa	1.91
Total	151.67		142.90		34.44

Source Nolte et al. (2016, p. 23). This paper and its data is downloadable from www.landmatrix.org

As far as cross-border Indian land deals are concerned, the Land matrix reports about 61 land deals for agriculture between 2000 and 2016. Out of these, 47 are in Africa of which 38 are in the Eastern region alone. The Western Region has 8 deals; whereas North Africa has only 1 Indian land investment between 2000 and 2016. Further, the analysis of the Land Matrix database also shows that China is far behind India in terms of agricultural land investments in Africa. The data show that while 21 Indian firms acquired land for agriculture in Africa, only 6 Chinese firms invested for the same purpose by 2012 (Moyo et al. 2015). Of the total deals done in East Africa between 2000 and 2012, 94.7% were done by transnational companies, in which big Indian conglomerates played a big role. Further, the data also show that Indian companies have invested in approximately 12.45 million ha between 2000 and 2016, but much of this (i.e. around 11.40 million ha) was acquired before 2012 (Nolte et al. 2016, p. 23).

Though the Reserve Bank of India provides some basic statistics, there is no comprehensive public disclosure system regarding FDI outflows. However, some rudimentary estimates can be made from the RBI statistics, 1995–2016 whose analysis yields the following (Table 5).

A large share of agricultural investments took place between 2009 and 2013. But as indicated in the table above, this conclusion is only sustained if the investment in Mozambican mines in 2014 is included as a part of the total investment by India. Thus, the period of high land acquisitions and the agricultural investments almost coincided with each other.

The extent of the FDI outflows in agriculture alone can be gauged by some data regarding specific company investments which are provided by Banks. For example, if we look at the long-term patterns of Indian investment for select five countries show the following trends.

Table 5 Phases of FDI outflows from India to Africa in agriculture and mining

Years	Investment USD/Million	Remarks
1995–2008	160.78	All these investments were of amounts that did not need prior approval
2009–2013	950.56	All these investments were of amounts that did not need prior approval
2013–2016	2939.38	Most of this investment was for Mining in Mozambique with USD 2643 being invested by Oil and Natural Gas Corporation of the Government of India and mining giants in 2014 alone. Hence rest of the investment was only USD 295.88
Total	4050.72	
Total after discounting 2014 Mozambican mining investments	1407.72	

Source Calculated from data provided by the Reserve Bank of India for different years

Table 6 Select country wise investments in Eastern Africa by Indian companies, 2000–2016 (USD million)

Country	Investment (USD million)	Percentage of total investment of five countries
Ethiopia	98.1	25.2
Kenya	164.3	42.3
Rwanda	25.6	6.5
Tanzania	70.2	18.0
Uganda	29.9	7.7
Total	388.1	100

Source Table created from data provided by EXIM Bank (2017)

Table 6 clearly shows that over the last two decades, the bulk of the investments are concentrated in Kenya and Ethiopia. These, along with Tanzania and Uganda are countries with long associations and settlements with people of Indian origin, a factor that facilitates Indian investments. As per the available data collected from Authorised Dealer Banks for the period 2009–2016, 21 companies invested about USD7.502 Million in five countries namely Ethiopia, Uganda, Mali, Tanzania and Mozambique. Of these, the greatest share of investments 58% (about USD4.34 Million) was in Ethiopia. Between 2011 and 2016, about half of this investment (i.e. about USD2 Million) was in five Ethiopian projects invested by Verdanta Harvests alone. The patterns of these investments showed that Indian businesses are largely confined to natural resource-rich pockets and concentrated in this region. Such a trend is symbolic of the new phase of capitalist development where the trans-national corporations are directly entering into resource-rich regions and coming into conflict with local people. The nature of investments in Africa shows that most Indian companies focus on farm management services and 'efficient farming'. They also claim to cater to the need for achieving food self-sufficiency in order to meet the objectives of African policymakers. This can be gauged from the credit provided to these companies by the EXIM Bank, which has opened 32 lines of credit for those investing in Africa. Of the USD1245.2 million given as credit to 32 countries between 2012 and 2016, about 60% (USD747.38 million) was for agricultural mechanisation and agro-processing. The focus was on sugar processing with Ethiopia being a special beneficiary with a credit line of USD632 million or nearly half of the total investment by EXIM bank in Ethiopia (EXIM Bank 2017).

The total FDI inflows into Africa increased, from USD432,408.7 million in 2008 to USD773,070.6 million in 2015, i.e. a total increase of 55.9%. The highest share was that of Northern Africa (about 40%) followed by Southern Africa (about 29.1%). East Africa, where Indian companies have more than 80% of their investments, had a consistent share of 5.94% of the total FDI inflow in Africa (UNCTAD 2016a, b, p. Table 3). This implies that Indian firms participating in direct land investments in Africa were only a small part of the overall trend of FDI inflows.

In the light of this macro-trend, it is interesting to note that even though the direct inflow of FDI was small in the Eastern region, the total value of mergers and takeovers went up from USD76 million in 2008 to USD336 million in 2015 (UNCTAD 2016a, b, pp. Table 9, 13). It appears that mergers and takeovers emerged as an important strategy for cross-border investments by Indian businesses. The main advantage of mergers and takeovers is that companies are not forced to invest in assets, land or technology and can, therefore, make relatively cheap investments.

The fact that Indian companies did not put sufficient finances into their agricultural investments becomes clear when the FDI inflows in the Eastern region are contextualised in the overall trajectories of foreign investments in the African subcontinent. The total FDI inflows into Africa increased substantially from 13.6% in 1995 to 32.1% in 2015 as a percentage of the total Gross Domestic Product. In East Africa, it went up from 5.9% in 1995 to 23.9% in 2015. The highest increase was in Central Africa with little Indian investment (i.e. from 8.7 in 1995 to 63.6 in 2015), thus indicating a large amount of foreign aids going to the region was not in the areas where Indians were making investments (UNCTAD 2016a, b, p. Africa Fact Sheet). The continental balance of trade as far as agricultural and livestock products are concerned shows that the gap between imports and exports increased substantially in between 2000 and 2013 (Table 7).

The table above shows that though Africa as a whole has a growing negative balance of payments in crops and livestock product trade, Eastern Africa has a relatively better regional balance. The gap between exports and imports has come down by more than 50% in Eastern Africa after the food crisis of 2008. Given these figures, the question what impact the acquisition of Ethiopian subsidiaries by transnational Indian agri-businesses has had both exports and imports in the region. Preliminary analysis shows that while commercial crops cultivated through these

Table 7 Continental balance of agricultural trade in Africa

Year	Export value (1000 USD)	Import value 1000 USD	Net balance of payments in agricultural trade
Africa Total			
2000	12,811,086	31,992,877	**−19,181,791**
2008	29,901,117	89,811,098	−59,909,981
2013	47,144,602	132,789,919	−85,645,317
Eastern Africa			
2000	4,090,219	2,594,996	1,495,223
2008	8,546,950	8,207,420	339,530
2013	13,901,249	13,363,327	537,922

Source Calculated from FAO Statistics for Different years www.faostats.org
The bold value signifies to contextualise eastern Africa in within the framework of the continent

acquisitions formed the bases of exports from such projects, food was also imported through the same entities for the local populations (Rakotoarisoa et al. 2011). In this sense, the promotion of agri-business did not necessarily result in food sufficiency that was articulated as one of the prime objectives of investments by both host governments as well as the companies. The bulk of the Indian investments have focused on biofuels, cereals, coffee, tea, and other commercial crops. Further, a major section of the growing investments was not in agriculture alone, but also in its allied sectors showing that the investment patterns are geared towards super-profits whose accumulation requires violations of several national and international standards.

Policy Framework for Investments

The FAO Guidelines

The extra-territorial territorial acquisitions are governed by both international guidelines as well as domestic laws. The international framework is largely guided by the formulation of the *Voluntary Guidelines on the Responsible Governance of Tenure of Land, Fisheries and Forests in the Context of National Food Security* (VGGT) which acknowledge that responsible public and private investments in land, fisheries, and forests should form the foundation of food security and secure tenurial rights in the contemporary world. By this, the VGGT means that large-scale investments 'should do no harm, safeguard against the dispossession of legitimate tenure right holders and environmental damage, and should respect human rights. Such investments should be made working in partnership with relevant levels of government and local holders of tenure rights to land, fisheries, and forests, respecting their legitimate tenure rights. They should strive to further contribute to policy objectives, such as poverty eradication; food security and sustainable use of land, fisheries and forests; support local communities; contribute to rural development; promote and secure local food production systems; enhance social and economic sustainable development; create employment; diversify livelihoods; provide benefits to the country and its people, including the poor and most vulnerable; and comply with national laws and international core labour standards as well as, when applicable, obligations related to standards of the International Labour Organisation' (FAO 2012a, b, p. 21). Apart from this, these Guidelines also suggest that the investments should be transparent and be guided by prior consent of the land losers. The VGGT is, however, not a regulatory mechanism, but it is a voluntary mechanism which can be used by scholars and activists to monitor and evaluate the impact of large-scale extra-territorial investments. The regulatory frameworks comprise of rules for foreign investment outflows in the investors home country on the one hand, and legal contracts governed by the laws of the investment receiving country on the other hand. Thus, these Guidelines cannot ensure socially just investment till they are enshrined and ratified by domestic laws.

The Regulatory and Institutional Framework in India

Broadly speaking the foreign investment policy of India can be divided into three phases. The first began in the early phase of the structural adjustment programme (1992–95), where firms were motivated to make foreign investments. The second phase from the mid-1990s till the turn of the century firmed up this intent by making fast-track laws to export capital under the Foreign Exchange Management Act, 1999 (FEMA), which allowed two types of overseas investments. The first was under the automatic route where joint ventures and wholly owned subsidiaries did not need prior government approval. The second was the approval route where an investment of more than USD1 billion would need prior approval of the Reserve Bank of India. The nature of investments in Eastern Africa shows that most investing companies make very small investments of less than INR one million at one time and investments are made in joint ventures or wholly owned subsidiaries at different points in time. Therefore, they avoid the prior approval route altogether.

In order to boost the outward investments into Africa, the African Development Bank and the EXIM Bank signed an MOU in 2004 for providing credit to investing companies. According to its own report, the EXIM Bank set up Lines of Credit to several agencies and governments in Africa. These supplemented the 'Focus Africa Programmes' and invested through financial institutions and Investors in the priority areas identified by the Government of India such as agri-business, alternative sources of energy like biofuels, infrastructure projects like hydroelectricity, food processing, textiles and retail. Their presence also ensures that Indian government and companies could contract terms of trade in a way that facilitated Indian exports of farm machinery and other technical inputs to Africa. It is obvious that such terms would help the Indian government to influence investment policies and deals for the Indian companies. Between 2006 and 31 December 2016, the Bank extended 154 operational lines of credit amounting to US$7.7 billion and covering 44 countries

(EXIM Bank 2017, p. 23). Credit was given for 32 agriculture and allied sector related projects with a total credit line of USD1638.74 million. Of this, the EXIM bank provided a direct disbursement of USD1245.2 million or 75.9%. In terms of private investments, about USD290 million was invested through companies and their subsidiaries in five companies, but only USD47.75 million was invested in agriculture and allied sectors (i.e. 16.4%). The bulk was invested in public sector projects through the Public Private–Partnership model (EXIM Bank 2017). Thus, it may be surmised that the EXIM Bank subsidised a large number of Indian investments in Africa with public money of the Indian exchequer. In this indirect sense, the Indian people subsidised the investments of the Indian corporates in Africa.

African States and the Land Rush: Some Case Studies

The African governments have been providing generous concessions, lease agreements and contracts to investor companies. The understanding was that these companies would boost the food security of the countries and also make the agricultural system more efficient. The main contracts are signed between the companies and the State who is the formal owner of all lands in most national contexts. The nature of these agreements is influenced by the fact that most small farms in Africa are on state-owned common lands and the customary rights of the people are hardly recognised by law. The World Bank endorses this approach when it outlines some advantages of this approach in at least three ways. The first land can be acquired in smaller slots and sold as one consolidated bloc to the private player. Second, acquisition by the state allows the rulers to hide the weaknesses of land administration and evade the question of rights. And third, it certainly reduces the transaction costs (Deininger and Byerlee 2011, p. 104). The authors of the Report argue that large-scale investments can benefit local people if proper investment areas are targeted and the private sector is regulated to ensure short-term benefits for local people. This can be done if project details are properly publicised and consultations are done adequately (Deininger and Byerlee 2011, p. 125). Other perspectives question such a process of negotiation (i.e. between the companies and the State) because it leaves little room for the involvement of local institutions and the affected people. Even in cases where customary rights are legitimate and recognised, studies show that the role of the local people is quite minimal (Cotula 2011, p. 16).

Despite this broad thumb rule, there is great diversity in the nature of concessions and contracts in land deals in a continent as vast as Africa. Some deals have been contracted between the Central governments and the companies. Prominent cases such as these are seen in Cameroon, Liberia, Mali and Sudan. In certain cases like Tanzania, the government itself has set up investment agencies to channel investments in land. Another trend is the signing of agreements between regional or provincial governments and the companies as seen in the case of five regions in

Ethiopia. There are other examples where local self-governments have had direct contracts with the companies. But these are only in regions where customary rights have been given legal sanctity. Of the 16 contracts analysed by Cotula, there is only one contract in Madagascar where 13 farmers associations have a direct dealing with the company (Cotula 2011, pp. 8–9) Within this broad framework, the Indian companies have largely worked through lease agreements and concessions. Some of these differences and commonalities are illustrated in the specific case studies analysed below.

Ethiopia

During the last couple of decades, the policy priority of the Ethiopian government has clearly moved away from small-scale agriculture and landholders to large-scale foreign investors. The first indication of this shift is seen in the 2001 rural development policy which argued that accelerated agricultural development was only possible if private players were made major partners in land investments. It stated that foreign investors should not only be encouraged in non-agriculture but also agriculture and agro-processing (Rahmato 2011, pp. 8–9). In the period between 2000 and 2009 foreign investors were given several incentives such as total remittances for salaries and profits for joint ventures, exemptions from import duties, and guarantee against expropriation through nationalisation. By 2008, the Ministry for Agriculture and Rural Development was designated as the nodal authority for agricultural land investments. The agency identified 54 million ha for investments in agriculture, and especially promoted investors with 'capital and technology'. In addition to this, the Ministry of Mining and Energy also identified 24 million ha for production of biofuels through large-scale investments.

By 2009 the investment processes were institutionalised through the formation of Regional Development Councils who were now authorised to sign land contracts with companies. The character of these contracts shows the way in which Indian companies got favourable deals from the government. For example, Verdanta harvests got a deal for 3072 ha for a period of 50 years at a price of Rs. 111 Birr or less than USD 4.8 (approximately INR 47.0) per hectare per year. A similar price was paid by Green Valley PLC in the same year for 5000 ha for the same period. Similarly Sannati International and JVL Overseas paid 158 Birr or about USD 6.7 (i.e. approximately Rs. 66.9) per hectare per year for 5000 ha of land. This range of pricing, however, did not hold true for Karuturi International who paid only 20 Birr or less than USD1 (approximately Rs. 8.47) per hectare per year for 100,000 ha in Gambella in 2010. Thus, the system of pricing shows that there was neither any regulation nor any minimum control price for the sale of land. The data collected by other studies also provide support for this (Table 8).

These differences in prices show that State institutions left the land markets unregulated in order to encourage foreign investments.

Table 8 Rent of land in selected regions (*Birr*/ha/year), 2009

Region	Maximum rent	Minimum rent
Amhara	79.37 (3.39 USD or INR 33.55)	14.21 (USD 0.60 or INR 6.02)
BeniShangul	25.00 (USD 1.05 or INR 10.5)	15.00 (USD 0.63 or INR 6.35)
Gambella	30.00 (USD 1.26 or INR 12.7)	20.00 (USD 0.84 or INR 55.5)
Oromia	135.00 (USD 5.68 or INR 57.2)	70.00 (USD 2.95 or INR 29.66)
SNNP	117.00 (USD 4.9 or INR 49.5)	30.00 (USD 1.26 or INR 12.71)
Tigrai	40.00 (USD 1.68 or INR 16.9)	30.00 (USD 1.26 or INR 12.71)

Source Rahmato (2011, p. 15) downloadable from www.landgovernance.org. 1 Ethiopian Birr = 23.75 USD and 2.36 INR

But apart from low prices, other provisions of the leases are also flexible. Leases vary from 20 to 50 years and from 5000 to 100 thousand ha. The lessees were given grace periods of 3–5 years for paying their rents. Contracts also ensured that individual lessors would not be able to embroil the investor in legal tangles or 'create disturbances' for them. However, the investor was obligated to develop the land in a particular period of time. Environmental and social impact assessments made certain claims that these projects were to conserve trees, water tables, etc.[1] Many companies like Karuturi international also made claims that they would create employment opportunities, healthcare facilities and other infrastructure. Unfortunately, these promises were never met by the company (Rowden 2011). This shows that the weak monitoring and compliance mechanism of the Ethiopian government was structured by pro-corporate tax breaks and incentives as well as an inadequately developed institutional mechanism. Though the local governments were responsible for land registration, the monitoring of the projects was very poor since the Regional Investment Offices (in charge of the investments) did not possess either staff or the capability to deal with this task.

These State policies and the consequent foreign investments created substantial dispossession within small farmers and also negatively affected their user rights. This was further accentuated by the fact that farmers had no formal land titles after the land nationalisation project of 1975. Further, there were environmental impacts of such investments impacted the livelihoods of communities like the Nuers and the Annauk who had usufruct rights on common lands and forests. But such impacts did not go unchallenged and local people used a number of interesting and creative methods to express their dissent. For example, protestors bypassed the local government and appealed directly to the federal government against Karuturi's land investments in the SNNP area (Rahmato 2011, p. 23). But such methods of petitioning did not follow any set pattern of appeal and the government's repressive tactics often led to the failure of such movements.

---

[1]These provisions are gathered from the study of land contracts of Karuturi, Verdanta, Sannati Agro, Green Valley, Ruchi, Saber, BH Bio and JV Overseas ltd, which are available on www.openlandcontracts.org and were accessed on 1 May 2017.

Mozambique

Mozambique is another important case study of newly developing Indian business interests in land. The institutional framework for land management and investment process is a complex one. After independence from the Portuguese in 1975, all Mozambican land was nationalised by the new government which meant to have a 'socialist outlook'. However, the first formal recognition of community land rights and the terms for private investments in agricultural land were enacted only in the Land law of 1997. This law set up the DUAT, or the right of use and benefit for lands that technically remain under the ownership control of the State. A DUAT could be acquired in three ways. First, it could be acquired through the right of traditional occupation or what is commonly known as the 'community right'. Second, the acquisition of a DUAT could be done by a private Mozambican citizen who could be given the right to occupy the land for at least ten years. Land acquired through both these means is inheritable and generally allotted for private or subsistence use. The third form of land acquisition is the allocation of land by the State to foreign investors after making a direct acquisition. This is the only route available to foreign investors who can apply for land investments to the National Directorate of Land and Forests. But the investors have to complete the process of public consultations with local communities before they make this application. However, these provisions are vague in the law and are often misused to have inadequate and 'formalistic' consultations. Ultimately the land investment process is completed with the consent of the Governor of the Province whose power to allocate has a ceiling of 1000 ha. Similarly, the Minister of Agriculture can allocate lands from 1000 to 10,000 ha. Land allocation above 10,000 ha is done by the Council of Ministers (Fairbairn 2013). This shows that the power to allocate land is concentrated in a few individuals, who have more often than not, had a pro-foreign investment bias in their decision-making process.

The following legislative guarantees have been granted to foreign investors:

1. Legal protection on the property and intellectual property rights;
2. No restriction on borrowing and payment of interest abroad;
3. Unrestricted transfer of dividends (payments to shareholders) abroad; and
4. Arbitration according to international rules for the resolutions of disputes on investments (Oakland Institute 2011).

These guarantees have ensured that foreign companies can accumulate profits in their own countries without making any substantial contribution to the development of the country in which they invest their capital. According to Annual Reports by the Investment Promotion Councils of Mozambique, investment in agriculture increased from approximately USD28.4 million in 2011 (Investment Promotion Centre 2011) to USD92.2 million in 2015 (Investment Promotion Centre 2015). Of these Indian investors had only three projects for land investment till 2011 and another five were added by 2014. Hence, the bulk of the Indian investment was not in agriculture or allied activities.

In the light of this, it is possible to make a more detailed assessment of Indian investments through the Land Matrix. This database records that about 62,300 ha have been acquired by five Indian companies. Out of these, HK Jalan group has the largest contracted holding of 30,000 ha which it has acquired for Eucalyptus production. In addition, it has also acquired 6000 ha for tea production. In the case of both, the Jalan group set up a subsidiary company, Cha de Magoma S.A. which it purchased from the Portuguese JFS group in 2006 by way of a 100% equity take-over. This company, in turn, set up a joint venture with the African Timber and Farming Company, U.K. to own timber plantations and purchase tea estates. Similarly, Tata Sons acquired Grown Energy, a South African Company, for setting up its biofuel plantations in 2011. It is pertinent to note that Tata Sons were not very successful in operationalizing investments till 2009. By 2013, only 3000 out of the acquired 24,000 ha were planted by Grown Energy (Andrew and Vlaenderen 2014, p. 6).

There is little public information on the nature of Indian contracts in the land. However, some reports clearly show that land laws were bypassed to get access to cheap land and resources. The land laws clearly stated that investors would not be permitted to transfer or sell lands once they had acquired them for a particular purpose. But this did not deter the investors because they were allowed to sell the shares and assets of their companies in order to recover their losses. In such cases, companies who made losses from land investments sold their entire company through mergers and takeovers. This meant that the buyer of the company got access to land at the original price at which it was acquired by the selling company. For example, Tata Sons bought Grown Energy Ptc for USD1.1 million in 2009 in order to produce 199 million L of ethanol per year. By doing this take over, they also inherited the 15,000 ha of land in Chemba of Sofala province at a one-time cost of USD73 (4398.5 MZN or about INR 4475) per hectare or just 7.3% of the entire deal. (Oakland Institute 2011, p. 25). Thus, Indian investors got land at throwaway prices through the strategy of takeover and mergers. This also absolved them of all responsibility towards the local area and its people.

Tanzania

According to the Tanzanian Investment Centre, agriculture employs about 80% of the working population and contributes about 40% of the export earnings of the country. It has about 44 million ha of land of which only 23% was cultivated annually in 2014 (Tanzanian Investment Council 2014, p. 39). This formed the basis of the government measures and policies to attract investments in Tanzania. Under the Tanzanian Land Law (1998), all land is vested in the President of the country and is classified into three categories: general, reserved and village lands. Village lands are those with customary rights, whereas the reserved lands are those which have been declared as National Parks and ecologically sensitive areas by the State and are under the control of particular ministers. General lands are under the direct control of the President. One of the main features of the land law is that it enables the transfer of land from the 'reserved' and 'village' categories to 'general lands' thereby making an acquisition by foreign investors possible (Government of Tanzania 1998, pp. 15–20).

Investments are made through the Tanzanian Investment Centre, which is like a 'one stop shop' for the investors. Under the provisions of the Tanzanian Investment Act (1997), the Centre makes a land bank and provides all types of assistance and services to investors. Though there are no specific criteria for choosing investors but employment creation, technology transfer and expansion of production seem to be some of the objectives (Oakland Institute 2012). As per the report of the Investment Centre, the total FDI inflows in Tanzanian agriculture increased from USD21.2 million in 2008 to USD34.5 million in 2011. India contributed about USD70.2 million to these overall agricultural investments between 2000 and 2016. However, a bulk of this investment was in poultry, farm services and inputs, and not in land acquisitions (EXIM Bank 2017). These were mainly done after 2012 when the Tanzanian government invited investments in partnership with the Rufiji Basin Authority. Though the Land Matrix shows that there were only three big land contracts by Indian firms after in the Rufiji Basin 2012, these contracts were much bigger in size (ranging from 10,000 to 12,000 ha) than the ones awarded to companies from other countries who were mostly awarded leases which were less than 5000 ha. For example, the Rufiji Sugar plant was initiated in partnership with the Indian investor, Mahakaushal Sugar, and Power Company which acquired 12,000 ha in the Basin and provided 25.25% of the total investment costs or USD30.36 million. Another company Euro Vistas also acquired 10,000 ha in the Basin for the development of cotton fields (Oakland Institute 2012). However, only 470 ha were operationalised because of lack of finance by 2014. Though the persistence of 'idle land' violated the terms of the contract, the extent of this violation is difficult to understand because there is little public information about the contracts.

The general picture that emerges out of these case studies is that most African States made policies that promoted the 'ease of doing business' without adequately protecting the rights of the local people. They allowed Indian companies the luxury of acquiring local subsidiary companies and therefore, enabling to get advantages without making minimal investments in infrastructure or job creation. International norms of transparency and consultation with the local people, institutions and communities have been ignored, thus having an adverse impact on the life and livelihood of people. Further, the norms of the VGGT were not respected by either the land investors or the African governments. Though the VGGT mandated public consultations are hardly respected by land investors even though this was required also by many national laws. Since compliance and monitoring systems have been inadequate, most local authorities and investors got away without doing a credible consultation. This also became easy because the lands were transferred to the state so the responsibility and rehabilitation came on the government instead of the investors. States, in turn, did not press the compliance of these provisions because they feared the loss of investments and their entire strategy for making African agriculture more 'productive and efficient' was based on an export-oriented strategy. Further, the VGGT's emphasis on food security has also been ignored in many projects. Even though 20 of 36 projects mention food crops as the main objective of their investments, they only concentrated on commercial export-oriented crops and biofuels once the projects were operationalised. As Timothy Wise noted, 'strapped for cash and investment, many countries have signed on, rewriting their laws on the vague promise of increased private investment. From Malawi's Green Belt Initiative to Tanzania's SAGCOT Corridor to Zambia's Farm Block Program, governments are taking some of their best agricultural lands and making it available to foreign investors under concessional terms. The land rights of current occupants are regularly violated, and the results thus far have been mediocre. When the investors come, they grow biofuels or flex crops like sugar, often for export, but create few jobs. They displace farmers and communities. Many projects fail, as is the case with biofuels projects in Tanzania (World Bank 2010). That creates the stunning paradox of hungry, land-poor smallholders in land-rich countries and the best available land are ceded to foreign investors (Wise 2015)'. In short, the development strategies of African States have given the investors concessions to the extent they have been able to evade their responsibilities towards local people.

Investments and the Accelerated Process of Semi-proletarianisation

The presence of large investors with big capital has obviously changed the dynamics of the local livelihood systems and laid the foundations of oppressive labour relations. This was done through a clear violation of contracts and promises of the creation of employment. Since most of the investment contracts were largely lease deals and land concessions with stated objectives of job creation and food security, these were hardly respected and most investors violated the terms of the contracts. In fact, none of the companies followed the agreed provisions of settling land rights and tenures before completing the contracting process. For example, the Mozambican Law was violated by Grown Energy when it did not settle the community tenures before acquiring lands (Andrew and Vlaenderen 2014). In the case of Karuturi of Ethiopia, the local communities challenged and protested against the investments because it took over their grazing lands and denied the pastoralists their rights (Rowden 2011).

Further, investors made claims that their projects would create employment in order to augment livelihood strategies. But this did not materialise because in many cases the land acquired by them remained idle. For example, in the case of Ethiopia, we have seen that Karuturi International was allotted land at throwaway prices without any substantial monitoring. Most of its land lay idle and unused and therefore the company was not able to meet the terms of the contract. Its license was eventually cancelled because only 1000 ha had been operationalised by 2016. The non-implementation of the project led to the non-fulfilment of the promises to create

20,000 jobs and social infrastructure. The investments had affected the livelihood of about 12,500 people (mainly landless people and labourers) who were dependent on common lands allotted to Karuturi. It also adversely impacted 150 small-scale peasants who did subsistence farming and were partly dependent for their daily needs on common lands. In lieu of this displacement, the Company created merely 60 permanent jobs and between 200 and 600 jobs at abysmal wage rates of 12 Birr, i.e. USD0.50 per day, which was far lower than even the cover given under the relevant social safety nets. At the peak season employment was rotational and a different set of labourers was employed in each week (Rahmato 2011, p. 25). Similarly, in Mozambique Tata Sons subsidiary Grown Energy employed only 2139 people and, Cha De Magoma SA, a subsidiary of the HK Jalan group employed only 1000 employees on 2500 ha of land (Sutton 2014, p. 61). This evidence shows that there was a creation of a large displaced labour reserve, which was forced to work at depressed wages because of expropriation from land.

A common model marketed by the investors was out grower model, which, it was hoped, would upgrade the agriculture and the income of small farmers. A good example of this model is the Grown Energy biofuel plantation operated in Mozambique. The plantation covers about 9000 ha of which 2300 ha are to be given to out-growers for producing soya beans and their own food crops. This plan was meant to compensate the farmers who had been displaced. The area has about 875 small farmers who originally owned their own lands but now are forced to work under the out-grower model (Andrew and Vlaenderen 2014, p. 25). Hence, the first impact of this is the loss of customary user right and ownership of land. The second impact is the conversion of independent and self-reliant farmers into disguised wage labour. By employing out-growers the investor saves on labour and infrastructure costs and therefore is able to maintain a low cost of production. However, this can only be successful if the utilisation of land is done in an optimal way. Unfortunately in the case of most of the Indian investments such as Grown Energy the full utilisation of land has not been possible as only 1000 ha was operationalised within seven years. This had an adverse impact of the entire out-grower model and also the generation of direct employment. Seasonal employment was generated for only 34 days per year for the affected 1600 sugar cutters. If machines were used then only 60–70 people got seasonal employment (Andrew and Vlaenderen 2014, p. 25). This shows that the out grower model neither enhanced the incomes of small farmers and nor did it create jobs. Rather it was embedded in processes of extraction which have been super-oppressive in character.

The lack of a compliance mechanism was evident from the fact that almost all investors like Tata Sons (Mozambique) and Euro Vistaa (Tanzania) operated only a part of their leased lands even though their contracts stated that at least half the land was to be developed within one year. Further, even when they did operate their lands the terms of the contract violated by changing the patterns of land use. For example, Euro Vistas (Tanzania) bought land to grow cotton but was largely growing maize thus converting land use from non-food crops to food crops. It is important to note that this conversion was done purely out of commercial interests as maize was being exported to Indian markets (Oakland Institute 2012).

Multiple case studies and reports also show that the promises of enhancing food security were also violated by the Indian investments. For example, the FAO study on the investments by Uttam Eurotech in Mali showed that the project shifted the land use from production of cereal crops to sugarcane by incentivizing the out-growers. Here the company transferred the risk of production to out growers in two ways: (a) the specialization in one crop would increase the market risks of the farmers and (b) the reduction in crop diversity would have an ecological impact that may lead to crop losses over time. Therefore it was decided that the contracted area would ensure that inter-cropping was done and food crops and vegetables were grown with sugarcane in an estimated area of 1,250 ha. It was estimated that the project would benefit about 150 thousand small farmers, but such tall promises were not fulfilled. Further created mere 8000 person days of work was created over a period of a decade, thus adversely impacting, both livelihood and food security (FAO 2012a, b; Feodoroff 2014).

The Anecdotal evidence provided from the above mentioned selected cases give a bird's eye view of the broad trends with regard to the impacts of Indian investments on African peasants and small farmers. The most obvious commonality that comes out is that there has been an intensification in the process of semi-proletarianisation of the small farmers after the increase in foreign land investments in the post 2008 period. A major responsibility for this rests on the lax implementation of laws and the pro-corporate policies of the African states and ruling classes.

Conclusion

The recent scramble for Africa's land illustrates powerfully that the rights of local people have been encroached and that the affected people are being made ever more vulnerable through adverse impacts on their livelihood and food security. This chapter shows that the alliance between African ruling classes and the Indian investors has accelerated the process of the semi-proletarianisation of the African peasantry. Four specific characteristics can be identified about Indian investments. First land investments are concentrated in particular pockets of the African sub-continents, particularly in Ethiopia. Second, though land investments form a small part of the overall Indian investments in Africa, a large part of the inflow of Indian capital is for services that help to increase the control of the company oversupply of inputs and markets. Third, the Indian investors have commonly used the strategy of acquiring regional and local companies in order to make relatively 'cheap investments' and also evade the nuances of the national land laws. Lastly, the Indian and African states have played very significant roles in facilitating 'cheap investments' by providing a highly lose and enabling legislative structure, that does not put an even a reasonable sense of responsibility on the investor. To this end the chapter has taken the example of three case studies to explore the specific policy and institutional adjustments that have been made by African governments to give massive concessions to foreign companies. The Indian companies have also enjoyed the benefits of this bonanza especially from the late 1990s onwards. Like other foreign investors, they too have ignored international norms like the VGGT which aim at making investments more socially responsible.

Indian and Chinese investments have often been marketed by both Indian and African governments as part of South–South cooperation. But this chapter has provided enough evidence to show that, as elsewhere in the world, the Indian firms exhibit all the characteristics of predatory transnational companies. It is well documented that low wages in these estates are maintained through large-scale displacements without adequate livelihood compensation. Further, in many cases, the companies have also hoarded land by not putting it to the intended use after purchase. This lack of financial investment by the Indian companies has sometimes forced the African governments to withdraw the leases of these firms because of growing protests. For example, because of massive protests forced the Ethiopian government to end license of Karuturi Global in 2016. The matter is now under litigation. The second example is that of Tata Sons which is now threatening to withdraw from its subsidiary because the cost of production has gone up. Its operations have not only ruined land because of changing land use but also displaced farmers who now form part of the 'labour reserve', which has expanded because of large-scale land investments in Africa.

It is apt to end with the words of the leader of Ethiopian Solidarity Movement Obang Metho who says in an open letter to the people of India: 'Ethiopians are pro-business and pro-investment; particularly as Ethiopia is reported to be the second poorest country in the world with 90% of the people living under the poverty level. What we oppose is the daylight robbery of Ethiopia by modern day bandits who are willing to make secret deals with a corrupt government that would be illegal in India and other more developed countries…. Into this environment, have come over 500 Indian companies—more than from any other country in the world—to capitalize on this 'goldmine of opportunity'. One Ethiopian from the Oromia region protested: 'Our land is being given to the Indian companies and anyone who speaks out against it is labelled as a terrorist who is not supposed to have any rights or question any actions by the government.'… Why would any Indian be part of this? Anyone who resents the colonial past of your own country, should know that it began through the British East India Trading Company; where some of the more unscrupulous [collaborators] often colluded with corrupt indigenous government officials. What would Gandhi say today were he to know that Indians, who were only freed from the shackles of colonialism in recent history, were now at the forefront of this 'land-grabbing' as part of the race for foreign control over African land and resources?' (Metho 2011).

References

Andrew, M., & Vlaenderen, H. V. (2014). *Commercial biofuel land deals & environment and social impact assessments in Africa: Three case studies in Mozambique and Sierra Leone.* Hague: Institute of Social Studies.

EXIM Bank. (2017). *India's investments in select East African countries: Prospects and opportunities.* s.l.: Export Import Bank of India.

Cotula, L. (2011). *Land deals in Africa: What do the contracts say.* London: International Institute of Environment and Development.

Deininger, K., & Byerlee, D. (2011). *Rising global interest in farmlands: Can it yield sustainable and equitable benefits?.* Washington DC: The World Bank.

Fairbairn, M. (2013). Indirect dispossession: Domestic power imbalances and foreign access in Mozambique. *Development and Change, 44*(2).

FAO. (2008). *The state of food insecurity in the world, 2008: High food prices and food security—Threats and opportunities.* Rome: Food and Agriculture Organisation of United Nations.

FAO. (2012a). *The markala sugar project.* Rome: Food And Agriculture Organisation.

FAO. (2012b). *Voluntary guidelines on the responsible governance of tenure (VGGT) of land, fisheries, and forests in the context of national food security.* Rome: Food and Agriculture Organisation of the United Nations.

Feodoroff, T. (2014). *The right to food: Impact of land grabbing in Mali.* s.l.: FIAN International.

Government of Tanzania. (1998). *Land law 1998.* Dar es Salaam: United Republic of Tanzania.

GRAIN. (2011). *Global land rush: What it means for customary rights.* Briefing paper no 5: Rights to Resources Group, Customary Land Tenure in Africa.

Hall, R., Scoones, I., & Tsikata, D. (2015). *Africas Land rush: Rural livelihoods and agrarian change.* UK: Broydell and Brewer, James Currey.

International Land Coalition. (2012). *Land Rights and Rush for Land: Findings of Global Commercial Pressures on Land Research Project*, International Land Coalition, London.

Investment Promotion Centre. (2011). *Annual report of investment and approved projects.* s.l.: Government of Mozambique.

Investment Promotion Centre. (2015). *Annual report of investment and approved projects.* s.l.: Government of Mozambique.

Knapman, C., Silici, L., Cotula, L., & Mayers, J. (2017). *Africa's farmlands in changing hands: Review of literature and case studies from Sub Saharan Africa.* UK: International Institute for Environment and Development.

Metho, O. (2011). An open letter to the people of India: Day light robbery in Ethiopia. [Online] Available at: www.solidaritymovement.org/11006150OpenLetterToThePeopleOfIndia.php. Retrieved May 1, 2017.

Moyo, S., Jha, P., & Yeros, P. (2013). The classical agrarian question: Myth, reality and relevance in the 21st Century. *Agrarian South: Journal of Political Economy, 2*(1).

Moyo, S., Jha, P., & Yeros, P. (2015). The agrarian question in the 21st Century. *Economic and Political Weekly, 50*(37).

Moyo, S., Yeros, P., & Jha, P. (2012). Imperialism and primitive accumulation: Notes on the new land grab in Africa. *Agrarian South: Journal of Political Economy, 1*(2).

Nolte, K., Chamberlin, W., & Giger, M. (2016). *Fresh insights from land matrix: Analytical report II.* s.l.: CDE/CIRAD/GIGA/University of Pretoria.

Oakland Institute. (2011). *Understanding land deals in Africa: Country report Mozambique.* Oakland, California: Oakland Institute.

Oakland Institute. (2012). *Understanding land deals in Africa: Country report Tanzania*. Oakland CA: Oakland Institute.

OXFAM. (2011). *Land and power: Growing scandals of new wave of land investments*. London: OXFAM.

Rahmato, D. (2011). *Land to investors: Largescale land transfers in Ethiopia*. Adis Ababa: Forum for Social Studies.

Rakotoarisoa, M., Iafrate, M., & Paschali, M. (2011). *Why has Africa become a net food importer? Explaining Africa's agricultural and food trade deficits*. Rome: Food and Agricultural Organisation of United Nations.

Rowden, R. (2011). *India's role in new farm land grab in Africa*. [Online] Retrieved April 30 2017.

Sutton, J. (2014). *An enterprise map of Mozambique*. London: International Growth Centre.

Tanzanian Investment Council. (2014). *Tanzania country special report, Dar Es Salam: Ministry of Industry*. Government of Tanzania: Trade and Investment.

UNCTAD. (2016a). *World investment report*. Geneva: United Nations Council for Trade and Development.

UNCTAD. (2016b). *World investment report series*. Geneva: United Nations Council for Trade and Development.

Wise, T. (2015). Two roads diverged in the food crisis: Global policy takes the one more travelled. *Canadian Food Studies, 2*(2).

World Bank. (2010). *Rising global interest in farmlands: Can it yield sustainable and equitable benefits*. Washington DC: World Bank.

Brazil's Re-encounter with Africa: The Externalization of Domestic Contradictions

Paris Yeros, Vitor E. Schincariol and Thiago Lima da Silva

Introduction

The troubled history of Brazil's relationship with Africa entered a new phase after the end of Brazil's military rule in the 1980s and gained momentum in the 2000s at the time of the coming to power of the Workers' Party (*Partido dos Trabalhadores*, PT). This new phase has been the subject of substantial research and debate—and it could not be otherwise. Brazil's relationship with its own African origins only began to be reconciled at official state level in the Constitution of 1988, and advanced over the following decade by the broad mobilization of the black movement, culminating in the preparations for the Conference on Racism and Racial Discrimination held in Durban, South Africa, in 2001 (Pereira 2003; Vida Gala 2007; Da Silva and Pereira 2013). This dynamic spawned a series of affirmative action policies concerning the teaching of African and Afro-Brazilian History and Culture in the educational system, signed into law in 2003, and the adoption of quota systems for university admissions (2012) and the civil service (2014). It is thus that the Brazilian state officially recognized, for the first time ever, the country's African origins and the existence of racism in Brazilian society and institutions.

This chapter has benefitted from comments provided by Jorge Américo.

P. Yeros (✉) · V. E. Schincariol
Federal University of ABC (UFABC), CECS, sala D337, Alameda da Universidade, s/nº, Bairro Anchieta, 09606-045, São Bernardo do Campo, SP, Brazil
e-mail: parisyeros@gmail.com

V. E. Schincariol
e-mail: veschincariol@riseup.net

T. L. da Silva
Federal University of Paraíba, João Pessoa, Brazil
e-mail: thiagolima3@gmail.com

S. Moyo et al. (eds.), *Reclaiming Africa*, Advances in African Economic, Social and Political Development, https://doi.org/10.1007/978-981-10-5840-0_5

During this transition, Brazil–Africa relations also shifted substantially from those which held under the governments of Fernando Collor de Mello (1990–1992) and Fernando Henrique Cardoso (1994–2002), which did not view Africa as a strategic or even relevant region (Ribeiro 2007: 103–39).[1] The Lula government inaugurated a dozen new embassies in Africa, and African countries reciprocated with a similar increase in diplomatic missions in Brasília. But the nature of the policy shift reflected a variety of pressures, and, in fact, economic interests overtook other considerations, as trade and investment relations expanded exponentially to become the motive force of a new foreign policy generally, aiming to diversify economic and diplomatic relations to the South (Boito and Berringer 2013). Given the role that business interests assumed, it was a matter of time before Brazil's expansion into Africa would come under scrutiny. Apart from the new experiences of technical cooperation in agriculture and social development, and the export of engineering and construction services, the expansion has been marred by the participation of Brazilian monopolies in the scramble for agricultural land in Africa, especially in Mozambique.

Meanwhile, scholarly debate on Brazil's Africa policy also shifted away from the original national question. The debate came to focus largely on whether Brazil's 'emergence' augurs a multipolar world and a new type of South–South cooperation, or constitutes a 'sub-imperialist' force in the reproduction of imperialism. However, such analysis of systemic dynamics has not necessarily yielded clarity on the nature of Brazil's changing society, or its semi-peripheral role in the world economy. Moreover, imputing systemic status to sub-imperialism, or otherwise extolling Brazil's 'emergence' and its South–South cooperation as a systemic game changer, has often been a moralistic exercise. Besides certain conceptual shortcomings to be discussed, such concerns have also done little to promote in Brazil the systematic study of the political economy of contemporary Africa, which would certainly improve the analysis of Brazil–Africa relations, if not also of Brazil's own national question.

Among the starkest shortcomings in the analysis has concerned precisely the character of the Brazilian social formation. Indeed, recognition of the country's white-settler colonial origins and contemporary neocolonial social structure would go a long way to explain Brazil's relationship with Africa, as well as with its neighbours, quite apart from the recent expansion of its aspiring monopolies. The analytical point of departure is that Brazil's settler colonial experience is comparable to South Africa's. Brazil's 1988 Constitution, as South Africa's of 1993, established universal suffrage for the first time, which in Brazil's case abolished the disenfranchisement of the illiterate population which historically had served to

---

[1]President Cardoso declared in 1998: 'A África, infelizmente, é um continente que parece à deriva' [Africa, unfortunately, is a continent that appears to be adrift'] (quoted by Ribeiro 2007: 140).

exclude a significant part of the black and indigenous population. The transition yielded a new set of contradictions resulting in highly conflicting—even schizo-phrenic—policy tendencies, in both domestic and foreign affairs. These tendencies have stemmed from contradictions inherent in constitutional guarantees for white-settler property and privilege, on the one hand, and the promise of devel-opment, on the other, impeding the resolution of the deep inequalities and violence that pertain quite patiently to a settler society in its neocolonial phase. What Brazil has exported to Africa are, above all, the contradictions inherent in this type of society. Larger systemic conclusions related to the emergence of peripheral monopolies need not be inferred, although they are significant in their own right and will be addressed in what follows.[2]

The first section below will trace the contours of Brazil's neocolonial transition, characterized by the continuous evolution of settler capitalism and its articulation with monopoly capital and finance. Above all, this long historical transition, which culminated in the 1988 Constitution, capped the accelerated and violent expulsion of Brazil's black majority population from the countryside, whose main route of migration became the Northeast-Southeast axis.[3] This set the stage for a new set of contradictions that have left their mark in domestic and foreign policy alike. The second section will argue that in its recent re-encounter with Africa, Brazil's externalization of domestic contradictions has been clearly manifest in the country's conflicted approach to agricultural cooperation. The main instruments and policies of cooperation in agriculture will be outlined here, together with some general trends in economic relations, with a view to clarify the tendencies which will continue to play out in the course of Brazil's current crisis and the semi-stagnation of the world economy.

---

[2]For the analysis of settler colonialism and the national question in South Africa and the Southern African region, see Magubane (1979, 1983), Mandaza (1987), Mafeje (1997), Moyo (1995), Moyo and Chambati (2013). In the case of Brazil, the specific terminology varies, but the essence of this colonial situation has been discerned most lucidly in the works of Abdias do Nascimento, Lélia Gonzalez, Joel Rufino dos Santos, and Wilson N. Barbosa, among others. Settler colonialism, in the way the term is used here, refers to a mode of rule under a settled, foreign ruling class, whose settlement involves extensive appropriation of land and, in most cases, genocide and substitution of populations. Under settler colonialism, extreme racial domination persists even despite the attainment of juridical independence by the state and the existence of parliamentary politics. In *apartheid* South Africa, related terms included 'colonialism of a special type' or 'internal colo-nialism'. Neo-colonialism, in turn, refers to a substantial shift in the relation of forces, which typically crystalizes in universal suffrage and a new bureaucratic dispensation, but remains subject to the overall requirements of monopoly capitalism. The complexities of these issues have been addressed more recently with reference to Zimbabwe's neo-colonial transition and subsequent re-radicalization, in Moyo and Yeros (2005, 2007, 2011, 2013).

[3]As per the country's official terminology, used here, the term 'black', or *negro*, includes *preto* and *pardo*.

Brazil's Re-encounter with Africa

The White-Settler Colonial Legacy

If most of the white-settler societies of the Americas obtained juridical independence in the 1820s, the slave systems established over prior centuries did not unravel for several more decades, the final being that of Brazil in 1888. Brazil was, by far, the largest importer of enslaved labour from Africa, receiving around 40% of the total number of Africans forcibly transported to the Americas between the sixteenth and nineteenth centuries (Furtado 2004 [1958]). The second half of the nineteenth century found the Brazilian Empire waging a struggle against England's new anti-slavery policies.

Despite formal independence, and even the founding of a Republic a year after the abolition of slavery, race relations persisted in oppressive colonial conditions, especially as the white-settler state resolved to build a new nation as explicitly European. Through a policy of financial support for European immigration, destined largely for the South and Southeast of the country, a systematic and enduring effort was undertaken to marginalize the black and remaining indigenous peoples and wipe out its African and indigenous origins, both physically and culturally. By contrast to the new white immigrants, the Brazilian state offered labour, subsidies and eventually land. Influenced by the eugenic trends in the North, the first option of the settler state, at this early stage, was to eliminate its non-European origins altogether (de Azevedo 1987; Skidmore 1974; Schwarcz 1995; do Nascimento Barbosa 2002).

This settler type of colonial society, in which juridical independence was not accompanied by the suppression of white supremacy, succumbed thereafter to persistent convulsions. The state proceeded to militarize its policy of containment of the indigenous, blacks, and the poor, beginning with the War of Canudos (1896–97) in the Northeast, as they continued to struggle for forms of autonomous existence in the countryside, in indigenous territories or as a peasantry, or otherwise fled to urban centres to constitute the lowest rung of the workforce, in informal, menial and domestic employment (Fernandes 1964; Teodoro 2008; dos Santos Gomes 2015; Américo 2015). Popular artistic and religious expressions of African origin were also criminalized.[4]

Yet, the quintessential white-settler dilemma between separation and assimilation on the terms of white supremacy eventually imposed itself on the Brazilian state when the world economic crisis struck in 1929, undermining the reproduction

---

[4]It is worthwhile recalling the prior to this, the war against Paraguay waged by Brazil, Uruguay, and Argentina (1864–1870), aided by Britain, not only left Paraguay in ruins and deprived it of access to the Atlantic, it also exterminated 70% of its indigenous male population. The wars on Paraguay and Canudos, together with a series of other acts of genocidal violence (Balaiada, Cabanos etc.) underpinned the reorganization of the settler states of the region after settler independence.

of the oligarchic export-dependent character of the settler colonial system. The dilemma was resolved, thereafter, in favour of subordinate assimilation of the black and indigenous peoples into a postulated nation that now professed 'racial democracy', not by recognition of white supremacy but by its denial. The policy of cultural and physical 'whitening' was thereby reinstated on new terms. The conjuncture required the projection of a new pseudo-national vision, which would not permit acknowledgement of white supremacy and genocide (do Nascimento 1978; Munanga 1999).

The structural economic requirements for the new national myth were given by the unexpected boost to industrialization that obtained by the collapse of world markets after 1929 and the shift in the accumulation strategy of settler agrarian capital towards industrial investment. This laid the basis for a dependent industrialization process that, although substantially introverted in its profit realization strategy, relied on the super-exploitation of a black majority workforce, with the exception of some areas of the South and in the state of São Paulo, where whites, as a result of the modern immigration flows, became the majority of the population under better off conditions (Fernandes 1964). A strategy of import-substitution industrialization was initiated by President Getúlio Vargas (1930–1945, 1951–1954) along more national lines, in an attempt to create a hegemonic domestic industrial bourgeoisie. Under the subsequent administration of Juscelino Kubitschek (1956–1961), closer association was sought with monopoly capital under the aegis of US imperialism. This guaranteed some temporary reprieve for domestic industrial capital, both state-owned and private, in the course of the Cold War (Fernandes 1976; Dos Santos 1978, 1991, 1995; Marini 2000).

Brazil's industrialization experience leveraged a process of continuous structural change over the following half-century, until the 1980s. The composition of class forces was transformed, as was the relative autonomy of the state to intervene and cultivate a domestic capitalist class and even renegotiate its relations with the foreign monopolies (Fernandes 1976). During the uninterrupted period of rule by Getúlio Vargas (1930–1945), the state embarked on the consolidation of bureaucratic power at federal level and the modernization of its capacity to arbitrate among the fractions of settler and imperialist capital, as well as to coopt, disorganize and repress a growing urban working class and recalcitrant peasantry, in line with the requirements of settler colonial capitalism.

Whatever recognition of African and Indigenous presence obtained, it was effectively reduced to cultural syncretism and folklore in terms of the new mythology of the nation, which now posited harmonious existence and miscegenation among the constitutive racial groups and, above all, a benevolent civilizational role for settler colonialism. In fact, 'racial democracy', such as it was, did not establish universal suffrage until the 1980s. Although women received the vote in 1932, suffrage was qualified by literacy until a 1985 constitutional amendment. The qualified vote effectively denied citizenship to a substantial part of the predominantly black and indigenous people, affecting especially the Northeast, and particularly women. Yet, even this restricted type of parliamentary politics would not provide security to the settler colonial order: as the contradictions of settler capitalism accumulated, the qualified vote was suppressed during two long periods of military rule, 1937–45 and 1964–85, traversing and superseding the Vargas period of state-making. It is in this long period that the relative autonomy of the settler state gained its concrete meaning: the agrarian and aspiring industrial fractions of settler capital, organized by the civil–military bureaucracy and supported by the judiciary, media, and the ideological apparatus of the state, effected the expulsion of the black majority population from the countryside and established the modern parameters of a permanent regime of super-exploitation and genocidal violence.

White-Settler Colonial Recalcitrance

The most concrete moment of contestation occurred in the early 1960s, with the advance of the Peasant Leagues, urban unrest, and the coming to power of the reformist government of João Goulart (1961–64). There also occurred, at this time, an attempted departure from the policy of alignment with imperialism, including from Brazil's habitual support for Portugal's colonial policy in Africa and for the *apartheid* regime in South Africa that had hitherto been extended on all occasions in which the colonial question had been brought to the General Assembly of the United Nations (Saraiva 1996). The explosive contradictions of this juncture were, in fact, the underlying cause of the second, and most decisive, period of military rule. This effectively aborted the neocolonial transition in Brazil and followed the trends underway in the Portuguese colonies of Africa and the settler colonies of Southern Africa, where decolonization was similarly averted. Thus, Brazil, together with Guiné-Bissau, Angola, Mozambique, Namibia, Zimbabwe and South Africa, would have to endure another generation of fascist violence.

Brazil's posture towards Africa, South America and the Caribbean obtained a higher level of geostrategic ambition in what was now seen as a 'South Atlantic' theatre of operations. Brazil deployed troops to the Dominican Republic in 1965–66 in support of the US invasion, under the aegis of the Organization of American States. It also embarked on technical cooperation with Rhodesia in support of the settler regime's ethanol production and energy security, in its sanctions-busting manoeuvres after its Unilateral Declaration Independence of 1965. Moreover, Brazil initiated a policy of mass settlement of Brazilian farmers of European origin in neighbouring Paraguay, especially after 1967, in support of the Paraguayan state's own settler capitalist policy of 'agricultural modernization'. Thereafter, as serial *coups d'état* swept across the region, the regional settler alliance was consolidated in a US-led counter-insurgency strategy codenamed Operation Condor. After 1974, under President Ernesto Geisel (1974–1979), Brazil's military regime also tested a more 'independent' geostrategic agenda, by recognizing the governments of newly independent Angola and Mozambique and negotiating a nuclear deal with West Germany. But such geostrategic ambitions extended far beyond the limits set by US imperialism, as Brazil desisted from developing nuclear armaments and, in any case, as the grand ambitions were undermined internally by the boom and bust of the country's 'economic miracle' (1969–74).

This is the general economic and geostrategic context in which the theory of sub-imperialism was proposed (Marini 1969). Yet, it remains inadequate to impute a systemic 'sub-imperialism' to Brazil's transformation, whether on account of its emerging monopolies or its geostrategic ambitions. The development of the productive, bureaucratic, and military capabilities of this semi-peripheral state certainly enabled the implementation of a more expansive foreign policy, with consequences for the division of labour in the region as a whole. Nonetheless, this was by no means the determinant factor in the evolution of monopoly capitalism in the region, nor a newly acquired fascist posture, which was, after all, shared in the region under the settler dispensation. Nor, indeed, were the new material conditions sufficient to sustain a new systemic phase of 'sub-imperialism'. The tentative emergence of Brazil beyond the designs of imperialism was entirely quashed by imperialism itself. As soon as Brazil's debt crisis struck in the late 1970s, Brazil's economy was swiftly subordinated to the dictates of monopoly finance capital and systematically picked apart, in a process which Marini (1992) himself termed 'reconversion'.[5]

The transformations that occurred under military rule would have enduring consequences for the country's domestic and foreign affairs. A policy of rapid agricultural modernization of *latifundia* via Green Revolution technologies was implemented, after a prior reformist plan, the 'Alliance for Progress', designed by the US government for Latin America in response to the Cuban Revolution, was abandoned (Yeros 2007). The modernization policy effected the wholesale transformation of the countryside by means of state subsidies, mechanization, and accelerated expulsion of the peasantry from the countryside (da Silva 1982; Kageyama 1990). This was the context also of the expansion of the agricultural frontier (Velho 2009), not only into neighbouring Paraguay, but also into Brazil's Amazon Basin and the *Cerrado* (the country's savannah), the latter having been pursued by a joint venture with the Japanese government, under the Nipo-Brazilian Cooperation Programme for the Development of the Cerrados (PRODECER), for the production of soybeans. Furthermore, the state supported its modernization policy by establishing, in 1973, its own capacity in agricultural research, by the creation of the Brazilian Agricultural Research Agency (EMBRAPA). Thus, one of the key thrusts that decades later would be projected into the policy of South–South agricultural cooperation was to be driven by the monopolies promoted across the agro-food sector, which positioned Brazilian agribusiness as a major agricultural producer, exporter and investor, and EMBRAPA as an agent of modern know-how in tropical agriculture.

The policy in the countryside was accompanied by an overall strategy to direct investments to heavy industries, in response to bottlenecks created by the prior

---

[5]For two opposing interpretations regarding the trajectory of 'sub-imperialism', see Luce (2011, 2014) and Martins (2016), although in neither case is the conceptual basis of Marini's formulation contested.

policy of import-substitution. Investments were channelled into the steel industry, naval construction, civil engineering, telecommunications, petrochemicals and hydroelectric and nuclear plants, by a combination of foreign and domestic finance. The latter source occurred mainly through the National Bank of Economic Development (BNDE), which had initially promoted the expansion of state-owned enterprises—such as Petrobras in the petroleum sector, Vale do Rio Doce in mining, Companhia Siderúrgica Nacional (CSN) in steel—but now came to focus on the strengthening of the domestic and foreign private monopolies. The whole of the economy thus gravitated to the circuit of monopoly finance, with external finance retaining the overall supervision of the economy and eventually transmitting its general crisis via the liquidity crunch of the late 1970s, thereby laying bare the profound dependence of the Brazilian economy. Whatever economic expansion would subsequently occur, not least in a South–South policy direction, would either carry the stamp of monopoly finance capital or become a threat to imperialist rents by seeking to broaden membership in the club—itself a highly unlikely strategy.

The Neocolonial Transition

The transition to neocolonialism in Brazil, as in Southern Africa (Moyo and Yeros 2011), was conditional upon the country's subordination to monopoly finance capital in these closing years of the Cold War. Given the dictates of monopoly capital, the return to parliamentary politics with universal suffrage could only occur with guarantees for settler property and privilege and unfettered access by foreign creditors and multinational firms to the country's assets and natural resources. Notably, the Communist parties remained illegal until the end of the 1980s, with their leadership and those of other radical movements having been subjected to an extermination campaign in the 1970s. New political parties and forces of the left, such as the PT, emerged in their place, but renounced Leninism and maintained proximity to the Catholic Church. Yet, the guarantees demanded in the transition were not a foregone conclusion, given the scale and depth of popular struggle against military rule in the late 1970s. The industrial trade unions, the rural landless workers' movement, the women's movement, the student movement, the indigenous movement, and not least the reborn black movement (Pereira 2008), all advanced and synergized in this struggle, gaining organizational force and capacity to place new demands on the transition.

The result was a modern, progressive constitution with guarantees for basic rights and liberties, recognition of racism as a crime, responsibilities for social development and agrarian reform and protections for indigenous, *quilombola* and traditional communities. This marked a tectonic shift in the relation of forces and bestowed constitutional leverage to a wide range of social struggles. However, the debt crisis that ravaged the economy imposed an unsavoury option on the hitherto recalcitrant settler bourgeoisie, namely to abandon its autonomous industrial ambitions and accept, unequivocally, the hegemony of monopoly finance capital.

Evidently, this option was only less unsavoury to the prospect of a domestic pact with the emergent social forces that could spell the end of white-settler privilege and permit the birth of a genuinely popular national project.

The pact between settler capital and imperialism set the stage for the evolution of conflicts and policies over next 30 years. The state apparatus entered a process of bureaucratic reorganization to position the executive and legislature in the institutional epicentre of policymaking. Eventually, new ministries and secretariats were created in the executive, with responsibilities for the environment (1992), agricultural development for small-scale producers (2000), racial equality (2003), cities (2003) and social development (2004). Generally, it was in the 2000s, with the election of the PT government of Luiz Inácio Lula da Silva (2003–2011), that the social clauses of the 1988 Constitution began to be addressed in earnest, resulting in the amplification of pre-existing cash transfer programmes, such as what came to be known as the Family Fund (*Bolsa Familia*), two-thirds of which came to target black women, and in large part the Northeast; and support for 'family agriculture' through special funds and state procurement programmes, which went on to gain international recognition. Yet, social policy remained within the remit of the neo-colonial pact, especially with regards to property guarantees and white privilege, steering clear of substantive redistribution of assets beyond income transfers, such as through land reform, urban reform, protection of indigenous territories and *quilombos*, or empowerment of indigenous and black people, and particularly women.

Meanwhile, the repressive branches of the state, spanning the military, police, prisons, and the judiciary, escaped substantial reorganization, with their higher echelons given amnesty in spite of the cruelty of the crimes committed under military rule. These branches were retained as the main instruments of social control in the neocolonial state, alongside the evolving social programmes, and on a warpath with rural and urban working people, especially black youth, the rural and urban landless, and indigenous people. The incarceration rate rose exponentially in 1990–2016, registering a stunning 707% growth of the prison population, from 90,000 to 726,700 people, with two-thirds of the national total being composed of blacks and 74% of youth between the age of 18 and 34 (INFOPEN 2017: 9, 30–32). The homicide rate also spiked to top world rankings, amounting to over half a million homicides in just one decade, 2006–16, with the country's black population and youth being especially victimized, at 75 and 70% of the total, respectively, in 2016 (IPEA and FBSP 2018: 20–44; PdR 2018: 14). Both incarceration and homicide have been strongly related to the policy of criminalization of drugs, the collusion of security forces in the drug trade and the profit requirements of the security industry (the private security enterprises and military–industrial complex) which itself has systematically accounted for between 1.1 and 1.6% of the GDP in 1996–2015 (PdR 2018: 22). Thus, the hiatus between the state's social and racial equality policies, on the one hand, and its ongoing genocide of black youth, on the other, has represented the essence of Brazil's neocolonial crisis.

The structural conditions which have spawned a world of precarious labour and illicit trade have been addressed elsewhere (Schincariol 2016; Schincariol et al. 2017). Suffice it to note that the neocolonial transition witnessed serial privatizations since the 1990s, and a secular process of deindustrialization, outsourcing and informalization of labour which peaked in the 2000s, in an overall process that led to the re-primarization of the economy and the hypertrophy of the service sector. Although there were positive trends in economic growth, employment and minimum wages in the 2000s, these trends weakened in the aftermath of the 2008 global crisis and collapsed with the commodity bust in 2014. Thus, the brief period of Brazil's 're-emergence', which rode the commodity boom of 2005–2014, must be seen in the light of the escalating contradictions internally and the superficiality and fragility of the 'social pact' sought by the PT administrations (Singer 2012; Boito 2018). Despite the improvement in socio-economic indices, there was no national vision capable of taking hold to replace the 'racial democracy' of the country's settler colonial past. On the contrary, the most remarkable ideological advance was scored by fundamentalist evangelical churches, for which an informalized and insecure labour force has been their ideal terrain of contestation.

The schizophrenic tendencies internally were matched by an equally schizophrenic foreign policy, which defended closer South–South relations and regional autonomy for Latin America and the Southern Cone, while maintaining large trade surpluses with neighbours and projecting Brazil's state and private monopolies to dominant positions in the region, thereby reinforcing the tendency to re-primarization generally. The private and state monopolies that had consolidated their positions in the transition—including the state-controlled Petrobras, the privatized Vale do Rio Doce and CSN, the various construction firms, Odebrecht, Andrade and Gutierrez and Camargo Correa, and the agro-industrial food and beverage conglomerates, JBS, BRF and Ambev—were actively supported in their regional and global expansion by the state development bank (renamed BNDES to include 'social' objectives), which massively channelled national savings into their external operations. But the clearest sign of rot in Brazil's overall external thrust was the invasion and occupation of Haiti in 2004–2017, after the US-staged coup, in which Brazil took the commanding role of the UN mission, in an operation which rekindled, in the cruellest manner, the regional settler pacts of the past.

If the invasion of Haiti was the opportunity to demonstrate 'responsibility' in the UN Security Council, Brazil's foreign expansion was still to overstep the boundaries set by imperialism. The overtures to China and Russia in the formation of the BRICS, coupled with the discovery of vast pre-salt oil deposits off the Brazilian coast, for which Petrobras exercised operational control, laid the basis for what was to become the country's 'second reconversion'. As soon as the commodity prices plummeted in 2014, the internal contradictions were easily manipulated to bring the largest South American country to its knees, in the course of the country's most prolonged economic crisis to date and by means of an institutional *coup*. The latter was led by the judiciary, the media, and precisely the most reactionary and majoritarian parliamentary forces of the neocolonial period composed most emblematically by the 'BBB lobby' ('*Bíblia, Boi e Bala*', or 'Bible, Ox and

Bullet'), representing the fundamentalist churches, agribusiness, and the security industry. The *coup* impeached Dilma Rousseff, a popularly elected president (2011–2016) on trumped-up charges, and swiftly turned on removing the remaining fetters placed on monopoly finance capital, especially its access to the country's energy sector and natural resources, and undermined the social and political gains obtained since the 1988 Constitution. In an ominous gesture, the interim president, Michel Temer, extinguished the Ministry of Agrarian Development on the same day in which he assumed office, in the course of the impeachment process, as well as the Ministry for Women, Racial Equality and Youth and Human Rights.

Brazil–Arica Cooperation: Agriculture, Trade and Direct Investment

Brazil's engagement with Africa on new terms essentially began after 2003, under the Lula administration. This was the time in which China and other semi-peripheral countries were also entering the fray, driven predominantly by the profit requirements of their aspiring monopolies and taking advantage of neoliberal policy frameworks already in place throughout the continent (Mkandawire and Soludo 1999). Neoliberal policies in Africa promoted the titling and privatization of communal lands, while removing barriers on trade and investment. By the turn of the century, the African countryside had sustained a 'second wave' of land grabs to the benefit of emergent domestic bourgeoisie linked to external finance and markets (Moyo 2008; Moyo et al.: Chap. 1, this volume). These tendencies converged substantially, giving impetus to rural differentiation and undermining the lineage-based systems of control over land and labour, especially at the expense of women and youth. In the course of the 2000s, a 'third wave' of land grabs marked a turning-point by the direct involvement of large foreign investors, which set off a general tendency towards a 'tri-modal' agrarian structure, composed of the poor peasantry, preponderantly female, an intermediary small capitalist class, and large estates (Moyo et al., Chap. 1, this volume).

Divergent regional tendencies, nonetheless, were also at play, associated with shifting strategic factors. Central Africa became embroiled in a prolonged region-wide war in the mid-1990s, after the fracture of the state in the Democratic Republic of Congo (DRC), under a US-led campaign to retake control of the region. And after 9/11, large swathes of East, West and North Africa also succumbed to US designs and its 'war on terror', including its new militarization campaign spear-headed by AFRICOM. Meanwhile, Southern Africa, post-*apartheid*, gained unprecedented room for strategic manoeuvre whose most concrete result has been the re-radicalization of nationalism in Zimbabwe and the implementation of fast track land reform (Moyo et al. 2012).

The moment was thus ripe for emergent semi-peripheries to engage with Africa and propose a different type of cooperation based on principles of mutual respect and non-interference in domestic affairs (Amanor 2013). At the turn of the century, the African Union was also launching its New Partnership for Africa's Development (NEPAD), and within it, the Comprehensive Africa Agriculture Development Programme (CAADP), both of which invited new partnerships and foreign investors. It was in this propitious context that Brazilian diplomacy proposed its own South–South cooperation, although it proceeded to feed upon its own internal contradictions in the making of policy, which in turn interacted with conditions in the countries concerned. Recent debates have indicated some of the ways in which Brazil's internal contradictions, together with local conditions in African countries, have played out in the design and implementation of policy (Pierri 2013; Cabral and Shankland 2013; Leite et al. 2014; Cesarino 2015; Cabral et al. 2016).

Cooperation in Agriculture

The flagship programmes of Brazil's international cooperation in Africa have undoubtedly been developed in the agricultural sector. These include More Food International (MFI), led by the Ministry of Agrarian Development; the Food Acquisition Programme for Africa (PAA-Africa, *Programa de Aquisição de Alimentos para África*), led by the Ministry of Foreign Affairs and the Ministry of Social Development; and the Cotton-4 (C-4) Project in West Africa and ProSavana in Mozambique, which have been spearheaded by Brazilian Cooperation Agency (ABC, *Agência Brasileira de Cooperação*), EMBRAPA, and other agencies. With the exception of ProSavana, Brazil's policy has touted a focus on small-scale 'family' producers.

In the particular conjuncture of the 2000s, marked by the commodity boom and the social policy innovations of the PT government, agriculture and food and nutritional security became amongst the main spheres of Brazilian action abroad, apart from public health, social security and education (Ventura 2013; Milani et al. 2016). As Lula's government sought to establish itself as an international champion in the fight against hunger by supporting family farming, while also promoting the Brazilian model of agribusiness (in foods, feeds, fibres and agro fuels), technical cooperation emerged as an important approach to cooperation (de Albuquerque 2013; Brasil 2013). Thus, some initiatives focused more directly on small-scale producers and others more clearly served international agribusiness interests, while all revolved around technical cooperation.

African countries also looked to Brazil for assistance to boost their agricultural performance. As a country that struggled with underdevelopment and poverty but was now positioning itself among emerging powers, Brazil was able to project its cooperation policy within the South–South mould. Although criticism now abounds about such claims (Clements and Fernandes 2013; Castro 2014; Cesarino 2015; Vaz 2015; Nogueira et al. 2017), the whole picture was attractive for African countries, especially as the North's serial imposition of conditionalities reached exhaustion and entered a new phase of militarism. There was, therefore, considerable demand for Brazilian cooperation in Africa, and that demand met a domestic bureaucratic scenario that was open to it and which, indeed, was organized in good part to respond to that very demand (Leite et al. 2015).

The PAA-Africa was launched in May 2010, during the 'Brazil–Africa Dialogue on Food Security, Fighting Hunger and Rural Development', and its execution began in February 2012. The programme was inspired on the domestic programme with the same name (Food Acquisition Programme), whose objective was to create an institutionalized market for products from family farming. The basic idea was that supply should be more planned according to the local demands of public schools in rural areas, and that the government should guarantee that the foods are purchased from local family farmers at a 'fair price', usually above market prices. The process sought to bring together stakeholders from communities, schools, producers and the government to discuss demand and supply and create a more stable market for farmers and school-feeding programmes.

PAA-Africa has included five countries—Ethiopia, Malawi, Mozambique, Niger and Senegal—and has been conducted in partnership with the World Food Programme (WFP), the Food and Agriculture Organization (FAO) and the UK's Department for International Development (DFID). As the agreements with each country have been designed via multi-stakeholder processes, each has its own characteristics. The differences among projects have been seen as an important feature of Brazilian style 'demand-driven' cooperation, against the 'one size fits all' approach conventionally put forth by the North. Besides the MDA, the Ministry of Social Development (MDS) and CGFome (the coordinating organ for Humanitarian Cooperation and Fight against Hunger of the Ministry of Foreign Affairs) took leading roles in the negotiation process. As such, the PAA-Africa was intentionally created as a foreign policy initiative to externalize a successful Brazilian public policy.

More Food International (MFI) was also launched in 2010 (under its earlier name, More Food Africa), having been inspired on another of Brazil's domestic programmes (More Food Programme, *Programa Mais Alimentos*) (Pierri 2013; Patriota and Pierri 2013; Cabral et al. 2016). The MFI was led by the Ministry of Agrarian Development (MDA), becoming its main instrument of cooperation with Africa and focusing on upgrading the production capacities of small-scale farmers. The MFI created an export credit facility with concessional loans for the purchase of agricultural machinery from Brazil such as tractors, motocultivators, irrigation equipment and storage facilities (Pierri 2013), bringing onboard many other actors for its operationalization such as the Bank of Brazil, Ministry of External Relations, Chamber of Commerce (CAMEX) and business interests. In theory, the main purpose of the MFI has been to foster the upgrading of production by financing the acquisition of Brazilian-made equipment and machinery by African countries. In 2011, US$640 million was made available in export credits to finance MFI in Ghana, Kenya, Mozambique, Senegal and Zimbabwe, with the first deliveries being made in Zimbabwe in 2015, after some procedural difficulties and prolonged negotiations.

The MFI has been the culmination of Brazilian policymaking experiences geared towards 'family agriculture', whose principal objective, even in Brazil, has in fact been the reinforcement of a middle layer of peasant producers who survived the transformation of the Green Revolution (Kageyama et al. 2013; Favareto 2016). Thus, as the MFI policy dynamic gained force, and regardless of the competing visions around its design, the commercial thrust built into it naturally interacted with the evolving agrarian political economy of Africa, especially the tri-modal differentiation tendencies. In Ghana, while the procurement of Brazilian equipment faced competition from other sources, the Ghanaian government saw in MFI one further possibility to procure equipment for the strengthening of its own middle layer of small-scale producers (Amanor and Chichava 2016; Cabral et al. 2016). In Mozambique, despite the 'family farm' pronouncements of MFI, it was the commercial thrust of the programme that was most suitable to the ProSavana project, in which the other Brazilian agencies were heavily invested (Cabral et al. 2016).

Perhaps, the more complex case has been that of Zimbabwe. Zimbabwe's post-land reform situation (post-2000), which has struggled under unilateral sanctions imposed by the West (Moyo and Yeros 2011), has been especially open to any South–South engagement in support of the recovery of production. One of the effects of the land reform was to deprive the small-scale capitalist farming class of cheap labour, even though this intermediary farming category (the 'A2' farmers in Zimbabwe's policy terminology) had actually benefited from land reform (Moyo et al. 2009). The fiscal crisis of the state under sanctions was eventually to tilt the policy orientation towards the support of the A2 sector through mechanization, which could easily fit into the MFI design. Yet, equipment for irrigation was also procured, and this has also been channelled to peasant production. Most notably, the government's more recent policy of 'Command Agriculture', to which the MFI has contributed, has produced a concrete success story in the expansion of medium- and small-scale agricultural production in Africa (Chambati et al. 2018).

The remaining cooperation experiences have been more ambiguous, or have clearly tended in the opposite direction. The countries participating in the C-4 Project were initially Benin, Burkina Faso, Chad, and Mali, with Togo joining the group in 2013. This project has been led by EMBRAPA. Its main objective has been to support the development of cotton value chains, by adapting and improving seed varieties, developing infrastructure and logistics and controlling pests (Suyama and Rigout (n/d); Anunciato 2014; Cesarino 2015). The C-4 Project has its origins in the dispute over cotton subsidies between Brazil and the United States at the World Trade Organization (WTO) (2003–2010), when the C-4 countries joined Brazil in denouncing the adverse effects of US subsidies on the international cotton market. After 2006, Brazilian cotton experts from EMBRAPA analysed the production processes of the C-4 countries and initiated a project termed 'Assistance to the Development of the Cotton Sector in the C-4 Countries', with the support of the United Nations Development Programme. Originally, the project was to be funded by the Brazilian Cooperation Agency alone. However, additional funding came in

2012, from compensations paid by the United States upon losing the cotton dispute at the WTO. In 2009–2013, the total budget was USD 5.2 million, of which USD 1.35 million came from US compensations and the rest from Brazil. Brazil did not transfer any funds to the C-4 countries; the budget was to finance technical consultancy and the acquisition of equipment and materials, generally in the Brazilian market.

The project took the form of collaborative research initiatives among partner institutes in the partner countries for the purpose of adapting Brazilian technologies (Cesarino 2015). Although the conception and execution of the project has been pitched as 'horizontal', African countries have tended to see it as a Brazilian project and not one also owned by them. And even though, to date, it has been free of controversy, the question remains as to its future, given the reflux of social policy and international cooperation initiatives in Brazil in the aftermath of the 2016 *coup*, if not also the overall policy orientation of integration into global value chains under the control of foreign monopolies.

The ProSavana, officially called 'Triangular Cooperation for Agricultural Development of the Tropical Savannah in Mozambique', is a project between Brazil, Japan and Mozambique. The planning phase was inaugurated in 2009, but it is still undergoing reformulations mainly because of fierce domestic contestation (Cesarino 2015). It has been inspired on the Japanese-Brazilian technical cooperation that was fundamental for the development of agribusiness in Brazil's *Cerrado* in the 1970s (Santos 2016). The alleged geographical similarities between the Nacala region in Mozambique and the *Cerrado* opened the way for an approach that bridges the interests of the three governments and of transnational agribusinesses in increasing grain production and exports at a lower cost. Some of the project's modules are directed to cash crops and some are supposed to engage small-scale farmers in food production. Brazil's EMBRAPA has led the technical effort, with the support of the ABC and Fundação Getúlio Vargas, a private university which conducted the initial study and has sourced investors. ProSavana has a long-run perspective of around 20 years, within which it intends to develop the production of different grains such as wheat, rice, maize, beans, and, most importantly, soybeans.

However, the dramatic changes in the possession and use of lands have raised strong popular criticism and opposition from peasants' organizations, civil society generally, and university researchers (Shankland and Gonçalves 2016). Critics have complained that the formulation and execution of the project have not been conducted under adequate consultations with communities affected. Researchers have also argued that the Nacala Fund, which is private and headed by Brazilian business interests, plays a very important role in attracting foreign investments and raises concerns about the real nature of Brazil's South–South Cooperation. Besides, other Brazilian monopolies already operate in the region in construction and mining, specifically Vale and the civil engineering firms, which in fact opened space for ProSavana as an adjunct to mining, and these operations have very substantial adverse effects (Nogueira et al. 2017). This is the most concrete case of land-grabbing by Brazilian capital in Africa (Clements and Fernandes 2013; Cesarino 2015).

Trends in Trade and Foreign Direct Investment

As the commodity boom of the 2000s brought relief in terms of hard currency, both trade and direct investment grew with the support of the Brazilian government, which expanded its budget allocations, credit emissions, and diplomacy. The financial position of the BNDES improved significantly, and the bank gained a decisive role in the strengthening of the Brazilian monopolies. The Lula administration made a political decision to stimulate systematically the external expansion of the big Brazilian firms and boost their profit margins by diversifying operations in the South. Brazilian firms were understood to be competitive in the construction, engineering, energy, and mining sectors.[6]

Latin America and Africa were obvious destinations for Brazilian capital. Many of the Brazilian firms were already operating in Latin America and Africa before 2003, and even in the Middle East such as Iraq. Brazilian firms penetrated economic spaces not occupied by US or European firms, but remained vulnerable and, in fact, were forced out of the Iraqi market when the US invaded that country (Bandeira 2006). It was generally supposed that, in the long run, the expansion to Latin American and Africa would compensate for the exposure of the Brazilian economy to foreign capital. And although there was a remarkable expansion post-2003, Brazil's emergence would not be sustained after 2014, when it succumbed to the commodity bust and when its own monopolies came under attack in a series of corruption scandals, at the centre of which were precisely Petrobras and agro-industrial and civil engineering firms.

According to the Brazilian Ministry of Industry, Foreign Trade and Services, the total foreign trade between Brazil and Africa accounted for USD 4.2 billion in 2000, and expanded rapidly thereafter. BNDES has played an important role in this expansion by extending credit to exporters (Banco Mundial and IPEA 2010). In 2010, exports to Africa accounted for 6% of Brazil's total exports. In 2017, total trade reached USD 26 billion, a sixfold increase since 2000. This was a notable growth trend, especially when compared to Brazil's exports to China, a much larger economy, which reached approximately USD 40 billion in the same period.

---

[6]The main firms have included: Petrobras in crude oil and natural gas and petrochemicals, a state-owned company which nonetheless traded approximately 40% of its shares in stock exchange markets; Odebrecht in engineering, construction, chemicals, and petrochemicals; Andrade Gutierrez in engineering, construction, telecommunications, and energy; Camargo Correa in cement, siderurgy, real estate, construction, crude oil and natural gas, electric energy, transportation; Vale do Rio Doce in metals and mining; Weg in engineering, power, and automation technologies; and Marco Polo in coach and bus manufacturing.

During 2003–2015, Brazil maintained a trade deficit with Africa as a whole, reaching USD 1.5 billion in 2000 and USD 7.4 billion in 2014 (see Fig. 1). However, this trade deficit was mainly accounted for by oil purchases from Algeria and Nigeria, the main commodities involved in Brazil's foreign trade with Africa. With regard to Brazil's other main trade partners, South Africa, Angola and Mozambique, there was a repetition of the same existing pattern of trade found in South America, where Brazilian trade surpluses have prevailed. Brazil maintained trade surpluses with these three countries from 2003 until very recently, when the effects of the international (and then domestic) crisis began to appear, in 2014/15, although throughout the crisis trade surpluses remained with South Africa and Angola. As Fig. 1 shows the elasticity of the oil imports from Algeria and Nigeria in light of Brazil's declining rates of economic growth, in 2014–2018 was particularly relevant, marking a rapid fall.

As a result of Brazil's economic crisis after 2014, the country's total trade deficit with Africa declined to USD 500 million by 2015. In 2016 and 2017, and largely due to declining oil imports, Brazil obtained trade surpluses of USD 3.2 and USD 3.8 billion with Africa as a whole. Despite Brazil's relatively advanced technological capacity, the pattern of trade between these regions can be considered essentially as intra-periphery (Table 1): in the first half of 2018, 53% of Brazil's exports consisted of sugar, iron ore and meat, while 47% of Africa's exports consisted of oil and its byproducts (including the activities of Petrobras in Angola, Tanzania, Namibia and Nigeria). Machines, optic instruments and transport equipment reached only 11% of Brazilian exports in 2018, while these same items composed only 1% of the African exports to Brazil.

Official statistics on Brazilian investments in Africa—excluding those registered in tax havens—tend to underestimate the real flows, yet they remain low on a world scale, consisting of less than 3% of the total.[7] These investments have been substantially monopolistic, with 50% of the total values in 2016 corresponding to 0.1% of total number of investors.[8] The main sectors of Brazilian foreign investment in Africa are infrastructure, energy and mining, led by the big state and private firms, namely Petrobras, Vale do Rio Doce, Camargo Correa, Odebrecht and Andrade Gutierrez among others such as the Marco Polo Company which manufactures vehicles in South Africa. Some of these investments were made through credit provided by the BNDES during the 2000s. Petrobras invested in deepwater oil extraction in Angola, Libya, Nigeria and Tanzania (Banco Mundial and IPEA

---

[7]See 'Capitais Brasileiros no Exterior', Tables 2007–2016, 'Table 1-B, 'Estoque de Ativos regularizados', at http://www4.bcb.gov.br/rex/cbe/port/ResultadoCBE2016.asp?idpai=CBE, accessed 6 June 2018. A significant part of investments is registered in tax havens. Brazilian Central Bank statistics regarding Brazilian foreign investments via tax havens are reported as follows: the British Islands registered alone 26% of the Brazilian stock of investment abroad in 2016; Panama, Bahamas, Switzerland, and Cayman, registered 17, 14, 12, and 7%, respectively.

[8]See 'Capitais Brasileiros no Exterior', Tables 2007–2016, Table III, 'Capitais brasileiros no exterior, estoque, distribuição por faixa de valor', at http://www4.bcb.gov.br/rex/cbe/port/ResultadoCBE2016.asp?idpai=CBE, accessed 6 June 2018.

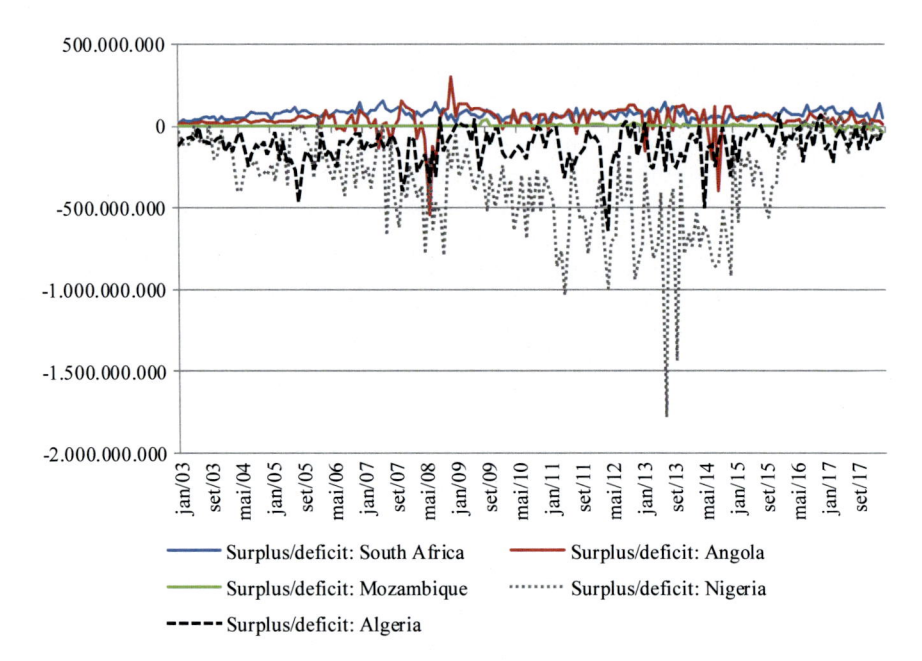

Fig. 1 Brazil–Africa foreign trade (surplus/deficit), by main trade partners (USD billions).
Source Ministry of Industry, Services and Foreign Trade, http://www.mdic.gov.br/index.php/comercio-exterior/estatisticas-de-comercio-exterior/balanca-comercial-brasileira-mensal-2, accessed 6 June 2018

Table 1 Brazil–Africa foreign trade, by main groups of sectors

2018	Brazil to Africa (%)	Africa to Brazil (%)
Live animals and other animals	16	1
Vegetables	25	1
Food, beverage and tobacco	38	6
Minerals	13	61
Chemicals	2	19
Plastics	1	1
Textiles	0.01	1
Jewellery and gems	0	3

Source Ministry of Industry, Services and Foreign Trade, http://www.mdic.gov.br/index.php/comercio-exterior/estatisticas-de-comercio-exterior/balanca-comercial-brasileira-mensal-2, accessed 6 June 2018

2010). The main destination of foreign investment was Angola, which received 0.1 and 0.4% of Brazil's total in 2007 and 2014, respectively.[9] Inter-firm investments in Africa suffered the consequences of Brazil's recent economic decline (and of the world economy, generally). Excluding Angola, which saw an increase from USD 148 billion to USD 234 billion in 2012–2014, there was a general decline or stagnation in investments after 2014. Mozambique saw a fall from USD 98 billion to USD 48 in 2012–2016; Morocco, from USD 7 billion to one; and South Africa and Nigeria received a relatively stagnant flow.[10]

There is no specific information by African countries regarding operations in stock markets, public debt or portfolio. When relating to real estate investments, Brazilian Central Bank reports that the total investments of Brazilian companies (and individuals) abroad amounted to USD 6.1 billion 2016; in Angola, these values reached USD 21 million in 2016 (up from one million in 2007), and in South Africa, 13 million in 2016 (up from thee million in 2007). Table 2 shows a sector-based summary of the Brazilian investments in Africa, according to available statistics.[11] The data shows that construction and infrastructure are the main areas of foreign investment in Africa, followed by trade and repair of vehicles and apparently insignificant flows in the majority of the other fields, such as agriculture, manufacturing, arts and culture.

The commodity bust and corruption scandals that rocked Brazil in 2014, as well as its operations in Africa and Latin America, led to declining rates of investment and employment, with catastrophic consequences for the Brazilian economy as well as the country's multinational firms, which rapidly ceded space to foreign competitors in the affected fields. Overall, the rise of Brazilian investments in Africa created some room for manoeuvre in sectors which had been dominated by US and European firms, or in countries under sanctions such as Zimbabwe, yet they also tended to reinforce a primary goods export-led pattern of economic performance. Whatever the effects in specific countries and sectors, Brazil's 'emergence' into the monopoly club could not be sustained and would be roundly defeated as the country sank, once again, into depression.

---

[9]See 'Capitais Brasileiros no Exterior', Tables 2007–2016, Table III, 'Investimento brasileiro direto, participação no capital', at http://www4.bcb.gov.br/rex/cbe/port/ResultadoCBE2016.asp?idpai=CBE, accessed 6 June 2018.

[10]See 'Capitais Brasileiros no Exterior', Tables 2007–2016, 'Quadro IX—Investimento brasileiro direto—operações intercompanhia', Table IX, 'Investimento brasileiro direto—operações intercompanhia', at http://www4.bcb.gov.br/rex/cbe/port/ResultadoCBE2016.asp?idpai=CBE, accessed 6 June 2018.

[11]Data concerning Nigeria, Tanzania, Algeria, Libya, or other countries are not available. Some data are regarded as 'confidential', allegedly relating to only three (or less) companies.

Table 2 Brazil–Africa foreign direct investment, by main groups of sectors for selected countries

2016	Angola	South Africa	Mozambique	Ghana
Agriculture and related activities			Confidential	
Mining		Confidential	Confidential	
Manufacturing		Confidential		
Electricity				
Construction and infrastructure	300	Confidential	52	30
Trade and repair of vehicles	1	103		
Food and housing				
Communications and information	Confidential		Confidential	
Finance and related activities		Confidential		
Real state				
Professional activities and other services		Confidential	Confidential	
Administration activities and other services		Confidential		
Arts, culture, sports				
Other		18	5	

Source Brazilian Central Bank (CBE, *Capitais Brasileiros no Exterior*), http://www4.bcb.gov.br/rex/cbe/port/ResultadoCBE2016.asp?idpai=CBE, accessed 6 June 2018

Conclusion

Brazil's re-encounter with Africa has entailed an internal process of struggle for the resolution of the national question, as well as an external vent for the accumulated contradictions of its neocolonial transition. It has certainly been a phase qualitatively different from previous ones, when the settler perspective was directly aligned to the colonial establishment. In the current phase, the schizophrenic tendencies have manifested themselves as much in support of Zimbabwe's radical land reform against the settler establishment, as in the direct involvement of Brazil's own settler capital in massive land-grabbing in Mozambique. Nonetheless, the prior thrust of this overall relationship has not been sustained post-2014, as Brazil's 'emergence' has been beaten back for a second time. It is still possible that the worst tendencies of the settler orientation will prevail more strongly in the current dispensation. Yet, it is also true that the black movement in Brazil has been advancing towards a new level of organizational capacity in the current crisis, which is laying the seeds for a new relationship with Africa. It is the next generation that stands to reap the benefits.

References

Amanor, K. S. (2013). South-south cooperation in Africa: Historical, geopolitical and political economy dimensions of international development. *IDS Bulletin, 44*(4), 20–30.

Amanor, K. S., & Chichava, S. (2016). South-south cooperation, agribusiness and African agricultural development: Brazil and China in Ghana and Mozambique. *World Development, 81,* 13–23.

Américo, J. L. T. (2015). Redemocratização e Racismo: Novas Formas de Genocídio no Brasil Pós-Ditadura. *Masters Dissertation in Human and Social Sciences.* Santo André, Brasil: Federal Universidade of ABC.

Anunciato, R. O. (2014). Política Externa Brasileira e a atuação da EMBRAPA no Caso do Cotton-4. *Masters Dissertation, Post-graduate Programme in Political Science.* Porto Alegre: Universidade Federal do Rio Grande do Sul.

Banco Mundial and IPEA. (2010). *Ponte sobre o Atlântico: Brasil e África Subsaariana, Parceria Sul-Sul para o Crescimento.* Brasília: Banco Mundial and IPEA.

Bandeira, L. A. M. (2006). *Formação do império americano.* Rio de Janeiro: Civilização Brasileira.

Boito, A., Jr. (2018). *Reforma e Crise Política no Brasil: Os Conflitos de Classe nos Governos do PT.* São Paulo: Editora UNESP and UNICAMP.

Boito, A., Jr., & Berringer, T. (2013). Classes Sociais, Neodesenvolvimentismo e Política Externa nos Governos Lula e Dilma. *Revista de Sociologia e Política, 21*(47), 31–38.

Brasil, P. F. (2013). O Brasil e a insegurança alimentar global: forças sociais e política externa (2003–2010). *Masters Dissertation,* Institute of International Relations, University of Brasília.

Cabral, L., Favareto, A., Mukwereza, L., & Amanor, K. (2016). More food international and the disputed meanings of 'family farming'. *World Development, 81,* 47–60.

Cabral, L., & Shankland, A. (2013). Narratives of Brazil-Africa cooperation for agricultural development: New paradigms? *FAC Working Paper,* No. 51, Future Agricultures Consortium, Brighton.

Castro, C. M. (2014). Brazil's cooperation with sub-saharan Africa in the rural sector. *Latin American Perspectives, 41*(5), 75–93.

Cesarino, L. (2015). Brazil as an emerging donor in Africa's agricultural sector: Comparing two projects. *Agrarian South: Journal of Political Economy, 4*(3), 1–23.

Chambati, W., Mazwi, F., Mudimu, G., & Chemura, A. (2018). *The political economy of command agriculture in Zimbabwe. Monograph series of the Sam Moyo African Institute for Agrarian Studies.* Harare: SMAIAS.

Clements, E., & Fernandes, B. M. (2013). Land grabbing, agribusiness and the peasantry in Brazil and Mozambique. *Agrarian South: Journal of Political Economy, 2*(1), 41–69.

da Silva, J. F. F. (1982). *A Modernização Dolorosa.* Rio de Janeiro: Zahar.

Da Silva, J., & Pereira, A. M. (2013). *Olhares sobre a Mobilização Brasileira para a 3ª Conferência Mundial contra o Racismo, a Discriminação Racial, a Xenofobia e Intolerâncias Correlatas.* Belo Horizonte: Nandyala.

de Albuquerque, F. L. R. (2013). Atores e Agendas da Política Externa Brasileira para a África e a Instrumentalização da Cooperação em Segurança Alimentar (2003–2010). *Masters Dissertation in International Relations,* Institute of Philosophy and Human Sciences, University of the State of Rio de Janeiro.

de Azevedo, C. M. M. (1987). *Onda Negra, Medo Branco.* São Paulo: Annablumme.

do Nascimento, A. (1978). *O Genocídio do Negro Brasileiro.* Rio de Janeiro: Paz e Terra.

do Nascimento Barbosa, W. (2002). *Cultura Negra e Dominação.* São Leopoldo: Unisinos.

Dos Santos, T. (1978). *Imperialismo y Dependencia.* México: Era.

Dos Santos, T. (1991). *Democracia e Socialismo no Capitalismo Dependente.* Petrópolis, RJ: Editora Vozes.

Dos Santos, T. (1995). *Evolução Histórica do Brasil: Da Colônia à Crise da 'Nova República'.* Petrópolis, RJ: Editora Vozes.

dos Santos Gomes, F. (2015). *Mocambos e Quilombos: Uma História do Campesinato Negro no Brasil*. São Paulo: Claro Enigma.

Favareto, A. (2016). Beyond "family farming versus agribusiness" dualism: Unpacking the complexity of Brazil's agricultural model. *CBAA Working Paper*, No. 138, Future Agricultures Consortium, Brighton.

Fernandes, F. (1964). *A Integração do Negro na Sociedade de Classes* (Vol. I). São Paulo: USP.

Fernandes, F. (1976). *A Revolução Burguesa no Brasil* (2nd ed.). Rio de Janeiro: Zahar Editores.

Furtado, C. (2004 [1958]). *Formação Econômica do Brasil*. São Paulo: Companhia das Letras.

INFOPEN. (2017). *Levantamento Nacional de Informações Penitenciárias*. Brasília: Ministério da Justiça e Segurança Pública & Departamento Penitenciário Nacional.

IPEA and FBSP. (2018). *Atlas da Violência*. Rio de Janeiro: IPEA & FBSP.

Kageyama, A. (1990). 'O Novo Padrão Agrícola Brasileiro: Do Complexo Rural aos Complexos Agro-industriais'. In G. C. Delgado, J. G. Gasques, & C.M.V. Verde (Eds.), *Agricultura e Políticas Públicas* (pp. 113–223). Brasília: IPEA.

Kageyama, A. A., Bergamasco, S. M. P. P., & de Oliveira, J. T. A. (2013). Uma Tipologia dos Estabelecimentos Agropecuários do Brasil a partir do Censo de 2006. *Revista de Economia e Sociologia Rural, 51*(1), 105–122.

Leite, I. C., Pomeroy, M., & Suyama, B. (2015). Brazilian south-south development cooperation: The case of the Ministry of Social Development in Africa. *Journal of International Development, 27*(8), 1446–1461.

Leite, I. C., Suyama, B., Waisbich, L. T., Pomeroy, M., Constantine, J., Navas-Alemán, L., Younis, A. S. M. (2014). Brazil's engagement in international development cooperation: The state of the Debate. *Evidence Report*, No. 59. Brighton: IDS.

Luce, M. S. L. (2011). A Economia Política do Subimperialismo em Ruy Mauro Marini: Uma História Conceitual. *Anais do XXVI Simpósio Nacional de História (ANPUH)*, São Paulo, July.

Luce, M. S. L. (2014). O Subimperialismo, Etapa Superior do Capitalismo Dependente. *Tensões Mundiais, 10*(18/19), 43–65.

Mafeje, A. (1997). *The national question in Southern Africa*. Harare: SAPES.

Magubane, B. (1979). *The political economy of race and class in Southern Africa*. New York, NY: Monthly Review.

Magubane, B. (1983). Imperialism and the making of the South African working class. In: B. Magubane & G. Nzongola-Ntalaja (Eds.), *Proletarianization and class struggle in Africa* (pp. 18–56). San Francisco, CA: Synthesis Publications.

Mandaza, I. (Ed.). (1987). *Zimbabwe: The political economy of transition, 1980–1986*. Dakar: CODESRIA.

Marini, R. M. (1969). *Subdesarrollo y Revolución*. México DF: Siglo XXI.

Marini, R. M. (1992). *América Latina: Dependência e Integração*. São Paulo: Editora Página Aberta.

Marini, R. M. (2000). *Dialética da Dependência: Uma Antologia da Obra de Ruy Mauro Marini*. E. Sader (Eds.). Petrópolis, RJ, Buenos Aires: Editora Vozes and CLACSO.

Martins, C. E. (2016). O Legado de Ruy Mauro Marini para as Ciências Sociais: A Economia Política do Capitalismo Dependente. *Cadernos Cemarx, 9*, 13–31.

Milani, C. R. S., Conceição, F. C., & M'Bunde, T. S. (2016). Cooperação Sul-sul em Educação e Relações Brasil-PALOP. *Carderno CRH, 29*(76), 13–32.

Mkandawire, T., & Soludo, C. (Eds.). (1999). Our continent, our future: African perspectives on structural adjustment, CODESRIA, IDRC and AWP, Dakar, Ottawa and Asmara.

Moyo, S. (1995). *The land question in Zimbabwe*. Harare: SAPES.

Moyo, S. (2008). *African land questions, agrarian transitions and the state: Contradictions of neoliberal land reforms*. Dakar: CODESRIA.

Moyo, S., & Chambati, W. (Eds.). (2013). *Land and agrarian reform in Zimbabwe: Beyond white-settler capitalism*. Dakar: CODESRIA.

Moyo, S., Chambati, W., Murisa, T., Siziba, D., Dangwa, C., Mujeyi, K., et al. (2009). *Fast track land reform baseline survey in Zimbabwe: Trends and tendencies, 2005/06*. Harare: African Institute for Agrarian Studies.

Moyo, S., & Yeros, P. (2005). Land occupations and land reform in Zimbabwe: Towards the national democratic revolution. In S. Moyo & P. Yeros (Eds.), *Reclaiming the land: The resurgence of rural movements in Africa, Asia and Latin America* (pp. 165–205). London and Cape Town: Zed Books and David Philip.

Moyo, S., & Yeros, P. (2007). The radicalised state: Zimbabwe's interrupted revolution. *Review of African Political Economy, 34*(111), 103–121.

Moyo, S., & Yeros, P. (2011). After Zimbabwe: State, nation and region in africa. In S. Moyo & P. Yeros (Eds.), *Reclaiming the nation: The return of the national question in Africa, Asia and Latin America* (pp. 78–102). London: Pluto Press.

Moyo, S., & Yeros, P. (2013). The Zimbabwe model: Radicalisation, reform and resistance. In S. Moyo & W. Chambati (Eds.), *Land and agrarian reform in Zimbabwe: Beyond white-settler capitalism* (pp. 331–357). Dakar: CODESRIA.

Moyo, S., Yeros, P., & Jha, Praveen. (2012). Imperialism and primitive accumulation: Notes on the new scramble for Africa. *Agrarian South: Journal of Political Economy, 1*(2), 181–203.

Munanga, K. (1999). *Rediscutindo a Mestiçagem no Brasil: Identidade Nacional versus Identidade Negra.* Petrópolis, RJ: Vozes.

Nogueira, I., Ollinaho, O., Pinto, E. C., Baruco, G., Saludjian, A., Pinto, J. P. G., et al. (2017). Mozambican economic porosity and the role of Brazilian capital: A political economy analysis. *Review of African Political Economy, 44*(151), 104–121.

Patriota, T. C., & Pierri, F. M. (2013). Brazil's Cooperation in African Agricultural Development and Food Security. In F. Cheru & R. Modi (Eds.), *Agriculural Development and Food Security in Africa* (pp. 125–144). London: Zed Books.

PdR [Presidência da Republica] (2018). Custos Econômicos da Criminalidade no Brasil. Brasília: Presidência da República, Secretaria Especial de Assuntos Estratégicos.

Pereira, A. M. (2003). "Um Raio em Céu Azul": Reflexões sobre a Política de Cotas e a Identidade Nacional Brasileira. *Estudos Afro-Asiáticos, 25*(3), 463–482.

Pereira, A. M. (2008). *Trajetória e Perspectivas do Movimento Negro Brasileiro.* Belo Horizonte: Nandyala.

Pierri, F. (2013). How Brazil's agrarian dynamics shape development cooperation in Africa. *IDS Bulletin, 44*(4), 69–79.

Ribeiro, C. O. (2007). *Relações Político-Comerciais Brasil-África, 1985–2006.* PhD Thesis, University of São Paulo, Brazil.

Santos, dos C. C. (2016). Programa de Cooperação Nipo-Brasileira para o Desenvolvimento dos Cerrados – PRODECER: um espectro ronda os cerrados brasileiros. *Estudos Sociedade e Agricultura, 24*(2), 384–416.

Saraiva, J. F. S. (1996). *O Lugar da África: A Dimensão Atlântica da Políticas Exterior Brasileira.* Brasília: UNB.

Schincariol, V. (2016). *Economia e Política Econômica no Governo Dilma (2011–2014).* São Paulo: Raízes da América.

Schincariol, V., Barbosa, M. S., & Yeros, P. (2017). Labour trends in Latin Ameica and the Caribbean in the current crisis (2008–2016). *Agrarian South: Journal of Political Economy, 6*(1), 113–141.

Schwarcz, L. M. (1995). *O Espetáculo das Raças: Cientistas, Instituições e Questão Racial no Brasil, 1870–1930.* São Paulo: Companhia das Letras.

Shankland, A., & Gonçalves, E. (2016). Imagining agricultural development in south-south cooperation: the contestation and transformation of ProSAVANA. *World Development, 81,* 35–46.

Singer, A. (2012). *Os Sentidos do Lulismo: Reforma Gradual e Pacto Conservador.* São Paulo: Companhia das Letras.

Skidmore, T. (1974). *Black into white: Race and nationality in Brazilian thought.* Oxford: Oxford University Press.

Suyama, B., & Rigout, F. (n/d). *Avaliação do Projeto "Apoio ao Desenvolvimento do Setor Algodoeiro dos Países do C-4" (Benin, Burquina Faso, Chade e Mali).* Plan Políticas Públicas and Centro de Estudos e Articulação da Cooperação Sul-Sul: São Paulo.

Teodoro, M. (2008). A Formação do Mercado de Trabalho no Brasil. In M. Teodoro (Ed.), *As Políticas Públicas e a Desigualdade Racial no Brasil 120 Anos após a Abolição* (pp. 15–44). Brasília: IPEA.

Vaz, A. C. (2015). International drivers of Brazilian agricultural cooperation in Africa in the post-2008 economic crisis. *Revista Brasileira de Política Internacional, 58*(1), 164–190.

Velho, O. G. (2009). *Capitalismo Autoritário e Campesinato: Um Estudo Comparativo a partir da Fronteira em Movimento*. Rio de Janeiro: Centro Edelstein.

Ventura, D. (2013). Public health and Brazilian foreign policy. *SUR, 10*(9), 95–113.

Vida Gala, I. (2007). A Política Externa do Governo Lula para a África. 51° Curso de Altos Estudos, Instituto Rio Branco, Ministério das Relações Exteriores, Brasília.

Yeros, P. (2007). A Geopolítica da Reforma Agrária. In B. M. Fernandes, M. I. M. Marques, & J. C. Suzuki (Eds.), *Geografia Agrária: Teoria e a Poder* (pp. 151–176). São Paulo: Expressão Popular.

Part III
National Experiences in West, East & Southern Africa

Land Grabbing, a Virus in the Fruit of Food Sovereignty in West Africa: A Case Study from 'Office du Niger' Zone in Mali

Mamadou Goïta

Introduction

In Africa, and notably West and Central Africa, agriculture is a principal source of productive activity for the majority of the population. The type of agriculture in question is structured around rural farming produced by family farmers. The socio-economic relations within these types of farming enterprises are based on family and kinship relations. Family members pool their knowledge and financial and material resources around the primary objective of providing for household requirements, and, second, to produce wealth through commercial activities around surplus production.

This model of production is primarily geared towards providing for the food consumption needs of the family, while sales of surplus production to meet other non-food requirements assume a secondary role. This differs principally from the private agricultural enterprise model, where the share capital of one or several investors represents the principal linkage between interested parties.

The Malian economy depends mainly on the rural sector—agriculture, livestock production, forestry and fishing—which provides about 80% of all productive employment for the active population and contributes an average of 40–45% of the Gross Domestic Product (GDP), based on an average annual growth level of 3.6%. By contrast, gold, which is the country's principal mining resource, contributes only 10% of GDP.

Mali possesses a substantial agro-sylvo pastoral resource base for the development of agriculture, livestock, forestry and fishery activities, with a physical land area of 46.6 million hectares (ha), of which 12.2 million ha are suitable for agriculture and 30 million ha for pastures/grazing, along with 3.3 million ha of wildlife

M. Goïta (✉)
Institute for Research and Promotion of Alternatives in Development—Africa,
ACI 2000, Rue non codifiée, Lot N° AG/6011, BP 2729, Bamako, Mali
e-mail: mamadou_goita@yahoo.fr; mgoita@irpadafrique.ml

© Springer Nature Singapore Pte Ltd. 2019
S. Moyo et al. (eds.), *Reclaiming Africa*, Advances in African Economic,
Social and Political Development, https://doi.org/10.1007/978-981-10-5840-0_6

reserves and 1.1 million ha of forestry reserves, plus a wealth of biological diversity in forestry and wildlife/animal/livestock resources. Water is another important resource, comprising 2600 km of rivers, substantial biodiversity, vast resources in forestry, fauna and livestock, including 7.1 million bovine animals, 19 million sheep and goats, 0.6 million camels and 25 million heads of poultry. According to a 2006 study, updated in 2013, the country also has 900,000 agricultural enterprises, the majority of which are family farms (Ministry of Agriculture 2013).

Some major challenges have emerged in recent years, such as good land governance, access to and securing land tenure for family farms, capacity-building for land management actors, massive appropriation of land mainly by private national and especially, international companies in areas with high agricultural potential. These challenges are related to the current trends in the privatization of agricultural land in Mali.

The land legislation of Mali, which is being reformed, is based on public estate land which recognizes individual private property. It recognizes customary rights but emphasizes the issue of land registration. Since 2010, the state has been undertaking alternative land reform that aims gradually to do away with public estate land, to recognize customary rights in their diversity and to develop new tools for securing customary possessions and land transactions. Other measures are being adopted, such as the decentralization of land management through the creation of local land institutions, the introduction of compulsory procedures for resolving conflicts and affirmative action in favour of women and young people.

There are new threats to the coherence of land-related policies in Mali, in the context of the transfer of large tracts of land, particularly in irrigated and irrigable areas, to private international and local players. This is accompanied by the misuse of the 'virtuous' model of decentralization, the increase in land speculation, and the growth of protest movements by non-state actors. This chapter will begin with some conceptual issues related to sustainable natural resource management, before focusing on the land question in Mali and the specific case of land appropriation in the Office du Niger (ON) zone.

The Challenge of Sustainable Natural Resource Management

Natural resource management, including land, has been at the centre of policy debates as well as environmental and social justice movements. Development requires not only better global economic conditions but also a cleaner environment with the sustainable use of natural resources, such as land, water, soil, energy and minerals, and their security at both the global and national level, including availability, affordability, and accessibility to all. Natural resource exploitation and economic activities have played a role in fueling many violent conflicts. To prevent violent conflicts, environmental and social movements have emerged to advocate better policy reforms.

The struggles of social movements in natural resources management can be situated in a political ecology approach that analyses social forms of organization in interaction with the environment. Political ecology queries the relationship between economics, politics and nature, and stands at the confluence of ecologically rooted social science and principles of political economy. Political ecology thus encompasses, on the one hand, issues of conflict of individual interests and the possibility of collusion that lie at the heart of political economy, and on the other hand, the concerns of ecology with our biological and physical environment, emphasizing the need for a holistic analysis that connects with the more social and power-centred field of political economy.

There are three key assumptions in political ecology: (a) the costs and benefits associated with land and natural resource management are distributed unevenly; (b) changes in the environment do not affect society homogenously but are subject to political, social and economic inequalities, which account for the uneven distribution of costs and benefits; and (c) political power plays an important role in such inequalities. Inevitably, the uneven distribution of land and environmental conditions either reinforces or reduces existing social and economic inequalities. In this sense, political ecology joins political economy, as any change in environmental conditions must affect the political and economic status quo. The uneven distribution of costs and benefits and the reinforcing or reducing of pre-existing inequalities hold political implications in terms of the power relationships that are produced.

In terms of struggle, political ecology can be used to inform policymakers and organizations of the complexities surrounding environment and development, thereby contributing to better environmental governance. It can inform the decisions that communities make about their natural environment, in the context of their political conditions, economic pressure and societal regulations. It can also shed light on how the unequal relations in and among societies affect the natural environment, especially in the context of government policy frameworks. The management of natural resources should lead to a development path that is economically viable, socially beneficial and ecologically sustainable. Key issues related to sustainable natural resources management are resources tenure, ownership structure and governing laws.

The concept of environmental governance, from a political ecology perspective, advocates sustainability as the supreme consideration for managing all human activities—political, social and economic. As such, even if the concept remains inadequately defined, as discussed below, it considers the separation of environmental issues from political processes as erroneous.

Sustainable development has been defined in many ways. According to the Brundtland Report (WCED 1987: 16), sustainable development is that which 'meets the needs of the present without compromising the ability of future generations to meet their own needs'. Two key concepts within it are those of (a) needs, in particular, the essential needs of the world's poor, to which overriding priority should be given and (b) the limitations imposed by the state of technology and social organization on the environment's ability to meet present and future needs.

This resonates with the Rio+20 meeting held in 2012 when the global community reconvened in an effort to secure agreement on 'greening' world economies through a range of smart measures for clean energy, decent jobs and more sustainable and fair use of resources.

Another dimension of the above theoretical framework remains linked to theories concerning the evolution of property rights which stipulate that private property, when anchored in legal documents inspires confidence and encourages both investment and the use of bank credits and other sources of finance (Forsyth 2008). Once the gains from such investments have been realized, they produce improvements in productivity. Largely elaborated by the World Bank during the 1970s, the policy of land titling proved controversial, and has subsequently been strongly contested. In Mali, as elsewhere in Africa, the evidence suggests the supposed link between security of private property and granting of legal documents is highly questionable. On the contrary, other factors come into play: notably, local legitimacy and the presence of a functioning administrative and judicial system.

In many cases, there appears to be no automatic link between private property and investment. On the contrary, the example of real estate speculation in peri-urban areas illustrates the point that investment in agricultural production does not necessarily result from land acquisitions within the regime of private property. In the context of 'imperfect markets', other factors, such as the cost of inputs in relation to agricultural prices, the cost and availability of labour, and dysfunctional value chains also act as obstacles to investment.

Agricultural Land in Mali

Mali's past reflects a rich history of multi-culturalism, accommodating populations of diverse customs and habits. Composed of small satellite kingdoms to larger empires, the country has traditionally maintained a sense of national cohesion in managing conflictual relations between different populations, notably those involved in agriculture. However, in recent years, in view of the flaws of land administration and of the land-grabbing system in general, the country has had great difficulties in organizing its national land tenure system. Indeed, significant inconsistencies are noted through the poor definition of roles.

In particular, this is observed between the public authority represented by the state and its decentralized departments responsible for issuing different legal documents for accessing and securing different types of land (rural and urban). The state also collects property taxes in a very fragmented way and organizes, with difficulty, the prevention and management of land disputes. Land management agents have been very limited in terms of skills to meet the expectations of land actors. Some officials have been at the heart of land scandals in complicity with landowners.

Second, decentralized communities have the responsibility of granting land exclusively for housing purposes, but also the collection of part of the property taxes or costs of acquisition of urban land. They have been major sources of land disputes in the country. They are renowned for very weak technical skills in land management. Some of them have even 'given' themselves the right to allocate agricultural land that is outside their area of expertise.

Third, the customary land authority, which is another major actor in access to land—agricultural, pastoral, forestry, fisheries and forests—also presents problems. Due to the recognition of customary practices by the Land and Property Law (CDF) as a legal way of access to land, major difficulties have arisen in recent years with the increased 'monetization' of land transactions and the very noticeable involvement of local customary power.

We are witnessing a gradual deterioration in the general management of land in Mali, and of agricultural land in particular. Land administration remains relatively weak and poorly organized. Notable weaknesses of the current management system of agro-sylvo-pastoral land include the low level of distribution of roles, or the poor distribution of roles; ignorance of existing laws (even though imperfect and incoherent overall); and the low level of transparency, added to the very limited competence of judges/lawyers on the management of land issues. There is, therefore, a need to redefine the institutional and organizational framework for the management of agricultural land and to make it an area of specialization for men and women who are supposed to be involved in preventing and managing conflicts of use, access and security.

Historically, the land has always been a fundamental factor for agricultural development in the country. In the period before French colonization, there were collective land rights that were different from customary law. These customary land tenure rights were also referred to as 'rights of the axe' and allowed the management of community land. The collective customary tenure rights of villages and families (local rights) were respected by the communities according to socio-land areas.

In the period of colonization, the land became a tool of domination. Property rights based on registration and land title by decree began to give ownership of all land to the dominant state apparatus. Thus, Article 1 of the decree of 23 October 1904, defined the public land components in the colonies and territories of the AOF as follows: 'from the seashore to the highest tides ..., navigable watercourses ... and non-navigable watercourses ... lakes, lagoons and ponds ..., and generally, property of any kind which the civil code and French laws declare non-susceptible to private property'. This vast field, with its imprecise boundaries, given that Article 10 of the same decree also adds 'vacant lands without an owner', were subject to the exclusive management of the colonial administration through the colonial ministry, the Governors-General and the Lieutenant-Governors of the colony.

In the independence period, from 1960 onwards, significant changes have occurred, often toned down but often also radical, to meet the demands of the environment. At the risk of generalizing trends in Africa, four periods have marked significant changes on the continent. The first period, from 1960 to 1970, was the first decade of development, proclaimed by the United Nations. The second period, from 1970 to 1980, was that in which basic needs began to be recognized as an objective, but also when indebtedness rose and the debt crisis began. The third period, from 1980 to 1990, marked the beginning of Structural Adjustment Programmes (SAPs), which produced the first results of SAPS, as well as reflections on their social dimensions. And the fourth period, from 1990 to date, characterized by the advance of economic globalization.

In the case of Mali, as elsewhere, the early 1980s were marked by recognition of the debt crisis. The country had difficulty in repaying loans, while the International Financial Institutions (IFIs) and civil society began to hold the nation-state responsible for the crisis: its practices and its inability to drive development were identified as the main causes of bankruptcy. The entrepreneurial state had to give way to private initiative, and the market had to be able to regulate the levers of development.

The shortcomings of the state thus exposed, not least in an international economic context characterized by deep economic and financial crisis and the onset of globalization, Mali, like other African countries, was assigned new tasks that went beyond 'the normal tasks of economic management'. SAPs became a dominant paradigm in Mali, alongside regulatory stabilization programmes. According to Hugon (1994), the SAPs are based on three principles, as follows:

(a) The opening up of African markets to the world market, based on the liberal principle of comparative advantage. The direct consequence of such opening is that states have been obliged to focus on cash crops, to the detriment of other crops, in the same way as some did in the 1960s, which, in turn, has aggravated drought and produced more dramatic consequences. A further consequence has been speculation in non-manufactured raw materials, which has limited the scope for industrial development.
(b) Internal liberalization through the recognition of the mismanagement of the state, its corruption and its inefficiency, which has led to a poor redistribution of resources and aggravated poverty. The role of the state in the economy has thus been reduced.
(c) Reduction and a restructuring of public expenditure to restore macroeconomic balances.

The SAPs have had a number of consequences on the lives of the people in Mali, among them the increase in the unemployment rate, the impoverishment of the predominantly rural population, and the exclusion of a large part of the population from education and health services. The period from 1990 to the present has seen a further increase in the impoverishment of the population, which has led to different types of public policy reforms aimed at strengthening the 'Public-Private Partnership'. It is structured on the agrarian plan and around the 'Green Revolution' model, which has been devastating in Asia and Latin America in terms of worsening poverty, employment trends and labour conditions, among others.

It is in this historical trajectory that the agrarian system of Mali has evolved. In addition to the complexity of customary tenure systems—such as village/lineage organizations and authorities, the coexistence of individual and collective rights, the superimposition of rights over time and space (agriculture, livestock farming, picking, etc.), the social entrenchment of land rights, migrations and land dependencies—an incoherent land system coexists with positive law, which has led to the individualization of rights and the commoditization of land through its monetarization.

Access to Land in Mali

In general, there are two means of access to land in Mali: (a) through the procedures set up by the Land and Property Law; and (b) through devices of customary rights (intra-lineage access, loan, donation, etc.). These two legal sources coexist and are fully recognized in Mali. With regards to the Land and Property Law (CDF), Article 35 of the Law stipulates that land in the private domain of the state is to be allocated according to a number of modalities, whose corresponding documents may be different. They range from the tenancy at will (less binding) to the land title which is the definitive title and legally more binding. According to the CDF, there are the following titles:

(a) The rural concession, which is the right granted by the public authority, the grantor, to a person called a concessionary, to enjoy, provisionally, the use of land and develop it according to the conditions and specifications stipulated in the concession.
(b) An emphyteutic lease, by which the lessor confers on the lessee, on payment of an annual royalty, a long-term real estate right called emphyteusis, which may be mortgaged. It is important to note the mortgageable nature of the emphyteutic lease (mortgageability).
(c) A lease with a promise to sell, which is a contract by which the state grants tenure for the tenant to develop it, and commits to, at the expiry of the lease and provided that the land has been developed according to the conditions set out in the lease, sell to the lessee for a price fixed by decree of the Council of Ministers.
(d) The title deed, which, by virtue of Article 169 of the Land and Property Law, is the definitive and 'unassailable' title. It constitutes, before the Malian courts, the sole starting point of all the real rights existing on the immovable property at the time of registration.

Article 42 of the CDF stipulates that other forms of allocation may be fixed by the decree of the Council of Ministers on the proposal of the Minister of Lands.

As regards customary rights to land, it is important to mention that the land to which these rights belong is part of the private domain of the state. However, the

Land and Property Law recognizes and confirms them, whether exercised collectively or individually, and even provides for their finding following a public and contradictory inquiry which gives rise to the issue of a title opposable to third parties (Articles 43 and 44).

Article 45 provides that individual customary land rights, where they have an obvious and permanent right of way on the ground, may be transformed into a right of ownership for the benefit of their owner, who must apply for registration or may be conceded for the benefit of an owner, a third party; the latter must also request the registration of the immovable property without delay. All natural resource management texts recognize user rights for communities alongside natural resources, as well as licensing rights. By way of illustration, the regulation regarding the management and harvesting of forest resources has three categories of rights: usage rights, rights conferred by operating licences and property rights (exercised only on forests artificially planted on self-owned land).

In addition to legislation on Natural Resource Management, Mali has an environmental law that clearly affects the area. In 2003, it was made mandatory for project initiators to conduct environmental studies. Any project likely to have an impact on the environment must be preceded by an environmental and social impact assessment that specifies the negative impacts and proposes solutions to prevent them. The environmental and social impact assessment is 'the identification, description and evaluation of the effects of projects on human being, flora and fauna, soil, water, air, climate and the landscape, including interactions among these factors, cultural, socio-economic and other material aspects' (Décret N°08-346/PRM, 26 June 2008). Projects subject to environmental and social impact assessment should only be implemented if there is an authorization from the Minister of the Environment in the form of an environmental permit. There must be two types of public consultations before this permit can be issued: (a) the proponent must inform the people, especially those likely to be affected by the project and (b) a public consultation is organized around the project by the representative of the state or the mayor of the area in order to allow people to raise their concerns.

This procedure is compulsory and is enshrined in the laws in force in Mali. Other important laws in force in the country are also to be taken into account in the current context. These include Law No. 95-004 laying down conditions for the management of forestry resources; Law No. 95-003 on the organization of the harvesting, transportation and trade of timber; Decree No. 01-404 determining the terms and conditions for the exercise of the rights conferred by the titles of the harvesting of forestry resources.

Despite the many laws, there is a great deal of inconsistency in land management in Mali. This is manifested in decisions which are in blatant contradiction with the laws in force.

The Issue of the Office du Niger

Created in 1932, in the interior delta of the Niger River, the Office du Niger (ON) was meant, according to initial plans, to become the main supplier of cotton to the textile industries of colonial France, the rice granary of West Africa, as well as a place of technical and social innovations. The objectives were ambitious, with nearly one million hectares to be prepared in 50 years. The major structures were designed and built to meet these objectives. These include the Markala dam on the Niger River. Today, almost 87,692 ha of land is managed and developed (rice growing, market gardening and sugar cane) through the old ponds and a dense network of irrigation and drainage canals.

The ON has the monopoly of the management of the lands that are the subject of a land title of the state. Decree No. 94-004 of 9 March 1994 stipulates that the Office du Niger is a commercial public establishment (EPIC) responsible for the management of the lands in the Central Delta of the Niger River. Decree No. 96-188/PRM of 1 July 1996 on the organization of the management of land allocated to the ON (later Decree 96/188) enshrines the right of way of the ON not only on managed and equipped lands, but also those in undeveloped areas, in this case those irrigated and those that can be irrigated from the Markala dam.

Means of Land Management at ON Zone

There are five major ways of access to land in the ON area. These means are governed by Chap. 3 of the Management Decree, as follows.

The annual operating contract. Article 24 stipulates that the Office may allocate to a natural or legal person a plot of irrigated land for rice cultivation purposes. The holder of the annual contract is expected to pay a fee based on the area of the allocated plots and taking into account the quality of land management. The rate of royalty shall be fixed by order of the responsible Minister, on the proposal of the ON, after consultation with the operators. Failure to comply with the obligations relating to the maintenance of the network and the non-payment of the fee shall result in the cancellation of the annual operating contract.

The farm license. This license is mandatorily granted by the Office du Niger to the operator holding an annual contract and who has proved his capacity to meet the standards of intensification of production and compliance with all other contractual clauses.

The residential lease. The residential lease may be awarded to land title holders of the Office du Niger. It is land for residential use in one of the villages or agglomerations located on the domain of the Office.

The emphyteutic lease. For the purposes of production, processing, trade or service enterprises, or any other activities related to agro-industry, the ON may conclude an emphyteutic lease with natural or legal persons on the land it manages.

The emphyteutic lease is granted on undeveloped land and is a guarantee against the eviction of the already established operators for the benefit of agro-industrial companies. Article 45 stipulates that land management, the creation of the water supply system and all other installations to facilitate farming are the responsibility of the lessee. The emphyteutic lease has a duration of 50 years. It is renewable by express agreement of the parties. It is granted on payment of an annual fee, the rate of which is fixed by a decree of the Council of Ministers.

The ordinary lease. This licence can be allocated to natural and legal persons on undeveloped land and covers a maximum period of 30 years. It is renewable indefinitely, by agreement of the parties. It is granted against the payment of a royalty. Failure to pay the fee and failure to maintain the water supply system will result in termination of the contract. There are two situations: that of 'settlers', usually family farms, located on the perimeters developed and benefiting from the annual operating contract or operating license and that of investors benefiting from emphyteutic or ordinary leases.

Regarding the issue of access, Mali has the following six (6) access modes: intra-lineage access, donation, loan, leasing, sharecropping and sale, which is becoming increasingly practised in the country. Faced with the situation of legal dualism, the main issue is to reconcile the state and customary systems. This form of management allows a balanced management of agricultural land in Mali.

Massive Land Cessions in the ON Zone

Over the past few year,s family farms of the ON zone have faced crisis such as land fragmentation, the indebtedness of farmers and farmers' organizations, underequipment, yield declines (less than four tons per hectare on average), welding period problems (with 54% of heads of households experiencing welding period problems), the breakdown of families that once farmed together and the relatively small size of plots, which is a key factor.

Research carried out in collaboration with SEXAGON (Office du Niger Rice Producers Trade Union) under the supervision of the Institute for Research and Promotion of Alternatives in Development (IRPAD) and the scientific commission of SEXAGON, between 2006 and 2009, revealed a number of concerns regarding land fragmentation (Table 1):

Table 1 shows that the average area of land held by family farms (rice fields, non-rice fields and market gardens) is 3.73 ha. Approximately, 50% of the holdings awarded are less than 2.5 ha, and holdings under 2.5 ha cover 16.6% of the total rice area of the ON. Moreover, 56% of the farms are beneficiaries of less than 3 ha, and this group of family farms measuring less than 3 ha covers 21% of the total rice area of the ON.

In 2000 (9 years prior to the IRPAD study), another study conducted by ON-Urdoc on a sample of 3,004 farms reached very similar conclusions, with 44% of the farms measuring less than 2.5 ha and 52% measuring less than 3 ha, thus

Table 1 Land fragmentation

Categories established in function of irrigated plots
(rice fields + non-rice fields + market gardens)

Acreage	% operations per category	% total operations per category	% acreage per category	% total acreage per category
−1 ha	16	16	2	2
From 1 to 2 ha	24	40	9	11
From 2 to 3 ha	16	56	10	21
From 3 to 4 ha	9	65	8	29
From 4 to 5 ha	12	77	14	43
From 5 to 6 ha	6	83	8	51
From 6 to 7 ha	5	88	9	60
From 7 to 8 ha	2	90	4	64
From 8 to 9 ha	2	92	5	69
From 9 to 10 ha	2	94	5	74
+10 ha	6	100	26	100

Table 2 Land fragmentation

Number of plots held or farmed by the same family (excl. market gardening plots)	
0 plot	1.4%
1 plot	44.4%
2 plots	32.4%
3 plots	14.4%
+3 plots	7.4%
Total	100.0%

concluding that there was an increase in land fragmentation between 2000 and 2006.

The reasons for the fragmentation include the policy of allocating very small plots to the increase in family separation, with 28% of the farms surveyed having experienced a 'real family separation'; and sales of land under the argument of family separation (false family separation). In this respect, out of 396 respondents, 48 transactions were noted for 39 farms, or 10% of the farms surveyed. Another cause stated relates to the policy of reallocation of land as a result of the developments carried out (Table 2).

As a result of the transactions (purchases, sales, leases and sharecropping) and multiple allocations within the same family, there is a significant dispersion of land holdings on ON households, with approximately 54% of households having two or more plots.

There is also a correlation between the size of family farms and the level of equipment of these farms (Table 3). This trend is confirmed with 84% of farms

Table 3 Underequipment of the farms

	Rice fields ≤ 3 ha (%)	Rice fields >3 ha (%)	Total fields (%)
% farms with a complete team	37	84	55

measuring more than 3 ha having a complete team, compared to 37% of those farms measuring 3 ha having the same. This data can be compared with the size of the farms in the area with a very large majority below 3 ha.

Furthermore, Table 4 shows a relative correlation between land transaction indices, farm equipment level and consumption indices. This implies taking labour and employment issues into account in relation to the size of plots.

According to the agreements signed with the authorities of Mali, Map 1 and Table 5 show that agro industries have been allocated a total 493,572 ha. These allocations represent more than one-third of the total area that can be developed in the whole area (in terms of potential).

Table 4 Plot size as a revenue determinant

	Average index of land transaction	% of agricultural plots not equipped with a team (%)	Number of livestock (cattle equivalent)	Consumption index
Plot with acreage <1 ha	0.25	83	0.69	39
Plot with acreage ≥ 1 ha and <2 ha	0.05	61	2.23	71
Plot with acreage ≥ 2 ha and <3 ha	−0.09	48	4.52	72
Plot with acreage ≥ 3 ha and <4 ha	−0.09	21	2.79	81
Plot with acreage ≥ 4 ha and < 5 ha	−0.04	23	4.91	106
Plot with acreage ≥ 5 ha and <6 ha	0.11	10	5.15	104
Plot with acreage ≥ 6 ha and <7 ha	0.20	30	4.99	115
Plot with acreage ≥ 7 ha and <8 ha	−0.11	14	11.14	151
Plot with acreage ≥ 8 ha and <9 ha	0.78	13	5.8	171
Plot with acreage ≥ 9 ha and <10 ha	1.43	0	13.03	159
Plot with acreage ≥ 10 ha	1.27	0	29.04	182
All categories	0.16	43	5.1	88

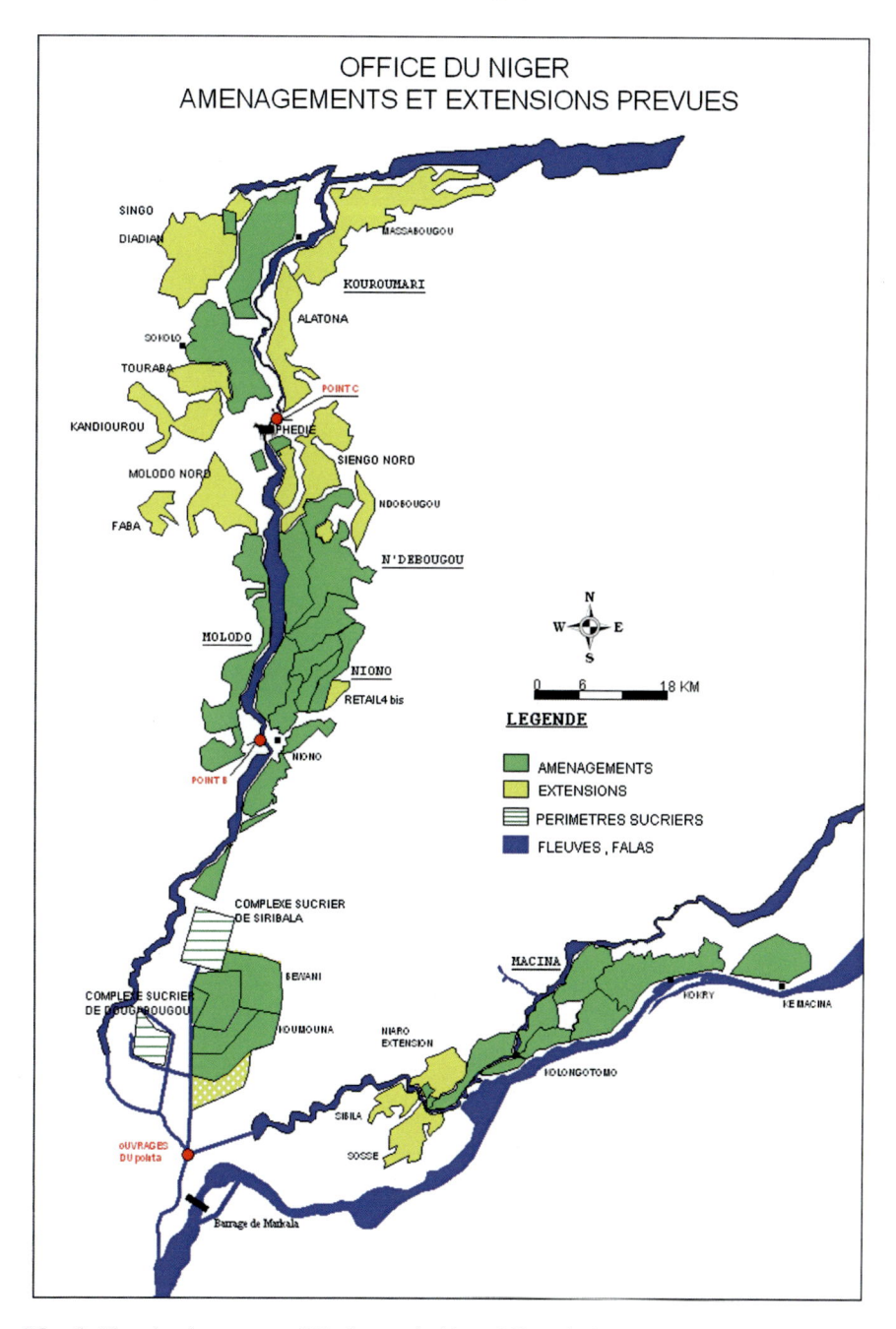

Map 1 New developments at ON *Source* Archives Office of Niger (2009)

Table 5 Allocations from 2003 to 2009: agro-industries' developments

Investor	Country of origin	Acreage (ha)	Area	Land usage	Date of acquisition
LONHRO	South Africa/RU	20,000	Kouroumari (ON)	Sugar and ethanol production	ND
CAMEX	ND Brazil?	20,000	Sabalibougou (ON)	ND	ND
DUNKAFA	Mali	358	Sabalibougou (ON)	Rice cultivation	2008
Physical person	Mali	143	N'Debougou (ON)	ND	2005
AGROENER-BIO	Mali	40,000	Massabougou (ON)	Biofuels, Oilseeds	Letter of agreement
SOCOGEM	Mali	20,000	Macina	ND	ND
Physical person	Mali	10,000	Macina	ND	ND
SAPA	ND	20,000	Macina	ND	ND
Physical person	Etranger (pays nd)	5,000	Macina	ND	ND
SNF	Mali	15,000	Macina	Agrocarburants	ND
Physical person	Mali	5,000	Macina		ND
HUICOMA	Mali	100,000	Macina	Oilseeds, Biofuels	Letter of agreement
SUDAN	Foreign country	5,000	Macina	ND	ND
ASSIL	ND	5,000	Macina	ND	ND
Société Yatassaye	Mali	20,000	Macina	ND	ND
Malibya	Libya	100,000	Macina	Agricultural production, livestock, manufacturing	2008
SUKALA	Mali/Private Chinese	5,800	Kala supérieur	Sugar cane	1996

(continued)

Table 5 (continued)

Investor	Country of origin	Acreage (ha)	Area	Land usage	Date of acquisition
SOPROMIE	ND	5,000	M'Bewani	ND	ND
BURKINA FASO	Foreign country	2,500	M'Bewani	ND	ND
FORAS	Saudi Arabia	5,000	M'Bewani	Rice production	2009
Co-entreprise	ND	1,000	Sansanding	ND	ND
Moulins Modernes du Mali Modibo Keita	Mali	7,400	Sansanding	ND	ND
N-SUKALA	China/Mali	20,000	Kala supérieur	Sugar cane	2009
AED	France	2,600	Dougabougou	Biofuels	ND
Illovo, Schaffer, Etat malien (SOSUMAR)	Mali/Private (South Africa)	14,000	Sansanding	Sugar cane, ethanol	2007
PETROTECH	Mali	10,000	Macina	Biofuels	ND
SOCIMEX	Mali	10,000	Macina	Biofuels	
Ferme COVEC	China	1,000	Koumouna	Rice production, Tests	1999
Sambalagnon Association villageoise	Mali	90	Touraba	Rice production	2008
Physical person	Mali	60	Macina	ND	2005
Physical person	Mali	50	Kouroumari	ND	2005
Physical person	Mali	50	Kouroumari	ND	2005
Physical person	Mali	70	Macina	ND	2003
Physical person	Mali	200	Kouroumari	ND	2009
Physical person	Mali	50	Kouroumari	ND	2009

In total, over 26,994 ha of land were allocated to agro-entrepreneurs to undertake agricultural activities (Table 6). All these areas have been granted at the expense of the family farmers in the different zones. These projects are financed by Mali's technical and financial partners through an approach based on the Green Revolution model and Public–Private Partnership (PPP). The total area under development for family farms is 9,346 ha. These improvements are for seven projects financed by the state and its partners (Tables 7 and 8).

The different development projects were allocated particularly to agro-food industries by the authorities at different levels (the management of the Office du Niger, the Ministry of Agriculture, the Ministry of Lands and the Presidency). This situation shows the inconsistencies in land governance in Mali, often with some illegal and illegitimate decisions.

Table 6 Allocations from 2003 to 2009: agro-entrepreneurs' developments

Millenium challenge account (USA)	Alatona/ Kouroumari	14,000 ha Phase 1: 5,200 ha Plots from 5/ 10/30/60/ 90 ha **Land title**	Rice/ market garden	Tenders for development currently under review
TEST DE KOUMOUNA I (BM)	Koumouna/ Bewani	390 ha Plots from 3 ha **Land title**	Rice	Completed
TEST DE KOUMOUNA II (BM)	Koumouna/ Bewani	444 ha Big surface **Land title**	Rice	Abandoned no more concrete actions
UEMOA	Kandiourou/ Tourouba/ Kouroumari	11.288 ha Phase 1: 5.500 ha Plots from 4/ 9/21/48 ha Emphyteutic lease	Rice	Technical studies in progress and almost complete
Dunkafa/Pays-bas	Sabalibougou Kouroumari	358 ha Ordinary emphyteutic lease	Rice	Completed in June 2009
BSI	Seribala Nord	514 ha Emphyteutic lease	Rices	Completed in June 2009
Total	26.994 ha			

Table 7 Allocations from 2003 to 2009: community managed lands for rice production development

Project name	Area
Bewani D	2007 ha BOAD Finished
Siengo Ext.	520 ha BID Finished
Siengo Ext. II	1700 ha KFW Funding agreement 2009
Siengo Nord	514 ha No funding yet
Siengo/Apej	155 ha Government Studies launched February 2009
N'débougou III	1950 ha KFW Farming expected in 2011
Bewani D—UE	2500 ha European Union Farming in 2011
Total	9.346 ha

Table 8 Summary of the acreages allocated by the authorities per category

	Ha in project (ha)	Size of plots issued (ha)	Cost to farmer per ha	Land status	Types of farming	Type of crop
Agro industries	493,572	+2500	2,500,000 to 4,000,000	Emphyteutic lease	Agro industrials often foreign	Rice, Cane Wheat, Oilseeds, agro fuels
Agro entreprises	26,994	From 3 to 90	1,250,000 to 2,500,000	Land title or Emphyt. lease	Traders Civil servants, Cooperatives, family farmers	Rice Market gardening
Community developments	9,346	From 0 to 3	300,000 to 500,000	Annual lease or PEA	Family farmers	Rice Market gardening

The Case of Malibya

The field study carried out in 2010 by the IRPAD/Africa Research Institute team focused on the case of Malibya, which is in the Macina area. This study supplemented the work carried out on the mapping of massive land transfers in the same area. The case in question is included in the list of assignments.

Several villages affected by the lands allocated to Malibya were threatened with expulsion or condemned to suffer the consequences of the arrival of a new Libyan investor, all in the name of cooperation between Mali and Libya. This case reveals the threats to the peasantry of the ON in particular and that of Mali in general. It also reveals practices of land grabbing by foreign firms.

The Malibya project began when, at a meeting of the community of Sahel-Saharan States, Mali's president, Amadou Toumani Touré, gave 100,000 ha of land located in the NO zone to Libya. The latter directly developed a sovereign fund called 'Libya Africa Investment Portfolio'. The Malibya Group became responsible for the implementation of the project in the country. A more precise agreement was reached in 2009 between Mali and Libya under a bilateral investment treaty. It provided for a right of use of over 100,000 ha of land to Malibya for a period of 50 years. This contract could be renewed for a total of 99 years. The main objective stated was the development of agricultural activities, agro-industry and livestock.

This important project has affected 75,000 people who live in the area, and has had two components. The 'infrastructure' component consists of the construction of a canal and a road, both about 40 km long. This work was entrusted to the Chinese company 'CGC' which belongs to the Chinese oil giant SINOPEC. The canal, with a capacity of 130 m^3, should make it possible to circulate 11 million m^3 of water per day. This first component was completed at the time of the research. The second part concerns production. It includes the production of rice, meat (25,000 tons per year) and tomato concentrate. The rice seed used would be a hybrid rice species that would allow yields of eight or nine tons per hectare (instead of four tons/ha on average during field work). Another Chinese company, Yuan Longping High-tech Agriculture, has been awarded a contract for the supply of hybrid rice seed. This second phase is to start with the development of 25,000 ha of agricultural land. Malibya plans to employ wage labour mainly among the peasants of these expropriated lands.

This Libyan operation seems to have been motivated by a need for rice. Indeed, figures published by the Food and Agriculture Organization (FAO) on this subject reported that Libya imported 177,000 tons of rice in 2005. Libya had launched the development of its infrastructure, injecting around 130 billion for this purpose. This work led to a huge recruitment of foreign labour. With the arrival of many Asian workers on its territory, the demand for cheap rice began to rise.

On reading the agreement signed between Mali and Libya, many questions can be raised. The agreement seems unbalanced. Mali received very little compared to what it offered to its Libyan partner. Apart from the payment of a water fee and

Malibya's obligation to respect Malian law, no obligation on the part of the Libyan partner was actually specified; no obligation to use local labour or to allocate part of the produce to the national market. Malibya presents food safety as a priority. The project was created to meet the food needs of the Malians, as well as those of Libya and all other CEN-SAD member states. However, there is no clause in the contract specifying in what proportion the produce will be distributed. Nothing prevents consequent exports to Libya, leaving little for the Malian population already experiencing problems of food self-sufficiency. The contract also provides unrestricted access to the Macina Canal water and groundwater on payment of an annual fee, which can be renegotiated annually. Water supply priority is, therefore, given to Malibya, which could be at the expense of other farmers in the area.

The Malibya venture in the region was underway at the time of the research. Work began in 2009 with the construction of the road and canal which was completed. Malibya was preparing to set up the first cultivation area of 25,000 ha, but this was being done in a brutal way. No environmental and social impact studies have been carried out, contrary to Malian law. No consultation of local populations was done. The little information provided to the various actors is unclear. In 2009, with the beginning of the work, conflicts broke out. Following this, meetings were held with about 30 villages. These meetings replaced an environmental and social impact study. The project continued despite tensions and disagreements with local communities. The villagers who lived along the canal and the road were promptly evicted at the beginning of the work. The evictions took place without compensation. Of the 150 families evicted (listed as 'peasant organizations'), only 58 of them have been compensated. Malibya has offloaded all responsibilities to this effect in the contract and the Malian government is slow to assume these responsibilities. Only some villages have been compensated, which creates discrimination between villages which have received compensation and those which have not received anything. Moreover, the amount of compensation, when this was done, was significantly lower than the value of the lost real estate.

The arrival of Malibya has not been without risks. Among the proven economic and social risks, the deployment of Malibya resulted in the destruction of cemeteries, dwellings, orchards and vegetable gardens. Some evicted peasants found themselves without shelter and without land. According to a report written by La Via Campesina in October 2009, 150 families were evicted from their areas. The loss of land by these peasants was exacerbating the already strong land pressure in the region. This threat to access to land is all the more worrying because many villagers depend on land for their survival and food security. Some competition between new investors and local farmers for access to resources is likely to emerge. This is mainly because the newcomers will be in possession of an emphyteutic lease, whereas the peasants who have been working on these lands for decades will always be in this precarious situation of the right use of land belonging to the state.

Immigration of agricultural workers from other regions can also be expected in search of employment. These arrivals will increase competition for existing natural resources, opening the door to conflicts between newcomers and the inhabitants of the area. One can even imagine that these tensions take the form of conflicts with ethnic references. Other tensions may also arise from differences in wages that could occur between poorly paid locals and foreign project managers receiving higher remuneration.

Increased competition for access to water is likely. It will be seen in the short term, especially in the dry season, but also in the long term, with the drying up of some existing water points. Water supply could put private investors in competition with local producers.

The obstruction of 7 km of the runway used by the animals, from the commune of Kolongo to that of Boky-Wèrè, also poses serious problems. In view of the many tensions already present between livestock farmers and crop farmers, the disappearance of a passage zone for animals can prove problematic. The destruction of pastures or transhumance roads is likely to reignite the ancestral tensions between livestock farmers and crop farmers.

On a more general note, the arrival of new investors occupying enormous areas will trigger very profound changes (such as in lifestyle) and identity (loss of tradition, disruption of identity and weakening of the family unit) among the concerned peasants. The indigenous culture can be directly threatened by the arrival of these foreign elements.

Further risks of environmental nature may be advanced. First, Malibya's land management contributes to the destruction of biodiversity. Forest areas are doomed to disappear. The disappearance of these forests implies the loss of various resources which are very valuable to the villagers of the area (timber, heating, medicinal plants and food). This will increase pressure on the remaining resources. New varieties of hybrid rice will be used by Malibya (for example the Nerica rice variety). These will destabilize the use of the peasant varieties over which they have control. In addition, hybrid rice seed cannot be conserved. It will, therefore, have to be redeemed every year, which creates a certain dependency of the area on the outside. The arrival of this new species could eliminate any diversity in terms of rice, eliminating many traditional varieties. Traditionally cultivated species (sorghum, millet and peanuts) will be replaced by more water-hungry species. The issue of water is also essential. Water resource management and sharing could become problematic. Moreover, one wonders about the soil, water and air pollution that will result from the new activities using more chemical inputs. What care will these newcomers grant to a land which does not belong to them, to a land situated in a foreign land?

Finally, risks related to food safety can be highlighted. The Nerica rice that Malibya is considering cultivating has a poor taste and demands more water than traditional crops. The export of produce to the country of origin of the investors, Libya, or elsewhere cannot be ruled out. Vulnerability of the poorest groups is inevitable: their access to water resources, forest resources, and land can only diminish, undermining their food sovereignty. The standard of living of the rural population is threatened, threatening their ability to feed themselves.

Thus, Malibya has occupied this new territory little by little. Its arrival has disrupted local communities. Some villages have already come face to face with the facts through the investments made. Others will only do as the work progresses. But this new development has been changing the environment.

Social movements led by farmers' organizations, NGOs and human rights organizations have mobilized to address the situation. In addition to the mobilization and advocacy activities organized in the area, particularly in Kolongo (project area), they prepared to file complaints with the national and international courts.

The crisis situation in Libya has now led to the suspension of the project. However, land activists in Mali are cautious about the necessity to continue the fight to influence policymakers for the future of the lands in question and their infrastructure. Two main texts have been adopted to take into account some of the main concerns: the Agricultural Land Policy and the Agricultural Land Law. They include instruments not only to facilitate access to agricultural land by smallholder farmers, but also to secure their access with two different certificates. The land tenure regime finally includes community lands in addition to private lands within the rural areas.

Conclusion

This initial mapping out of the situation has laid the groundwork for understanding the general phenomenon. Further research should indicate ways and means to defend family farms in the area of the Office du Niger, in particular, and in Mali, in general. Other important studies on impact anticipation must be carried out in order to argue better the positions taken by the social movements of Mali and to act on the phenomenon.

References

Djiré, M., & Keïta, A. (2010). *Diagnosis of agricultural land in Mali, Bamako.*

Escobar, A. (1996). Construction nature: Elements for a post-structuralist political ecology. *Futures, 28*(4), 325–343.

Forsyth, T. (2008). Political ecology and the epistemology of social justice. *Geoforum, 39*(2), 756–764.

Hugon, P. (1994). Ajustement structurel dans les pays en développement. In X. Greffe, et al. (Eds.), *Encyclopédie économique* (pp. 2015–2056). Paris: Économica.

Ministry of Agriculture of Mali. (2013). *Etude nationale sur les exploitations Agricoles au Mali.*

Ministry of Agriculture of Mali. (2014). *Agricultural land policy.*

Parliement of Mali. (2017). *Agricultural land law.*

Peet, R., & Watts, M. (1996). *Liberation ecologies: Environment, development, social movements.* London: Routledge.

Robbins, P. (2004). *Political ecology.* Oxford: Blackwell Publishers.

Watts, M. J. (1985). Social theory and environmental degradation: the case of Sudano-Sahelian West Africa. In Y. Gradus (Ed.), *Desert development: Man and technology in sparselands*. Dordrecht: D. Reidel.

WCED [World Commission on Environment and Development]. (1987). *Our common future*. Available at http://www.un-documents.net/wced-ocf.htm. Retrieved November 29, 2017.

The Scramble for Agricultural Land in Senegal: Land Privatisation and Inclusion?

Abdourahmane Ndiaye

Introduction

In the wake of the food crisis in 2008 and the uncertainties which accompanied it, globalised capitalism has defined a number of new responses; among them a new scramble for agricultural land in Africa. This solution ostensibly fulfils the demands from wealthy countries for food products, facilitates the development of biofuels, while simultaneously providing a safe investment haven for global financial interests. It is in this context that the land question is, more than ever before, at the centre of agrarian policies. Indeed, land constitutes an important basis for economic and institutional activity of both market and non-market institutions. In Senegal, the status of land and the division of rights to its use is a major area of interest in a legal context which superimposes different sources of legitimacy on a path of conflict (Dahou and Ndiaye 2008). On one hand, land grabbing is at the centre of many controversies. On the other, while land grabbing is itself as yet ill-defined, the statistics reveal its existence as a problem of significant magnitude. In the meantime, its effects remain contentious.

The purpose of this chapter is to consider whether land grabbing, as a set of principles and a system of actors, has the capacity to operate as a lever for development. First, our aim is to bring forward and discuss the foundations and challenges of the land question. Second, taking as the point of departure the contradictions linked to the plurality of legal systems governing land and the conflicts they generate, we question the role of public policies and land policies in the scramble for agricultural land in Senegal. Third, we present the details of land grabbing/acquisitions in Senegal. This makes it possible to assess land utilisation

A. Ndiaye (✉)
National Centre of Scientific Research, Bordeaux Montaigne University, UMR 5319
PASSAGES CNRS, Bordeaux, France
e-mail: yadondiaye@hotmail.fr

© Springer Nature Singapore Pte Ltd. 2019   143
S. Moyo et al. (eds.), *Reclaiming Africa*, Advances in African Economic,
Social and Political Development, https://doi.org/10.1007/978-981-10-5840-0_7

between 2006 and 2010, map out a typology of investment projects, and evaluate tentatively their early impacts on economic, social and environmental development in Senegal.

Agricultural Land Grabbing

What Is Land Grabbing?

Land grabbing implies a weak, unclear, incomplete and misunderstood legislative order around land rights and a weak institutional capacity within local government. It can be defined as a process of compulsory acquisition which is characterised by manipulative practices, or a fraudulent manoeuvre intended to secure the uninformed consent of the other party to a contract without giving the relevant information which would be required to make an informed decision. Land grabbing can be based on misleading or false information, under dubious conditions of acquisition, and unclear or inequitable conditions of termination established in a long-term emphyteutic lease.[1] Large-scale acquisitions of agricultural land are also considered as land grabbing. The question must be asked about the extent to which these definitions provide workable concepts which can be operationalised in the analysis.

What is certain is that the acquisition of large surfaces of land, through both leases and direct purchases by local and foreign investors in many African countries, has significantly increased during the past decade (GRAIN 2008). Land grabbing is occurring with the agreement, whether tacit or explicit, of governments and the complicity of certain segments of the elite (Alden Wily 2008), and manifests itself in the establishment of numerous enclaves comprising plantations and agricultural domains. These are frequently located in the best-suited areas for agriculture, those endowed with irrigation systems and infrastructure. The purpose is to create value fundamentals for markets external to Africa, or to provide a safe haven for international finance interests (Papazian 2011).

It appears that governments play a major role in large-scale land acquisitions (Burnod et al. 2011) through their activities to promote and welcome investors (Cotula et al. 2009) within the framework of creating an attractive environment for business. The entrance of multiple waves of direct investment into the countries of the Global South raises important questions as to whether this appetite for land

---

[1]The emphyteutic lease (referring to 'the act of planting') is a long term lease, generally for 99 years, although in certain instances such as in Kenya and Rhodesia (now Zimbabwe) its duration could be up to 999 years. This lease confers rights and obligations on the tenant (lease holder) to develop the lease object and to pay a nominal rent. At the end of the lease, however, the benefits of such improvements accrue solely to the lease holder without obligation to indemnify the emphyteutic lessor. The position of the parties to an emphyteutic lease is thus quite peculiar, since it endows the tenant with concrete rights in the lease object which make him a virtual owner.

translates into access to resources and whether the emergence of new relationships defines the rules and norms of engagement at the global level, both in terms of adaptation and productive capacity. It appears that methodical and systematic efforts are currently underway to consolidate transitional institutions in the so-called developing countries of the South. Development suggests changing trajectories of economic, institutional and social structures which are closely linked to the phenomenon of globalisation, both in terms of competitiveness and attractiveness (Piveteau and Rougier 2010). In this context, the hypothesis that land grabbing can be used as a lever for development necessitates nuanced consideration, notably in view of the fact that pressures on land can bring about both a substantial reduction in the amount of land under family farm production (Beliere et al. 2003) and the informal commodification of usage rights (Coulibaly and Belieres 2006).

Controversies About the Extent of Land Grabbing

The exact size of areas directly affected by land grabbing is difficult to quantify. The relevant contracts are generally shrouded in secrecy, and the lack of dependable statistics makes it difficult to verify data and make a comprehensive assessment of the extent of the problem (Delcourt 2012). At least 5 million ha have been made available to foreign investors in more than 20 African countries (Von Braun and Meinzen-Dick 2009; Cotula et al. 2009; Tabb 2008). China, South Korea, the United Arab Emirates, Japan and Saudi Arabia, dispose of over 7.6 million ha of agricultural land outside of their own national territories, and a large part of these are in Africa (IPAR 2011). Delcourt (2010) has established that about 20 million ha in total have already changed hands in Africa, or are in the process of doing so. According to the World Bank (2010), transactions involving 45 million ha of agricultural land were carried out in 2009 alone. This figure represents ten times the total area of land transacted during the course of the preceding decade. Agricultural land grabbing is primarily an African problem since 70% of transactions are taking place in Africa (Anseeuw et al. 2011).

Some analysts have warned against alarmism or media-driven hysteria (Gabas 2011; Burnod et al. 2010), calling for a sober assessment of the facts. They argue that the empirically anchored knowledge about land grabbing in the countries of the South is still very distant from initial assessments and that distinction must be made amongst investors' diverse motives/interests, which include the production of agro fuels and bio-energy; securing the supply of raw materials to stabilise trading conditions on international markets; contributing to food security; supplying agro-food enterprises; and tourism and environmentally orientated activities.

Even if there is a degree of exaggeration of the problem, the undeniable fact is that using land as an investment haven deprives peasants of their principal means of production and cannot, therefore, be justified on the pretext that land grabbing/accumulation can leverage development through the channels of private investment. The wider impacts of land investments in terms of food security, agricultural sector investment and rural poverty remain highly controversial, and not insignificant. Moreover, recent studies point to the multiplication of land acquisition contracts concluded and an increase in the size of land areas to which they relate (Burnod et al. 2010). Given that these investments operate over a diversity of agricultural- and non-agricultural-based economic activities which must be documented, the quality of the land in question is known. Data reveals that in Madagascar, Mali and Senegal they are located on land with the best endowments including infrastructure and irrigation equipment (Bagayogo 2012; Burnod et al. 2010; IPAR 2011; Ndiaye 2012).

The scramble for African land to benefit intensive agricultural production, mining and the extraction of natural resources are the causes for concern not only on account of its extent and concentration but especially, because of the subjugation of rural populations and their labour which it accelerates. This is aside from the fact that the scramble for land detracts attention from the scramble for other natural resources such as water, forest and underground resources.

According to the World Bank (2003), the scramble for land is justifiable because it is capable of attracting investment, improving productivity, and enabling the poor to profit from new opportunities for economic activity and social participation which become available to them. According to its proponents, land acquisition is justified by the generation of tax revenues, incomes, jobs, agricultural investments, food production for local markets, technology transfers, improved infrastructure and greater economic dynamism. On the other hand, peasant organisations (POs) and social movements resist this phenomenon, which manifests itself as widespread land dispossession and a massive exodus of small producers and growers from the countryside (GRAIN 2008).[2] The ensuing resistance and struggles, which in some instances have culminated in death, place peasants and their allies among local authorities in confrontation with public governance bodies, in disputes as to which instance has the primary decision-making authority in questions of land governance.

The Challenges

Family farming is the principal driver of Senegalese agriculture. Indeed, as has been noted by the National Council for Rural Concertation Concentration (CNCR 2010: 2, *our translation*),

> 95 percent of farms engaged in agricultural production are family farms; family farming is the dominant mode of agricultural production and also produces the largest share of food

---

[2]The issue of agricultural land grabbing in developing countries, and especially in Africa, was one of the central themes which mobilised civil society actors during the World Social Forum in Dakar, in 2011. These concerns were also explicit in the Dakar Manifesto and the World Social Forum in Tunis, in 2013.

originating domestically. Family farms have the capacity to provide for over 60 percent of national food demand, and the families themselves also provide 91 percent of the productive labour force on these farms (57 percent male and 43 percent female). Family farms employ around 50 percent of the national population.

Small-scale agriculture geared towards food production accounts for 4.6% of the Gross Domestic Product (GDP), whereas the figure for industrial agriculture stands at only 1.3% (ANSD 2013). Family farming is extensive, while land rationing is reducing its productive capacity to only 38.4%, covering 5 months of the total estimated annual food requirement (ANSD 2013).

A review of the literature on land governance shows that questions concerning the regulations which are supposed to mediate the increasing competition over land and renewable resources for agricultural, forestry and pastoral uses are themselves a central problem (Founou-Tchuigoua and Ndiaye 2012). The challenge principally refers to how to avoid, limit and manage conflicts over rights of usage; consolidate property rights, their modes and modalities of transmission; and limit parcel sizes and guarantee the effective and equitable division/allocation of land. The contentions revolve around the best mode of governing the land; in other words, how simultaneously to ensure the optimal exploitation of the land's productive possibilities, an equitable distribution of land and the consolidation of secure land rights.

Following the views espoused by the World Bank, market-led land reforms are perceived in some quarters as the most efficient tool for addressing these issues. One argument is that market-led reforms create land markets which increase the valuation of the country's land assets, thereby anchoring the economy in stronger market fundamentals. The assumption that the mere existence of land markets generates investment because it creates opportunities for large-scale acquisitions is a key problem. The passage from 99-year emphytheutic leases to the outright privatisation of land title, displaces the systems of customary rights, thereby resolving the issues of conflicting legitimacy. Private land markets thus opens up the possibility for multinationals to acquire large areas of land on which to satisfy the appetite of wealthy countries for tropical agricultural products and biofuels.

Even though it is well recognised that land privatisation is neither synonymous with security of tenure nor productivity, the literature on this topic nonetheless asserts a causal relationship between market-led privatisation, security of title and improvements in agricultural productivity. This dichotomy is linked to the historical dominance of a belief in fixed land tenure systems which classifies African customary tenure arrangements as inefficient (Lavigne Delville 1998) and, therefore, antagonistic to the system of private land rights. It is further assumed that since they are geared primarily to meeting the consumption needs of the community, they encourage an extensive and unproductive form of production which prohibits surplus production. For these reasons, the organisational and institutional structures of customary land governance are deemed unsuitable for creating an enabling environment for profit-driven value-added agriculture, and thus also incapable of attracting investment to the sector. This view tends to dislocate market and financial rationales from social logics by assuming that private property on its own can be an efficient model of governance which is better suited to modernity and more appropriate in addressing the contemporary challenges of demographic growth and increasing competition in the context of liberalised global markets.

This unrealistic vision of customary markets does not stand up to analysis. On the contrary, the experience with market-led land reforms in Brazil, Colombia and the Philippines suggest the need for a differentiated approach (Borras 2002), because land reforms conducted under the liberal paradigm are often biased, or emptied of substance, by powerful private interest lobbies (Amin 2012). It is through such mechanisms that the land reforms in South Africa and Zimbabwe created opportunities for a Black capitalist middle class to emerge without either reducing poverty or inequality (Moyo 2005). By their insistence on private property rights, such land reforms promote the legal framework around positivist rights; however, the realm of rights to be protected under the law are not limited to positivist rights, but to the collectivity of legal practices including the issues of traditional or customary rights, even though these may be less accessible by virtue of being expressed in the vernacular languages—notably, as is the case with Wolof in Senegal (Plançon 2009). Private rights in land are legal constructions linked to the rights to use land. On this basis, rights to land are not only a legal instrument but also an expression of policy preferences.

Customary law is not a static system. Community control does not mean the absence of permanent and transferable family rights to productive land. Extensive farming can be a coherent/appropriate response in certain agro-climatic and economic settings (Lavigne Delville 1998). The rules of customary management of land are flexible, dynamic and capable of adapting to changes in the socio-economic context, including an expanding population, changing influences from the market and changes in the modalities of state intervention. By comparison, market-led agrarian reforms do not seem capable of responding simultaneously to the triple challenge of delivering economic efficiency and profit, social justice and food sovereignty. On the contrary, the establishment of intensive agriculture in some developing countries has been accompanied by the deterioration in food availability for small farmers (Borras 2002; Moyo 2005) and a new scramble for land (Niasse 2012).

According to the Survey of Poverty in Senegal (ANSD 2007), 58.4% of the population lives in the rural areas and is engaged in agricultural activity. Amongst households owning productive land, about 56.7% of them have farms smaller than 1 ha, and only 24.3% have farms which are larger than 4 ha. These figures lead to the conclusion that 75% of rural households control productive land parcels of four hectares or less, while the majority of urban owners of productive land (96.9% for Dakar and 89% for other towns) own parcels of less than one hectare. Fewer than 1% in Dakar and 5% in other towns own land parcels larger than four hectares. Conversely, in the rural areas where land ownership is more meaningful, the proportions are considerably larger, reaching 24.6 and 43.3%, respectively.

These findings reveal that important changes have taken place in the structures of access to agricultural land. The number of productive farms under six hectares has significantly increased between 2001 and 2006, while the ownership of larger areas of land has fallen from 72.1 to 27.4% of households between 2001–02 and 2005–06. These changes have benefitted small landowners.

From these tendencies, one can surmise that a greater concentration of large farms is developing. However, the drop in ownership of larger land parcels from 72 to 27% of households reflects an increase in the number of very small owners who now make up over half of the total number of productive landowners. These figures actually reveal that the majority of small owners do not have a sufficient amount of land to generate agricultural activities capable of returning any profits/ surplus.

Land and Institutional Reforms in Senegal

Even if a hybrid regime of customary rights remains as the dominant land model in Senegal, the privatisation of land is creating serious contradictions for land governance. Land tenure regimes are characterised by a plurality of norms which coexist across customary law and Islamic law, whose application largely depends on collective decisions by rural entities, a series of rules and conventions which originated in systems of patronage and a land legislation which is assumed to be modern, but whose roots lie in Roman law handed down from the days of colonialism. The reality of the situation is that questions of land access are regulated at three levels by rules and norms which operate in a more or less conflictual manner towards each other (Dahou and Ndiaye 2008).

First of all, the regulation of customary authorities attempts to perpetuate, while also reformulating, the application of customary laws/rights in the manner in which it supposedly existed historically. Within this model, the Lamanes, or owners and traditional elites are endowed with historical legitimacy as descendents of kings or land chiefs. This mode of governance is complemented by Muslim law and its application through conduits of patronage is well recognised amongst the Senegalese.

Next, the norm of governance by rural communities is represented by directly elected representatives and fits in with the first model. This has occurred because locally elected representatives have negotiated a right to apply a positivist approach which constitutes the basis of their legitimacy, by carefully avoiding rupture with local customary laws. This has enabled them to maintain clientelist relations with representatives in the central state who also hold key positions in the political party in power, to distribute resources and patronage functions towards bases of solid electoral control. Finally, the norm of public administration formulates and applies land policy based on Roman law.

These different levels reveal the complexity of potential contradictions shaped by the plurality of norms which can be exploited by actors within the hybrid land governance system (Lavigne Delville et al. 2000).

Senegal has undertaken two major land reforms since 1960 (Dahou and Ndiaye 2008), in addition to territorial and local administration reforms in 1972 and 1990.

Applicable Law on the National Territory

The law concerning the National Territory (LDN) aims to make land the property of the state, under decree as imminent property of the state.[3] Conceived in 1964, the provisions of the LDN departed from the African conceptualisation that land rights were part of a national legacy which was sacred, inalienable, and belonged to the collective, and which were, in this sense, a fundamental element of the system of African socialism. Collective control over land is, in this perspective, not only in conformity with custom and tradition, it also poses a direct challenge to the modern imperatives of economic development.

The promotion of the socialist model provides an option both to simplify customary hereditary rights based on lineage and descendence for the families actually settled on the land, and enable the modification of rules concerning land access. Since the passage into law of the LDN, no transaction can be made without the approval of the State, which, while seeking a greater security in these transactions, also uses its position to consolidate its own hegemony. The LDN's objective is to improve productivity by securing land rights. DN land cannot be transformed into individual (private) property since the legislation which governs its existence is based on customary modes of tenure which prioritise use rights.

On the other hand, the DN does not belong to the state, which, as stipulated in Article 2 of the Legal Statute 64–46, retains only legal rights as Holder of the land: The State is the holder of the lands included in the national territory in order to ensure their rational use and evaluation, in accordance with development strategies (*our translation*). The designation as Holder does not imply Ownership, nor the right of assignment. This is also the conclusion handed down in a judgement in favour of the residents of Sebikotane, in their case against the multinational BUD-Senegal and their allies in the state (Sow-Sidibé 1997). This legal conclusion illustrates the complexity surrounding the question of rights to land and to its use in Senegal.

The local and territorial administrative changes intended to complete the socialist reform, have occurred in two stages. First, the legal statute Number 72–25 of 25 April 1972, consolidated the DN's role in governance by endowing it with the rights to administer lands held by Rural Communities, and granting legal authority to decide on land-related litigations to locally elected functionaries (Campal 2004). This realignment of powers was intended to manage conflicts between rural councils and the *Préfet* (District Administrator). In the lands held by rural communities, two principal categories of DN can be observed: those assigned to the DN and those which derive their value added from the (work/activities/presence of) rural communities, but whose productive exploitation is conducted under the control of the state. According to the decree No. 72–1288 of 27 October 1972, the execution of assignment of customary lands and decisions made by the rural councils concerning their reclamation or value generating activities are

---

[3]The State acts as Trustee and Guarantor, but not Owner of land.

subordinated to the final validation of the state. This suggests that legal statutes concerning the organisation of power between the rural councils and the *préfet* do not actually transfer power to collective rural bodies since the final validation of any decisions always rests with the *préfet* (Diop and Diouf 1990).

The contemporary form of land governance is reminiscent of that prevailing in colonial times. In a land litigation case in West Africa, a British judge observed that 'the Indigenous Customary law [...] has virtually the same status as foreign law: it must be confirmed by an expert before tribunals other than the indigenous tribunals' (cited in Mamdani 2004: 161). In this context, it appears that, in spite of independence, access to political and civic rights applies only to a small part of the population and marginalises the vast rural majority. The laws currently in existence do not promote transparency in governance, and they enjoy little popular support or acceptance.

In spite of attempts to maintain the status quo, the legal amendment No. 90–37 of 8 October 1990 transferred the effective administration of national land resources away from the public authorities of the central state, to the President of the Rural Council, and the Senegalese Socialists used these texts to endorse the idea of granting a dominant role to the Rural Council in the assignment or reassignment of land and the resolution of conflicts over land. Nonetheless, effective power still remains in the hands of the *préfet*. The situation is further aggravated in the current context by the Agro-Sylvo Pastoral Guidance Law (LOASP) which aims to formalise individual, communal and business rights through a new set of legal provisions concerning the agricultural modernisation of agro-forestry and pastoral domains; these could further weaken the governance system around land.

The LOASP

Ratified in 2004, the LOASP establishes grand principles: the protection of business/productive and land rights of both individual actors and communities, rights to cede over land, inheritance rights, as well as provisions which enable land to be used as collateral to obtain credit. It also proposes a land reform, while also preserving the status quo on the LDN's role. Although it was initially integrated into the first version of the law, the intended land reform was removed due to various controversies during debates over the bill (to make the proposal into law). A delay for deliberation and dialogue with rural entities was requested by the Peasant Organisations (POs) of the National Council for Dialogue and Cooperation with the rural sector, which considers their involvement in decision-making to be crucial, given the significant implications of the type of agricultural development in question. The task of successfully managing dialogue on the land question is the major challenge faced by the LOASP.

The LOASP aims to transform the rural areas into an attractive environment for investment, with the intention of replacing extensive agriculture under family farming with an intensive, diversified and sustainable model of agriculture which also preserves and respects the country's natural resources. By promoting a new form of market-assisted land governance, the 2004 reform has provided the main stimulus, triggering the scramble for land in Senegal.

The LOASP rests on the liberal ideological assumption that a land market intrinsically exists and only requires to be governed. For this purpose, it prescribes a logic of creating incentives to attract investors, thereby clearing the way for private capitalist enterprise. The will to encourage the emergence of agrarian-based capitalism is reaffirmed through various agreements such as the Great Agricultural Offensive for Nutrition and Abundance (GOANA), the plan for a Return towards Agriculture (REVA), the Strategy for Accelerated Growth (SCA) and the programme concerning biofuels, which are to be implemented using a three-pronged strategy of stabilisation, liberalisation and privatisation. This does not, however, imply the dissolution of customary rights; the resulting situation is one of uncertainty and insecurity for beneficiaries of land which may be unfavourable to investment, to become exposed to the risks of overexploitation of natural resources and the erosion of their land. The daily news media reveals increasing levels of violence and conflict around land, which have resulted in many deaths since 2008.

Doing Business

Since 2003, the World Bank has been producing a report which purports to measure the business climate and rate the ease of Doing Business (DB) on the basis of an index of quantitative indicators.[4] Its focus, however, suggests a greater interest in eliminating informal activity than reducing poverty. The underlying hypothesis is that economic growth reduces poverty through the workings of the so-called 'trickle-down effect'. It is through this legal-institutional formulation that informal activities are transformed into legal ones. The DB indicators enable a comparative analysis of 183 economies to be made. The 2011 report underlines the notion that the development of private investment initiatives is absolutely essential to address the challenges of the current economic crisis. During 2010, a number of states adopted measures to encourage the development of domestic business enterprises. Between June 2009 and May 2010, of the 183 economies within the DB's classification, 117 had implemented 216 regulatory reforms to promote business enterprise, consolidate transparency and property rights, and simplify the resolution procedures applicable to commercial disputes and bankruptcies. These reforms resulted in the creation of new businesses enterprises, cross-border trading and the payment of duties and taxes. The World Bank thus employs the DB to methodically pursue its objective of liberalising the world economy in a more subtle manner; the

---

[4]The 11 indicators are: creation of businesses, construction permit grants, transfers of property, access to credit, investor protection, tax and duty payments, cross border trade, contract execution, business foreclosures/insolvencies, and access to electricity and employment.

assumption is that to convince countries to join the 'global competitive' system, they must satisfy conditions of entry which are contingent on 'improving the climate for doing business'. Chart 1 illustrates the DB measurements concerning Senegal, in 2012.

In 2012, Senegal moved up to 154th position in the DB index, up from 157th in 2011. This minimal improvement does not substantially alter Senegal's mediocre position in the overall rankings (154/183). As concerns property transfers, Senegal's position is in fact 171st; the causal assumption is that if the execution of contracts (enforcing contracts) is low, investor protection (protecting investors) must also be poor. Evidence which mitigates these assumptions has been presented in recent research, however. Commander and Svejnar (2007) and Dramani and Laye (2008) conclude that only in a few instances can correlation between the DB indicators, constraints to doing business, and business performance measured in terms of profitability be established. Commander and Tinn (2007) found no significant statistical correlation between the DB 2004 indicators and growth figures. On the other hand, a weak correlation was observed between investment and the DB indicators for 'enforcing contracts', while no significant correlation was established between the indicators for 'registering property' and 'dealing with construction permits'; between 'cross border trading' and import/export; between 'starting a new business' and the importance of the informal sector; or between the indicator for 'new jobs created' and the overall level of employment in the economy (Dramani and Laye 2008). Interestingly, recent research also suggests that there is no significant correlation between the DB indicators of growth and global changes in levels of investment and employment creation (Eiffert 2007). Nonetheless, Senegal will be compelled to liberalise its markets, notably land markets, if it is to address the issues highlighted by the DB index. This is in spite of the fact that privatisation of land assets, in a weak regulatory environment, is more likely to accelerate the rate of large-scale acquisition, which could, in turn, fuel food insecurity and aggravate rural poverty.

The political will of international institutions to develop economic initiatives occurs in a complex situation characterised by a plethora of economic, social, political and technological factors which vary significantly from place to place. The institutional environment confronting entrepreneurs in different locations/situations has evolved through a long historical progression which cannot be changed at will (Ndiaye and Boutillier 2011). These factors make it doubtful that reforms undertaken in the framework of DB can lead to substantial improvements.

Agricultural Land Grabbing Mechanisms and Impacts in Senegal in the 2000s

Who is involved in land grabbing in Senegal? Who monopolises agricultural land in Senegal? Multinational corporations, foreign investors, individuals closely connected to those in power, or ordinary private investors? How is a threshold to be

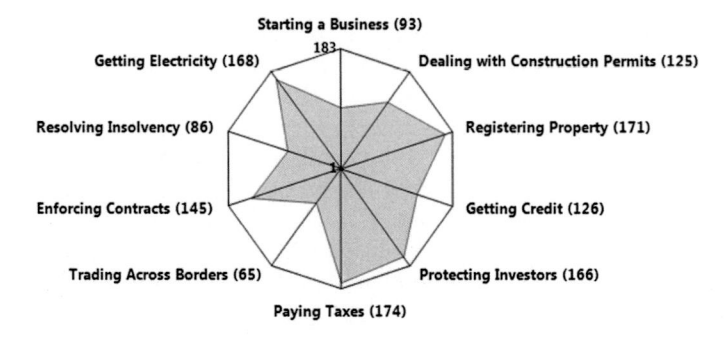

Chart 1 2012 classification of Senegal DB performance indicators in different categories *Source* DB 2012 Database

defined for marking the difference between land acquisition and land grabbing or large-scale land concentration? Vigilance at this level is especially necessary to differentiate between land accumulation, the scramble for land, land concentration and large-scale land acquisition. The current increase in the use of different terminologies to describe the phenomenon reveals a lack of coherence or consistency in understanding what is substantively at stake. Recognising the fact that complex and diverse land appropriations have occurred in countries of the Global South since the mid-2000s does not make it easier to quantify them or qualify what their implications might be (Burnod et al. 2010). Taking into account the country-specific variations and configurations, the phenomenon of land grabbing must necessarily be contextualised and the analysis must be contingent on those differences.

Land grabbing in Senegal currently affects at least 654,063 ha of arable/agricultural land, which represents about 30% of the country's available arable land (see Table 1).[5] About 2.5 million ha out of a potential 3.8 million are currently under cultivation. Private external investors account for 61.4% of allocations, with the balance being divided up between indigenous private investors. Conflicts of interest between domestic, external elites and front/shell companies have not been well studied, but are nonetheless very present and their existence is undeniable. These factors obscure the data and makes it difficult to gain an accurate picture of who is involved in land grabbing and how.

At the national level, large-scale land acquisitions have especially benefitted high-ranking state actors, the political class and religious authorities. In this context, programmes such as *Retour vers l'agriculture* (REVA) and *Grande Offensive*

---

[5]The underlying statistics in our analysis are principally those produced by civil society organisations, such as CICODEV, ENDA Tiers Monde, GRAIN, and IPAR, in conducting campaigns to lobby both governments actively promoting large-scale land acquisitions and public opinion nationally and internationally. However, the underlying conceptual frameworks, the manner in which they are produced, their units of analysis and reference, are not significantly considered, and a certain degree of caution is exercised with respect to the actual conclusions that can be drawn.

agricole pour la nourriture et l'abondance (GOANA), the programme for accelerated growth, initiated by the Government under the banner of agricultural modernisation and biofuel development, appears to have facilitated many of the large-scale acquisitions.

The scale of agricultural land transfers to investors is greater than the allocations made to domestic investors. Foreign/external investors are being granted on average approximately 36,500 ha. In Mbane, 232,208 ha have been allocated to domestic private investor, which pushes up the national average; however, when the actual number of 34 beneficiaries from this grant is taken into account, the average drops from 28,000 to 5,800 ha per person. Furthermore, even the average figure of 5,800 ha obscures serious disparities, since some recipients were allocated 10,000 ha while others obtained only 20 ha. The largest areas of the best pieces of land were distributed to religious chiefs and political leaders. In comparison with Senegalese peasants, the farms placed at the disposal of private investors resemble large colonial estates, almost feudal in scale. Large-scale acquisitions have been organised by the government and facilitated by local politicians, within the framework of an agricultural policy geared towards development and modernisation.[6] However, the experience of the majority of small producers and peasants whose access to parcels of land has been reduced to six hectares or less reflects a tendency towards the very opposite.

To examine the tendencies more closely, we consider different sets of variables concerning utilisation of land acquired within the context of large-scale acquisitions. First, we examine the logic of the land grabbers relating to their geographical location. Second, we consider the types of production which have been developed on these areas. The implied questions about food sovereignty will not be addressed here.

A careful study of the land allocated in Senegal since 2008 reveals land acquisitions are concentrated in the Senegal River Valley where the agricultural land parcels are equipped with irrigation infrastructure. These attractive areas have not been the prerogative of foreign investors since only about 62% of their total number has obtained land in the valley; by far the greatest beneficiaries as a group are the domestic investors, 95% of whom have received land in the valley. 75% of the total amount of land granted for investment is situated in the Senegal River Valley, which suggests an underlying interest on the part of both sets of investors to

---

[6]The example of Mbane, located on the Guiers Lake at the heart of the Senegal River Valley, illustrates the refusal of certain elected rural representatives to comply with government decisions. In the minutes of a meeting dated 7 June 2011, the Rural Council confirmed that about 230,000 hectares of land were distributed by previous Rural Councils (in power until 16 November 2009), when, in fact, the total rural community area covers only 190,000 ha. This scandal came to public attention as a result of the decision of the President of the Rural Community in Mbane to reverse the designation of the affected lands. The state, however, through the intervention of its *Sous Préfet* (Deputy Commissioner), has refused to sign the executive order to allow this decision to be enacted.

Table 1 Review of land transfers to external/foreign and local/domestic private investors in Senegal in 2006–10

Region	Locality	Attribute	Beneficiaries	Area (ha)	Pattern
			National Private Investors		
Saint Louis	Ross Béthio	Rural Council	Private Investor	5,000	Agriculture
	Diama	RC	Private Investor	1,800	Agriculture
	Mbane	RC	Private Investor and Politicians	232,208	GOANA and Jatropha
Ziguinchor	Kafountine	RC	Minister	20	GOANA
Diourbel	Ngom Ngom	CNRA	Minister	100	GOANA
Thiès	F.C Thiès et Pout	Government	General Khalifa	10,000	Agriculture
	Tassèt	RC	General Khalifa	125	Agriculture
Louga	Kër Momar Sarr	RC	Gafari	100	Cherry Tomatoes, Dairy cow farming and Ostriches
	Diokoul	RC	Politicians and Religious Leaders	3,000	
Total allocated to national private investors				252,353 (38.6%)	
			Foreign Private Investors		
Kédougou	Saraya	RC	Spanish Private	80,000	Tourism
	Bandafassi	RC	Investor Spanish Private Investor		
	Tombronkoto	RC	Spanish Private Investor		
Saint Louis	Mbane	RC	Nigerian Private Investor	40,000	Sugarcane
	Bokhal	RC	Nigerian Private Investor		Jatropha
	Fass Ngom	RC	Afrinvest	10,000	Jatropha
	Gandon	RC	Saudi Private Investor	200,000	Rie
Thiès	Beude Dieng		Saudi Private Investor	10,000	Agriculture
Kolda	Coumbakara	R	Saudi Private Investor	600	Agriculture
	Kounkané	RC	Saudi Private Investor	10,000	Jatropha
Fatick	Ouror		Jatropha Technology Farm (Italy)	700	Jatropha

(continued)

Table 1 (continued)

Region	Locality	Attribute	Beneficiaries	Area (ha)	Pattern
			National Private Investors		
Tambacounda	Neteboulou/Missira		Jatropha Technology Farm (Italy)	50,000	Jatropha
			SCL (France–Morocco–England)	300	But Sweet
			STS (Italy)	110	Tomato
Total allocated to foreign private investors				401,710 (61.4%)	
Total allocated to private investors				654.063	

Source Compiled by author based on data from CICODEV, ENDA Tiers Monde, IPAR gain control over the other natural resources; water, land resources and underground resources as well.

On the other hand, it is difficult to undertake a rigorous analysis of the motives underlying the actual allocation of land to different parties due to the weakness of data. Some beneficiaries simply describe their interest in relation to GOANA. However, the specifics of this programme hinge on various major issues which are supposed to mobilise actors from the agricultural sector to ensure that they are adequately provided with the inputs necessary for the production of special and sectoral food programmes (maize, rice, cassava, millet, sorghum, sunflower, wheat, fonio, cotton and horticultural products) and with the material support in terms of equipment supply and production inputs required for the establishment of sufficient and accessible Shared Agricultural Areas. In light of the diversity of cultures represented, the GOANA targets local and international markets in an undifferentiated manner.

Others declare 'agriculture' as their primary motive, without any further explanation. Others still use keywords which generally describe the nature of their business without specifying the actual areas they have been allocated, or the actual type of production being carried out. Since only explicit statements can be analysed, it is impossible under the current circumstances to conduct any study which purports to really shed light on the reality of what is happening in Senegal in any exhaustive way. That said, it appears that the majority of land allocated is being used for the production of jatropha trees (used in the production of biodiesel), rice and tourism. The rice projects operate under the auspices of Saudi interests and occupy about 200,000 ha; 70% of the production output is exported to Saudi Arabia. Spanish interests control the tourism projects at Kedougou. This profile suggests that land grabbing/acquisitions by foreign interests are poorly adapted to ensure the country's food sovereignty. Finally, we consider the conclusions which can be drawn from the current manifestations of the problem of land grabbing, knowing that over the long term, such land acquisitions are virtually irreversible.

Whether they involve external direct investors or investors from the national agricultural sector, the majority of private projects tend to be located in the irrigated areas supplied with good infrastructure around Senegal River Valley. We do not yet have longitudinal data covering a sufficient period of time to conclusively evaluate the effect of these projects in a detailed and objective manner. However, based on the statements from project leaders and data from available early evaluations, the following lessons can be drawn from two representative projects.

Through the Agro-Industrial Society of Senegal, Saudi interests currently operate an agricultural project on 120,000 ha in the Senegal River Valley. The objective of this project is to produce one million tons of rice, 70% of which will be destined for export to Saudi Arabia, with the balance of 30% to be sold on urban domestic markets (GRAIN 2010). Saudi interests control 90% of the Agro-Industrial Society of Senegal's share capital, while Senegalese interests hold only 10%, which is allocated to them in kind as agricultural land. Saudi investors envisage being able to pay off the entire amount of debts incurred on this project within 5 years, with an expected annual return on investment of 36.7%.

Additionally, in accordance with the provisions of GOANA, investors expect to receive subsidies and tax exemptions from the state.

By comparison, the Sen Oil-Sen Ethanol project is minimal in scale, covering only 20,000 ha granted to by the state in the Senegal River Valley. Its capital is principally controlled by Italian investors. According to the company's Administrative Director/CEO, the project is making a significant economic impact on regional development through the creation of 8,500 jobs, of which 2,500–3,000 were to come into effect before the end of 2013.[7] The reality looks rather different: 500 seasonal positions and 80 fulltime jobs have actually been created. The scheme has also taken on 35 trainees. Seasonal workers receive a daily wage of FCFA 3,000 (or EUR 4.5). The anticipated revenues from the export of agriculture products from this project should generate revenue for the national economy and also reduce the trade deficit. From a social perspective, a health centre offering free health checks, medical care, and medicines has been established. Amongst other initiatives, a Bilharzia vaccination campaign has been arranged in two villages. According to the Sen Oil-Sen Ethanol Administration Director/CEO, the company's corporate social responsibility programmes also include environmental initiatives.

In the cases studied, the mechanisms of land transmission seem to operate in the same way. Foreign investors ally themselves with local private investors, politicians or religious leaders to form part of the policies initiated and accompanied by the state. Land allocation decisions are taken at the central state level and imposed on rural councils. The growing interest of foreign investors for Senegalese lands is validated by a complex and poorly regulated system of land governance. This system results in the programmed decline in arable land available to family farmers.

Conclusion

Our objective in this article has been to illustrate how neoliberal approaches embodied in public policies such as 'Doing Business', REVA, the programme for accelerated growth (SCA), GOANA and LOASP lead to land privatisation and how the latter promotes the scramble for land in Senegal. Given the changes they are precipitating, large-scale acquisitions are of concern to all actors. Strong peasant mobilisation has led to serious confrontations with political leaders, and has resulted in four deaths since 2008.

This account of large-scale acquisitions suggests several conclusions. On one hand, the government of Senegal has displayed its willingness to develop policies to attract direct foreign investment in the agricultural sector and has elected to do so

---

[7]This evaluation was made public during a press conference in March 2013. An account of this conference is accessible under: https://www.farmlandgrab.org/post/print/21884, accessed 21 July 2017.

by allocating vast areas of arable land in the geographical parts of the country which are best endowed, equipped and irrigated for this purpose. Private investors have access to credit, innovation, equipment and markets. Large-scale land acquisitions are occurring in regal conditions. Labour costs are more than competitive. The fiscal support commitments under the GOANA, SCA and REVA create conditions of optimal profitability.

On the other hand, the agricultural output is clearly not directed towards domestic markets. External investors are interested in producing agricultural goods to supply their home markets. Jatropha trees, which are the main components of biofuel, are grown over approximately 300,000 ha. Labour costs are low (less than EUR 5 per day) and the public revenues are limited by the generous fiscal allowances granted. Surpluses are not necessarily reinvested, or even put back into the local economy as consumption since a large part of the profits are repatriated. Large-scale acquisitions create landlessness in the peasant population and compromise food sovereignty. They bring to evidence Prebisch–Singer's theory that productivity gains in the primary activities of developing countries translate into price reductions which benefit wealthy countries (Prebisch 1950; Singer 1950).

Can the exclusionary appropriation of agricultural land by private interests really be necessary to increase the performance of peasant production, or should land rather be a 'common good'? The proposition that private property is the only efficient way to assign resources because it allows them to be managed optimally is as dogmatic as the assertion that transferring land to the state is the only way to ensure rigorous planning of agricultural activities. Land is collective and no economic logic can reasonably demand its total privatisation. The principal argument advanced by proponents of privatisation rests on the hypothesis that productive sector capitalisation and development funding is organised exclusively by the logic of globalised capitalism. However, there is nothing to justify such a hypothesis, since experiences to date have shown that it is not borne out by reality and as such the assertions themselves remain empty of meaning.

References

Alden Wily, L. (2008). *Whose land is it? Commons and conflict states: Why the ownership of the commons matters in making and keeping peace.* Washington, DC: Rights and Resources Initiative.

Amin, S. (2012). Préface. Agriculture paysanne, agriculture familiale moderne. Agricultures capitalistes ou agricultures dans le capitalisme: les réformes foncières nécessaires en Asie et en Afrique. In B. Founou-Tchuigoua & A. Ndiaye (Eds.), *Réponses radicales à la crise agraire et rurale en Afrique. Agriculture paysanne, démocratisation des sociétés rurales et souveraineté alimentaire* (pp. xiii-xxxiii). Dakar: CODESRIA.

ANSD [Agence Nationale de la Statistique et de la Demographie]. (2007). *Enquête de suivi de la pauvreté au Sénégal, 2005–2006.* Dakar: ANSD.

ANSD [Agence Nationale de la Statistique et de la Demographie]. (2013). *Situation économique et sociale du Sénégal en 2011.* Dakar: ANSD.

Anseeuw, W., Alden Wily, L., Cotula, L., & Taylor, M. (2011). *Land rights and the rush for land*. Rome: IIED, CIRAD, ILC.

Bagayogo, I. (2012). Le Delta intérieur du Niger: un gage majeur de la souveraineté alimentaire pour le Mali et la CEDEAO. In B. Founou-Tchuigoua & A. Ndiaye (Eds.), *Réponses radicales à la crise agraire et rurale en Afrique. Agriculture paysanne, démocratisation des sociétés rurales et souveraineté alimentaire* (pp. 121–68). Dakar: CODESRIA.

Beliere, J. F., Coulibaly, Y., Keita, A., & Sanogo, M. K. (2003). *Caractérisation des exploitations agricoles de la zone de l'Office du Niger en 2000*. Ségou: URDOC/ON Nyeta Conseils.

Borras, J. (2002). La réforme agraire assistée par le marché: les cas du Brésil, de l'Afrique du Sud et de la Colombie et leurs implications pour les Philippines. *Alternatives Sud, 9*(4), 119–183.

Burnod, P., Anseeuw, W., Bosc, P.-M., & Even, M. A. (2010). Appropriations foncières dans les pays du Sud: bilan et perspectives. Centre d'études et de prospective. *Analyse, 16*. Paris: Ministère de l'Alimentation, de l'Agriculture et de la Pêche, https://agritrop.cirad.fr/555882/1/document_555882.pdf. Retrieved July 20, 2017.

Burnod, P., Bosc, P.-M., Tonneau, J.-P., & Jamin, J.-Y. (2011). Régulations des investissements agricoles à grande échelle. *Études de Madagascar et du Mali, Afrique Contemporaine, 237*(1), 111–129.

Campal, A. (2004). Enjeux et contraintes de la décentralisation: les communautés rurales du département de Mbour. In M. Niang (Ed.), *Participation paysanne et développement rural au Sénégal* (pp. 97–126). Dakar: CODESRIA.

CNCR [Conseil National de Concertation des Ruraux]. (2010). *Les exploitations familiales peuvent nourrir le Sénégal. Nos positions*. Dakar: CNCR.

Commander, S., & Svejnar, J. (2007). Do institutions, ownership, exporting and competition explain firm performance? Evidence from 26 transition countries. *IZA Working Paper*, No. 2637. Bonn: Institute for the Study of Labor.

Commander, S., & Tinn, K. (2007). Evaluating doing business. *Paper prepared for the World Bank IEG Working Paper*.

Cotula, L., Vermeulen, S., Leonard, R., & Keeley, J. (2009). *Land grab or development? Agricultural investments and international land deals in Africa*. Rome: IIED, FAO, IFAD.

Coulibaly, Y., & Belieres, J. F. (2006). Les exploitations agricoles familiales du périmètre irrigué de l'Office du Niger au Mali: évolutions et perspectives. *Cahiers Agricultures, 15*(6), 562–569.

Dahou, T., & Ndiaye, A. (2008). Les enjeux d'une réforme foncière. In T. Dahou (Ed.), *Libéralisation et politique agricole au Sénégal* (pp. 49–69). Dakar and Paris: CREPOS, ENDA GRAF DIAPOL and Karthala.

Delcourt, L. (2010). L'avenir des agricultures paysannes face aux nouvelles pressions sur la terre. *Alternatives Sud, 17*(3), 7–34.

Diop, M. C., & Diouf, M. (1990). *Le Sénégal sous Abdou Diouf*. Dakar: Karthala.

Dramani, L., & Laye, O. (2008). *Les déterminants de l'investissement privé au Sénégal: une approche VAR Structurel*. Dakar: Direction des Statistiques Économiques et de la Comptabilité Nationale, Agence Nationale de la Statistique et de la Démographie, Ministère de l'Économie et des Finances du Sénégal.

Eiffert, B. (2007). *The economic response to regulatory reform, 2003–06*. Washington, DC: Paper commissioned by the Center for Global Development.

Founou-Tchuigoua, B., & Ndiaye, A. (Eds.). (2012). *Réponses radicales à la crise agraire et rurale en Afrique: Agriculture paysanne, démocratisation des sociétés rurales et souveraineté alimentaire*. Dakar: CODESRIA.

Gabas, J. J. (2011). Les investissements agricoles en Afrique: introduction thématique. *Afrique contemporaine, 237*(1), 45–55.

GRAIN. (2008). Main basse sur les terres agricoles en pleine crise alimentaire et financière. www.grain.org/e/140-main-basse-sur-les-terres-agricoles-en-pleine-crise-alimentaire-et-financiere. Retrieved July 21, 2017.

GRAIN. (2010). Les nouveaux propriétaires fonciers: les sociétés d'investissement en tête de la course aux terres agricoles à l'étranger, www.grain.org/fr/article/entries/4407-les-nouveauxproprietaires-fonciers-les-societes-d-investissement-en-tete-de-la-course-aux-terres-agricoles-a-l-etranger. Retrieved July 21, 2017.

IPAR. (2011). *Les acquisitions de terres à grande échelle au Sénégal: description d'un nouveau phénomène*. Dakar: Initiative Prospective Agricole et Rurale.

Lavigne Delville, P. (Ed.). (1998). *Quelles politiques foncières en Afrique noire rurale? Réconcilier pratiques, légitimité et légalité*. Dakar: Ministère de la Coopération and Karthala.

Lavigne Delville, P., Toulmin, C., & Traore, S. (Eds.). (2000). *Gérer le foncier rural en Afrique de l'Ouest: dynamiques foncières et interventions publiques*. Dakar: Karthala/URED.

Mamdani, M. (2004). *Citoyen et sujet: L'Afrique contemporaine et l'héritage du colonialisme tardif*. Dakar: Karthala.

Moyo, S. (2005). La nouvelle question paysanne au Zimbabwe et en Afrique du Sud. In S. Amin (Ed.), *Les luttes paysannes et ouvrières face aux défis du XXIe siècle* (pp. 109–177). Dakar: NENA.

Ndiaye, A. (2012). La réforme des régimes fonciers au Sénégal: condition de l'éradication de la pauvreté et de la souveraineté alimentaires. In B. Founou-Tchuigoua & A. Ndiaye (Eds.), *Réponses radicales à la crise agraire et rurale en Afrique: agriculture paysanne, démocratisation des sociétés rurales et souveraineté alimentaire* (pp. 93–120). Dakar: CODESRIA.

Ndiaye, A., & Boutillier, S. (2011). De l'économie sociale à l'économie populaire solidaire via l'économie solidaire: quelles leçons tirer du *social business*? In A. Ndiaye (Ed.), *Économie sociale et solidaire: animation et dynamiques des territoires* (pp. 83–106). Paris: L'Harmattan.

Niasse, M. (2012). Une terre donnée à bail pour 99 ans est une terre pratiquement perdue à jamais. *Planète Science, 10*(2), 15–16.

Papazian, V. (2011). Notes de lecture. *Afrique contemporaine, 237*(1), 163–165.

Piveteau, A., & Rougier, E. (2010). *Émergence*, l'économie du développement interpellée. *Revue de la régulation, 7*. http://regulation.revues.org/7734. Retrieved July 21, 2017.

Plançon, C. (2009). Droit, foncier et développement: les enjeux de la notion de propriété étude de cas au Sénégal. *Revue Tiers Monde, 200*(4), 837–851.

Prebisch, R. (1950). *The economic development of Latin America and its principal problems*. Lake Success, NY: United Nations Department of Economic Affairs.

Singer, H. W. (1950). The distribution of gains between investing and borrowing countries. *American Economic Review, 15*(2), 473–485.

Sow-Sidibé, A. (1997). Le domaine national, la loi et le projet de réforme. *La Revue du Conseil économique et social, 2*, 55–65.

Tabb, W. K. (2008). *The global good crisis and what has capitalism to do with it*. http://www.networkideas.org/feathm/jul2008/Global_Food_Crisis.pdf. Retrieved July 21, 2017.

Von Braun, J., & Meinzen-dick, R. (2009). 'Land grabbing' by foreign investors in developing countries: risks and opportunities, *IFPRI Policy Brief, 13*, 1–4. http://www.landcoalition.org/sites/default/files/documents/resources/ifpri_land_grabbing_apr_09-2.pdf. Retrieved July 21, 2017.

World Bank. (2010). *Rising global interest in farmland: can it yield sustainable and equitable benefits?*. Washington, DC: World Bank.

World Bank [Banque Mondiale]. (2003). *Des politiques foncières pour promouvoir la croissance et réduire la pauvreté*. Washington, DC: World Bank.

Land-Based Investments in Tanzania: Legal Framework and Realities on the Ground

Godfrey Eliseus Massay and Telemu Kassile

Introduction

At independence in 1961, the economy of the then Tanganyika (now mainland Tanzania) was at an early stage of growth, characterised by inadequate human capital and physical infrastructure, less established administrative institutions and feeble private institutions with restricted capacity (Nyerere 1974). As a result, during the first five years of independence, there were concerted efforts to establish effective government institutions. The second half of the decade was characterised by a quest for a plan for national social and economic development (ibid.), promulgated in the Arusha Declaration of 1967, which committed Tanzania to a policy of socialism and self-reliance (Collins 1974). Because the new government had limited financial resources, foreign capital inflow was the most important means of building and developing the economy during the 1960s and 1970s (Biermann and Wagao 1986).[1]

From the mid-1970s to the 1980s, Tanzania experienced a grave socio-economic crisis whose impact was manifested at both micro- and macro levels. At the micro level, the crisis resulted in a breakdown of the social structure and worsening living

---

[1]An earlier version of this chapter appeared as a Working Paper of the Land Deal Politics Initiative (LDPI); see https://www.iss.nl/fileadmin/ASSETS/iss/Research_and_projects/Research_networks/LDPI/LDPI_WP_56.pdf. The authors wish to acknowledge the LDPI collective for its support in preparing the initial paper for publication. In particular, the authors acknowledge with gratitude the helpful comments made by Prof. Ruth Hall, Happiness George and Emmanuel Sulle.

G. E. Massay (✉)
Tanzania Natural Resource Forum, P.O. Box 15605, Arusha, Tanzania
e-mail: massayg@gmail.com

T. Kassile
Department of Mathematics, Informatics and Computational Sciences,
Solomon Mahlangu College of Science and Education, Sokoine University
of Agriculture, P.O. Box 3038, Morogoro, Tanzania
e-mail: telemuk@yahoo.com

© Springer Nature Singapore Pte Ltd. 2019
S. Moyo et al. (eds.), *Reclaiming Africa*, Advances in African Economic,
Social and Political Development, https://doi.org/10.1007/978-981-10-5840-0_8

conditions, while at the macro level, it resulted in severe shortage of foreign exchange, balance of payment problems and large budget deficits (Meena 1989). Overall, the 1960s and 1970s were epitomised by undue government borrowing and bad debts accumulated by commercial banks, and this was attributed partially to excessive government interference, in adequate supervision of financial institutions and pursuit of multiple policy objectives, among others (BoT 2011).

In an attempt to turn things around and accelerate economic growth, the government embarked on a broad range of economic, legislative and institutional reforms. These include the National Economic Survival Plan, Structural Adjustment Programmes (SAPs), Economic Recovery Programmes I (1986) and II (1989) and the Economic and Social Action Plan and Priority Social Action Plan (1989) (Lugalla 1995). These changes were seen to be necessary because previous development initiatives were not commensurate with the ideology of market-led economy and progress in technology, which were taking part in the world. Through these and other reforms,[2] doors were opened to FDIs and initiatives were taken to create an enabling environment for investment in response to the dynamics of the world and local economic conditions. The agriculture, energy, mining, tourism and transportation sectors experienced major policy, legislative and institutional reforms. Most likely because of initiatives such as these, a number of both foreign and domestic investors have been attracted to, and now operate in, Tanzania, in various sectors, including agriculture, agrofuels and agroforestry.

This chapter highlights policy and legal frameworks that govern land-based investments in Tanzania. It discusses some land deals and the impacts of these investments in the context of poverty eradication in Tanzania. The chapter attempts to answer the following questions: has the Tanzanian investment legal framework achieved its objectives? Are land deals in Tanzania guided by the free, prior and informed consent principle? Is there a win-win situation in Tanzanian land deals? What should be done to make land-based investments work in Tanzania?

At the outset, we add a disclaimer that we draw on evidence from a number of studies conducted previously and that, as noted elsewhere (Locher and Sulle 2013), data on land deals in Tanzania is not entirely reliable and up to date. One main reason is the lack of coordination and transparency among government institutions and ministries responsible for investment in the country, hence making it hard to have authentic data (Sulle and Nelson 2009; Makwarimba and Ngowi 2012). Nonetheless, this chapter aims to examine the realities of land investments in Tanzania, despite the challenges.

---

[2]For example, parastatal reforms were designed to diminish the dominance and monopoly of state-owned enterprises, as part of wider structural adjustment initiatives. Reforms also included allowing the private sector to compete in marketing and processing cash crops in the increasingly liberalised market environment. Revisions in the land law rules enabled long-term leasehold property rights for up to 99 years for domestic and foreign investors. Financial reforms enhanced the investment climate, enabling 26 licensed banks (foreign and domestic) to operate in the country (FAO 2012).

Theoretical Legal Framework Governing Investment in Tanzania

From Independence to 1967

After independence, the government of then Tanganyika, under President Julius Nyerere's leadership, desisted from the inclusion of the Bills of Rights in both the Independent Government and the Republic Constitutions of 1961 and 1962, respectively. This was because it was believed that a Bill of Rights would assure private property ownership, which would hamper government development plans and create conflict between the Executive and Judiciary, which was still under the control of some foreign expatriates (Maina 1994; Maina and Mwakaje 2004).

The lack of a Bill of Rights in the constitution did not dissuade investors from investing in Tanzania, nor did it dissuade the government from pursuing investment in the public interest.[3] The government showed its determination when it prepared and passed the Foreign Investment (Protection) Act, 1963, which aimed to provide a legal warranty for foreign investors, so that they would be persuaded to invest in the country. The government also entered mutual arrangements with foreign governments to support, promote and protect investment (Maina 1994).

Arusha Declaration and Its Aftermath

The heart of the social policy in Tanzania, which began by promulgating the Arusha Declaration in 1967, was to promote mass nationalisation (Court 1976). In this respect, to ensure that the objectives of the Arusha Declarations were met, various laws were enacted, including the Land Acquisition Act of 1967 (Act No. 47), which intended to simplify the land acquisition process in the public/state interest. The government also guaranteed and compensated for nationalised property (Maina 1994).

However, with the turn of events in the 1980s, including the SAPs, the collapse of the Soviet Union and the reign of the capitalist block, Tanzania failed to sustain its commitment to the Arusha Declaration. In 1984, the fifth Constitutional Amendment included the Bill of Rights, and in 1985, with the change in the presidency from Nyerere to Ali Hassan Mwinyi, a new investment climate was

---

[3]President Nyerere, while addressing the meeting of the Association of Chambers of Commerce of Eastern Africa on 11 February 1963, said 'the government wishes to work with private investors for the development of Tanganyika'; and again, on 11 February 1965, while laying the foundation stone for the ENI Oil Refinery at Kigamboni, Dar es Salaam, he said: '[t]he government of Tanzania is determined to have an oil refinery in Tanzania rather than continue to import the end products of crude oil, and therefore we have worked hard to interest those who might be able to undertake such an investment under conditions which would benefit Tanzania' (cited in Maina 1994: 5–6).

promoted. The enactment of the Investment (Promotion and Protection) Act, in April 1990, marked the climax of economic liberalisation. The Act covers the investment promotion centre, application procedures, areas of investment, investment incentives, investment protection, dispute settlement and transfer of foreign currency; it covers both foreign and local investors but excludes investment in petroleum and minerals from the scope of the Act. The Act is silent on investors' duties, and provides procedures to avoid double taxation (Maina 1994).

Current Investment Legal Regime

The third presidency, of Benjamin Mkapa, starting in 1995, focused on scaling up the market-led economy through privatisation, commensurate with SAP principles, to transform the state-managed economy into a market economy and promote economic growth. The new investment regime saw the enactment of the Tanzania Investment Act, Act No. 26 of 1997, which must be read together with the Financial Laws (Miscellaneous Amendments) Act of the same year.[4] The new Investment Act aimed to correct some aspects of the National Investment (Promotion and Protection) Act of 1990, which restricted potential investors (Maina and Mwakaje 2004). The Investment Act of 1997 provides more detail than its precursor regarding the investment process and investment opportunities in Tanzania, but has some shortcomings, including failure to spell out the duties of the investor, double taxation (Maina 1994; Maina and Mwakaje 2004), and two separate statutes[5] to govern investment which makes it hard for investors to understand. The Act also has a weak dispute settlement mechanism, and only addresses foreign investors, not domestic investors (Maina and Mwakaje 2004).

Land Investment Laws

Land law reforms in the 1990s were internally driven by increased land conflicts and, externally, by the market economy, and were funded by International Financial Institutions (IFIs) and donor communities (Tsikata 2003). The Village Land Act, Act No. 5 of 1999, prohibits foreigners from owning land in Tanzania except for investment purposes under the Tanzania Investment Act. Land to be designated for investment purposes must be identified, gazetted, and allocated to the Tanzania Investment Centre (TIC), which then creates derivative rights for investors.

---

[4]Amended laws include the Income Tax Act, 1973, Customs Tariff Act, 1976, Sales Tax Act, 1976, and Immigration Act, 1995.

[5]The Investment Act of 1997 and the Financial Laws (Miscellaneous Amendments) Act of 1997.

However, the Village Land Act allows the President to transfer village land to general land for public interest, including investment for national interest.

According to the Land Act of 1999, general land includes unoccupied or unused village land.[6] The Land Acquisition Act of 1967 also allows the President to acquire land for 'public interest', which entails fair or a win-win land acquisition in the context of the laws, national development, and poverty reduction initiatives. Unfortunately, *public interest* has never been satisfactorily defined either by the Constitution or the by land registration regulations (Larsson 2006).

The Mining Act of 2010, which revoked and replaced the Mining Act of 1998, responds to some issues side-lined by its predecessor such as allocation of areas for exclusive use of artisan and small-scale miners. The Act, like its predecessor, requires the recognition of granted and customary rights of occupancy. In practice, however, owners' land rights are often disregarded, due simply to an absence of data on village land, land occupants, and existing rights to mineral resources to inform the granting of concessions. Even where such information is accessible, it is ignored (Makwarimba and Ngowi 2012).

Other legislation relevant to land-based investments includes the Export Processing Zones Act of 2002, which makes provisions to establish, develop and manage Export Processing Zones (EPZs), and the Special Economic Zones Act of 2006, which makes provisions to establish, develop and manage EPZs to create an attractive environment for local and foreign investment.

Context of Investment

Manifestation of External Forces for Investment in Tanzania

The Government of Tanzania, like many governments, seems to believe that investment could provide solutions to its economic problems. In this regard, the government created a favourable environment for foreign direct investment (FDI) and created institutions to promote, coordinate and facilitate investment into Tanzania such as the Tanzania Investment Centre (TIC) and THE Export Processing Zones Authority (EPZA). A core function of TIC, for example includes 'to identify investment sites, estates, or land together with associated facilities of any sites, estates, or land for the purposes of investors and investments in general.[7]' On the other hand, the EPZA is responsible for land acquisition and putting in place all necessary infrastructures for investors to start a business. Such institutions work diligently to ensure investors are attracted to Tanzania. We briefly discuss below investments in agriculture for food production, agrofuels, agroforestry and mining

---

[6]S. 2 of the Land Ac of 1999 states that general land means all public land, which is not reserved land or village land and includes unoccupied or unused village land.

[7]Section 6(c) of the Investment Act of 1997.

with a view to provide an understanding of the extent of land-based investments in Tanzania in the context of the existing policy and legal framework. However, as discussed below, unlike other sectors, the government has allowed investments in biofuels and Reducing Emission from Deforestation and Forest Degradation (REDD) schemes without creating a policy and legal framework to guide investment in these sectors.

Agriculture for Food Security

Investment in agriculture for food production is growing. The Rufiji River Basin, which represents about 20% of all Tanzanian land, and which is under the authority of the Rufiji Basin Development Cooperation (RUBADA),[8] is the area most coveted for investment in the agricultural sector. Tanzanian districts in which many agricultural land acquisitions deals have been reported in the last decade includes Kisarawe, Bagamoyo, Rufiji, Morogoro Rural and Kilombero.

Both internal and external forces drive the quest for food security in Tanzania. Internally, the government has created the Agricultural Sector Development Programme (ASDP), since 2003, which has an agricultural transformation programme from national to district level. Several international development partners joined hands with government in support of agricultural sector development, including the Danish International Development Agency (DANIDA), Japanese International Cooperation Agency (JICA), the European Union (EU), Irish Aid (IA), the International Fund for Agricultural Development (IFAD) and the International Development Association (IDA). This was followed by the Kilimo Kwanza (Agriculture First) initiative in 2009, which intends to develop large-, medium- and small-scale farmers. Funds have been allocated through Tanzania Investment Bank, and farmers can access agricultural inputs. Despite these initiatives, poverty remains widespread in Tanzania, especially in rural areas. More recently, as part of implementing Kilimo Kwanza, Tanzania is developing the Southern Agricultural Growth Corridor of Tanzania (SAGCOT), an agricultural partnership investment project with an area amounting to 300,000 km^2, launched at the World Economic Forum Africa meeting in Dar es Salaam, in 2010. SAGCOT aims to increase agricultural productivity and food security and improve livelihoods in Tanzania. Other initiatives include the Alliance for Green Revolution in Africa (AGRA) and the Comprehensive Africa Agriculture Development Programme (CAADP), whose stated objective is to emancipate small-scale farmers through research on the best agronomy, seed development, soil fertility and commercialisation of the agricultural sector. The government produced a strategic Investment Blueprint for SACCOT, in 2011, to promote commercial farming in the areas known to be the granary of good production in Tanzania. Foreign investors are

---

[8]The RUBADA was established by the The Rufiji Basin Development Authority Act of 1975.

increasing in the country in search of good arable land and have been allocated thousands of hectares (Locher and Sulle 2013). This might seriously affect small-scale farmers, if an alternative strategy for the farmers is not adopted.

While plans such as the SAGCOT may reflect the government's commitment to transform the agricultural sector and, thus, contribute to realising the National Strategy for Growth and Reduction of Poverty and the National Development Vision 2025, analysts are wondering whether the initiative will meet the objectives and be sustainable, given that many similar previous large-scale investments in groundnuts in Dodoma and wheat plantations in Hanang, or programmes such as ASDP and CAADP, have mostly failed to meet the objective of changing the livelihoods of most Tanzanians. Statistics from the 2007 Household Budget Survey (National Bureau of Statistics 2009) show that poverty remains widespread, especially in rural areas. Between 2000/01 and 2007, the proportion of Tanzanians unable to meet basic needs only marginally decreased, from 35.6 to 33.4%. In the same period, the incidence of poverty in rural areas decreased from 38.7 to 37.4, while in urban areas (excluding Dar es Salaam), it decreased from 25.8 to 24.1%.

The failure of the agricultural initiatives to achieve a significant impact on rural livelihoods could be attributed to many factors, but a close look at these initiatives shows that they are top-down projects, devoid of small-scale farmers' consultations (Cooksey 2012; Maghimbi et al. 2010).

Agriculture for Energy Security

Tanzania, like other countries around the world, ventured into the production of biofuels based on four main assumptions that have driven the global bioenergy industry. The first assumption is that bioenergy is a more economical and renewable alternative source of energy than fossil fuels; the second is that bioenergy can reduce carbon emissions; the third is that bioenergy provides countries with the prospect of being energy independent, by reducing or even cutting out dependence on imported fossil fuels; the forth is that bioenergy offers new avenues to farmers in developing countries to reduce poverty and improve their livelihoods (Sosovele 2010). After a study conducted by German Technical Cooperation (GTZ) in 2005 (GTZ 2005), the doors were opened to biofuel investment in Tanzania. As of 2011, more than 40 companies, mostly with foreign capital, were involved in biofuel development activities in Tanzania, while only a few and small local companies were engaged in such activities (Mshandete 2011). Yet, it has been shown that to realise poverty reduction and sustainable development programmes through biofuel investment, engaging and promoting small-scale farmer productivity is indispensable (Arndt et al. 2010).

While investors have acquired, and others seeking to acquire, thousands of hectares of land for biofuels (Veit et al. 2012), and while awaiting a national policy on biofuels, the government formed the National Bioenergy Task Force (NBTF) to prepare biofuels guidelines as an interim measure (ActionAid 2009). The guidelines, released in 2010, provide general statements with no binding force, enforcement mechanism, and legal teeth. The wave of investors in the biofuels sector scared the government and it suspended new biofuel development until appropriate policies, regulatory frameworks, and laws are in place to guide the process (Sulle and Nelson 2009). In September 2012, the government issued the first draft of the National Liquid Biofuel Policy for public comments, but the policy is still in its draft form.

Several studies have explored issues related to biofuel investment in Tanzania. For example, Mshandete (2011) examines players in biofuels projects and their roles, value chains, social-economic and environmental impacts, tenure issues, food security, sustainability and research and development. Evidence shows that the role of the state in facilitating land deals is higher than in enforcing the terms on the deals. For instance, state agencies more often assist investors to obtain land, mobilise villagers to give land to investors and draft contract terms or Memoranda of Understandings (MoUs) than make public all the contract terms and enforce the obligations made in such deals (Kweka 2012).

Poverty and illiteracy in local communities have been used to the advantage of the local elites, politicians, and investors in negotiating land deals (HAKIARDHI 2011b; ActionAid 2011). In some land deals (for example Bagamoyo and Rufiji), in the process of the negotiations meals (rice meat) and bribes (giving tips) were reportedly given to the village leaders (Massay 2012). In Songea, an investor offered an allowance of 2000 shillings to any villager to attend the village assembly as a consideration to approve his request for land (HAKIARDHI 2012). This is not surprising, given the high level of poverty in rural areas.

Studies show that politicians and district officials have been instrumental in land acquisitions for biofuels companies such as Sunbiofuels in Kisarawe, African Green Oil in Rufiji and BioShape in Kilwa, but the same state has given people a cold shoulder when investors fail to deliver the pledged benefits (ActionAid 2011; HAKIARDHI 2011a; Veit et al. 2012). This casts a shadow of doubt as to whether their active participation in the land acquisition process is really for the 'public interest'. Moreover, government agency interference has created fear among villagers and their leaders, but it has also made villagers and leaders trust the government officials and politicians who they know best when giving land for investment. There is evidence that negotiations for land deals, supervised by government agencies, have been done in a very short period (HAKIARDHI 2012). To date, much less land (641,179 ha), has already been allocated for biofuel investments. Only 100,000 ha have been fully secured by biofuel investors following the land acquisition procedures (Sulle and Nelson 2009; Mshandete 2011).

Because most companies engaged in biofuel activities in Tanzania are foreign companies and because of the lack of a national policy on biofuels, there are increasing concerns both within and outside the country that the industry may not be of much benefit to local people, or the nation at large. For example, the Evert Vermeer Foundation (van Teeffelen 2013) reveals that European biofuel companies operating in Tanzania have caused problems for rural communities; it calls for a change in EU biofuel policy to ensure that it is commensurate with country development objectives (including those of Tanzania), minimises the likelihood of food insecurity, and ensures people's land rights. This is especially important as many European companies invest in Tanzania because of EU support for Tanzania's biofuel industry (ibid).

Forest Plantations for Carbon Market

Forest plantation investments are new in Tanzania, but agroforestry investors are looking forward to using the opportunities of the Clean Development Mechanism (CDM), as provided in the United Nations Framework for Climate Change Convention (UNFCCC), of 1992.[9] Tanzania is a signatory to the UNFCCC and the Kyoto Protocol—two international legal instruments that provide a framework for industrialised countries to incentivise developing countries to conserve forests to increase carbon stock, which absorbs carbon dioxide and other greenhouse gases (GHG) from the atmosphere.

Tanzania, with over 33.5 million ha of forestry reserves and a sizable rural land under forest cover, formulated a National Climate Change Strategy in 2012, which delineates strategic interventions to guarantee that the communities and the nation at large benefit from the global initiatives (for example UNFCCC) to mitigate the effects of climate change (URT 2012). Climate change mitigation and adaptation programmes have been encouraged worldwide. More funds are channelled to programmes that have climate change adaptation or mitigation objectives, and funding proposals sent to donor agencies or development partners are only accepted if they include climate change adaptation and mitigation objectives. The Carbon Market can now be accessed through REDD projects.[10] In Tanzania, foreign companies have acquired land for agroforestry projects in Mufindi, Kilombero, and Kilolo districts. Projects are now extending to Muheza, Songea and Njombe districts (see Locher and Sulle 2013).

Deals around this kind of investment are hindered with lack of *consensus ad idem* principle in contract law—or 'meeting of minds'. That is, contracting parties must be on the same level of understanding of the terms of contract before entering into a contract. In Idete village, where a Norwegian-based Green Resource Limited (GRL) entered into an agreement with Idete Village, in Mufindi district, Iringa

---

[9]According to an anonymous interview, '[a]s far as I know, there is no single CDM project approved yet in Tanzania. As far as I know, GRAS has so far sold carbon certificates on the voluntary market instead. However, I think the company's application for being accepted as CDM project might be pending at the respective Tanzanian government authority' (19 February 2013).

[10]REDD is an effort to create a financial value for the carbon stored in forests, offering incentives for developing countries to reduce emissions from forested lands and invest in low-carbon paths to sustainable development. REDD + goes beyond deforestation and forest degradation, and includes conservation, sustainable forest management and enhanced forest carbon stocks; see http://www.un-redd.org.

region, the village chairperson, who signed the contract, confessed to the team of researchers that he did not understand the terms of the contract because the whole contract was written in English and not translated for him.

Investments in Mining Sector

The mining sector is considered likely to contribute to Gross Domestic Product (GDP) if sustainably exploited and effectively managed, and is currently the second fastest growing sector after tourism (Makwarimba and Ngowi 2012). Confirmed deposits in Tanzania include gold, diamonds, tanzanite, ruby, tin, copper, nickel, iron, soda, phosphate, gypsum, kaolite, coal, natural gas and uranium (LHRC 2012). However, even after the Mining Act of 2010 was enacted, despite the enormous investments taking place, the mining sector has not met expectations in terms of income generation for Tanzania, since government is losing substantial tax revenue from the mining sector (Curtis and Lissu 2008; LHRC 2012).

Land Acquisition Procedures

Land Transfer

The President of Tanzania has powers to acquire any piece of land for public interest, including investment for public interest. To make that possible, the President has to transfer village land (which is appropriate for investment) to general land.[11] This has to go through several stages as per the Village Land Act of 1999. Villagers, through village and district councils, and any representations on the matter, may endorse or reject to endorse the proposed transfer. However, the village assembly can only refuse a transfer of less than 250 ha. Although there is a provision for villagers or a group of villagers who are allocated with the right to use the land (referred to as 'the affected') to register their unwillingness to support a transfer, they cannot in effect refuse the proposal, because the decision to approve or disapprove a proposed transfer is at the discretion of the Village Assembly or the Minister responsible for land depending on the area involved (although it is not clear if the President can override a Village Assembly's decision to refuse on areas less than 250 ha). Ultimately, the President

---

[11]The Village Land Act of 1999 vests administrative powers of village land under the Village Council. Village land is one of the three categories of land in Tanzania, the others being general and reserved land.

can resort to lawful expropriation, subject to payment of compensation. In effect, a transfer of land can be a form of land acquisition giving rise to involuntary resettlement (Makwarimba and Ngowi 2012).

Access to Land Through TIC

In Tanzania, land can be acquired through granted or customary right of occupancy through the TIC, which holds granted right of occupancy, but gives investors derivative rights of occupancy. According to the Land Act, 1999 (Section 2), derivative right is a right to occupy and use land created out of a right of occupancy and includes a lease, a sublease, a license, a usufructuary right, and any interest analogous to those interests. In regard to this, Section 20 of the Land Act, 1999[12] provides a detailed account on land ownership issues vis-à-vis foreigners. However, of particular interest to the ongoing discussion is that the Act does not attach any value to all lands acquired by foreigners prior to the enactment of the Act except in situations where unexhausted improvements have been made.

Alternative Process Commonly Used to Access Village Land for Investment

Olenasha (2011, cited in Makwarimba and Ngowi 2012) identifies an alternative procedure that investors use to access land, which emerged simply to meet a need, but is not guided by any law or official procedure. It is not clear whether the full land transfer procedures as laid down in the Village Land Act of 1999 are followed at the point when this process kicks in. Through this procedure, a potential investor identifies a place (e.g., a village) where a suitable land for the intended investment is likely to be found; this is usually done with the help of local brokers, or by officials from TIC or a local Member of Parliament. Otherwise, an investor might approach and seek approval from Village Council first, before other processes ensue (Sulle and Nelson 2009: 41). An investor may also acquire land through some established institutions (authorities) that have administrative authority over land and can invite and enter into contract with an investor—one of such authorities being RUBADA. EPZA also seeks land for investments through district and regional governments. So far, as per EPZA websites, over 23,000 ha of land has been earmarked in Tanzania for investment.[13]

---

[12]This section is read together with amendment made under Sections 2 and 4 of Act 12 of 2004.

[13]See http://www.epza.co.tz, accessed 14 August 2012.

Analysis of Land Investment Practices in Tanzania

Land Acquisition

As noted earlier, foreign investors are attracted to Tanzania and many other countries in Africa because they assume there is abundant land. In the case of Tanzania, however, this assumption is not supported by any nationwide survey. According to ActionAid (2009), the GoT considers 29.4 million ha to be suitable for irrigation development, or 31.8% of Tanzania's total land mass, of which 2.3 million ha are of high irrigation development potential, 4.8 million ha are of medium potential, and 22.3 million ha are of low irrigation development potential. Tanzania is estimated to have more than 30 million ha of land suitable for cultivating energy crops, with corresponding areas of 570,000 ha, 24 million ha, and 14 million ha suitable for sugarcane, cereals and root crops, respectively (FAO 2007, cited in OI 2011).

The aforementioned statistics are not supported by land use maps/plans, to clearly show what amount of land has been identified and where it is located. Tanzania currently has about 12,000 villages, and statistics show that only 1,000 villages have been surveyed and planned (URT 2011). As a result, some investors have spent more time in land acquisition process because of the absence of a land bank; for example it took three years for Sunbiofuels to acquire land in Kisarawe district.

Community Participation

Local and international legal instruments require local community participation in any investment projects that involve their land. The noble idea behind this requirement is to have their free, prior and informed consent to such projects, which will help to avoid any future conflicts between investors and local communities. It also intends to pave way for negotiation and integration of local communities in such projects. Studies have shown that most of the land deals have been transacted without full participation of local community. Where local communities are involved, it is because their political leaders have asked them to participate and some investors have furnished some considerations. Sometimes local communities have been deprived of the right to understand (lack of transparency) terms of land deals and the legal implications,[14] and some local leaders have entered into an

---

[14]Most villages are not made aware that when the land is taken by an investor it has to be transferred to general land, which comes under the control of the Commissioner of Lands and not Village Council.

agreement with foreign investors without understanding the language of the contract, as mentioned above in the case of Green Resources Company (Ltd.) in Idete Village.

Compensation

Full, prompt and fair compensation of the landholder is the right, which is not only provided by land laws,[15] but also guaranteed by the constitution.[16]

While the Village Land Act guarantees compensation to the affected parties, there are many practical problems, which surround the compensation procedures in Tanzania. Compensation practices are not inclusive, lack participation of local communities, monitoring and record keeping (Mtoni 2010). Moreover, the compensation process involves middlemen (including elites) who are not part of the deal, but take part in the process because of private financial gains and do not protect the interests of the landholders or local communities (affected parties). Compensation processes in Tanzania have also been observed to be associated with high transaction costs, which limit the maximisation of well-being among the affected parties.

For example, Bioshape made a compensation of about USD 647,000, but only 40% reached the targeted people, while Kilwa District Council took the remaining 60% (Veit et al. 2012; HAKIARDHI 2011a). Sunbiofuels had recently (December 2013) paid TZS 577,708,870 as compensation for bare land, eight years after the valuation report for payment was made public and the land was acquired. Geita Gold Mine has not compensated over 20 people, delayed payment for over 30 villagers and over 50 households living near the mine suffered from mining operations due to cracks in their houses and pollution of their water sources, yet they are not resettled and compensated. Experience shows that compensation, which needs to be presided by participatory processes of land valuation, has never put the victims in a better position, but instead worsens their situation because land valuers are trained to use minimal standards (Bergius 2012). Sometimes the victims have been vacated forcefully and their properties destroyed in the name of paving the way for investment. For example, AgriSol tried to give half of the compensation to the victims of a land deal and only promised to pay the remaining sum after the victims have vacated the area, which is against the requirements provided by law.

---

[15]Land Act and Village Land Act of 1999, Investment Act of 1997, Road Act of 2007, Mining Act of 2010, and Town Planning Act of 2007, among others.

[16]Article 24 of the Constitution of the United Republic of Tanzania of 1977, as amended periodically.

Impacts of Land Investments

Economic Impact

In 2011, EPZA registered 16 new investors who put up industries in the country, created about 8,000 new employment opportunities and increased exports to USD 130 million (*The Guardian*, 10 January 2012, p. 3). Statistics show that in 2010, 8 new investors were registered under EPZA with about USD 39 million capital investments, which created 3,000 employment opportunities for Tanzanians (*The Citizen*, 25 January 2010, p. 10). Although this appears to be positive, when considering the costs that EPZA incurred in developing the necessary infrastructure for the investments to take off and the 10-year tax grace period for investors, one may conclude that such economic benefits take a long time to be realised.

Studies show that Tanzania provides an assortment of tax incentives and exceptions, especially for mining companies and firms operating in EPZs. Many of these exemptions represent an unnecessary loss of revenue. Exemptions given to corporations have deprived Tanzania an average of TZS 458.6 billion (USD 288 million) a year in 3 years 2008/09–2010/2011 (Curtis et al. 2012).

Impact to Livelihoods and Food Security

Over the past few decades, pressure on pastoral grazing lands and water resources have increased due to increased interests in investment, which demands more land for cultivation, and conservation areas. This culminated in the eviction of pastoralists residing in Usangu/Ihefu in 2006, and in Loliondo in 2009. These evictions are characterised as violent, having disregarded the human and land rights of the pastoralists. Such relocations of pastoralists from their original areas have caused serious livelihoods issues, as they have failed to cope with the dry season and their movements have fuelled constant confrontation with other land users such as farmers.

Agrofuel and agroforestry are posing a challenge to the food security of the communities around such investments, because of acquisitions of areas that are good quality for growing food crops. Areas such as Kisarawe, Mpanda, Bagamoyo, Kilwa, Kilolo, Mufindi and Morogoro have fertile soil and good climatic conditions for food crop production, but these areas have reported deals in biofuels and agroforestry, such that the latter may jeopardise food security. There is also evidence that, in such areas, the labour force which was used for food crops production is now used for biofuel and agroforestry productions. This has resulted in hunger in such areas, for example in Kilwa the Bioshape-hunger (*njaa ya Bioshape*) (HAKIARDHI 2011a). Project impacts correlate with compensation and worsening natural, physical, human, financial and social capitals of households (Mtoni 2010).

Furthermore, land loss for investment purposes has resulted in deteriorating livelihoods for rural communities due to declining agricultural productivity.

Social Impact

Land-based investments estrange local communities from their land, so that all traditional values attached to community land are disrupted. For example, in Kisarawe district, it became hard for the community to have access to medicinal plants and graveyards located in areas under investor control. In Mishamo and Katumba refugee camps, villagers (former refugees) have criticised the resettlement plan, as it would detach them from their land and relatives with whom they have lived for decades, which, in turn, threaten to destroy their traditional ways of living. Land deals typically have little involvement with local communities, and men are more involved in the process than women, making it hard for women to benefit from such deals (LEAT 2011).

Environmental Impact

Environmental justice is a vital criterion that must be adhered to by all investment projects in the country. Corporate entities have a duty to manage and conserve the environment, not only to preserve nature and the quality of the environment but to benefit mankind. On this basis, every entity is urged to look at the environment with a holistic eye, considering the possible chain of consequences triggered by a single action (LHRC 2012).

Although both international environmental legal instruments and local environmental laws require the aforementioned condition, the practices are quite different. Allegations suggest that mining and manufacturing have caused land degradation, and factories near residential areas have caused air pollution. North Mara Gold mine had sustained impact on the surrounding environment of north Mara, as a toxic spill made the area dangerous for people and animals,[17] and there are concerns that the area around the tailing dam—in effect, between the Tighite and Mara rivers—might be contaminated and harmful to people (LHRC 2012).

In Mkwajuni hamlet, located in Nzega district, wastewater from the mine has created serious environmental pollution, with the water from the nearby stream producing a bad smell due to the contained chemicals from mines' dams. Also, in Nyakabale village, pollution due to the mining activities of Geita Gold Mine was a noted problem, as well as heavy dust caused by rock blasting. Barrick Buzwagi area

---

[17]Specifically, nine cows died due to consumption of water from the ponds which contained water mixed with chemicals from the mine (LHRC 2012).

is also largely affected by mine pollution, with severe complaints from the nearby residents (LHRC 2012).

In agribusiness investments, the situation is not advantageous as some companies have not conducted Environmental Impact Assessments (EIA) in the way that the law requires, and others have not followed recommendations from EIA reports. Agro Eco energy[18] and Sunbiofuels are criticised for not following the recommendations given by EIA reports, which are decried for lacking community participation (LEAT 2011; ActionAid 2011; OI 2012). As a result, local communities in Kisarawe district are facing serious water shortages, and donors are reluctant to finance Eco energy projects.[19] Clearing of miombo forest to pave way for jatropha farm in Kilwa by Bioshape caused serious environmental impact to the community.

At Kilombero, Illovo, a sugar-growing company, used aeroplanes to spray pesticides on its farm, while taking no effective environmental and health precautions, thereby causing local crops to dry before maturity. Also, in Mufindi district, Tanzania Pyrethrum is blamed for air pollution caused by dust generated from mining, with nearby communities suffering from chronic coughing (LHRC 2012).

The Environmental Management Act of 2004 provides for various prohibitions and corresponding penalties, but despite being comprehensive, the Act is not followed in letter or spirit. Despite many violations, law enforcement machinery is ineffective, although the entire public bears the burden, as it has a stake in environment management (LHRC 2012).

Conclusion

Large-scale land-based investments are happening at an extraordinary pace in Tanzania, and are a reality for many local communities. Many issues need to be tackled to permit realisation of the benefits of land-based investments in the country. Challenges around land investments have made the local communities living around these projects believe that investment is not the goose that lay the golden egg. Much as the government is working hard to attract investors for development, there is a need to learn from the past, be more cautious and ensure that the project objectives are realised at all levels. Local communities and institutional empowerment and participation are equally essential to have profitable land deal discussions and sustainable investment for the benefits of the present and future generations.

Several policy initiatives remain necessary. First, a wide-ranging land use plan is needed in all villages, especially those targeted for investment. Land use plans can help villages know the size of their village land and plan for current and future land use. With a village land use plan, villagers can identify land to be leased to potential

---

[18]See Matondi et al. (2011), for more detailed information.

[19]SIDA recently commissioned a study to investigate on EIA process of Agro Eco Energy.

investors. Second, land has to be given constitutional protection and the constitution should state how land-based investment should be governed. This is the biggest challenge because the current land legal regime, governed by the Land Act and Village Land Act (both of 1999), has centralised power in government. These land laws declare all land in Tanzania as public, vested under the President as the trustee. The laws allow acquisition of any piece of land by the state for public interest, which can be an investment for the public interest. The definition of the term *public interest* has not been clearly defined by these laws. Related to this is that biofuels policy and associated legal framework, which is in harmony with other sector legislations, need to be in place.

Third, compensation should shift from monetary compensation, because money cannot compensate poor people when their land is taken. A partnership approach may be needed whereby a farmer can lease their land to the investor and get a regular income from it. Finally, all land deals need to be entered into transparently. Documents related to the proposed land deals should be made public, contract documents should be written in an accessible language (Swahili) that is widely spoken by most Tanzanians to permit easy understanding of the contents by all parties involved. In addition, local institutions need to build capacity to interact and negotiate better with investors in order to achieve a win-win situation in all land deals.

References

ActionAid. (2009). *Implication of biofuels production on food security in Tanzania.* Available: http://www.actionaidusa.org/sites/files/actionaid/implications_of_biofuels_in_tanzania.pdf http://www.actionaidusa.org/sites/files/actionaid/implications_of_biofuels_in_tanzania.pdf. Retrieved October 19, 2013.

ActionAid. (2011). *Impact of biofuel investment in Kisarawe district.* Available: http://letstalklandtanzania.com/s/download/case_studies/Impact%20of%20Biofuel%20Investment%20in%20Kisarawe%20July%202011.pdf. Retrieved October 19, 2013.

Arndt, C., Pauw, K., & Thurlow, J. (2010). *Biofuels and economic development in Tanzania.* IFPRI Discussion Paper 00966. Available: http://www.ifpri.org/sites/default/files/publications/ifpridp00966.pdf. Retrieved October 18, 2013.

Bergius, M. (2012). *Large scale agro-industrial for biofuel development in Tanzania. Impact on rural households.* Institute of Development Studies. University of Agder.

Biermann, W., & Wagao, J. (1986). The quest for adjustment: Tanzania and the IMF, 1980–1986. *African Studies Review, 29,* 89–103.

BoT (2011) *Tanzania mainland's 50 years of independence: A review of the role and functions of the Bank of Tanzania (1961–2011).* United Republic of Tanzania: Bank of Tanzania.

Collins, P. (1974). Decentralisation and local administration for development in Tanzania. *Africa Today, 21,* 15–25.

Cooksey, B. (2012). *Politics, patronage and projects: The political economy of agricultural policy in Tanzania.* Available: http://www.future-agricultures.org/publications/research-and-analysis/working-papers?start=10#.UUlzQhemjoI. Retrieved October 19, 2013.

Court, D. (1976). The education system as a response to inequality in Tanzania and Kenya. *The Journal of Modern African Studies, 14,* 661–690.

Curtis, M., & Lissu, T. (2008). *A golden opportunity? How Tanzania is failing to benefit from gold mining.* Available: http://www.pambazuka.org/images/articles/407/goldenopp.pdf. Retrieved October 19, 2013.

Curtis, M., Ngowi, P., & Warris, A. (2012). *The one billion dollar question: How can Tanzania stop losing so much tax revenue.* Available: http://www.curtisresearch.org/ONE%20BILLION %20DOLLAR%20QUESTION.Final%20text.%20June%202012.pdf. Retrieved October 19, 2013.

Food and Agricultural Organisation (FAO). (2012). *Trends and impacts of foreign investment in developing country agriculture: Evidence from case studies.* Rome: FAO.

German Technical Cooperation (GTZ). (2005). *A study on liquid biofuels for transportation in Tanzania: Potential and implications for sustainable agriculture and energy in the 21st Century,* August 2005, Tanzania (p. 21).

HAKIARDHI. (2011a). *Accumulation by land dispossession and labour devaluation in Tanzania. A case of biofuel and forest investments in Kilwa and Kilolo.*

HAKIARDHI. (2011b). *Land grabbing in a post investment period and popular reactions in the Rufiji River Basin.*

HAKIARDHI. (2012). *Report of the fact finding mission on the conflict between the Lutukira Mixed Farm Limited and Lutukira villagers in Songea District.*

Kweka, O. L. (2012). On whose interest is the state intervention in biofuel investment in Tanzania? *Cross-Cultural Communication, 8,* 80–85.

Larsson, P. (2006). *The challenging Tanzanian land law reform: A study of the implementation of the village land act.* Royal Institute of Technology. Available: http://www.kth.se/polopoly_fs/ 1.158660!/Menu/general/column-content/attachment/EX-06-160.pdf. Retrieved January 14, 2014.

Lawyers' Environmental Action Team (LEAT). (2011). *Land acquisition for agribusiness in Tanzania: Prospects and challenges.*

Legal and Human Rights Centre (LHRC). (2012). *Human rights and business in Tanzania: Stock taking of labour rights, land rights, environmental justice and consumers' rights protection.*

Locher, M., & Sulle, E. (2013). Foreign land deals in Tanzania: An update and a critical view on the challenges of data (re)production. *LDPI Working Paper 31.* Available: http://www.plaas. org.za/sites/default/files/publications-pdf/LDPI31Locher%26Sulle.pdf. Retrieved January 14, 2014.

Lugalla, J. L. P. (1995). The impact of structural adjustment policies on women's and children's health in Tanzania. *Review of African Political Economy, 22,* 43–53.

Maghimbi, S., Lokina, R. B., & Senga, M. A. (2010). *The agrarian question in Tanzania: A state of the art paper.* Available: http://nai.diva-portal.org/smash/get/diva2:405966/FULLTEXT01. pdf. Retrieved October 19, 2013.

Maina, C. P. (1994). *Foreign investments in Tanzania: The mainland and Zanzibar.* Dar es Salaam: Friedrich Ebert Stiftung.

Maina, C. P., & Mwakaje, S. J. (2004). *Investments in Tanzania: Some comments—some issues.* Dar es Salaam: Friedrich Ebert Stiftung.

Makwarimba, M., & Ngowi, P. (2012). *Making land investment work for Tanzania: Scoping assessment for multi-stakeholder dialogue initiative.* Available: https://s3.amazonaws.com/ landesa_production/resource/381/Makwarimba_Making-Land-Investment-Work-for-Tanzania_2012.pdf?AWSAccessKeyId=AKIAICR3ICC22CMP7DPA&Expires= 1391343922&Signature=WA6UfOpaqMcAovFVO1y94cH92EA%3D. Retrieved October 19, 2013.

Massay, G. (2012). *Energy and food demands, drivers of land grab: A case of Rufiji River Basin in Tanzania.*

Matondi, P. B., Havnevik, K., & Beyene, A. (2011). *Biofuels, land grabbing and food security in Africa.* London: Zed Books.

Meena, R. (1989). Crisis and structural adjustment: Tanzanian women's politics. *A Journal of Opinion, 17,* 29–31.

Mshandete, A. M. (2011). Biofuels in Tanzania: Status, opportunities and challenges. *J. Appl. Biosci., 40,* 2677–2705.

Mtoni, P. E. (2010). *A compensatory framework for sustainable development: the case of Tanzania.* This thesis is submitted in full fulfilment of the requirements for the doctoral degree. Cranfield University.

National Bureau of Statistics. (2009). *Household Budget Survey 2007.* Tanzania Mainland: United Republic of Tanzania.

Nyerere, J. K. (1974). From Uhuru to Ujamaa. *Africa Today, 21,* 3–8.

Oakland Institute. (OI 2011). *Understanding land investment deals in Africa: country report: Tanzania.* Available: http://www.oaklandinstitute.org/sites/oaklandinstitute.org/files/OI_country_report_tanzania.pdf. Retrieved October 19, 2013.

Oakland Institute. (OI 2012). *Understanding land investment deals in Africa: Tanzanian villagers pay for sunbiofuels investment disaster. Land Deal Brief.* Available: http://www.oaklandinstitute.org/sites/oaklandinstitute.org/files/OI_Land_Deals_Brief_Sun_Biofuels.pdf. Retrieved October 19, 2013.

Sosovele, H. (2010). Policy challenges related to biofuel development in Tanzania. *Africa Spectrum, 45,* 117–129.

Sulle, E., & Nelson, F. (2009). *Biofuels, land tenure, and rural livelihoods in Tanzania.* London: International Institute for Environment and Development. Available: http://pubs.iied.org/pdfs/12560IIED.pdf. Retrieved October 19, 2013.

Tsikata, D. (2003). *Securing women's interests within land tenure reforms: Recent debates in Tanzania.* In S. Razavi (Ed.), *Agrarian change, gender and land rights.* Oxford: Blackwell Publishing Ltd.

United Republic of Tanzania. (URT 2012). National climate change strategy. Available: http://tanzania.um.dk/en/ ~ /media/Tanzania/Documents/Environment/TANZANIA%20CLIMATE%20CHANGE%20STRATEGY/TANZANIA%20CLIMATE%20CHANGE%20STRATEGY.pdf.

United Republic of Tanzania (URT). (2011). *Taarifa ya Miaka 50 ya Uhuru wa Tanzania Bara 1961-2011.* Wizara ya Ardhi, Nyumba na Maendeleo ya Makazi: Dar es Salaam.

van Teeffelen, J. (2013). *Fuelling progress or poverty? The EU and Biofuels in Tanzania policy coherence for development in practice.* Available: http://www.fairpolitics.nl/doc/Impact%20Study%20DEF.pdf. Retrieved January 20, 2014.

Veit, P. G., Stickler, M., Schibli, C., & Easton, C. (2012). *Biofuel investments threaten local land rights in Tanzania.* Available: http://www.wri.org/stories/2012/02/biofuel-investments-threaten-local-land-rights-tanzania.Retrieved October 19, 2013.

Accumulation by Dispossession and Resistance in Uganda

Giuliano Martiniello

Introduction

This chapter explores the dynamics of escalating large-scale land acquisitions in Uganda, their impact on the agrarian social structure and their underlying political and social struggles. In so doing, it seeks to shed light on the drivers, agents and implications of large-scale land enclosures, as well as the related social struggles, which have all been amplified by neo-liberalism. It is important to ask 'why' and 'how' land enclosures are occurring in Uganda, while simultaneously inquiring into the ways in which everyday struggles are shaped by, and are shaping, the mechanisms for uneven capitalist development. Framing land struggles at the core of social analysis serve to illuminate the relational character of accumulation, dispossession and resistance.

In the sections that follows, the historical lineages of the tensions that emerge in the case of Uganda will be presented, while underlining the contextual trends, national and international, economic and political, within which land grabs are embedded.

The Political Economy of Land Enclosures in Uganda

Large-scale land enclosures have been a global phenomenon, involving transnational corporations, financial speculators, hedge funds and food insecure countries, voraciously searching for land for a variety of purposes. Sparheaded by converging and mutually reinforcing food, financial and ecological crises, and driven by nar-

G. Martiniello (✉)
Faculty of Agricultural and Food Sciences, American University
of Beirut, P.O. Box 11-0236, Riad El Solh, Beirut 1107 2020, Lebanon
e-mail: gm43@aub.edu.lb

© Springer Nature Singapore Pte Ltd. 2019
S. Moyo et al. (eds.), *Reclaiming Africa*, Advances in African Economic,
Social and Political Development, https://doi.org/10.1007/978-981-10-5840-0_9

ratives of alleged abundance of unutilized, underutilized and 'idle' land, land grabs have predominantly targeted the African continent, with Eastern Africa accounting for the highest number of commercial land deals (White et al. 2012; Friis and Reenberg 2010). Ethiopia, Sudan, Tanzania and Uganda features among the most targeted in terms of the number of land deals and the magnitude of hectares involved. Although sources are themselves problematic and sometimes contradictory, there is a convergence of evidence which reinforces the view that Eastern Africa is one of the main foci of the current wave of land grabbing. The magnitude of land grabbing covered is approximately 2 million ha of land in Uganda, between two and 11 million in Tanzania, between 3 and 5 million in Sudan and about 3.5 million in Ethiopia (Friis and Reenberg 2010: 11).

In Uganda, large-scale commercial land deals represent 14.6% of the national agricultural land (Friis and Reenberg 2010: 12). Land acquisitions in Uganda assume multiple forms and may be intended for the production of food and biofuel; carbon capture schemes and the demarcation of forests, conservation areas and game reserves for tourism; oil and other mineral exploration and extractive activities; or cattle ranching and other commercial agriculture schemes. Land acquisitions may involve state-driven unlawful land deals by domestic elite and high-ranking government and military officials, or deals to the advantage of politically affiliated local capitalists and speculators. Moreover, many of these deals often involve the acquisition of rights of exploitation of water resources, especially in cases where access to abundant water supply is a necessary condition such as in heavily irrigated sugar and palm oil plantations and mining. This has raised concerns with respect to 'water or blue grabs' (Benjaminsen and Bryceson 2012).

The complexity of land enclosures in Uganda emerges through a quick look at the different sources and documents available. The Land Matrix, a public database funded by organizations of the International Land Coalition with an interest in promoting transparency and accountability on land/agricultural deals, reports six medium/large-scale agricultural deals, between 1,000 and 40,000 ha. These mainly involve European companies from the Netherlands, the United Kingdom (UK), Germany and Norway, in the form of joint ventures with the Ugandan government and with the support of major global financial players such as HSBC, the International Finance Corporation and the World Bank. The intent, among others, is to develop commercial timber plantations, mainly pine and eucalyptus trees, as well as to produce palm oil, coffee and sugar for the export market.

Other sources report the involvement of big agri-business companies, such as the AgriSA, the association of South African capitalist-corporate farmers, in large-scale land acquisitions which amount to 170,000 ha (Friis and Reenberg 2010). In 2009, The Ugandan government reportedly leased 840,127 ha, or 2.2% of Uganda's total area, in various parts of the country, to Egypt, so that the Egyptian private sector can produce wheat and meat and export it back to Cairo (Graham et al. 2009). Reports from local NGOs campaigning for social and environmental justice and human rights, such as the Uganda Land Alliance, the National Association of Professional Environmentalists and the Advocates Coalition on Development and the Environment, warn that its extent and diffusion represents a challenge to the social and environmental sustainability of the country. The most stricken areas are especially those located in the central, western and northern regions which historically have been relatively marginal to the colonial political economy and where customary land tenure systems prevail (Martiniello 2015b).

The mushrooming of land grabbing incidents, evictions, localized struggles of resistance are reported daily by media and civil society and community-based organizations: in Mubende, in centre-west Uganda, the UK's NFC and Germany's Neumann Kaffee setting up of coffee plantations determined the eviction of 24,000 people (Graham et al. 2009); Mount Elgon and Luwunga Forest Reserves, the Bukaleeba and Mabira Forest have been, and are, the locus of intense struggles between international afforestation companies, mainly from the UK and Norway and local populations (NAPE 2011); conservation projects supported by the Uganda Wildlife Authority involving the demarcation and enclosure of protected land, let to the displacement of thousands of indigenous and rural populations which depends for their livelihoods on collecting wild fruits and food from the forests (Lyons and Westoby 2014); in Kamwenge, in the west, the government evicted 30,000 people to establish commercial ranching schemes (*The Independent* 2012); in Kalangala, an island on Victoria Lake, the United Nations International Fund for Agricultural Development (IFAD) and the World Bank are actively promoting deforestation and people's displacement by sponsoring the development of palm trees and production of palm oil by BIDCO and Wilmar International (NAPE 2010); in Amuru district, in northern Uganda, the establishment of a sugar plantation on a surface of 10,000 ha by the Madhvani Group, an Asian–Ugandan company, is threatening to evict 20,000 Acholi people (Martiniello 2015b).

We need also to note that dispossession does not occur only through spectacular manifestations which involve influent political and economic actors at national and international levels. It also takes place on a small- and medium scale (Kandel 2015), as a result of the power and wealth imbalances and inequalities emerging among local social classes in the context of neoliberal restructuring of land and agriculture (Martiniello 2015b). Yet, the diversity and plurality of modes of dispossession and the heterogeneity of its manifestations should not detract us from a deeper understanding of its inner causes, social and economic driving forces, political and discursive formations and legal mechanisms.

Starting from the latter, the World Bank, the FAO, IFAD and UNCTAD defined large-scale land acquisitions as a 'development opportunity' and designed a code of conduct for land deals to fulfil such expectations. The guidelines emphasize such principles of responsible agricultural investment (RAI) as transparency, respect for land rights, consultation and promotion of social and environmental sustainability (FAO et al. 2010). Moreover, it is argued that by increasing the rate of commercialization of agriculture—the main objective of the current policies and target of international development institutions and donors—land deals promote infrastructural development and create employment opportunities. The development of land markets is seen as a necessary driver of factor mobility and economic development.

On the other hand, civil society organizations argue that large-scale land acquisitions dramatically impact on local populations and ecosystems, in multiple ways: the destruction of natural habitats, ecosystems, biodiversity and wetlands through monocropping; the increasing use of fertilizers and pesticides; the pollution of Lake Victoria and the decline of fish stocks and associated livelihoods; and the erosion of indigenous knowledge and values, loss of medicinal plants, declining food and water security and rising poverty among displaced rural populations.

Similarly, a growing body of literature has shown that land grabs convert forest lands and areas originally and currently devoted to food production for subsistence and domestic consumption to land for food production for export and biofuel production mainly for export as well as national consumption (Borras and Franco 2012). Land grabs also trigger dynamics of change in, and struggles over, land use and property relations (Borras and Franco 2013), in accordance with the transformation of the world food system and its approximation to a food-for-fuel regime (McMicheal 2010). Moreover, land grabs reinforce linkages between finance, food, and farmland (Clapp 2014; Fairbairn 2014) and propel the crystallization of an agro-imperial pattern of neocolonial exploitation and domination (Petras 2008) in the context of a triple financial, food, and energy crisis. In all, land gabs represent a new scramble for land and natural resources in Africa fuelled by imperialist interests and geopolitical and inter-capitalist rivalries (Moyo et al. 2012). This is a competition not simply within the traditional politico-economic framework structured around the North/South dichotomy, but within a wider geographical spectrum that now includes the BRICS countries (Martiniello 2016).

Land Enclosure as Primitive Accumulation in Uganda: An Historical Perspective

The wave of land enclosures in Uganda represents a form of primitive accumulation, a process in which (state) violence and coercion are used as instruments of appropriation of land and accumulation of capital. This is a process by which people are separated from the means of production and transformed into landless proletarians, in a manner similar to that analysed by Karl Marx in his radical critique of classical political economy. Focusing on the enclosures of sixteenth-century England, Marx revealed the inherently conflictual and violent nature of the development of capitalism, in order to counter the 'idyllic' argument of the harmonious origins of capitalism constructed by Adam Smith in his analysis of 'previous accumulation of stock' (Smith 1776: 277). There is nothing natural in the process of selling labour power as the only means for survival, Marx defended; primitive accumulation 'is written into the annals of mankind in letters of blood and fire' (1858: 669) and is driven by capital's endless drive for accumulation.

Yet there has been a fierce debate as to whether Marx's argument was of historical or logical nature, and whether violence characterized capitalism only in its 'prehistory' or was instead a persistent feature of capital accumulation. Differently from Marx, Rosa Luxembourg made a clear argument according to which capitalism expanded to a non-capitalist social environment that she saw in non-capitalist social stratums in Europe and non-capitalist countries. In her view, capitalism lives by exploiting its non-capitalist periphery at the same time as it destroys it, bringing it within the capitalist economic orbit. By emphasizing the role played by land enclosures in the transition from feudalism to capitalism, the concept of primitive accumulation has been turned by orthodox Marxist interpretations into a corner stone of a monumental 'stage theory', obscuring that this separation occurs continuously, at any time, even within a mature capitalist mode of production, when the conditions for an *ex novo* separation are posited (De Angelis 1999).

Harvey (2003) labelled the resurgence of coercive mechanisms, in their legal, political, and military forms, as constituting a process of 'accumulation by dispossession'. The centrality and persistence of violence and coercion in the contemporary dynamics of capital accumulation, an aspect that, according to Harvey, emanates from the crisis of capital accumulation and discloses the fallacy of the neoliberal ideology, manifests itself concretely in (ibid.: 74):

> [c]ommoditisation and privatization of land and the forceful expulsion of peasant populations, conversions of various forms of property rights, suppression of rights to the commons; commoditization of labour power and the suppression of alternative indigenous forms of production and consumption.

Yet land grabbing is not just an epiphenomenon, nor does it occur in a vacuum. Despite the fact that it involves new practices and a new set of actors, it is the outcome of long-term, historical, and systemic dynamics initiated during colonialism and continued in the post-colonial era. Seen from African peripheries, the deployment of violence and coercion is hardly a novelty, as it represents a structural element in the processes of capital accumulation (Shivji 2009). The current wave of land acquisitions are situated in the long-term consolidation of a transnational agri-business complex, which was propelled by neoliberal economic and political reforms in the country. For land enclosures to take place, a set of legal and political mechanisms, as well as new economic dispositions and social configurations, are necessary. Thus, the neoliberal agricultural and land reforms in Uganda, and the economic and political relationship which they created represents an effort to consolidate agri-business and other agricultural capitalist entrepreneurial classes at the expenses of small-scale rural producers.

The history of primitive accumulation in Uganda can be traced back to 1894 when the logic of inter-imperialist rivalries at the apex of the 'scramble for Africa' led to the proclamation of Uganda as a British protectorate. The violence and coercion of the colonial state deepened the incorporation of the region in the world capitalist economy, expanding upon the prior integration through the capture of peoples as slaves rather than the enclosure of lands (Rodney 1972). The problem that the new colonial state faced was dual: create the preconditions for profitable production and exploitation and setting up the metropolitan state apparatus in a conquered territory. As in India and Natal before, a class of local collaborators had to be carved up from local power structures. This was the dawn of indirect rule in Uganda, a policy implemented through the Buganda Agreement of 1900, which created a class of local notables among the Baganda oligarchy: a landed gentry chosen by, and dependent upon, the colonial masters (Mamdani 1976: 41). This Land Settlement, which parcelled out land throughout the entire hierarchy of Buganda chiefs, involved the recognition of 'occupied' land as belonging to the natives, whereas 'waste and uncultivated' portions would be labelled as Crown Land and made available for sale or lease to incoming settler planters or farmers (Wrigley 1959: 23). The total amount of land allocated among 'tribal' groups was 9,000 square miles, nearly half the supposed total area of the Buganda chiefdom. The redesign of the landholding structure had a profound impact on the class structure of the colony by consolidating the power of the chiefs and transforming them into a class of landlords. These landlords were actually not involved in direct production; rather they represented a *rentier* class extracting rents from a tenant peasantry.

Commodity production for export was to become the main sector around which the structure of the colonial economy was constructed. In 1902, the ties with the world economy were deepened through the completion of the Ugandan railway, which facilitated the circulation of commodities which could now be exported at advantageous costs. Cotton, which better suited the conditions of soil and climate in Uganda, and which was prevalently grown on small plots by peasants alongside British plantation production, became the principal crop in the export sector in the first three decades of the colony. In 1920–21, 81,000 lb of lint were produced in Uganda, of which 85% were grown in the Southern regions (Mamdani 1976: 47). Peasant households embraced cotton production mostly in order to respond to the coercive measures of the colonial government, as well as to find means to pay increasing rents to landlords and taxes to the colonial state. The use of coercion was necessary, moreover, to ensure the supply of cheap labour for the making of roads, the carriage of official stores and other public works. The chronic lack of labour was resolved by making the northern districts the source of cheap migrant labour, not only for planters and municipal works but also for the military forces of the colonial state (Mamdani 1987: 71).

However, the cumulative effect of these multiple coercive measures and demands on peasants was manifested in the crystallization in 1922 of an agitation struggle known as the Bataka movement (Wrigley 1959: 52; Mamdani 1976: 123–124). The struggle movement, which represented the demands of tenants and won strong political support, gained an important political victory, embodied in 1928 in the Basulu and Envujjo Law. The law was passed to entrench tenants' rights, especially the permanency of their tenancy rights, reduce demands on their labour dues (busulu), and, finally, fix tribute on cash crops to 4 sh. (Mafeje 1991: 138–139).

Differently from primitive accumulation in England which resulted in displacement and eviction, in Uganda, in light of the small numbers of incoming settlers and the absence of a massive coercive apparatus, the basis of economic exploitation of the colony was built around the aggregate output of a mass of rural smallholders. Similarly to the 'enclosure model', Uganda's system of protected areas, which began in 1900 with the Buganda Memorandum of Agreement, brought 1,500 square miles of forest under the control of the British Uganda Administration (Himmelfarb 2006). The British justified these large-scale appropriations by claiming that the land was not held privately in the individualized British tenurial manner. Despite long histories of land use, management and cohabitation of African populations in livelihoods and forests, the assumption was that African populations were unable to manage their lands. Throughout subsequent agreements in the Toro, Ankole and Bunyoro regions, the British government assumed control of 'all forest and waste and uncultivated land encompassing many thousands of square miles' (Webster and Osmaston 2003: 125). Neumann (2004) argues that the creation of national parks was one component of the wider process of colonial appropriation of land and natural resources, as well as a symbolic legitimization of that process. Colonial officials re-invented land use histories based on their erroneous assumption that certain areas designated for conservation had no history of human occupation, or that native residents had left no historical ecological imprint. Officials considered traditional patterns of land use to be detrimental to protected ecosystems, thinking that forests existed in their pristine state, rather than being highly anthropogenic, produced by human activities rather than in isolation from them. By categorizing them as threats to protected resources, the colonial state could justify the exclusion of local residents from protected area planning, as well as their forced displacement.

The northern regions instead did not follow the same path. As a marginal, remote geoeconomic area, these regions did not undergo the same kind of changes in the landholding pattern (Atkinson 2010), which prevalently followed customary patterns of land access and use (Girlings 1960). When cotton, in fact, was forcefully introduced into the area in the late 1930s by colonial authorities, it was met by substantial obstructionism. It is common to hear histories in which peasants used to fry cottonseeds before seedling so to simulate soil infertility and involve colonial developers to search for more suitable lands (Isaacman 1990). Moreover, different instances of the 'art of not being governed' (Scott 2009) can be also found in the Lamogi rebellion of 1911, which represented one of the most resilient struggles of contestation of British colonialism in Acholiland. The causes of rebellion, according to Adimola (1954: 169) must be seen in the attempt by British colonial administrators to require and register firearms in possession of Acholi clans as well as in the attempt to recruit forced labour in the form of porters for public services and traders' caravans. The refusal to return firearms was interpreted as an act of open defiance by the colonial authority. Local residents recall that colonial army poisoned the caves' water by generating an escalation of dysentery and diarrhoea on a very large scale. Approximately, 700 people died of dysentery, from bullets or starvation, according to local chiefs, and more than 1,000 were deported and imprisoned, while police reported two deaths and eight wounded officials (ibid.: 175). The movement of resistance, which emerged as an instance of the wider attempt of refutation and contestation of the imposition of colonial authority and its demands in the forms of taxes, forced labour and land requisitions can be seen as a moment in the more complex and long-term confrontation with external political and economic forces, to maintain the political and economic sovereignty and autonomy over a specific geographical territory and social group.

In other cases, movements to more remote areas and exit strategies were undertaken (Tosh 1978). Whereas cotton succeeded, it did not monopolize farming, although it may have played an important part to the social reproduction of the household, as it facilitated colonial taxation and other monetary duties. Nonetheless, it never supplanted food production. Rather, it was integrated within the usual cycle of production, which at its core placed food crops planted in this sequence: millet, pigeon peas, sesame, sorghum and cassava. The work involved was intermittent but hard, plus clearing, planting, singling, four weeding, two or three spraying and picking (Leys 1967: 49). At the same time, the family must have cleared, planted and weeded enough food crops to live on for the next year. Rather than a transition from subsistence to cash crops, Acholi peasants opted for a partial combination of the two, although they gave large priority to food crops (Tosh 1978).

The introduction of cotton enhanced the creation of a minority of 'progressive' medium and large-scale farmers who used to plant it with commercial intents. A group of emergent progressive farmers took up farming for profit often after a period of salaried employment. As late as the end of the 1950s, colonial officials still perceived Acholiland as an area in which the development of commercial enterprise had so far played only a negligible part (Branch 2011: 50). In 1964, after independence, it was estimated that there were 'fewer than ten successful farmers of this kind in Acholi' (Leys 1967: 50). Acholi peasants depended on family labour and had few incentives to produce cash crop surpluses. The result was low cotton production and a small cash economy (Mamdani 1976: 46).

Land and Agriculture in the Post-colonial Era

At the eve of independence in 1962, Uganda's economy was still dependent on subsistence agriculture and export of cash crops, such as cotton, coffee, tea, tobacco and sugar. By replicating and widening the efforts of the colonial state, the post-colonial state developed means to extract surplus produce from peasants through taxes and the establishment of Marketing Boards, which monopolized the purchase of cash crops in the countryside (below international market price) and its sale on international markets. The creation of Cooperative Marketing Boards dates back to the colonial period when the 1946 Ordinance allowed cooperatives to register for the first time (Ahikire et al. 2013). Uganda inherited these cooperatives at independence. Marketing boards and parastatals in Africa were meant to service peasants' input requirements, enforce commodity standards and provide single channel marketing facilities and controlled prices (Bryceson 1999). In this connection, the creation of the East Africa Community, in 1964, placed Uganda at an advantage in accessing outlets for her exports and imports at a cheaper cost (Mukiibi 2001: 201). During the post-independence, in 1962–71, Uganda experienced considerable economic prosperity with a remarkable degree of growth, stability and partial industrialization.

The country was viewed as the most promising economy in Sub-Saharan Africa with an economic growth rate averaged at 4.5%, from 1963 to 71 (Mukiibi 2001: 202). The prices of commodities were relatively stable, the balance of payments was in surplus, the inflation was as low as 10% for that decade, and, most importantly, the country had a very stable foreign exchange rate. Yet, a combination of global oil shocks and worsening terms of trade for agricultural commodities, on one side, and the 1972 expulsion of Ugandans of Asian origin, especially Indian, who controlled much of the plantation and commercial sectors, led to the collapse of the manufacturing and commercial sectors. Conjunctly, the process of erosion of customary land tenure, consolidated by Idi Amin's Land Reform Act of 1975, which claimed all land to be state-owned, aimed to turn peasants into tenants of the state (Mamdani 1987). The Land Reform Act, therefore, erased all the forms of security of tenure that peasants struggles had secured, while simultaneously representing an effort to consolidate state capture of customarily redistributed land. The production of export crops was completely disrupted: coffee shipment declined by 34% between 1976/77 and 1986/89, while cotton fell by 55% and tea production dropped by 70% in 1978–89 (Ngategize and Kayobyo 2001: 205). In the period 1981–83, foreign donors gave Uganda an estimated USD 350 million not only in the form of grants but also, more importantly, in loans, in the effort to revitalize the economy (Mukiibi 2001: 204).

In 1986, President Museveni came to power inheriting an economy tattered by the effects of colonialism and post-colonial mismanagement and insecurity, and with the general population in a state of dire despondency. Under the pressures of international donors, the Ugandan government accepted a market-led reform programme, involving devaluation of the currency, a reduction in budget deficits, liberalization of the marketing system and privatization of many parastatals (Brett 1998: 324). The reforms in the framework of implementation included liberalization of agricultural input trade, liquidation of cooperatives, removal of domestic and export tariff barriers, and, lastly, the abolition of taxes on most agricultural products. In light of these agricultural reforms, the government progressively reduced its public spending in agriculture from 10 to 3.7% between 1980 and 2008/09 (Okello 2009:13). A tiny minority of politically well-connected individuals monopolized the remaining fragments of state support in agriculture, especially in coffee production and other cash crops for export. The National Resistance Movement (NRM) government pledged Shs 60 billion to support agricultural mechanization and agro-processing, as well as Shs 30 billion to establish an agricultural credit facility to be accessed by commercial farmers and agro-processors (ibid.: 15–16).

The privatization of land was to be the first task of Structural Adjustment Programmes (SAPs), which the International Monetary Fund (IMF) and the World Bank demanded. Conditionalities written into these programmes—the shift from food production to export-oriented agriculture, the opening of African lands to foreign investments, the privileging of cash crops over subsistence agriculture— were presumed on the success of a new privatization drive, which was to formalize land tenure through individual titling and registration. In the two decades, the Poverty Eradication Programmes (1997/98–2008/09) and the Plan for Modernization of Agriculture (2001–09) supported enterprise development, agricultural zoning and support to large-scale agriculture. Under the slogan of 'securing food security through the market', the plan increased commercialization of agriculture through diversification and specialization, by abolishing the traditional systems of agricultural extension services and marketing boards, which, although focused on major export cash crops, had reduced price volatility and provided inputs and credits to farmers (Bategka et al. 2013: 2). The stated objective was to increase farmers' income-price by reducing taxation and to establish private marketing agencies. Liberalization of agricultural input trade was another policy recommendation to improve agricultural stagnation in Uganda. Since 1990, the policy has enabled foreign private firms to participate in seed sector and acquire local-based seed companies involved in production, processing and marketing (Lwakuba 2012: 10). Driven by the ideological objective of fostering state withdrawal from economic activities, the goal was to create space for market capitalism with a particular focus on private sector development.

The policy of agricultural liberalization and restructuring, one of the priorities of the SAPs, reinforced processes of social differentiation in the countryside by favouring the thriving of a tiny minority of politically well-connected and commercially oriented medium- and large-scale farmers in Uganda. Income inequality measured through the Gini coefficient increased from 0.365 to 0.408 from 1992 to 2005/2006 and to 0.426 in 2009/10 (Makoba 2011: 48). Furthermore, in northern districts, consumption levels and growth remains below the national average for all but the richer 10% in the rural North (World Bank 2012: 21). These developments led to criticism of a growth trend without development and equity (Makoba 2011: 55–56).

The Contradictions of Land Reforms in a Neoliberal Era

Land privatization was one of the main items on the agenda, whose purpose was to formalize land tenure through individual titling and registration. Land reforms based on 'willing-buyer willing-seller' market logic were framed in a way as to prevent land redistribution. The 1998 Land Act recognized the existence of different land tenure systems: communal, *mailo*, leasehold, and freehold. Land activists and non-governmental organizations (NGOs) welcomed the recognition of customary ownership, incorporated also in the last World Bank vision on land tenure regimes (World Bank 2012). Yet, behind this recognition lies a vehement effort to map and title land and formalize land tenure systems. In fact, the general trend and recent policy efforts have pushed towards the uniformization of the land tenure regimes towards private property (Batungi 2000). In this framework, the value of the property tends to increase upon the issuing of the title. Large landowners and speculators gain immediately from the increased value of property. Small owners of property see no benefit from increased value. By the 1990s, only a small percentage of African communal land had been registered, because small farmers saw no need to register their land, as their access was often already secure though customary land tenure regimes, and because the high fees and taxes required by titling and formalizing land tenure were unaffordable (Bategka et al. 2013). As Mitchell notes, 'the creation of formal legal title and property registration becomes a machinery for transferring property from small owners and concentration it into larger and larger hands' (2005: 29). According to Mamdani (2012), the aim of the 1998 Act to recognize customary land tenure must be seen as the latest phase in the modern state endeavour to colonize society. It is not aimed at protecting customary land, but to target it for immediate control and eventual elimination. The aim of the 1998 Land Act is to expand the logic of 1900 Buganda Agreement to the entire country.

The recently issued land policy document entitled 'Land Reforms: Enhancing Economic Productivity and Commercial Competitiveness for Wealth Creation' (Government of Uganda 2014), elaborated in collaboration with the World Bank, the Ford Foundation, and the National Agricultural Research Unit, has further entrenched existing trends. In its approach, land is considered to be a crucial asset in enhancing competitiveness and productivity and transforming the country from a peasant nation into a middle-income country. In a context where only 5% of the population has land titles, 20% of land is titled, and 80% is communally owned, the document presents a 2040 vision based on a process of titling and property registration intended to enable people use of land and access to credit. The use of land as collateral is further seen as critical for the commercialization of agriculture and exploitation of natural resources. In this scheme of things, the problem is the absence of dynamic markets and reliable information systems to improve the attractiveness of the country to foreign direct investments. As such, the policy proposes forms of decentralized governance, land tax, digitalized cadastral systems, and the elaboration of client charters. The plan foresees the creation of six zonal offices to consolidate the national land information systems and bring land and agriculture to the market. Freehold is considered as the best mode of social organization of land access and use, and as perfect for Northern and Eastern Uganda, which would represent a step further to bring them in the market economy.

The liberal approach anchored in market principles has been vehemently criticized for its inability to re-dress historical landlord–tenant grievances, especially in relation to security of tenure and rent, by maintaining the status quo and favouring absentee landlords (Bategeka et al. 2013). On the other hand, feminist scholars have questioned the notion that women can beneficially participate in, or gain, as a result of formalization of their land rights (Manji 2006; Ossome 2014). This approach interrogates some of the formalist assumptions underlying liberal orthodox policy approaches to women's land rights in Africa, arguing that liberal formulations of the law are limited by a set of silences regarding women's position in the political economy (Ossome 2014). It is important, therefore, to engage in sociocultural analysis of economic relations understanding how this shapes distinct modes of social organization and cultural modes of understanding. It challenges the idea of the efficacy of law in protecting women's right to land, as this is not accompanied by larger contestation in the wider politico-economic and discursive arenas. This entails asking questions about the type of political and economic relations in which land is situated, particularly with reference to relations of inequality—class, ethnicity, gender and age. The question of women's access to land in the context of land commoditization is not simply enhancing the process of class formation, but shaping, reshaping, redefining and transforming pre-existing social and cultural ideas, practices and relations, even as it is shaped by them (Peters 2004).

The notion that individual tenure is the only possible mode of social organization for agricultural production, irrespective of its cultural context and historical peculiarities, may be traced back to a set of presuppositions based on the European historical experience. This recurrent emphasis on law, on the framing of appropriate and conducive legal frameworks, produced the (un)intended consequence of abstracting the debate from land redistribution and land-based social inequities and exclusionary practices in access to land (Manji 2006). These legalistic discourses on land law tenure reforms are, therefore, restricted to the form of land tenure rather than preoccupied with its content, treating land as a thing and neglecting the more salient aspect of land-based social relations. The intrinsically normative character of the analysis, the technicist nature of the debate, the increasing emphasis on the legal architecture, the focus on appearance rather than substance, amounts to a de-politicization of land issues. Global development institutions are framing the debate on the basis of principles, anchored in development economics, which interpret land mainly as an economic asset. This has the effect of abstracting the socially embedded character of land, as well as ignoring the socio-relational, political and cultural character of land (Mafeje 2003: 13; Borras and Franco 2012: 270–71).

Political Responses from Below to Land Enclosures

The attempt by the Ugandan state to dispossess 10,000 ha in Acholiland and lease it to the Madhvani Group, the largest sugar processing company in Uganda, to develop a sugar plantation and processing factory, represents an illuminating entry point in the debates on escalating land enclosures. Behind the appearance of what is termed a 'Private–Public Partnership' the Amuru Sugar Works conceals e profound involvement and investment by the state itself. Although unsuccessful so far, by virtue of communities' resistance to the project, the state deployed its usual arsenal of violence and bribery in an effort to evict the inhabitants and secure the land for the company. The Madhvani land grab is, indeed, characterized by alliances between private capital holders and state violence. The role played by the state is not limited to the creation of the necessary legal and physical infrastructure to attract capital investments through fiscal exemption and preferential land lease. Its action enhances and actively shapes the making of the social conditions that affect markets and their functioning.

Practices of resistance to dispossession emerged vigorously in the context of rampant and protracted attempts at enclosing territories and excluding people. In a context where about 80% of the population survives on agricultural-based livelihoods, the threat of dispossession is leading to a recrudescence of political action across the Amuru district such as women peasants attacking the Madhvani caravan of surveyors and technicians and the Resident District Commissioner upon their attempt to enter the area in Lakang; people in Paboo breaking down boundary makers created by the Uganda Police Defense Force; and persistent skirmishes with game wardens and rangers of the Uganda Wildlife Authority around conservation areas in Apaa. Land with its embedded resources is the most important productive asset to which rural populations have access. Of course, for many of them land is much more than that. It is a way of life, a territory, geographical and symbolic, of huge historical and cultural relevance. Local communities have been mobilizing themselves against persistent attempts at dispossession and displacement.

Notwithstanding government pressures since 2007—President Museveni himself visited the district at least three times in 2012—rural communities in Kololo and Lakang have resurrected and sustained forms of local organization and mobilization and intercommunity solidarity. In April 2012, in order to prevent the initiation of surveying work for the instalment of the sugar plantation by Madhvani representatives and local councillors escorted by soldiers, people organized a demonstration of protest, physically prohibiting them to enter the area. Eighty women took the lead of the protest, while men occupied the second rows with spears. Besides physically opposing the intruders, women undressed themselves as a sign of hunger and displeasure, but also an invitation to respect moral obligations towards women in their reproductive and nurturing capacity. Acts of resistance here occurred at interconnected levels, material and symbolic. Symbolic resistance here reinforces physical resistance by providing it with an ideological justification, a whole of beliefs and social norms embedded in local culture. The response of the government was to increase militarization, by patrolling the area, occupying the local school and checking movements in and out of the communities. Rural communities, which are, of course, internally segmented along class, gender and generational lines, held regular meetings involving the participation of neighbouring clans, dealing with interpretations of the actors and power and developing their own narratives of resistance and measures of permanent alert and tactics.

One of the immediate mobilizing factors among rural social constituencies has been the non-recognition of clan authority over land by the state. Community members and clan leaders claim not having been informed of the government intention to allocate land to Madhvani, nor invited to participate and discuss the terms of the contract. It is not surprising, therefore, that clan leaders are becoming catalysts for struggles of resistance and contestation, as they are considered the paramount authority in land matters. Another related question concerns the reason why this instance of rural social protest has been successful in preventing land dispossession and displacement for affected communities. Five reasons may be identified for its success, even if temporary: the capacity to maintain a relative unity of the community in the face of mounting pressures from within and without to fragment its constituent parts; the ability of 'peasant intellectuals' (Feierman 1990) to articulate views and narratives that framed a common platform of multi-class interests; the successful utilization of inter-elites rivalry and cleavages within structures of authority (state and traditional authorities) and the ability to reach the wider public and mobilize other sympathetic sections of civil society, exploiting the possibilities of the political opportunity framework (Borras and Franco 2013); the combined utilization of non-violent tactics and militant forms of struggle; the extent of the spreading of rural protests in the country which subtracted important terrains of legitimization to state action; and last but not least, the remoteness of the area posed challenges to state rule which might have stimulated what Scott (1975) refers to as 'geographical resistance'.

Acholi peasants have been impoverished by years of forced reclusion in Internally Displaced People camps, due to the decade of military confrontations between the Museveni-led NRM and some rebel formations in the North. Rural populations in Amuru have always been at the margins of commercial agriculture. Indeed, they tend to sell only between 10 and 20% of their agricultural production (Bureau of Statistics 2010a, b) and use the remainder for different forms of consumption, including food, as well as ceremonial and replacement funds (Wolf 1966). In Acholi, moreover, 80% of the population practices shifting cultivation (Atkinson 2008) and the average landholding is 1.8 ha. With an average availability of nearly two hectares per household, peasants are able to produce a basket of food crops, including finger millet, pigeon and cowpeas, sesame, sorghum and cassava, which are aimed at ensuring food self-provisioning, as well as rice, which is partially sold (Bureau of Statistics 2010b).

In Acholi, involvement in national markets is the lowest in the country. The low degree of monetization of economic relationships and the low mobility of factors of production provide another form of resistance to capitalist commodification. This does not mean that peasants could retreat in complete isolation from negative external pressures. Peasants are embedded in powerful and exploitative political, social and economic networks. In this condition, they could still be reached by the squeezing mechanisms of uneven exchange with local merchants and middlemen or through farm-gate prices, but they could still maintain autonomy over the mobilization and use of labour and land, as well as deciding when and what channels to use to market their agricultural surplus. In fact, peasant households switched to the supply of local food markets as these provided avenues for cash income, which were less exploitative than export crops.

In Amuru, where the majority of people access land by means of inheritance (87%) and hold land in customary tenure (98%), and where certificate of customary ownership amounts only to 1.4% and freehold property to 0.4%, commercialization of land seems not to be proceeding as in the rest of the country (Ravnborg et al. 2013: 18–22). Access to labour power is normally secured through family labour or through the *awak* (working groups) at times of clearance and harvest, and only very rarely through hiring within the community. Occasional income is derived from the sale of agricultural produce, generally taken on a bicycle or by renting a wagon, to the nearest market in Amuru. Seeds are generally secured by the labour of women, who at harvest time dedicate energy and care in selecting and storing them.

If we add that 94% of the population does not have access to credit, and that those who do, spend it on non-productive activities, we may conclude that the degree of commoditization of subsistence is almost inexistent. Informal markets, petty trade, petty commodity production, forms of bartering within the community, links of reciprocity and mutuality, and labour cooperation all provide an obstacle to generalized commodity production (Bush 2007). If access to land, labour, credit and product markets is mediated through direct non-monetary ties to other households or classes, and if these ties are reproduced through stable institutional mechanisms, then commodity relations are limited in their ability to penetrate the cycle of reproduction (Friedmann 1980: 163). Village organization and cohesion, maintained through a set of rituals, customs and mores of marriage, reciprocity with neighbours and kinship groups, has allowed for limited penetration of market imperatives, as social reproduction can be enhanced through customary non-market practices.

Grassroots struggles have been increasingly centred on the role of women. As agricultural producers in the communities, they respond to pressure to commodify self-provisioning by attempting to retain control over household assets, such as land, food production, and access to communal resources. As in the past, when cash crop production had marginalized women's authority in household decision-making and put the control of agricultural produce in the hands of men, thereby exacerbating their labour burden, women have struggled to preserve the food security of the households. Women struggle over land, as this represents their system of social security (Federici 2004: 49). Women's loss of access to land, therefore, has less to do with tradition or customary systems of land management than with the pressures resulting from the commercialization of agriculture and the consequent loss of communal land. The pattern of accumulation by dispossession is confronted by communal ownership of resources, as it denies that private property rights are universal in human society (Hall and Fenelon 2003: 174). Women can, indeed, negotiate a better deal of access to land than what would be left to them in a system of private property rights, as their tiny purchasing power does not allow them to access land through the markets. For women, struggles over land are more important than struggles over law.

Social struggles around land, in this case, has changed or narrowed the policy option available to the state and surplus appropriators of various types. As Scott has argued (1985: 36), it is in this fashion, and not through revolts, let alone legal pressure, that the peasantry has classically made its political presence felt. These insights advance the deepening of our understanding of peasant agency in land and agrarian struggles. Debates over the relationship between struggles over social relations of production and social reproduction, and those over forms of political consciousness are, however, beyond the scope of this study. For what concerns the line of argument of this chapter, the two moments of resistance, hidden or open, daily or occasional, work as a continuum of social struggles whose form changes as conditions to which they respond to change. The emergence of episodes of open rebellion lays on a substratum of everyday social struggles. Making recourse to more violent and manifest forms of physical or symbolic resistance signals that the largely covert forms of struggle are failing, or have reached a crisis point which does not allow them to be effective against new challenges that emerge. Such declaration of open war normally comes only after a protracted struggle on a different terrain.

Conclusions

This chapter explored the character and origins of proliferating capitalist land enclosures and the recrudescence of rural social struggles in Uganda. It showed that by challenging the attempts by the state and agri-business to transform peasants into rural landless, underpaid, and overexploited agricultural labourers, or as subordinate and dependent out-growers, Acholi rural populations have been engaged in a long-term struggle against the commodification of land. They are also struggling to maintain relative autonomy over the mobilization of family labour and access to communal resources. These insights into the agricultural social reproduction strategies of Acholi peasants illuminate the dual character of contemporary social struggles, which embody and manifest both political and socio-economic strategies diachronically and synchronically. Although social struggles can be expressed through protests and land occupations, they are also manifested in the everyday efforts at the household level to ensure social reproduction and the improvement of available resources through constant adaptations in a context of increased politico-economic and ecological pressures. These localized struggles illuminate the different geographies and patterns of commoditization and allow us to recognize the existence of multiple practices of resistance and the necessary synergies between different *loci* of struggle.

References

Adimola, A. B. (1954). The Lamogi rebellion. *Uganda Journal, 18*(2), 166–177.
Ahikire, J., Kafureeka, L., & Murari-Muhwezi, M. (2013). *The cooperative movement and the challenges of development: A search for alternative wealth creation and citizen vitality approaches in Uganda*. Kampala: Action Aid, CBR and the Uhuru Institute.
Atkinson, R. (2008). Land issues in Acholi in the transition from war to peace. *The Examiner, 4*, 3–25.
Atkinson, R. R. (2010). *The roots of ethnicity: Origins of the Acholi of Uganda before 1800*. Kampala: Fountain Publishers.
Bategeka, L., Kiiza, J., & Kasirye, I. (2013). Institutional constraints to agriculture development in Uganda. Research Series, No. 100. Kampala: Economic Policy Research Centre.
Batungi, N. (2000). *Land reform in Uganda: Towards an harmonised tenure system*. Kampala: Fountain Publishers.

Benjaminsen, T. A., & Bryceson, I. (2012). Conservation, green/blue grabbing and accumulation by dispossession in Tanzania. *Journal of Peasant Studies, 39*(2), 335–355.

Borras, J. S., & Franco, J. (2012). Global land grabbing and trajectories of agrarian change: A preliminary analysis. *Journal of Agrarian Change, 12*(1), 34–59.

Borras, J. S., & Franco, J. (2013). Global land grabbing and political reactions from below. *Third World Quarterly, 34*(9), 1723–1747.

Branch, A. (2011). *Displacing human rights: War and intervention in northern Uganda*. Oxford: Oxford University Press.

Brett, E. A. (1998). Responding to poverty in Uganda: Structures, policies and prospects. *Journal of International Affairs, 52*(1), 313–337.

Bryceson, D. (1999). African rural labour, income diversification and livelihood approaches: A long term development perspective. *Review of African Political Economy, 80,* 171–189.

Bush, R. (2007). *Poverty and neoliberalism: Persistence and reproduction in the global south.* London: Pluto Press.

Clapp, J. (2014). Financialization, distance and global food politics. *Journal of Peasant Studies, 41*(5), 797–814. (Special issue on 'Global Agrarian transformation, Vol. 1: New directions in political economy').

De Angelis, M. (1999). *Marx's theory of primitive accumulation: A suggested reinterpretation.* Working paper no. 29, available at University of East London, Department of Economics. https://www.researchgate.net/publication/266446934_Marx's_Theory_of_Primitive_ Accumulation_A_Suggested_Reinterpretation. Retrieved July 19, 2017.

Fairbairn, M. (2014). Like gold with yield: Evolving intersections between farmland and finance. *Journal of Peasant Studies, 41*(5), 777–795. (Special issue on 'Global Agrarian transformation, Vol. 1: New directions in political economy).

FAO, Ifad, UNCTAD and World Bank. (2010). *Principles for responsible agricultural investments that respect rights, livelihoods and resources.* Washington, DC: World Bank.

Federici, S. (2004). Women land struggles and the reconstruction of the commons. *The Journal of Labour and Society, 14,* 41–56.

Feierman, S. (1990). *Peasant intellectuals: Anthropology and history in Tanzania.* Madison, WI: University of Wisconsin.

Friedmann, H. (1980). Household production and the national economy: Concepts for the analysis of agrarian formations. *Journal of Peasant Studies, 7*(2), 158–184.

Friis, C., & Reenberg, A. (2010). *Land grab in Africa: Emerging land system drivers in a teleconnected world* (GLP Report No. 1). Copenhagen: GLP-IPO.

Girlings, F. (1960). *The Acholi of Uganda.* London: Her Majesty Stationery Office.

Government of Uganda (2014). *Land reforms: Enhancing economic productivity and commercial competitiveness for wealth creation.* Kampala: Ministry of Lands, Housing and Urban Development.

Graham, A., Aubry, S., Kunnemann, R., & Monsalve Suarez, S. (2009). *Land grab study. CSO Monitoring 2009–2010 on advancing African agriculture (AAA): The impact of Europe's policies and practices on African agriculture and food security.* Heidelberg: FIAN.

Hall, T. D., & Fenelon, J. (2003). Indigenous resistance to globalization: What does the future hold. In W. A. Dunaway (Ed.), *Emerging issues in the 21st century world system: Crises and resistance in the 21st century world system.* Westport, CT: Praeger.

Harvey, D. (2003). *The new imperialism.* Oxford: Oxford University Press.

Himmelfarb, D. (2006). Moving people, moving boundaries: The socio-economic effects of protectionist conservation, involuntary resettlement and tenure insecurity on the edge of Mt. Elgon national park, Uganda. In *Agroforestry in landscape mosaics working paper series.* World Agroforestry Centre. http://www.worldagroforestry.org/programmes/african-highlands/ pdfs/wps/ahiwp_24.pdf. Retrieved June 19, 2017.

Isaacman, A. (1990). Peasants and rural social protest in Africa. *African Studies Review, 33,* 1–120.

Kandel, M. (2015). Politics from below? Small-, mid- and large-scale land dispossession in Teso, Uganda, and the relevance of scale. *The Journal of Peasant Studies, 42*(3–4), 635–652.

Leys, C. (1967). *Politicians and policies: An essay on politics in Acholi Uganda, 1962–65.* Nairobi: East Africa Publishing House.

Lwakuba, A. (2012). *The seed sector of Uganda: Is the future of the small-scale farmers bleak or bright.* Kampala: PELUM MISEREOR.

Lyons, K., & Westoby, P. (2014). Carbon colonialism and the new land grab: Plantation forestry in Uganda and its livelihood impacts. *Journal of Rural Studies, 36,* 13–21.

Mafeje, A. (1991). *The theory and ethnography of African social formations: The case of interlacustrine kingdoms.* London: Codesria Book Series.

Mafeje, A. (2003). *The agrarian question, access to land and peasant responses in sub-Saharan Africa.* Geneva: United Nations Research Institute for Social Development.

Makoba, J. W. (2011). *Rethinking development strategies in Africa: The triple partnership as an alternative approach—The case of Uganda.* Bern: Peter Lang.

Mamdani, M. (1976). *Politics and class formation in Uganda.* New York, NY and London: Monthly Review Press.

Mamdani, M. (1987). Extreme but not exceptional: Towards an analysis of the agrarian question in Uganda. *Journal of Peasant Studies, 14*(2), 191–225.

Mamdani, M. (2012). *The contemporary Ugandan discourse on customary tenure: Some historical and theoretical considerations.* Paper presented at the workshop on 'The Land Question: Socialism, Capitalism and the Market', Makerere Institute of Social Research, Kampala, August 9–10.

Manji, A. (2006). *The politics of land reform in Africa: From communal tenure to free markets.* London: Zed Books.

Martiniello, G. (2015a). Food sovereignty as a praxis? Rethinking the food question in Uganda. *Third World Quarterly, 36*(3), 508–525. (Special issue on 'Food sovereignty: Convergence and contradictions, condition and challenges').

Martiniello, G. (2015b). Social struggles in Uganda's Acholiland: Understanding responses and resistance to Amuru sugar works. *Journal of Peasant Studies, 42*(3–4), 653–669. (Special issue on 'Land grabs and politics from below').

Martiniello, G. (2016). 'Don't stop the mill': South African capital and agrarian change in Tanzania. *Third World Thematics: A TWQ Journal,* 1–20. http://dx.doi.org/10.1080/23802014.2016.1243017 (online).

McMicheal, P. (2010). Agrofuels in the food regime. *Journal of Peasant Studies, 37,* 609–629.

Moyo, S., Yeros, P., & Jha, P. (2012). Imperialism and primitive accumulation: Notes on the new scramble for Africa. *Agrarian South: Journal of Political Economy, 1*(2), 181–203.

Mukiibi, J. K. (2001). *Agriculture in Uganda* (Vol. 1). Kampala: Fountain Publishers.

NAPE [National Association of Professional Environmentalists] (2010). A case study of World Bank investments in agribusiness in Uganda.

NAPE [National Association of Professional Environmentalists] (2011). A study on land grabbing cases in Uganda.

Neumann, R. (2004). Nature-state-territory: Toward a critical theorization of conservation enclosures. In M. Watts & R. Peet (Eds.), *Liberation ecologies: Environment, development, social movements* (2nd ed., pp. 195–217). London: Routledge.

Ngategize, P. K., & Kayobyo, G. (2001). Agricultural marketing. In J. K. Mukiibi (Ed.), *Agriculture in Uganda.* Kampala: Fountain Publishers.

Okello, O. A. C. (2009). *Opposition response to the government budget statement FY 2009/10.* Presented by A. C. Okoman & M. P. Okello. (FDC).

Ossome, L. (2014). Can the law secure women's right to land in Africa? Revisiting tensions between culture and land commercialization. *Feminist Economics, 20*(1), 157–177. https://doi.org/10.1080/13545701.2013.876506.

Peters, P. (2004). Inequality and social conflict over land in Africa. *Journal of Agrarian Change, 4*(3), 269–314.

Petras, J. (2008). The great land giveaway: Neocolonialism by invitation. *Global Research, 1.* http://www.globalresearch.ca/the-great-land-giveaway-neo-colonialism-by-invitation/11231. Retrieved July 19, 2017.

Ravnborg, H. M., Bashaasha, B., Pedersen, R. H., Spichiger, R., & Turinawe, A. (2013). *Land tenure under transition: Tenure security, land institutions and economic activity in Uganda.* Copenhagen: Danish Institute for International Studies.

Rodney, W. (1972). *How Europe underdeveloped Africa.* Dar es Salaam: Tanzania Publishing House.

Scott, J. (1975). *The moral economy of the peasant.* New Haven, CT: Yale University Press.

Scott, J. C. (1985). *Weapons of the weak: Everyday forms of peasant resistance.* New Heaven, CT and London: Yale University Press.

Scott, J. (2009) *The art of not being governed: An anarchist history of upland Southeast Asia.* New Heaven, CT and London: Yale University Press.

Shivji, I. (2009). *Accumulation in an African periphery.* Dar es Salaam: Mkuki na Nyota Publishers.

Smith, A. (1776). *An enquiry into the nature and causes of the wealth of nations.* New York, NY: Oxford University Press.

The Independent (2012). Uganda: Museveni angry over ngo report on land grabbing. May 6.

Tosh, J. (1978). Lango agriculture during the early colonial period: Land and labour in a cash crop economy. *Journal of African History, 19*(3), 415–439.

Uganda Bureau of Statistics (2010a). *Uganda census of agriculture: Agricultural household and holding characteristics report* (Vol. III). Kampala: Ministry of Agriculture, Animal Industry and Fisheries.

Uganda Bureau of Statistics (2010b). *Uganda census of agriculture: Crop area and production report* (Vol. IV). Kampala: Ministry of Agriculture, Animal Industry and Fisheries.

Webster, G., & Osmaston, H. A. (2003). *A history of the Uganda forest department.* London: Commonwealth Secretariat.

White, B., Borras, S. M. Jr, Hall, R., Scoones, I., & Wolford, W. (2012). The new enclosures: critical perspectives on corporate land deals. *Journal of Peasant Studies, 39*(3–4), 619–647.

Wolf, E. (1966). *Peasants.* Englewoods Cliffs: Prentice-Hall.

World Bank. (2012). *Uganda: Promoting inclusive growth.* Washington, DC: World Bank.

Wrigley, C. C. (1959). *Crops and wealth in Uganda.* Kampala: East African Institute of Social Research.

Customary Land in Zambia: The New Scramble and the Evolving Socio-political Relations

Horman Chitonge

Introduction

Land is a key asset for the majority of people in Africa and the Global South in general, especially in rural areas. The Zambian Land Administration and Management Draft Policy (Draft Land Policy 2006) makes this clear by recognising that land is the 'greatest resource' that the country has, and that land resources (which includes minerals, water, forest and wildlife) are at the centre of all economic activities and development.[1] In the Zambian context, the importance of land lies in the fact that the majority of the population (82%), and 95% of the rural population, derive their livelihood directly from land-related activities (CSO 2011). Over the last two decades, the demand for land has increased due to various reasons including population growth, the growing global interest in farmland and also the government development strategy of 'opening up the countryside' for development, which have created pressure on the available land resources, especially in areas with developed economic and social infrastructure. While the global media have focused on the foreign acquisition of farmland by various groups of investors, including sovereign wealth funds, foreign governments and multinational corporations (Cotula 2011), there is now emerging evidence that the growing middle class are also acquiring considerable amounts of land, targeting customary land, and it has been suggested that the total land acquired by local investors is actually larger than what has been acquired by foreign investors (Honig and Mulenga 2015; Brown 2005).

---

[1]There is a more recent draft policy on land which was circulated at the beginning of 2016 for comments, but has not yet been finalised.

H. Chitonge (✉)
Centre for African Studies, University of Cape Town, Rondebosch,
Cape Town 7701, South Africa
e-mail: Horman.Chitonge@uct.ac.za

© Springer Nature Singapore Pte Ltd. 2019
S. Moyo et al. (eds.), *Reclaiming Africa*, Advances in African Economic,
Social and Political Development, https://doi.org/10.1007/978-981-10-5840-0_10

This growing demand for land, in more recent years, has created pressure which is now directed towards customary land, largely as result of the policy and practice of converting customary land into leasehold tenure (Chitonge 2015; Kabilika 2010; USAID 2010; Brown 2005).[2] The conversion of customary land, which is part of the broader land grabbing trend supported by the government, is creating many challenges within the Zambian agrarian setting. Conversion of customary land into leasehold tenure may appear as a genuine attempt by the state to stimulate rural development, but a close analysis of the situation suggests a deep-seated struggle for the control of resources between the state and the traditional authorities, resulting in tension and conflicts in rural and peri-urban communities. This chapter discusses some of these challenges locating them in the broader social, political and economic relations which this practice is engendering. It is argued here that the policy and practice of converting customary land into leasehold title has introduced an open contest for land and other resources, thereby compromising the current and future livelihoods of the rural poor, and promotes social segregation in the countryside. Conversion of customary land into leasehold tenure is broadly analysed in the context of large-scale land acquisitions occurring in the country and the various social and political processes which trigger this development.

The paper is divided into five sections. The first section provides the background to the current land tenure policy and legal framework. The second section briefly addresses the question of land availability in Zambia against the claims that Zambia is a land-surplus country with large tracks of empty land which are not being utilised or are under-utilised. The third section looks at the current policy and practice of converting customary land into leasehold tenure. The fourth section draws out some of the socio-political and economic implications of converting customary land into leasehold tenure; this section also identifies some of the drivers of the practice of converting customary land. The final section offers some concluding remarks.

Land Policy and Tenure Reforms in Zambia

Since the introduction of colonial rule, the land tenure and administration systems in Zambia have gone through three main phases, to which I refer here as bifurcation, nationalisation, and privatisation and consolidation.

---

[2]Although there are no official figures on how much customary land has so far been converted into state land (leasehold), available estimates suggest that conversion has been widespread since 1995 (USAID 2010: 4; Honig and Mulenga 2015).

Bifurcation

The first phase, which started in 1924, when Zambia became a British Protectorate, resulted in all land (except Barotseland,[3] currently Western Province) being transferred from the British South African Company (BSA Co.) to the British government under the Northern Rhodesia colonial administration.[4] Following this agreement with the BSA Co., the Northern Rhodesia Government, in 1928, through the *Northern Rhodesia (Crown and Native Lands) Order in Council 1928–1963*, reserved fertile land along the line of rail, from Livingstone to the Copperbelt, for European settlers. This land was designated 'crown land' and was administered separately from 'reserve land'—reserved for indigenous people. Indigenous people who were living on the land that was classified 'crown land' were forcibly removed and resettled on land which was often less fertile and infested with tsetse flies (Draft Land Policy 2006: 3). This effectively created a dual tenure system, whereby crown land was administered through English Common Law, while reserve land was administered under customary law (Bruce and Dorner 1982; Roth et al. 1995; Adams 2003). In addition to crown and reserve land, there was a category of 'unclassified land', part of which was later used to create 'trust land' in 1947, the remainder being classified later as 'silent land' (Bruce and Dorner 1982: 5). Compared to settler colonies such as Zimbabwe, South Africa, Kenya, Algeria and Namibia, relatively small amounts of land were grabbed from the indigenous people. Crown land constituted six percent (about 4.5 million ha), while land for indigenous people accounted for the remaining 94%, including reserve lands (27.2 million ha) and trust lands (43.3 million ha). To a large extent, the current land tenure system in Zambia, as in many other African countries, has failed to decolonise this tenure system, perpetuating the dualism in land administration (Adams and Palmer 2007; Bruce and Migot-Adholla 1994), with customary tenure perceived as insecure, with unclear rights. Failure to transform the colonial agrarian structure is probably more apparent in Zambia than elsewhere on the continent; as the Draft Land Policy (2006: 3–4) states:

> [t]he attainment of independence did not radically change the administration of land. The areas that were designated as reserves and trust land remained so designated and controlled by the same rules (Orders-in-Council).... [I]n effect the designation still exists, though the land is collectively now referred to as customary areas. This is the way in which Zambia's colonial legacy created the conditions for persistent subsistence production and poverty in rural areas.

---

[3]Although Barotseland became a British Protectorate, it retained autonomy over the administration of land under the Lozi paramount Chief Lewanika as stipulated in the 1898 Barotse Agreement between Lewanika and John Cecil Rhodes; see Bruce and Dorner (1982).

[4]The BSA Co. was a chartered company that administered Northern Rhodesia on behalf of the British Government from 1889 to 1924.

Nationalisation of Land

The second phase of land tenure and administration reforms began after independence, culminating in the *Land (Conversion of Title)* Act No. 20 of 1975. Some of the key changes introduced by the Land Act include the nationalisation of land, which cancelled all freehold titles and vested all land, including reserve and trust lands, in the Head of State. The other notable reforms include the decommodification of land, by placing a moratorium on the sale of undeveloped land which was deemed to have no value (Chizyuka et al. 2006; Adams 2003). It seems that these measures were introduced to curb speculation in land (Draft Land Policy 2006), and to promote equitable access to land and prevent alienation of land, particularly customary land, for individual gain at the expense of the community (ZLA 2008). However, these reforms did little to change the dual nature of land tenure in Zambia, which ironically was introduced for the purposes of promoting the interest of European settlers (Chizyuka et al. 2006: 6). Even if freehold titles were abolished and the sale of undeveloped land prohibited, land continued to be administered through two systems: state land (former crown land) was administered under statutory law, while reserve and trust lands were administered under customary law.

Privatisation and Consolidation

The third phase, which actually started in 1985, culminated in the enactment of the controversial Lands Act No. 29 of 1995, which repealed the 1975 Land Act and other earlier pieces of legislation.[5] Although the 1995 Lands Act retained several provisions—vesting of the land in the Head of State (Section 3(I)), the abolishment of freehold title (Sections 6 and 10(1)), the requirement for presidential consent with regard to the transfer of any piece of land (Section 5(1)) and the maximum limit for leasehold of 99 years (Section 6)—it introduced some new reforms. One of the major changes introduced includes the combination of trust and reserve lands to create one category called 'customary land'. Perhaps, the most important reform was the provision that allows for the conversion of customary land into leasehold tenure. Section 8(1) states that '... any person who holds land under customary tenure may convert it into leasehold tenure not exceeding ninety-nine years on application ...'.

Under the current policy and legal framework, any person (local or foreign) who obtains the consent of a traditional leader and local councillor can convert customary land into leasehold tenure. The crucial point here is that once customary

---

[5]The 1995 Lands Act was widely opposed by many Zambians, but the Movement for Multiparty Democracy (MMD) government ignored public concerns and passed the bill, using its two-thirds majority advantage (ZLA 2002; Adams 2003; USAID 2010; CAL 2009).

land is converted into leasehold, it does not revert back to customary land after expiry or cancellation of the lease (Adams 2003; Mudenda 2006; Kabilika 2010; Honig and Mulenga 2015). Unlike in countries such as Tanzania, Botswana and Ghana, where leases are issued on customary land, in Zambia the state promotes the conversion of customary land into leasehold tenure even in cases where there is no expressed private interest in the land (German et al. 2011); and once the land is converted, it permanently becomes state land.

This phase of agrarian transformation in Zambia effectively leads to the consolidation of state control over land through privatisation of customary land. This is one of the reasons why the state is actively pushing for the 'opening up' of customary land to investors in the name of bringing development to rural areas. The other reason is the need to increase state revenue through land rent which is paid on any leased piece of land. Of course, many traditional leaders are realising that they are losing control over land and, subsequently, power, and some have opposed these policies and practices (Kanyanta 2014). This has resulted in tensions and open confrontation with councillors (Brown 2005), Ministry of Lands' officials (Mudenda 2006) and local communities (FSRP 2010).[6]

The three phases of agrarian reforms outlined above should be seen in the broader political and economic context that underpins each phase. During colonial rule, dispossession of indigenous people of their land (first order land grabbing) was a common practice by most imperialist governments, especially in Southern Africa (Moyo 2010; Mafeje 2003). Although the magnitude of dispossession of indigenous populations differs in different countries in the region, displacement of indigenous people from fertile land was a common political and economic strategy.

Post-colonial African governments, in such countries as Zambia, Tanzania, Mozambique, Ghana and Angola, nationalised land. Nationalisation of land was seen as a way of promoting equal access to land, preventing speculation in land and the privatisation of common resources, enhancing social cohesion and promoting collective, as opposed to private, ownership (Kabilika 2010: 9; ZLA 2002). But in Zambia, this policy was soon replaced with the policy of privatisation (including land), starting from the 1980s with the onset of Structural Adjustment Programmes (SAPs) sponsored by international financial institutions, mainly the Word Bank and the International Monetary Fund (Moyo 2010).

In Zambia, the privatisation of land, which was formalised by the 1995 Lands Act, has also to be located in the dominant political and economic ideology of the time. Although the implementation of the SAPs was reluctantly started by the Kaunda government (Fundanga and Mwaba 1996), a full-scale liberalisation policy was implemented by the Movement for Multiparty Democracy (MMD) in 1992, as promised in the party's election manifesto (Simutanyi 1996; CAL 2009). The commitment of the MMD government to the liberalisation programme is evident in

---

[6]It must be noted here that it is not only the state that is promoting land alienation but some traditional leaders are actively engaging in land deals, which has created conflict in communities between the people and traditional leaders (Sitko 2010).

the scale of privatisation after 1992, but also in the policies that covered almost all sectors of society, including water services. The MMD's commitment to liberalisation is also clear from the address of the MMD President to the donor community in Lusaka, just after the 1991 elections: '[a]s far as the privatisation programme is concerned there is no sacred lamb. In other words, the government is committed to total privatisation of the parastatal sector' (quoted in Fundanga and Mwaba 1996: 7).

Land Resources in Zambia: How Much Land Is Available?

As noted above, there is a widespread perception that Zambia is a land-surplus country. For example, a prominent member of the Zambia National Farmers Union (ZNFU) once referred to Zambia as 'the empty country' because 'our country has vast areas of unused land' (Hudson 2007: 4). Similarly, the former Minister of Agriculture and Cooperatives, Dr. Brian Chituwo, in a media briefing on the sidelines of the World Economic Forum on Africa, in Cape Town, in 2009, told Reuters that, '[w]e have well over 30 million ha of land that is begging to be utilised. We are utilising only an estimated 14% of our land'; and referring specifically to land for growing sugarcane, Dr. Chituwo claimed that, 'we have 900,000 ha of prime land available, so the issue of land really should not be a problem. It is just a question of the mechanics of implementing this'.[7]

On this basis, the Zambian government, embarked on a campaign in the 2000s aiming to 'open up the countryside' to investment. However, there has been no updated data on how much land is available and for what purpose (Mudenda 2006; FSRP 2010). It is not clear whether the land to which such claims refer is occupied or not. What is clear is that state land has already been titled and allocated to commercial farms and urban development (Chizyuka et al. 2006: 5). This is why the state has 'considerable interest in conversion of customary land to leasehold tenure' (Draft Land Policy 2006: 14). Thus, it is apparent that the claims about unused land in Zambia refer to customary land.

However, evidence from the post-harvest survey of the Central Statistical Organisation (CSO) suggests that 'in many customary areas, unallocated land appears to be unavailable, particularly in areas close to urban areas, district towns and along major highways' (FSRP 2010: 3). Submissions made to the Parliamentary Committee on Agriculture and Land (CAL 2009) highlight the fact that land which is effectively under customary control has significantly shrunk over the past decades. A recent study also makes a similar observation, noting that land constraints are becoming common in many customary areas (Hichaambwa and Jayne 2014). A rough estimate of the share of different categories of land over time (Table 1), which excludes state land (which has been exhausted), the new and old

---

[7]See 'US, UAE firms eye Zambian farming land' (Reuters Africa, 12 June 2009), http://af.reuters.com/article/investingNews/idAFJOE55B0MB20090612, accessed on 28 June 2017.

Table 1 Estimates of different categories of land in Zambia, 1964–2010 (million ha)

Land category		1964	1975	2006	2010
State	A	4.5 (6)	4.5	9 (12)	15 (20)[c, a]
Reserve	B	27.2 (36.2)	27.2	N/A	N/A
Trust	C	43.3 (57.7)	43.3	N/A	N/A
Customary	B + C	70.5 (93.9)	70.5	32.8 (43.7)[b]	27.8 (37)[c]
Forest reserve	E	9 (12)	9	7 (9)[b]	7[b]
Game and nat. parks	F	13.8 (18.4)	13.8	13.8	13.8
Lake area	G	9 (12)	9	9	9
Urban		–	–	1.5 (2)	1.5
Arable		–	–	30.5 (40.6)	30.5
Agricultural		–	–	23.4 (31.1	23.4
Protected area	E + F + G	31.8 (42)	31.8	29.8	29.8 (40)[c]

Source Own calculation based on data from Chizyuka et al. (2006), Adams (2003), ILUA (2008), CAL (2009) and FAOstats figures for 2011 (www.faostats.org)
Note [–] Indicates no data available; figures in brackets are percentages
[a]Includes land under the farm block scheme
[b]Own estimates based on available data. The land effectively under customary control in 2006 was estimated based on the assumption that 10% of customary land had been converted to state land between 1985 and 2006 (USAID 2010; Chizyuka et al. 2006). Other estimates that include reserved lands under customary land are at 60% (see Honig and Mulenga 2015)
[c]Estimates based on figures from the Parliamentary Committee on Agriculture and Land (CAL 2009)
The figure for land under forest reserve in 2006 is estimated based on the assumption that deforestation has been taking place at the rate of 1% per annum, as per figures for arable and agricultural land for 2009, provided by FAOstats (www.faostats.org)

farm blocks, plus protected areas (administered and regulated by statutory bodies), suggests that current land under customary control is much smaller than the amount claimed by the outdated figures used to present Zambia as a land-surplus country.

Although official figures often cite 94% (or 71.5 million ha) as the proportion of land under customary tenure (Draft Land Policy 2006; Chizyuka et al. 2006), this figure is based on data from the 1970s and does not take into account customary land that has been converted into state land since 1985, including the land carved out for the farm block schemes. If the figures in Table 1 are anything to go by, the rate at which customary land is being alienated is indeed worrying. Between 2005 and 2010, almost 20% of customary land was converted into state land, with the latter increasing by more than 67% over the same period. At this rate, the call by the Parliamentary Committee on Agriculture and Land 'for Zambia to be more cautious when converting customary land to leasehold' (CAL 2009: 12), must be taken seriously. Although there has been no national land audit, submissions to Parliamentary Committee on Agriculture and Lands (CAL 2009) suggest that land effectively under customary tenure is much lower than the often quoted figure of 94%.

Table 2 Farm blocks in Zambia

Name	Size ('000 ha)	District	Province	Status
Kalumwange	100	Kaoma	Western	Proposal
Luena FB	100	Kawambwa	Luapula	Proposal
Manshya	147	Mpika	Northern	Proposal
Mikelenge	100	Solwezi	Noth-western	Proposal
Mungu	65	Kafue	Lusaka	Proposal
Musakashi	100	Mufulira	Copperbelt	Exploration
Mwase-Phangwe	100	Lundazi	Eastern	Proposal
Nansanga	100	Serenje	Central	Exploration
Senanga Citri	1.2	Senanga	Western	Proposal
Simango	100	Livingstone	Southern	Proposal
Total	913.2			

Source Zambia Development Agency (2010)
Note The different documents come up with different names and sizes of the proposed farm blocks. The figures here are taken from the most recent report

After accounting for state lands, commercial farms, wetlands, game management areas, national parks and the proposed farm block schemes, it becomes clear that the potential for expansion of customary farmland is not as great as commonly perceived. In addition, leasehold land has continued to increase in size (owing to the conversion of customary land to leasehold tenure), which leaves only an estimated 37% as customary land controlled by traditional leaders (CAL 2009: 12).

From Table 1, it is clear that a large proportion of the land which is often perceived to be under customary control is under protected areas, and this land is not available for use unless one has explicit permission from relevant authorities (ILUA 2008). If one excludes protected areas from land in customary areas, it is clear that land under customary control has often been overestimated. It is also clear that land pressure is expected in customary areas that are closer to the line of rail, where better infrastructure, since colonial times, has made the land more attractive to investors. Land away from the developed infrastructure and means of communication has low economic value, because such land cannot support commercially oriented activities (CAL 2009).[8] Farm blocks which are located away from the main communication lines have failed to attract investments (Deininger et al. 2011).

Creation of farm blocks, together with increasing large-scale land acquisition, has created more pressure on customary land, with many chiefs reporting that there is no more land left to allocate to local people. Considering the ten farm blocks created (Table 2), a total of nearly one million hectares of fertile land has been

---

[8]There are reports that most of the investors are actually refusing land far away from developed infrastructure and preferring land which is closer to communication facilities, mainly rail and road routes (German et al. 2011).

alienated from customary land since 2004, when the farm block scheme started, although most of the farm blocks are still at the planning stage (ZDA 2010).

Submissions to the Committee on Agriculture and Lands reveal that government did not consult the local communities when deciding to allocate land for farm blocks, with some farm blocks being created in areas which are already occupied. As a result, many local communities are being displaced to give way to the farm blocks (CAL 2009).

What seems to emerge from this is that customary land is under pressure, with little land remaining to accommodate the expanding rural population, especially communities along the line of rail and major roads (FSRP 2010: 3). Thus, claims that there is plenty of unutilised land can be misleading and dangerous. While it might be true that there is a lot of under-utilised land in customary areas, it is important to distinguish unutilised from under-utilised land.

Conversion of Customary Land to Leasehold Title

'Buying' and 'selling' of customary land to Zambians and foreign investors is not a new phenomenon, as this story from the 1994 *Zambia Daily Mail* shows (quoted in Roth et al. 1995: 30):

> In Zambia ... land is being dished out to foreigners and investors without considering the long-term consequences such action will have on the people .... Zambia has entered a phase where land grabbing is escalating at an alarming rate .... In Chief Kabamba's area, for instance, Serenje district council has already given out 4,800 ha of land to a South African investor on grounds ... this will bring development to the district .... People from outside the province are coming to stake claims to land in the name of development and local people cannot fight Lusaka businessmen or South African Investors.

As noted above, Circular 1 of 1985 permitted customary rights holders to convert the usufruct right into leasehold title. This was further confirmed by the 1995 Lands Act. Under the latter, anyone who wishes to alienate land in a customary area can approach the chief under whom the land falls, and if the chief consents through a written letter (together with local council approval), the person can then approach the Commissioner of lands to begin the process of conversion. Although the 1985 circular had a limit on the size of land which can be converted (not more than 250 ha), the 1995 Lands Act does not specify such limits. At the moment, it is difficult to ascertain who is involved in these conversions, but available evidence on investments in agriculture, between 2000 and 2010, suggests that the majority of large-scale land investors are non-Zambian. Table 3 shows the number of agricultural projects together with the country ownership of the projects, since 2000, while Table 4 provides examples of large-scale acquisitions. Though not all the investment involves acquisition of farmland, the number of projects involving purchase or expansion of farmland has been the biggest, especially before 2009.

Table 3 Pledged investment in agriculture by project

Year	Total projects	Farms	Other	Projects by foreigner	Projects by Zambians	Joint projects	Amount (US$ M)	Jobs expected
2000	18	14	4	13	3	2	8.3	1,058
2001	13	12	1	11	2	0	25.5	1,735
2002	21	13	8	15	2	4	12.03	2,797
2003	33	19	14	27	1	5	35.8	6,964
2004	34	25	9	29	1	4	24.8	2,340
2005	20	12	8	16	0	4	32.2	1,669
2006	23	14	9	19	0	4	60.9	1,499
2007	6	4	2	5	0	1	63.3	491
2008	21	7	14	12	3	6	62.9	1,508
2009	21	5	16	9	0	12	315.03	4,506
2010	12	3	9	9	0	3	45.9	1,660

Source Zambia Development Agency (ZDA 2011)

Note These figures represent pledged investments in agriculture which are channelled through the Zambia Development Agency (ZDA). There are other acquisitions of land which do not go through the ZDA. The database does not specify if these pledges have actually been realised. These investments are mainly farm investments which require acquisition of a farm plot, although not all projects are farming projects

Table 4 Examples of large-scale land acquisition in Zambia

Company	Size ('000 ha)	Location	Purpose	Ownership	Title	Year	Status
BTC-Bio	55	Mpongwe	Various	South African	99 year lease	1985	Operating
Dangote	0.219	Masaiti	Cement production	Nigerian	99 year lease	2010	Planning
Dar Farms	66	Mpongwe	Ranching	South African/ Zambian	99 year lease	1985	Operating
Chayton Africa	4	Several	Soya/wheat	British	99 year lease	2009	Operating partially
Neha International	100	Several	Various	India	99 year lease	2010	Planning
D1 Oil	4	Several	Jatropha	British	99 year lease	2010	Operating
MAN Ferrostaal AG	150	Several	Biofuel	Germany	99 year lease	2009	Planning
DWS GALOF	27	Several	Cereal	Germany	99 year lease	2008	Operating
China	2000	Several	Jatropha	China	99 year lease	2007	Exploration

Source Various sources including newspaper articles

Note The figures are not based on official records and include projects which have not been finalised

From the ZDA data, it is clear that most of the investments are located in areas along the line of rail (Lusaka, Kitwe, Ndola, Serenje, Mukushi, Kabwe and Chibamba), with very few investments going to other areas. Notably, pledged investment for agriculture rose sharply (fivefold) between 2008 and 2009, which may be a reflection of the effect of the global food prices and the demand for farmland. Overall, there has been growing investments in the agricultural sector, which implies that more and more land is required to accommodate the growing demand. Most of these investments are taking place in areas under customary tenure and involve the conversion of customary land to leasehold. It is difficult at the moment to estimate the total number of hectares which have been converted as a result of large-scale land acquisition. This is mainly because there has been a great deal of secrecy around large-scale land deals (Cotula 2011). Efforts to secure official data on large-scale land deals failed, because government officials handling these deals are not ready to release data into the public domain. There seems to be a lot of sensitivity around large-scale land deals. Officials from ZDA noted that they are reluctant to make data on land acquisitions available because investors complain when they read about these stories in the newspapers.

Drivers of Conversion of Customary Land

Although conversion of customary land into state land via leasehold tenure has been going on since 1985, there have been reports of swelling demand to convert customary tenure into leasehold tenure by both Zambian and non-Zambian investors.[9] In recent years, the pace and spread of this practice is a cause for concern, especially regarding the land rights of the poor in rural areas. As noted by Kabilika (2010: 5–6):

> At present in many parts of the country, the rights of land holders and users in customary areas are threatened. Some headmen are known to have begun illegally selling parcels of land to people who have money including foreigners and allowing them to convert such pieces of land to leasehold. In Chief Mungule's area for example, there is rampant selling of land literally to anybody who has cash. In the process of doing so … customary land tenure is under serious threat from those who are looking for land to buy and sell. It is like rewinding the clock back to colonialism when the Africans lost their good land to whites. At present, investors are given priorities and the rights of indigenous people to the land and its resources are not considered.

This is creating a number of challenges within rural communities, but also between chiefs and the state: '[t]here is conflict of authority between chiefs and the President in whom land is vested … in the process of converting land from

---

[9]Although it is widely held that conversion of customary land to leasehold title began with the 1995 Lands Act, customary land conversion has been ongoing since 1985, when the Administrative Circular No. 1 of 1985, was published, which allowed conversion of customary, conditional upon approval by the Chief and the district councils (Chizyuka et al. 2006). There are no recent figures on the rate of conversion. Figures for the period 1985–97 suggest a sharp rise of fivefold (see Fig. 1, below).

customary to state land' (Draft Land Policy 2006: 13). One of the challenges is that while there is enough land in the country, the poor people are having problems accessing land even in their communities (Kabilika 2010).

Key Drivers of Conversion

There are several factors which help explain the growing practice of converting customary land into leasehold. Only a few are briefly discussed below.

Tenure Security Perception

One of the key factors responsible for the practice of converting customary land into leasehold is the common perception that customary tenure is insecure while leasehold is more secure. In the case of Zambia, Adams (2003: 13) suggests that the applications for leasehold rights continue to grow presumably because the customary system is less secure and predictable than it used to be. Similarly, Roth et al. (1995) also indicate that the demand for leasehold has increased mainly because applicants see leasehold to be more secure, and that it has the advantage of being used as collateral. It is, however, not surprising that this perception has gained wide acceptance given the campaign since the 1970s to replace customary tenure with leasehold title (Deininger and Binswanger 1999). This view has persisted within policy circles despite empirical studies showing that there is, at best, mixed evidence regarding the correlation between titling and increased access to loans and investment (Jacoby and Minten 2007; Van den Brink et al. 2006; Chitonge 2012). Havnevik (1997: 8) also makes a similar observation arguing that:

> ... land registration creates increased insecurity for vulnerable parts of the population; it does not activate the land market, and if it does, it is mainly for speculative reasons; it does not bring about a reversal in land fragmentation nor does it improve land allocation; it does not in significant ways improve smallholders access to credit; and there is no significant correlation between land titling and increased agricultural yield.

In the Zambian case, a study conducted in the highly privatised parts of Southern Province concludes that there is no evidence suggesting that those with leasehold titles are using their titles to secure loans. The study shows that many farmers do not intend to use their land for collateral; they 'believe that they need them [titles] as a defensive measure, even on customary lands' (quoted in Adams 2003: 13). With regard to using land title as collateral, the poor people in customary land resist using their land as collateral for fear that in case of default they may lose their land (Kabilika 2010). However, the perception that customary land is insecure plays an important role in the decision to convert customary land into leasehold.

Table 5 Number of title deeds issued between 1985 and 1997

	Male	Female	Other	Total	Lusaka	Copperbelt	Annual average
1985–1991	145 (2.6)	22 (0.4)	5398 (97)	5565	1458 (26.2)	1357 (24.4)	771.1
1991–1997	18,651 (64.4)	3943 (14)	5513 (19.6)	28,107	11,046 (39.2)	6235 (22.2)	3513.4

Source Land Deeds Registry (cited in Kajoba 1997)
Note Numbers in brackets represent percentage of the total titles issued

The Role of the Lands Act of 1995

While there is not yet any empirical evidence gathered, there is a strong belief that the 1995 Lands Act has actually provided an enabling environment for alienating customary land into state land (leasehold tenure). Although the conversion of customary land into leasehold started in 1985 with the issuance of Circular, the 1995 Lands Act accelerated the conversion process (Mudenda 2006; Kabilika 2010). As Table 5 shows, the pace of issuing title deeds increased fivefold in 1991–97, compared to the earlier period of 1987–91.

While this increase may not entirely be attributed to the 1995 Lands Act, there is little reason to believe that this increase is a mere coincidence, or due to increased capacity of the deeds office (Roth et al. 1995). The 1995 Lands Act's provision to allow the conversion of customary land into leasehold title has led to 'wealthy Zambians and foreign investors buying up land previously held under customary tenancy by the rural poor' (Mudenda 2006: 5). Figure 1 shows that the number of title deeds issued doubled in 2000–02, and almost trebled by 2007, which partially reflects the increase in the conversion of customary land to leasehold.

A few well-educated and resourced local urban dwellers, as well as foreign investors, are therefore taking advantage of this provision to secure land for themselves. Many rural dwellers, however, may not be aware of this opportunity

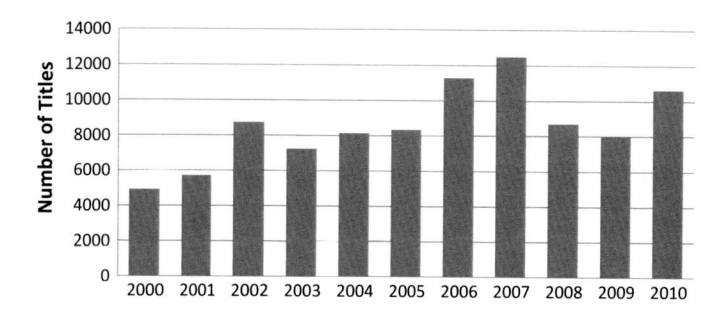

Fig. 1 Title deed issued per year 2000–10. *Source* Author, based on data from the Commissioner of Land Registry, 2011

(Brown 2005), or many simply cannot afford to pay the fees for processing land from customary land into leasehold title (USAID 2010; Honig and Mulenga 2015). The possibility to convert customary land into leasehold tenure which came with the 1995 Lands Act can be seen as something that has created the opportunity for a few to alienate customary land, while also institutionalising insecurity for many.

Growing Middle Class

Another factor which has contributed to the increase in demand for converting customary land into leasehold is the slowly growing middle class in Zambia. Following the years of SAP which saw rapid deindustrialisation and job losses, the middle class in Zambia almost disappeared. Since the beginning of the new millennium, the positive economic growth averaging 5.8% in 2000–10 (CSO 2011), the number of people with disposable income has increased, although still remaining very low, at 5.6% of the population (AfDB 2011: 5). Most of these local young professionals and business people seek to secure their future in areas not far from the urban areas where land can be economically productive, but also where they envision a future after retirement. These are people who are acquiring land in nearby customary areas, which they convert into leasehold in the form of small-holding. It is not entirely true that these people do not seek land from their area of origin because of weakening bonds, as suggested by Roth et al. (1995: 29), as well as Adams (2003: 13); it is actually the economic rationale that is behind the acquiring of customary land in nearby areas.

Speculation in Land Value

Speculative behaviour has also contributed to the increased rate of converting customary land, for the simple reason that the 1995 Lands Act does not have mechanisms to prevent or discourage speculation in land. Since the enactment of the 1995 Lands Act, there are reports that the number of absentee landowners (both Zambian and non-Zambians) has increased significantly (Brown 2005: 92). Although there is a provision to repossess undeveloped land, there is no clear stipulation of the period within which this can be done.[10] Even if the repossession of undeveloped land were possible, the low capacity and inadequate funding within the land administration and management department makes it unlikely that this would be implemented effectively. Given these loopholes, some investors, both

---

[10]This weakness arises from the mere fact that, since its promulgation in 1995, the Lands Act has never had a ministerial regulation to elaborate on its implementation (Kabilika 2010; Mudenda 2006; Adams 2003).

local and foreign, are taking advantage to acquire as much land as they can afford in the hope that the value of land will increase (in the not so distant future) to allow them make profit by hoarding land.[11]

Impact of Conversion

There are a number of challenges which arise from the conversion of customary land into leasehold tenure. Though at the moment there has not been a systematic study of the impact, some of the main issues are discussed briefly below.

Shifting Power Relations

Being able to allocate and settle disputes over land has been the main source of power and control for traditional leaders in Africa for centuries (Kabilika 2010; Mafeje 2003; Shipton and Coheen 1992). As noted (Jorgensen and Loudjeva 2005: v), the 'power to allocate land and judge disputes is the foundation of traditional authority. Transferring land to state control will remove this foundation and erect little in its place. [This practice] could thus spawn serious social disorder'. Kabilika has also made a similar observation arguing that this 'idea of converting customary land into state land has the potential to dethrone all the chiefs in Zambia. Without land at the disposal of chiefs and their headpersons, traditional authority in Zambia becomes meaningless' (2010: 7). Converting customary land into leasehold title essentially means that the land over which the chief used to exercise power is alienated from customary control, since in the current policy arrangement, once customary land is converted into state land, it cannot revert back to customary tenure after the expiry or termination of the lease.

Ironically, it has been reported that there are some traditional authorities who are happily engaging in alienating land through conversion to leasehold title (German et al. 2011; Brown 2005) in exchange for 'gifts', or the so-called 'token of appreciation' (USAID 2010).[12] It is thus clear that some chiefs have just fallen prey to the egoistic lure of money and the politics of patronage. However, there are some chiefs who from the beginning have opposed the conversion of customary land, arguing that leasehold title is 'something that makes them lose control over land and

---

[11]One example is of a South African investor who acquired land at no cost in Chief Nkanya's area, along the Luangwa Valley, to develop a Safari lodge, only to sell the land 2 years later for US $70,000, without even touching the land; see Brown (2005: 92), for more such examples.

[12]There have been several stories, especially in the print media, reporting that an increasing number of traditional leaders are being bribed into selling away land to foreign investors who have money. One example is an article in the *Pots Newspaper of Monday* (10 January 2011), which claims that many chiefs have become corrupt and selfish.

their subjects. Hence, they are reluctant to recommend applications for land' (Roth et al. 1995: 20). The Parliamentary Committee on Agriculture and Land also reports that 'traditional rulers, if not most of them, are not receptive to the practice of conversion of their land to statutory leasehold ...' (CAL 2009: 14). This view has been confirmed by a communique issued by a group of Traditional Leaders from different parts of Zambia who noted the loss of customary land as one of the challenges facing land administration in Zambia (ZLA 2008):

> Once land is converted from customary tenure to leasehold the land does not revert to customary tenure at the expiry or cancellation of the lease. This means that there is a net loss of customary land without corresponding benefits to local communities. There is insecurity on customary tenure as some people are displaced from their land due to large scale land acquisitions without regard to their land rights.... to ensure tenure security, some chiefs are issuing documents to ascertain user rights and ownership of pieces of land by families. However, such documents are not currently recognised by government.

A study by the Catholic Commission for Justice and Peace (CCJP) revealed that most people interviewed, even in urban centres, are not for the idea of conversion. 'Converting customary land to leasehold is a danger to the institution of chiefs and the culture of the people', they argue (quoted in Kabilika 2010: 8).

Increasing Insecurity

Converting customary land into leasehold tenure (state land) results in insecure access to land for most local people. This happens when traditional leaders, due to the increased demand for land, stop allocating land to local people in anticipation of big money from investors. Insecurity also arises when investors who convert customary land into leasehold evict the local people from the land. For example, in 2002, Chief Munkonchi approved the conversion of 26,000 ha of land, on which more than 2,000 people were living in five villages, and in 2003, the people were asked to vacate the land (Brown 2005: 93). In Chief Chiawa's area, local people lost their burial land to a Zambeef farmer who fenced off the area, including the burial site (Kabilika 2010: 9). When this happens, often the displaced people find it hard to obtain alternative land, mainly because all the land in the area has been allocated, or earmarked for investors. Thus, it has been observed that the 'leasehold system itself can be a source of insecurity because chiefs consent to outsiders being granted leases, transgressing the rights of local rights' holders, perhaps denying the right of parents to bequeath land to their offspring (Adams 2003: 12). This observation is not unique to titling in Zambia; it has been recorded in other parts of Africa where land privatisation has occurred (Havnevik 1997; Shipton and Coheen 1992; Place 2009; Platteau 1996).

Land Scarcity

Converting customary land into state land is also leading to land scarcity, especially in hotspot areas (those near developed infrastructure). There are cases of local people failing to find land, especially in areas where there is good infrastructure such as roads, access to markets, health care, education and water (FSRP 2010; Mudenda 2006). Effects of land scarcity have been felt more in areas where a lot of customary land has been converted into state land, and the chief has no more land to allocate. Key examples include the area outside Lusaka in Chieftainess Nkomesha's and Chiawa's areas, where Lusaka businessmen and professional workers, as well as foreign investors, have acquired most of the land for farming. Although scarcity may not be an immediate problem in most areas at the moment, it is likely to be a major problem in many parts of the country in the not so distant future. As more customary land disappears, it will no longer be easy for the poor to access land by exercising their right of avail, as the case has been over the centuries (Adams 2003).

Compromised Future Land Use

In Zambia, as in many other African countries, land in rural areas is acquired primarily through inheritance and through asking additional land from the chief. With the growing practice of converting customary land, it is probable that, in some areas, traditional leaders will run out of land to allocate to the people who may want more land in future. This compromises the land use of future generations in local communities, unless one assumes that the children of these people will be able to rent land from the state. If all customary land is converted into leasehold, the only source of land for families that need additional land is the land market, where they will have to compete with Chinese or Canadian investors. Future land use is also compromised by the ongoing land conversion, to the extent that people who are working in urban areas may not have a place to go to when they retire, and not all of them will have enough resources to acquire smallholdings close to the place where they work.

Weakening of Social Cohesion and Growing Conflict

The other key impact of land conversion is the weakening of social fabric in rural communities resulting in tensions and conflict. When a person new to the area obtains land through the village head or chief, s/he is introduced to the community by the community leader and s/he integrates into the community. With conversion of customary land, a person can obtain land without even seeing the village head, and this can weaken social cohesion. The fragmentation of rural communities into pockets of customary and state land may not only weaken social fabric, but is also likely to create a new social dynamic, with those on state land forming their own network which excludes residents on customary land who may be deemed traditional, poor and less sophisticated (Sitko 2010). Certainly, the equity of access which customary tenure ensures (German et al. 2011; ZLA 2008; Adams 2003) is likely to disappear, as land becomes accessible through the market. Open inequality in access to land can be a source of instability and conflict, especially during the period of transition. There are cases of increased tension and conflict over land in many rural communities, as more customary land is converted into leasehold tenure.

Rent-Seeking

Converting customary land in a context characterised by weak institutional capacity can lead to increase in what economists have euphemistically labelled rent-seeking, which in actual fact is corruption and abuse of public office. This is a phenomenon which has been reported in many instances in Zambia (Adams 2003; Brown 2005; Mudenda 2006; Jorgensen and Loudjeva 2005). In one case, the lease was so fraudulent that the Minister of Lands vetoed it, and the lease was eventually cancelled (Brown 2005). In another case, the President refused to approve the lease and referred the case to the anti-corruption commission for investigation (German et al. 2011). Given the low capacity to process the growing demand for titles at the Ministry of Lands (USAD 2010), well-resourced individuals may choose to jump the queue in the process of acquiring a title. The net effect of this is inequality in access to land and inefficient allocation of land resources. Speculation also may increase due to the fact that, when one acquires the lease, there is no incentive to use that land immediately. Even if there is a rule that undeveloped land will be repossessed, it is unlikely that this will be strictly applied. A study by the World Bank on large-scale land acquisition reveals that most of the lands acquired in 2006–10 have not been developed (Deininger et al. 2011).

Conclusion

This chapter has outlined the challenges of land tenure in Zambia in the context of the growing practice of converting customary land into leasehold title by both local and foreign investors. While it is the intention of government policy to 'open up' customary land to investors, there are a number of challenges that this strategy engenders. Key among them is the fact that, in the process of converting customary land into leasehold tenure, traditional leaders are slowly losing control over land. This has already created tension and open confrontation between the various stakeholders, including the state and chiefs, as well as between chiefs and their own people. Conversion of customary land into state land has also resulted in shifting power relations with the state consolidating its control over land. This power imbalance has generated a tacit struggle to regain control, on the one hand, and to consolidate control, on the other.

Second, as more customary land is converted into state land without a possibility of the converted land reverting back to customary land, more and more rural poor are beginning to face the problem of land scarcity, especially in areas close to well-developed economic and social infrastructure. This is becoming common in many areas along the line of rail, where infrastructure and services have attracted investments from well-resourced locals and non-Zambians (FSRP 2010; Mudenda 2006). If not carefully managed, this trend is likely to lead to a situation where many poor people will be landless.

One possible solution is to 'bring development' to rural areas by keeping land under customary administration (ZLA 2008, 2002); that is, to lease customary land without converting it into state land, so that the land remains under customary land when the lease expires. This has been done in countries such as Ghana, Tanzania and Botswana. In Ghana, foreign investors rent land under customary tenure directly from 'traditional councils', without alienating it into state land. Even in cases where traditional land is alienated, land can revert back to customary tenure after expiry or termination of the lease (German et al. 2011). In Zambia, such proposals have been made by civil society groups, but they have not been incorporated into policy documents and programmes. Civil society groups have been arguing that the answer to developing land under customary tenure 'does not lie in turning customary land into state land but rather in giving democratic local authorities/community leaders powers to lease land to individuals and institutions' (ZLA 2002: 7).

The policy and practice of converting customary land into state land has also revealed the weakness in the current framework with regard to the approval to transfer or alienate land. Assigning the power to approve alienation of land to one person (whether it is the Head of State or a traditional leader) makes the whole process prone to abuse and corruption. Again, there are important lessons from other countries, where the power to approve any form of land alienation is delegated to a 'village council' and 'traditional council'. Although imperfect, such arrangements help reduce the chances of abuse and corruption, which often disadvantage the poor and vulnerable in the community. Overall, in as much as the state's drive to bring growth and development to the rural areas may be a justifiable goal, there is need to balance the quest for development and the rights of local people whose land is being converted into state land.

References

Adams, M. (2003). *Land tenure policy and practice in Zambia: Issues relating to the development of the agricultural sector.* Unpublished manuscript.

Adams, M., & Palmer, R. (2007). *Independent review of land issues in eastern and southern Africa.* Mokoro: Oxford.

AfDB [African Development Bank] (2011). *The middle of the pyramid: Dynamics of the middle class in Africa, Market Brief.* https://www.afdb.org/fileadmin/uploads/afdb/Documents/Publications/The%20Middle%20of%20the%20Pyramid_The%20Middle%20of%20the%20Pyramid.pdf. Retrieved June 29, 2017.

Brown, T. (2005). Contestation, confusion and corruption: Market-based land reform in Zambia. In S. Evers, M. Spierenburg, & H. Wels (Eds.), *Competing jurisdictions: Settling land claims in Africa* (pp. 79–102). Boston, MA: Brill.

Bruce, J., & Dorner, P. (1982). Land Tenure in Zambia: Perspectives, Problems and Opportunities. Land Tenure Centre Research Paper No. 76, University of Wisconsin-Maidson.

Bruce, J. W., & Migot-Adholla, E. (1994). Introduction: Are indigenous African tenure systems insecure? In J.W. Bruce & E. Migot-Adholla (Eds.), *Searching for Land Tenure Security in Africa* (pp. 1–14). Washington, DC: World Bank.

CAL [Committee on Agriculture and Land] (2009). *Second report of the committee on agriculture and land.* Prepared for the Tenth Session of the National Assembly. Lusaka: Zambia National Assembly.

Chitonge, H. (2012). Land resource ownership and use in 'Africa of the labour reserves' (southern African development community). In C. Ben (Ed.), *Land relations policy in southern African development community* (pp. 57–88). London: Routledge.

Chitonge, H. (2015). Customary land at a crossroads: Contest for the control of customary land in Zambia. *SADC Law Journal, 4*(1), 45–67.

Chizyuka, R., Kamona, R. M., Ufwenuka, C., & Phiri, M. (2006). *Policies and strategies for agrarian reform and rural development to secure and improve access to natural resources: National report—Zambia.* Paper prepared for the International Conference on Agrarian Reform and Development (ICARRD), March 7–10, Porto Alegre, Brazil.

Cotula, L. (2011). *The outlook on farmland acquisition.* International Land Coalition (ILC). http://www.landcoalition.org/en/resources/outlook-farmland-acquisitions. Retrieved June 29, 2017.

CSO [Central Statistical Office] (2011). Population census preliminary results, 2010. http://www.mcaz.gov.zm/wp-content/uploads/2014/10/2010-Census-of-Population-Summary-Report.pdf. Retrieved June 29, 2017.

Deininger, K., & Binswanger, H. (1999). The evolution of the World Bank's land policy: Principles, experiences and future challenges. *The World Bank Research Observer, 14*(2), 247–276.

Deininger, K., Derek, B., Lindsay, J., Norton, A., Selod, H., & Sticker, M. (2011). *Rising global interest in farmland: Can it yield sustainable and equitable benefits?.* New York, NY: World Bank.

FRSP [Food Security Research Project] (2010). The status of customary land and how it affects the rights of indigenous local communities, submission to the Committee on Agriculture and Land Study.

Fundanga, C., & Mwaba, A. (1996). Privatization of public enterprises in Zambia: An evaluation of policies, procedures and experiences. *Economic Research Papers, 35.* Tunis: African Development Bank.

German, L., Schoneveld, G., & Mwangi, E. (2011). Processes of large-scale land acquisition by investors: case studies from sub-Saharan Africa. *A paper presented at the International Conference on Global Land Grabbing*, April 6–8, 2011. Institute of Development Studies, University of Sussex.

Havnevik, K. (1997). Land question in sub-Saharan Africa. In N.-I. Isaksson (Ed.), *Land question in sub-Saharan Africa.* Uppsala: Department of Rural Development Studies, Swedish University of Agricultural Sciences.

Hichaambwa, M., & Jayne, S. T. (2014). *Poverty reduction potential of increasing smallholder access to land.* Working Paper, No. 83. Lusaka: Indaba Agricultural Policy Research Institute (IAPRI).

Honig, L., & Mulenga, B. (2015). *The status of customary land and the future of smallholder farmers under current land administration system in Zambia.* Working Paper, No. 101. Lusaka: Indaba Agricultural Policy Research Institute (IAPRI).

Hudson, J. (2007). The empty country. *Journal Platform for Public Policy Analysis*. http://fsg.afre. msu.edu/zambia/resources/ZIPPALand_3rd_Quarter2007.pdf. Retrieved June 29, 2017.

ILUA [Integrated Land Use and Assessment]. (2008). *ILUA report, 2005–2008*. Lusaka: Department of Forestry and FAO.

Jacoby, H., & Minten, B. (2007). Is land titling in sub-Saharan Africa cost-effective? Evidence from Madagascar. *The World Bank Economic Review, 4*(3), 461–485.

Jorgensen, S., & Loudjeva, Z. (2005). *A poverty and social analysis impact of three programmes: Land, fertiliser and infrastructure*. Social Development Papers, No. 49. Washington, DC: World Bank.

Kabilika, E. (2010). *The status of customary land and how it affects the rights of indigenous local communities*. Zambia: Caritus.

Kajoba, G. M. (1997). *The landmarks of Zambia's land tenure system: From protectionism to empowerment*. Presented at the Conference on 'Land Tenure in Development Cooperation, January 27–29. Cape Town: University of Cape Town.

Kanyanta, C. (2014). The institution of chiefs is on slippery ground—Chitimukulu. *Lusaka Times*, July 3. https://www.lusakatimes.com/2014/07/03/institution-chiefs-slippery-ground-chitimukulu/. Retrieved June 29, 2017.

Mafeje, A. (2003). *The agrarian question: Access to land and peasant response in sub-Saharan Africa*. Civil Society and Social Movement Programme, UNRISD, Paper No. 6.

Moyo, S. (2010). Prospect for agrarian reform in southern Africa. *Opening society through advocacy*. Johannesburg: Open Society Initiative for Southern Africa (OSISA).

Mudenda, M. M. (2006). *The challenges of customary land tenure in Zambia*. Presented at the XXIII FIG Congress, October 8–13, Munich, Germany.

Place, F. (2009). Land tenure and agricultural productivity in Africa: a comperative analysis of the economic literature and recent policy strategies and reforms. *World Development, 37*(8), 132–136.

Platteau, J.-P. (1996). The evolutionary theory of land rights as applied to sub-Saharan Africa: A critical assessment. *Development and Change, 27*(1), 29–86.

Republic of Zambia. (2006). *Draft land administration and management policy*. Lusaka: Ministry of Lands.

Roth, M., Khan, A. M., & Zulu, M. C. (1995). Legal and administration of land policy in Zambia. In M. Roth (Ed.), *Land tenure, land markets and institutional transformation in Zambia* (LTC Research Report, No. 124) (pp. 1–46). Madison, WI: Land Tenure Centre, University of Wisconsin-Madison.

Shipton, P., & Coheen, M. (1992). Understanding African land-holding: Power and meaning. *Journal of International African Institute, 62*(3), 307–325.

Simutanyi, N. (1996). The politics of structural adjustment in Zambia. *Third World Quarterly, 17* (4), 825–839.

Sitko, N. (2010). Fractured governance and local frictions: The exclusionary nature of a clandestine land market in southern Zambia. *Africa, 80*(1), 36–54.

USAID (2010). Property rights and resource governance: Zambia country profile. www.usaid.org. Retrieved August 11, 2011.

Van den Brink, R., Thomas, G., Bruce, J., & Byamugisha, F. (2006). *Consensus, confusion and controversy: Selected land reform in sub-Saharan Africa*. Washington, DC: World Bank.

ZDA [Zambia Development Agency (2011). *Pledged land investment*. Unpublished.

ZDA [Zambia Development Agency] (2010). 'Development and commercialisation of Nansanga farm block', a Memorandum by the Multi-Sectoral Committee on Farm Block, Lusaka.

ZLA [Zambia Land Alliance] (2002). *Initial position paper on the draft land policy, civil society land policy review committee*. Presented to the Zambian Government Land Policy Technical Committee, Lusaka Province Workshop, December 16–21, Lusaka.

ZLA [Zambia Land Alliance] (2008). *Land policy options for development and poverty reduction: Civil society views for pro-poor land policies and laws in Zambia*. Lusaka: Civil Society Consultative Forum.

Land and Natural Resources in Zimbabwe: Scramble and Resistance

Sam Moyo, Walter Chambati and Paris Yeros

Introduction

The recent wave of land grabbing in Africa began soon after Zimbabwe initiated the Fast-Track Land Reform Programme (FTLRP) in 2000, following a decade of repression of popular pressure resulting from neoliberal policies. The FTLRP expropriated land from foreign and domestic white-owned capital in a reversal of settler-colonial land dispossession and the land concentration which was consolidated during the 1990s (J. Moyo 2011, S. Moyo 2011). This enabled peasants to acquire most of the agricultural land and domestic elites to appropriate some middle farms (J. Moyo 2011, S. Moyo 2011), altering the key agrarian relations typical of the settler-colonial labour reserve (Amin 1972; Chambati 2012). Subsequently, in 2004, the Government of Zimbabwe (GoZ) initiated the Look East Policy, which sought to accommodate foreign capital from the East and South. From 2006 onwards, the Indigenisation and Economic Empowerment Policy sought to increase domestic elite class participation in the mining, tourism, and manufacturing sectors. In the process state ownership of land, natural resources and minerals and its role in the economy were expanded.

These redistributive reforms directly challenged private property relations and transformed the agrarian structure, altering its erstwhile vertical integration with transnational capital from the West and South Africa and seeking to diversify

---

Sam Moyo (1954–2015).

S. Moyo · W. Chambati
The Sam Moyo African Institute for Agrarian Studies,
19 Bodle Avenue, Eastlea, Harare, Zimbabwe

P. Yeros (✉)
Federal University of ABC (UFABC), CECS, sala D337,
Alameda da Universidade, s/nº, Bairro Anchieta, 09606-045,
São Bernardo do Campo, SP, Brazil
e-mail: parisyeros@gmail.com

© Springer Nature Singapore Pte Ltd. 2019
S. Moyo et al. (eds.), *Reclaiming Africa*, Advances in African Economic,
Social and Political Development, https://doi.org/10.1007/978-981-10-5840-0_11

investments from the West. A trajectory of accumulation from below was initiated at the expense of Western and settler-colonial capital, which also created scope for new forms of accumulation through state enterprises. However, the capital was not fully ousted, as the state made concessions to some sections of capital which continue to control some agro-industrial estates and conservancies (J. Moyo 2011, S. Moyo 2011) and mining operations. Moreover, Zimbabwe has continued to be a target of the wider West–East scramble for agricultural resources and minerals, such as gold, chrome, platinum and diamonds, which is underway in Africa. This outcome unraveled the post-Independence political transition in Southern Africa as a whole and threatened the compromise especially in South Africa, by challenging Western hegemonic control over resources, while also shaking the hegemony of NATO in matters of regional security. Indeed, Zimbabwe was perceived as a quintessential model of 'bad governance' and labelled an 'unusual threat' to US interests. Consequently, a regime-change strategy was initiated by the West in Zimbabwe from the late 1990s onwards. This entailed military and economic sanctions and the use of soft power, in support of capital in some sectors, and providing support, more generally, for the political opposition party Movement for Democratic Change (MDC) and allied 'civil society' organisations. These measures to undermine the entire state apparatus persisted against both popular mobilisation and state-promoted radical nationalism.

Since the reconfiguration of global markets had increased the scale and sources of demand for Zimbabwe's products, the sanctions and the decline in overall production and investment created the expectation that Zimbabwe would open up to foreign capital in desperation, and in competition with its regional peers. But Zimbabwe's radicalised politics and heterodox economic policies did not permit this. While Western sanctions advanced, investments from the East into Zimbabwe increased, but these were limited in scale and also delayed, because the Indigenisation Policy and popular pressures sought to limit foreign ownership of land and mineral resources. Indeed, BRICS investors were initially hesitant due to both internal policy conditionalities and threats from the West. National resistance to foreign control and the changing class and racial interests had altered the political dynamics of the former settler-colony, leading the increasingly radicalised state toward inward and autonomous development (Moyo and Yeros 2007).

The resistance to capital from the West and the sanctions over the decade did stress the economy, but it also created room for the state to manoeuvre *vis-à-vis* foreign investment. Zimbabwe courted the East largely on its own terms, while experimenting with an introverted accumulation strategy. Consequently, investment and trade relations with the East rose gradually, led by the Chinese and, later, to a more limited extent, some countries from the South (such as India, Brazil and South Korea). These developments did not displace the dominance of capital from the West and South Africa, and the persistent Eurocentric pattern of trade. But trade patterns did diversify, as in the key agricultural commodities (tobacco and cotton) and, to a more limited extent, imports of agricultural inputs and manufactured goods. Investment patterns also diversified in some mining sectors (chrome, diamonds, platinum) and public construction projects, which had borne the brunt of financial sanctions and escalating debt.

The sanctions and the emerging shifts in the security order of Southern Africa provided a distinctive policy context for resistance against the ongoing scramble in Zimbabwe. In the wider context, and unlike the experience of other experiences of radical land reform—see, for example Borras (2005) on the Philippines–Zimbabwe did not remain in strategic alliance with the West; its military doctrine and arms procurement directly confronted NATO's security arrangements in the Southern African region. Nor did it maintain the neoliberal financialised regime, as it executed extensive state controls on the economy until 2009. Nor did it receive positive material support from external allies, as, for instance, Cuba had received from the Soviet Union, after its revolution. On the contrary, the reforms in Zimbabwe led to a reduction in the historical trade financing arrangements with South Africa. Indeed, one of the responses of white farmers and capital from Zimbabwe was to initiate a wave of land grabs in the region (Mozambique, Zambia). Moreover, the West sought to sow divisions among the Southern Africa Development Community (SADC) member-states (Moyo and Yeros 2009). As Thabo Mbeki later conceded, SADC had felt that the international balance of forces acting upon the SADC region were not in favour of a revolutionary approach to social transformation in Zimbabwe, and that market-based reforms were seen as the only feasible option. In the event, Zimbabwe's radicalisation opened up avenues for foreign policy innovation, and this has favoured a shift towards a new practice of non-alignment, as well as strategies of regional resistance within SADC.

Historical Context and Radical Reform in Zimbabwe

The colonial dispossession of indigenous Zimbabweans of their land and natural resources through British settlers began in the 1890s. Racially discriminatory and unequal land ownership structures (Palmer 1977; Moyana 2002) marginalised the majority of the population in 'Communal Areas' (Shivji et al. 1998), institutionalising a labour-reserve economy based largely on agriculture and mining. From the 1940s, a limited import-substitution industrialisation (ISI) was promoted, dependent on cheap migrant black labour from a stunted peasantry (Moyo and Yeros 2005). From 1966, the state-supported large-scale irrigated estate farming, with landholdings averaging more than 10,000 ha, through various infrastructures, in order to expand commodity exports and reduce food imports (Stoneman 1988). By 1999, post-Independence, the limited state-led land reforms had created over 1,000 middle-sized black farmers and 70,000 new peasants, alongside 4,500 large white farms (reduced from 6,000 in 1980), 8,000 small-scale black commercial farmers (SSCFs), and the pre-existing one million peasant families (Moyo 2000).

British and South African agrarian capital, and a variety of Western interests in mining, dominated the process of primitive accumulation in Zimbabwe. The land question was being popularly perceived as a matter of redressing race-based inequalities in the control of land, minerals, and various natural resources, holding the United Kingdom (UK) responsible for reparations of indigenous Zimbabweans and for any compensation to its 'kith and kin' arising from land reform. However, no legal suit for reparations was lodged, and the UK government opposed expro-priatory land reform, while refusing to recognise any colonial responsibility, or promises to pay for land redistribution.

Land and mineral resource grabbing in the former settler-colonies of Africa also deepened under neoliberalism, spreading European land ownership and widening the international front of land conflict in the Southern African region (Moyo 2008). Unlike in non-settler Africa, this process was built upon the historical alienation of land by racial minorities and foreign corporations, and the extensive private property regimes typical of these countries, as well as the long history of foreign mineral exploitation. Belated Independence from the late 1970s in the settler-colonies did not lead to redressing the injustices of unequal land and natural resource ownership. Rather, foreign control escalated. By the time the Western sanctions policy against Zimbabwe was implemented, from 1998, primitive accu-mulation in Zimbabwe was largely a preserve of Western capital orchestrated by neoliberal policies and settler networks. When radical land reform began, it was routinely labelled a 'violent and chaotic land grab' (Hammar et al. 2003), not an act of restitution or 'indigenisation'.

Despite the foreign investment profile, political relations between the GoZ and key Western nations (especially the UK, United States, Germany and France) were lukewarm until the late 1980s, when neoliberal policies were adopted, although relations with the Scandinavians remained buoyant. The balance of payments crisis of 1982 led to an agreement with the International Monetary Fund (IMF), and subsequently to the adoption ESAP in 1990, and together with the 1992 drought, led to increased Western aid and concessional lending. Liberalisation, however, limited the state's corporatist strategies and the fiscal capacity to co-opt labour (for example, in the public sector), the peasantry through a conservative land reform programme, and the wider public through free and cheap social services.

The relations between the UK and Zimbabwe took a major dip in 1997, when the GoZ listed 1,471 farms for expropriation, and the UK refused to fund Zimbabwe's newly proposed approach to land reform. The Blair government openly dissociated itself from any colonial obligation to fund land reform, alleging that the proposed land reform programme lacked a 'poverty focus' and 'transparency', and that it favoured elites. Expropriatory land reform at Zimbabwe's Lancaster House nego-tiations had been treated as inimical to the interests of international capital in settler Southern Africa and as a geopolitical threat to imperialism during the Cold War after the liberation of Mozambique and Angola (Moyo 1995). Despite unwritten 'promises' by the UK and United States, during informal side talks at Lancaster House (S. Moyo 2011), to fund a 'land settlement programme', the British gov-ernment had only provided GBP 30 million for market-based land reform by 1989.

Confrontation with West widened when Zimbabwe rejected a new structural adjustment programme in 1996, and the antagonism intensified over Zimbabwe's intervention in the Democratic Republic of Congo (DRC) war from 1998, drawing the United States more deeply into the conflict. By 1999, the West had lost its patience and openly began to support the political opposition and allied non-governmental organisations (NGOs) towards the 2000 elections. Even the white landowners placed their bets on an MDC electoral victory by also funding them.

Western Monopoly-Finance Capital Against Re-radicalised Nationalism

The Structural Features of Primitive Accumulation

After Independence, Zimbabwe's trade and investment relations were dominated by Europe, until 2005, when China, South Africa and the rest of Africa became significant actors. This Eurocentric focus was even more pronounced in terms of Foreign Direct Investment (FDI), aid and loans, largely from the Bretton Woods institutions. Between 1985 and 1996, the scale of foreign investments originating from the West increased, while the scope of investments diversified. Trade volumes also increased, with exports rising from USD 2.3 billion in 1980 to USD 4 billion in 1990, and a further increase to USD 5.2 billion by 1995. New exports rose sharply, especially in tourism and horticulture, as well as platinum and diamonds, reflecting new investors from Europe and Australian mining firms. Generally, there was an expansion of FDI until the late 1990s (see Fig. 1). During this period, perhaps a dozen new Bilateral Investment Promotion and Protection Agreements (BIPPAs) were also signed. Yet, after 1997, the net capital flight was dramatic. The first major disinvestment initiative was by BHP, which closed the Hartley Platinum mine and sold it for one US Dollar! New investments and loan transfers only re-emerged at a much lower level from 2006, reflecting growing Chinese interests, and interests in mining, mainly from South Africa (in platinum and gold), from China (into chrome and diamonds), and Chinese concessional loans.

Zimbabwe's confrontation with the West deepened around 1996, when the adverse effects of the structural adjustment programme took their toll on working people (Yeros 2002), and shifted the balance of power, as dependency on aid and IFI loans escalated, also threatening domestic black 'elite' class aspirations, ultimately leading to radical land reform initiatives and the abandonment of structural adjustment. In response, the key Western nations coalesced around a regime-change

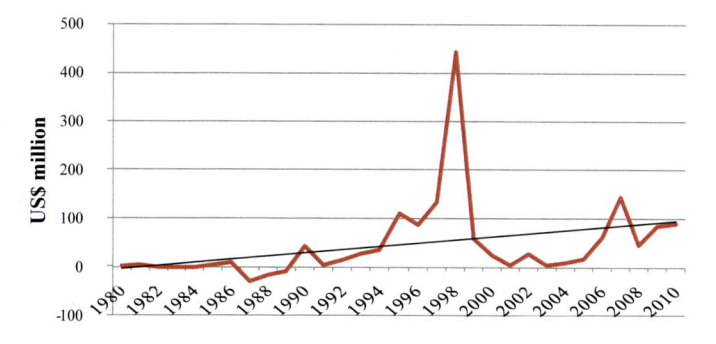

Fig. 1 Net foreign direct investments in Zimbabwe, 1980–2010. *Source* Reserve Bank of Zimbabwe (RBZ), International Monetary Fund (IMF), and United Nations Conference on Trade and Development (UNCTAD), various years

agenda which almost unseated the ruling party, ZANU-PF, in 2000. This reaction served to heighten resistance against foreign land and resources and the formalisation of radical reforms.

One of the consequences of this conflict was the withholding of concessional loans by the West to Zimbabwe, and the latter's defaulting on debt. This polarised the debate on 'debt management', and evoked new strategies to raise a new scale and forms of external loans. The MDC's finance minister had argued for a Heavily Indebted Poor Countries (HIPC) debt relief strategy managed by the Bretton Woods Institutions, while ZANU-PF called for new ways of borrowing against minerals (especially diamonds and platinum) through state joint ventures with foreign capital.

Initially, Zimbabwe's land redistribution policy, sought to unravel domestic white monopoly control of the agrarian economy and its ties to monopoly-finance capital, by targeting large-scale individual white-owned farms. The GoZ was ambiguous about expropriating large-scale foreign-owned agro-industrial estates, wildlife conservancies and forest plantations, and protected the state- and/or publicly-owned agricultural estates, as well as some large black-owned farms. Emphasising 'scale economies' and the preservation of integrated irrigation and agro-processing infrastructures on the estates, the policy envisioned agro-industrial development, exports, and employment growth being served by some large farms, while the smaller producers would ensure food security (GoZ 1998a, b). However, the GoZ also sought to revive state-owned agro-industrial estates to promote a renewed import-substitution industrialisation strategy, including reducing fuel imports through local agro-fuels and cutting food imports and dependence on food aid. The preservation and reconstitution of some large-scale estate farming was later seen to be required by the deteriorating economic situation, in the context of limited access to multilateral concessional loans and the 'balance of payments crisis', at a time when agricultural production and the supply of agricultural inputs were declining and world food prices were rising sharply (S. Moyo 2011).

Between 2003 and 2008, the state pursued heterodox economic plans (NEDPP 2006), intervening in trade and domestic markets, and rationing foreign-exchange use. Farming increasingly depended on government finance and credit, although the state's capacity to fund this was limited. The GoZ cajoled the remaining foreign and public agro-industrial estates to expand food and agro-fuel production, by 'allowing' them to retain their land, while incorporating black outgrowers around them. From 2005, contract farming was encouraged through new initiatives for the retention of export earnings. This shored up agricultural production to a limited degree and encouraged foreign investments in agricultural markets, especially involving Chinese, Indonesian, and Indian merchants (S. Moyo 2011). By 2007, the state was courting new foreign 'investors' and domestic capital, towards financing production on state-owned farming estates. However, at the height of hyperinflation in 2008, the currency, trade, and agricultural markets were liberalised to enhance imports and selectively attract foreign investment in agriculture and mining.

The retention of large-scale foreign-owned agro-industrial estates was resisted by many landless people and some elites who aspired to gain land. They lobbied the state to subdivide some of the estates for redistribution (S. Moyo 2011). Between 2000 and 2002, a large hectarage of the state-owned estates and parks had been 'illegally settled' (Utete 2003). While the GoZ discouraged popular 'illegal settlements', it did expropriate some of the private plantations and state-owned farms which faced such occupations, and redistributed them (S. Moyo 2011). In this context, foreign land grabbing was a rather contained affair, thwarted by radical redistributive policies and popular resistances, with the retained agro-industrial estates being subjected to an evolving Indigenisation Policy. This led some black elites to turn towards demanding the shareholdings of unexpropriated conservancies, at the expense of landless people.

The Indigenisation Policy escalated beyond agriculture in 2006, moving first towards the mining sector. Indigenisation has always been a multi-class strategy, whose class character oscillated as the correlation of forces changed (Moyo and Yeros 2011, 2013). In the late 1980s, it shifted from a popular land reform policy towards the creation of a black agrarian bourgeoisie with limited success. After implementation of the FTLRP, Indigenisation re-emerged as a bourgeois strategy geared towards creating majority shareholding amongst black capitalists. Since 2009, the policy envisioned joint ventures between state-owned enterprises and foreign firms, as reflected not only in the support for state-owned agro-estates and joint ventures in mining, but also in the provision of some shares to community trusts and employees.

The redistributive character of the Indigenisation Policy with regards to minerals and natural resources, unlike the redistribution of agricultural land which was eventually settled through mass physical land occupations, tended to remain abstract and led by the bureaucracy. Less clear has been the accumulation model that has informed the Indigenisation of mining, especially with regards to state capital formation and accumulation by domestic elites and smaller enterprises. The policy on the share equity to be held by Zimbabwean investors was driven by diverse views and competing class, racial and party political interests. Many feared that a dominant clique of ZANU-PF cadres would get them.

This ultimately created pressure by some on the state to retain 51%, instead of a few black individuals gaining such access. Others sought to increase the community shares to more than 20%, although this was challenged as excluding citizens outside those areas. By 2010, however, the state was proposing that five percent of the shares of foreign-owned firms be allocated to employees and another 10% to local community trusts in their area, while the remaining 36% of shares (to make up the majority share of 51%) was to be allocated to black domestic entrepreneurs. Most critically, the Indigenisation Policy lacked an organised social force—such as the peasants and war veterans who had mobilised during the FTLRP—to steer its redistributive character and the confrontation with capital, while facing opposition by the MDC and sections of civil society. Such agency gradually emerged but remained scattered (to be discussed further below).

Land and Resource Control by Capital from the West

Before the FTLRP, most large private estates were owned by South African-based transnational corporations such as Triangle Sugar Corporation and Hippo Valley (Sugar) Estate (EU 2007), and European and domestic white capital (such as Meikles, Tanganda Tea, Liebig's, Mazoe Estates and Ariston Holdings). Domestic agribusiness conglomerates and estates included pioneer white family owners, some of which held mining exploitation licenses.[1] The sugar estates had created white large-scale outgrower farmers called Independent Commercial Growers (ICGs), largely through Mauritian and South African immigrants, with average landholdings of 217 ha (EU 2007). Around 1971, Mkwasine Estate, owned by Triangle and Hippo Valley estates, created black sugar outgrowers with 10 ha. The tea estates had also created about 1,000 white and black outgrowers (USAID 2010).

Adding the settlers of British origin and European investors, Zimbabwe's prime lands, including water, natural resources and minerals were largely controlled by the West. Although the European landed investments were significant, their scale was much smaller than those of the British citizens, and they were widely differentiated by country and size. Out of 267 farms owned by persons from 13 European countries, 65% were owned by persons from European countries, while a few (two percent) were owned by Americans. In area terms, Europeans collectively held 70% of the total foreign-owned farms.[2] Three other countries from the South (South Africa, Mauritius and Indonesia) held 33% of the farms, corresponding to 27% of the hectarage. About 20% of the foreign-owned farms ranged in size from 2,000 to over 50,000 ha, although 70 of the farms (25%) were below 300 ha. This foreign ownership still predominates in the remaining plantation sector, including agro-industrial estates and conservancies.

Moreover, by 1999 numerous large farmers created seven wildlife conservancies on over 900,000 ha in the drier Lowveld region, and these involved white settlers and European partnerships (Moyo 2000; GoZ 2009b). In the early 1990s, the industrial forest plantations (owned by the state and private capital) covered about 110,000 ha, with 16 private forestry plantations holding about 70,000 ha, owned largely by foreign companies, such as Border Timbers, Mutare Pulp and Paper Mills, and Allied Timbers (Bradley and McNamara 1993). Over 100 timber outgrowers existed by 1999 (FAO 2001). Most of these agricultural and timber estates were connected to British and South African capital, while German interests were in the tourism sector.

This transnational land concentration escalated during the 1990s, with black elites as junior partners (Moyo 1999). Additionally, by 1999, over 250 large farms and estates were under the protection of BIPPAs. Thus, about half a million hectares amounting to three percent of the large farming area and one percent of the

---

[1]Notable are the Oppenheimer, Nicolle, Moxon and Charter Estates' families.

[2]The main countries of origins were Germany (45 farms), the Netherlands (39), Switzerland (28) and Italy (26).

agricultural land were foreign-owned. It is notable that this extent of foreign ownership in an individual country is larger than the scale of foreign land grabbing that is underway in most African countries without a settler-colonial history (see also GRAIN 2009). Furthermore, most of the foreign investments in Zimbabwe's agriculture, finance, mining and tourism, as well as in the few archaic import-substituting industries which survived de-industrialisation after structural adjustment (such as in agro-processing, agro-chemicals and farm machinery and equipment), and some in retail, were owned by Western capital, with limited indigenous participation in ownership. Official backing for these Western investments, through licensing protection and supportive state investments, as in infrastructure, was largely a pre-Independence state-led affair, and was built upon waves of migrant European networks after World War II. But state-backing to Western investments, through BIPPAs covering land and mining was also enhanced during the early 1990s.

The FTLRP significantly reduced the scale of the 'British-owned' estates in the Mashonaland, Matabeleland and Manicaland provinces, including white family-owned estates involved in the production of tobacco, livestock, wheat, and grain (such as Charter Estates, Ariston Holdings and Nicolle Brothers in Mashonaland). The Oppenheimer' estate in Matabeleland South was, however, subdivided and only partially redistributed. The Triangle and Hippo Valley sugar estates dominated by South African capital were mostly retained, although Mkwasine Estate lost all of its core estate of 16,643 ha, of which 9,000 ha were allocated to A2 cane growers, with average plots of 30 ha, and the remainder to A1 farmers. The tea estates in Manicaland lost over 50% of their area, although over 1,000 black outgrowers were already being promoted by Tanganda Tea Estates. Smaller sections of the forest plantations were expropriated and about 113 private and state plantations covering over 80,000 ha were retained.

The white outgrower farms in the Hippo Valley estates in Masvingo, mainly of Mauritian and South African origin, also had most of their land transferred to many more smaller sized black outgrowers. By 2010, the 47 white estate outgrowers had been replaced by over 239 black outgrowers through an A2 sugarcane scheme, with an average plot size of 29 ha each, while only one white outgrower with 61 ha remained by 2010. Altogether, there were now 560 black sugar outgrowers with average plot sizes ranging from 10 to 30 ha. A new black sugarcane outgrowers union had emerged in Chiredzi by 2006, as race-based struggles between new black and former white sugar outgrowers escalated, and outgrowers contested the EU aid policy and the methodology of the proposed by EU-funded National Sugar Adaptation Strategy intended to re-develop the sugar industry.

A number of British and South African multinational firms, such as Anglo-American Corporation, Lonrho, ZIMASCO, found most of their underutilised lands being expropriated, although the productive parts of the plantations (such as sugar and perennial crops) remained untouched. Many of these firms entered into direct negotiations with the GoZ to save their farms, while some offered land in exchange for saving their core production estates. Anglo-American Corporation, for instance, made an offer of approximately 30,000 ha in Insiza district to the GoZ's FTLRP and created a trust fund to finance the settlers' farming activities over time. Similarly, approximately 800 white large farmers had offered some of their lands in return for remaining on subdivided portions of the land or smaller sized single farms, and about 400 of them remained.

Since the BIPPA protection did not include the 3,000 farms which were owned by British nationals, most of whom retained dual citizenship, their claims against expropriation could not be pursued in external courts. However, it was felt that the 'property rights' of an estimated 15,000 and 30,000 (Hansard, House of Lords 1998) British citizens among the white persons living in Zimbabwe, were under threat.[3] This meant that while the UK had an explicit interest to protect its citizens' rights in general, as well as their land rights, it could not do so without conceding to its colonial responsibility, such that no formal attempt was made to stop the expropriation of land of UK citizens.

However, most of the European-owned farms under BIPPAs had become subject to expropriation from 1997. While all the Western nations engaged in diplomatic efforts to stop the expropriation of their citizens' lands, invoking the BIPPAs signed after Independence, as well as the need to harmonise EU–Zimbabwe economic and trade relations, such as through the Lomé Convention, in public they criticised Zimbabwe's 'governance' and 'human rights' practices and its method of land acquisition. Since many of the European farms facing expropriation were already occupied by land reform beneficiaries, and the GoZ only recognised 153 of the so-called BIPPA farms covering some 200,000 ha and belonging to nationals from Denmark, Germany, Italy, Netherlands and Switzerland, most of them were expropriated. Not surprisingly, the European Union became obsessed with defending the basic 'principles of foreign investment', (foreign) property rights and the 'rule of law' within Zimbabwe, although a few European diplomats (such as the French and Spanish) sought exemptions from land expropriation for their citizens' farms by dissociating themselves from the regime-change agenda.

When the 2005/6 Constitutional Amendment closed the doors to national litigation on land expropriation, 13 Dutch farmers took their BIPPA farms case to the International Centre for Settlement of Investment Disputes (ICSID) for arbitration. The ruling in their favour required that each farmer be compensated at an average of one million US Dollars, although, by 2012, this had not yet been paid. This exposed Zimbabwe to the potential forfeiture of state property in other territories, and set a high benchmark for the valuation of expropriated farms, suggesting that it would require about USD 4 billion to compensate 4,000 farms. Nonetheless, even an informal British parliamentary grouping (AAPPG 2009) found such compensation valuations to be unaffordable and unsustainable for Zimbabwe or the donors, while shielding the UK from responsibility to compensate, and argued that it would be a misuse of funds, which ought to focus on development and poverty reduction.

---

[3]Dual citizenship was abolished by the GoZ in the 1990s, and in 2001 the law was further tightened to restrict the rights of dual citizens by forcing them in law to choose their citizenship of preference. This mainly had implications for voting, passports and residency.

These events further polarised Zimbabwean politics and fueled the radicalisation of its indigenisation and foreign policies.

White Zimbabwe Farmers Scramble for Agricultural Land and Markets in the Region

Another strategy of isolating Zimbabwe by Western capital was to export white farmers and merchants to the SADC region. It was namely thought that large-scale farming could be easily replicated. Already from 1994, some large-scale white farmers in South Africa, anticipating an uncertain future under black majority rule, had begun to relocate to Mozambique, Zambia and the DRC. New partnerships between white Zimbabwean farmers whose land was now repossessed were now formed with foreign capital and key donor agencies towards the establishment of large-scale farmers by foreigners in the region. Indeed, a major impact of Zimbabwe's FTLRP has been the relocation of large-scale white farmers to various countries in the region, including to Mozambique, Zambia and Tanzania, and even as far as Nigeria, the Congo, DRC and Uganda. This relocation of about 400 white farmers appears to have been facilitated by both domestic and international forces, promoting the use of existing skills among white farmer through allocations of cheap land leaseholds, subsidised operating and investment capital, domestic credit and the exploitation of cheap labour.

In Zimbabwe, the relocations were promoted by both Commercial Farmers Union (CFU), representing the white farmers, and business firms, and also facilitated by some black business interests involving war veterans and some leaders in government (*Sunday Mirror*, 22 June 2003). The white farmers were reported to have left the country with some of their large tractors, combine harvesters, irrigation equipment and other implements, as well as with some of their skilled farm labourers. Domestic support to this relocation, through machinery export permits and secure storage facilities, was often accompanied by the payment of 'protection fees' by some white farmers with huge landed interests in Zimbabwe, to some officials, while some black 'fronts' kept some of their investments in large farms. New commercial farming partnerships involving black businesses and white farmers, or foreign firms, began to emerge. Essentially, there was substantial domestic and external collaboration in an effort to reproduce and ensure the survival of large-scale commercial farming and its ties to monopoly capital in the SADC region.

This regime-change campaign, coordinated among Western donors and NGOs in Zimbabwe and South Africa, only elicited an escalation of Zimbabwe's land expropriations among the remaining white farmers, until 2012. In fact, the implementation of the Indigenisation Policy alongside the mining reforms began with the South Africa-connected ZIMPLATS platinum mine, which was pressured in 2007 to release 30% of its underutilised mining concession. A Look East Policy was beginning to mature and big Chinese investments started trickling in.

The Look East Policy and Investments in Zimbabwe from the East and South

Radical Nationalism and the New Investments

When the Look East Policy was formally adopted in 2003–04, there were expectations and unsubstantiated allegations that Chinese investments in Zimbabwe had grown substantially to the extent of surpassing those of the West. Zimbabwe's foreign investment context was becoming more uncertain and less inclined to Western capital as the external confrontation grew, while demands for implementation of the Indigenisation Policy against foreign investment grew from 2005.

However, from 2007 Zimbabwe did cautiously open up to investments from the East and South, but mainly on the basis of shared equity holding in selected mining and industrial investments, as well as through concessional loans and partnerships in infrastructural development. Faced with hyperinflation, a balance of payments crisis and a political stalemate in 2009, the GoZ re-liberalised the economy through the policy of 'dollarisation', the reduction of trade barriers, and reduced intervention in agricultural and capital markets, initiating a re-insertion of foreign capital more broadly into the agrarian markets. Formal cross-border trade increased the imports of foods, beverages, and farm inputs, with South African capital gaining the most from this. Local agricultural products soon faced stiff competition from cheaper, GMO and duty-free, imports from South Africa, Brasil, China, and the West, leading to domestic demands for renewed protection. After two years of good rainfall, the production of maize, cotton, small grains, and tobacco was again on the rise, while wheat and oilseeds outputs remained in substantial deficits, leading to sustained food imports (MoF 2010; RBZ 2011). However, the recovery of agriculture remained constrained by the limited access by farmers to private credit, ostensibly due to the low levels of liquidity, but certainly due to the high interest rates charged as a consequence of limited external loans.

Yet foreign-owned estates, such as the South African-owned sugar firm Tongaat Hullet, were gradually enabled by the liberalisation policy to reinvest and borrow locally. A new but limited wave of foreign investments trickled in, largely in mining and retail from South African capital, in the state-owned Iron–Steel enterprise (New ZimSteel) by an Indian firm (Essar) registered in Mauritius, and in mining and infrastructure construction from China. But these were largely based on 50% partnerships derived from the 2007 Indigenisation Policy, while pre-existing foreign investments were more vigorously being compelled to cede 51% of their shares to domestic actors.

Landed Interests from the East: China's Rise?

Investment and trade relations between China and Zimbabwe were low between 1980 and 1996, including when structural adjustment was adopted. Economic relations started to grow when Western capital flight and the sanctions were at their peak, and especially in 2006–11 when the Look East Policy took operational effect and the wider global scramble for resources escalated. Yet, claims that large-scale land grabbing by the Chinese, Libyans, and other foreign nationals from the South has been growing has obtained little empirical evidence.

Chinese investments in Zimbabwe can be classified sectorally, ranging from the more socially oriented early investments (such as the Sports Stadium in the 1980s and Chinhoyi Hospital in the 1990s), to military exchange and cooperation (Defence College), private commercial relations, and the large state-backed investments projects in mining, infrastructure (roads, airports) and energy (coal, gas). Chinese investments have been more notable in the contracting and buying of tobacco and cotton, and in a few construction projects, especially road and airport runway expansion (as elaborated below). Since 2007, Chinese deals in the mining, diamonds and energy sector began to come to fruition. Moreover, China investments can be differentiated between those that are officially negotiated, protected and relatively large scale and those that are private individual arrangements focused on commerce and other businesses on a Small and Medium Enterprise (SME) basis, now involving an estimated 5,000–10,000 Chinese migrants.

Between 2000 and 2004, the Cement Plant by Sino-Zim was the key investment concluded. However, individual small and medium Chinese investments, particularly in commerce/trading and small manufacturing, escalated gradually from 2003. Government and/or bilateral agreements grew, as Chinese investments initially expanded in agriculture from 2005 and moved towards mining in 2007. By 2006/7, officially backed Chinese investors were also discussing with the GoZ the prospect of investments in farming, mainly around two ARDA farms, but this did not take off. In all, by 2010, there were over 80 Chinese firms registered with the Zimbabwe Investment Authority (ZIA). Additionally, from 2000 onwards, and in response to sanctions, Zimbabwe purchased arms only from non-Western countries, especially China, Ukraine, and Libya. In the period of 1980–1999, China already accounted for 35% of Zimbabwean imports of major conventional weapons, followed by the UK (26%), Brazil (11%), Italy (9%) and Spain (8%). In 2000–09, China accounted for 39%, followed by Ukraine (35%), and Libya (27%) (SIPRI 2011).

The bilateral trade between China and Zimbabwe grew in other sectors as well, but has remained well below Western trade. Exports to China increased from USD 100 million in 2000 to a peak of USD 167 million in 2003, before declining to about USD 158 million in 2005. These exports mainly constituted unprocessed tobacco and minerals. Imports also rose from about USD 30 million in 2000 to about USD 130 million in 2005, comprising textiles, fertilisers and small machines (motors, generators, etc.), which priced at 75% lower than other traditional markets, in Europe and the United States. Such trade grew from August 2006, when the GoZ received a USD 200 million Buyer's Credit Loan Facility from the Government of China for the procurement of agriculture inputs (fertilisers, agro-chemicals, agriculture equipment and tools, irrigation and other equipment) and animal health products (AFRODAD 2008). While this load facility was meant to boost agricultural productivity in support of the land reform programme, China also ventured into direct agricultural ventures, initially as a commodity buyer, on auctions, and then as an investor in contract farming for tobacco and its exportation. But even there, until 2011, China was second to the overall role of Western capital in tobacco.

From 2006, a new surge of formal bilateral negotiations led by the Ministry of Foreign Affairs (MFA) under the Bilateral Joint China–Zimbabwe Commission sought to broaden and increase Chinese investments, marking the operationalisation of official cooperation and investment protection under the Look East Policy. By 2011, up to 20 projects covering mining, trade, finance, industries and energy were being negotiated. Key among these large-scale investments was the purchase of ZIMASCO by Sinosteel Corporation of China. Despite having received all approvals by the Reserve Bank of Zimbabwe (RBZ), this deal reportedly created tensions within ZANU-PF, for it was not in good line with the Indigenisation Policy preference, since Sinosteel Corporation held the majority shareholding of 86.3%, with the balance of 13.7% being owned by China–Africa Development Fund. During 2012, negotiations were underway for Sinosteel to release 37% of its shares, as was the case with Western firms, indicating the greater degree of autonomy in implementing the Indigenisation Policy.

Other Chinese investments in infrastructure, energy and mining were increasing by 2012. The largest investments were in diamonds, and most involved loans guaranteed by the investments. Also, Sino-hydro was involved in the expansion of Kariba Dam South, investing USD 700 million to generate 300 MW by 2016. Reportedly, Anjin Corporation, consisting in a 50–50 investment with the Zimbabwe Defence Forces (represented by Army personnel as shareholders) had, in 2010–12, invested USD 400 million in one of the four Marange Diamond concessions, employing 1,000 workers, including a certain percent of Chinese, and had remitted up to USD 60 million in royalties, while paying off the capital. The state's dividends were being used to pay for various investment loans (such as the Defence College). Anjin was also investing in two hotels (Mutare and Harare), a supermarket, and large shopping mall in Harare.

Investments from the Wider South

Indian investments in Zimbabwe have a long precedent, dating back to the settlement of numerous Indians in Rhodesia, who came to be recognised as a dominant force in the secondary urban commercial hubs and in some rural areas, establishing a significant community, mainly Gujarat. Records on their investments in Zimbabwe are not available separately. There was a significant shift in economic relations between Zimbabwe and India from 2009, which included the acquisition of a 54% share in ZISCO Steel (now NewZim Steel) by Essar, registered in Mauritius, and investments such as Midex Global and Swat Rough Diamond Sowais India Ltd. (SRDSL) in the mining industry.

Brazilian exports to Zimbabwe emerged mainly from 2006, focusing largely on agricultural inputs (irrigation equipment) and farm machinery (tractors), with state-backed concessional credit from 2011 valued at USD 90 million, in support of efforts to improve agricultural productivity and reduce dependence on rain-fed agriculture. There have also been some food exports (chicken and meat). The only truly large-scale Brazilian investment (USD 600) has entailed cooperation in the supply of technology and machinery for the ethanol plant in Chiredzi, owned by Rating Investments Ltd. and Macdom Investment Ltd.

Other investments from the South have also been noted, albeit to a lesser degree. This has included interests form the Gulf region in Zimbabwe's diamonds, Russian interests in gold, diamonds and platinum, and South Korean interests in biofuel. Other investments have included a handful of farms already owned by Indonesians and Malaysians, these having been acquired in the 1990s under BIPPA protection, plus the 63 farms which had been acquired by white Mauritians around the South African-owned sugar estates long before Independence. It is also notable that, in the 2000s, a few Indonesian firms were seeking farming investment partnerships on state-owned estates to pursue beef exports, as well as a few South Korean private individuals seeking to lease a number of medium-sized farms owned by the black land reform beneficiaries, but these did not materialise.

The Indigenisation Policy Against the New Scramble for Natural Resources and Minerals

The Policy Context of the Resource Scramble

At the turn of the century, Zimbabwe offered a qualitatively hostile ground for foreign investments in natural resources and mineral resources, such that, while many foreign investments in these sectors persisted and a few new investments occurred, Western foreign capital was largely on guard, and increasingly compliant with the GoZ, while also actively in support of the regime-change agenda. There was limited scope by 2007 for land to be openly concessioned to foreign companies, while remaining estates remained under pressure of land occupations (Moyo 2011), and the state was now seeking to stabilise the investment climate in general, and to promote investments in the natural resources and minerals sector.

The 'opening up' of agricultural land enclosures historically created by white and foreign monopoly capital generated greater movement of indigenous Zimbabweans and involvement in trade, wildlife exploitation, small-scale natural resource extractive activities, including substantial small-scale mining activities, particularly in gold. This, in turn, generated a scattered and low-intensity scramble for natural resources and minerals. The popular perception was that the white landowners had been engaged exclusively in these wealth generating activities and that the formerly marginalised were entitled to exploiting these resources.

It became apparent that a much larger social momentum and activism for access to resources, especially the redistribution of rights to mining and resource exploitation, was underway, building upon the experiences of the land occupation movement and the acquiescence of the state to self-provisioning and confrontations with foreign and white capital.

As the increasingly radicalised state felt isolated around 2005, it sought to re-establish 'order', especially by the Murambatsvina forced urban removals of the same year, and to regulate resource extraction, while reformulating the mining, conservancies, and Indigenisation policies. Already the shortage of labour on A2 farms was being blamed on the tendency of former farmworkers and others to pursue non-farm work in gold panning, thus requiring regulation. By 2010, however, the state was now promoting small-scale activities as legitimate and in need of state support.

As the implementation of the Indigenisation Policy was becoming more structured around 2009, the popular agency was relegated to the sidelines. Besides, the media and political opposition vilified the Indigenisation Policy as being driven by the interests of ZANU-PF and corruption. Furthermore, many in the bureaucracy feared that a strategy of nationalising and/or occupying factories and mineral concessions would elicit renewed capital strike and other adverse effects on investments. However, from 2011, Community Share Trusts and Employee-Share Trusts became the only mobilising mechanism, that the state could muster in order to gain concessions from the capital and other domestic opponents. Various associations of indigenous entrepreneur associations were soon being formed, by 2012, demanding an equitable share of the foreign equity to be redistributed, while putting pressure on the state to pursue the Indigenisation Policy in earnest.

Struggles Over Wildlife Conservancies and Forests

The natural resources contained in the large-scale conservancies and agro-industrial landed estates were always sites of fierce land struggles before and after Independence (Murombedzi 1994; Moyana 2002; Hughes 2001), with the contestation going beyond farming land to include water (Hellum and Derman 2004), woodlands (Bradley and McNamara 1993), and wildlife (Wolmer 2003; Wolmer et al. 2004) natural resources. Wildlife was increasingly exploited for tourism by the mid-1990s, having effectively been privatised on white farms from 1975 (Moyo 2000), and it was only later that Government policy (GoZ 2004) proposed to 'indigenise' ownership of forest estates and wildlife conservancies through the redistribution of shareholdings, rather than subdivision. By 2009, most of the conservancies had been occupied by over 20,000 Communal Area families, which resisted government evictions (GoZ 2009a, b). The Public Parks and Forest Lands, including Gonarezhou Park in southeast Zimbabwe, were also occupied (Wolmer 2003; Wolmer et al. 2004).

The state was hesitant to evict illegal occupiers, but would not subdivide the conservancies for redistribution, promising to redistribute shares through the Indigenisation Policy. Disputes arose between the GoZ and various actors over who got the shares. Some of the former owners of the conservancies claimed compensation for the expropriated land and fixed improvements, as well as the wild animals, at market value. State officials argued that the natural resources (including wild animals) on large-scale white farms were public property, and that wild animals would constitute part of the shareholdings of black entrants into the conservancy partnerships with former landholders. By 2011, about half of the conservancies' shareholdings had been allocated to blacks, including some 'belonging' to 'other' provinces, fuelling an intra-elite class struggle over access to shares (J. Moyo 2011, S. Moyo 2011). Meanwhile, some excluded landless people and among the black middle class perceived the retention of conservancies as prioritising animals in a tourist industry dominated by white and foreign operators, to their own disadvantage (S. Moyo 2011).

One of the most highlighted and interesting cases of local level resistance over access to wildlife resources is the case of Save Conservancy, which blew up into a high-level political issue in 2012. The Parks Authority, which had been in charge of allocating the 51% share of the conservancy, had allocated these to 'elite' members of ZANU-PF and securocrats, largely from among Masvingo province, who were seen to represent one of the party's factions, leaving out the local chiefs and their 'communities'. The chiefs mobilised protests locally and among other excluded provincial party leaders, and also took this up in the private media. This fuelled intense debate in Cabinet based on factional fights over succession in ZANU-PF. The ruling party established a committee to review the 51% share of the Parks and Wildlife Authority and ensure that locals benefited from it.

Since German investors held major shares in the Save Conservancy, the German government threatened to step up the sanctions against Zimbabwe, cutting aid. Later, in 2012, when the German Foreign Minister visited Zimbabwe, he offered to fund the translocation of the wild animals to another trans-border park, involving South Africa and Mozambique (Gonarezhou-Kruger Parks). The GoZ retorted by suggesting that the German government consider assistance to promote the livelihoods of neighbouring communities in the existing Save Conservancy (so as to become a state park) and also promote back home the removal of EU sanctions on Zimbabwe.

Similarly, resistance over the control of forests was common. Some of the land of Border Timbers' forest estates (48,000 ha) had been 'pegged' for resettlement by 2001. Soon after, 'exotic' timber-producing companies stopped planting new trees, because the 'illegal land occupations were supported by big politicians' and their land tenure was uncertain (Abu-Basutu 2010). Timber (Sawn) outputs decreased from 374,779 m^3 to about 194,181 m^3 between 1998/99 and 2008/09, with over 90% of this coming from the core estates (Timber Producers Federation 2009). But the Forest-Based Land Reform Policy, adopted in 2004, brought a moratorium to 'illegal' timber estate occupations, and the state's Forest Commission of Zimbabwe

(FCZ) actually evicted the occupiers, who had sought acceptance as formal out-growers, promising to prevent new land invasions.

These struggles over land, forests and wildlife resources were also underlain by competing initiatives to control water resources. Struggles over access to water for irrigation, which the remaining large estates currently dominate, also raised wider regional and institutional questions, beyond the TNC estates and new sugar out-growers (EU 2007). A future scramble for water is expected, and it involves the private sugar estates, outgrowers, and the DTZ and ARDA estates, as well as other new black farmers upstream and downstream of the concerned waters, given their expansionary plans (S. Moyo 2011).

The Scramble for Minerals by Foreign Capital Facing Indigenisation

From 2007, the liberalised economic policy environment fuelled the scramble for Zimbabwe's mineral resources, although the state's radical stance on Indigenous ownership persisted, as did the sanctions and acrimonious relations with the West. Initially, mines owned by Australian, South African, British and former Rhodesians living abroad, were forced to indigenize. The Australian firm BHP had been the first to pull out of Zimbabwe in 1998, by selling its platinum mine in Hartley, now called ZIMPLATS, to a South African firm (Implants) for a pittance, arguing that its geological problems could not be overcome. Some Canadian gold-mining invest-ments in Mutoko were also sold off as the sanctions escalated around 2005. The pressure on these Western mining and agrarian interests, and the latter's public retaliation ostensibly in defence of 'human rights', 'good governance', and the 'rule of law', shaped a series of coordinated punitive international interventions against Zimbabwe. Yet, the sanctions elicited even more radical reforms around the existing mining sector and new investments.

The main new foreign investments in the mining sector since 2007 have been limited mainly to eight minerals, and most of these new investments have involved capital from the East and South Africa. However, existing mineral investments have continued to be dominated by Western capital. By 2010, the mining sector was being more vigorously subjected to inward-looking policies, based on the prior amendments to the Mining Act (2006) and the new Indigenisation Act (2007). Upon the open discovery of diamond deposits in the Marange area in 2007, a struggle ensued over the control of the industry. Initially, it involved small-scale miners competing with a corporate oligarchy of largely Western origin. Then, the state came in, through RBZ, the Minerals Marketing Corporation of Zimbabwe (MMCZ), and the Zimbabwe Mining Development Corporation (ZMDC), seeking to take control over the area. Some government elites soon joined the informal diamond mining process, until 2008, when the state formally took over the entire Marange concession. The strategy on diamonds, and the possibility of circumventing sanctions via diamonds sales, led to a confrontation with foreign capital and small miners, which entailed the repression of the latter. In the event, the West, ostensibly in solidarity with the repressed small miners, resolved to broaden its sanctions tactics by invoking the 'Kimberly Certification Process' with regards to 'blood diamonds'. Then, as Zimbabwe won the certification battle, the United States proceeded unilaterally to impose new sanctions on two mining firms in partnership with the mining parastatals.

Meanwhile, the fact that high-ranking state personnel have been well positioned in the state-owned ZMDC's ventures has undermined the legitimacy of the strategy, while the sanctions policy has also enabled poor transparency. Some 'pro-democracy' forces, have thus become opportunistic in their critique, calling for the nationalisation of black capital, but not Western capital! Yet, the elaboration of the Indigenisation Policy in the wake of popular agitation saw deeper redistribution of majority shareholding from the joint ventures and a higher degree of social access. This compelled foreign firms to invest in physical and social infrastructures such as roads, schools and clinics, and abide by the policy of allocating a 10% share to 'community trusts' and a 5% share to employee trusts. In practice, the state has also gained a larger share of the mining sector, mainly through partnerships involving the ZMDC and the MMCZ.

More recently, since the escalation of factional fighting within ZANU-PF and the forced resignation of President Mugabe, the Indigenisation Policy has again entered a new phase, with a renewed emphasis on liberalisation and the relaxation of conditionalities hitherto placed on foreign investors, with the exception of the diamonds and platinum industries.

Resistance to the Scramble

The Repositioning of State Capital in Joint Ventures

The reconfiguration of national strategy through Fast-Track Land Reform, Indigenisation, and the Look East Policy has created new sources of accumulation. The FTLRP initiated a platform for accumulation 'from below' among peasants, small and medium-scale capitalist farmers, and small-scale miners, as well as through state-owned farms and estates, despite retaining a number of large-scale privately owned agro-industrial estates and wildlife conservancies. The agrarian differentiation that has been emerging has promoted new structural conditions for capital accumulation along competing trajectories, while preserving significant enclaves of foreign-controlled estates, including the new investor and those based on remnants of the colonial land grab. Nonetheless, there have been sustained efforts to reposition state capital through direct control of land resources.

Since 1972, approximately 20% of Zimbabwe's entire land included parks and indigenous forests held by the state (GoZ 2009a, b). By 1999, the state held over 40 large estates, with ARDA holding 18 highly capitalised large estates, producing commodities such as tea, wheat and cotton, while the Cold Storage Commission (CSC) held 110,000 ha for livestock rearing for domestic and foreign markets, and the Forest Commission owned 44,830 ha of forest plantations (S. Moyo 2011). The very existence of state-owned estates was always contested, because it arose from colonial land grabbing, as well perceived corruption and incompetence, the 'negative reputation' of local white investors, and the apparent use by a few black (and white) elites of the CSC's and ARDA's underutilised grazing lands for their private livestocking. With the onset of land occupation, this discontent led to extensive resistance against the state-owned estates. About 4,255 local peasant families went on to occupy DTZ land 'illegally', although this included about 2,000 families that were expected to be displaced by the construction of the Tokwe Mukorsi Dam, intended to supply water to numerous estates.

The FTLRP proceeded to redistribute some of the lands pertaining to state-owned estates. By 2010, ARDA's total hectarage had decreased by 7,150–115,601 ha on 24 estates; the CSC and National Railways of Zimbabwe (NRZ) lost, respectively, about 55,277 and 7,099 ha (or 33 and 57%) of their land; and various local urban and rural authorities also lost land amounting to over 30% of their total (17,222 ha). Estates owned by public trusts were also included in the programme, with DTZ holdings being reduced by some 65,000 ha, leaving it with 300,000 ha. By contrast, security organs (defence, prisons and police) gained over 20,000 ha. Thus, alongside the large-scale privately owned estates retained, among the sugar, tea and timber holdings, and the reconfiguration of outgrower farming, conservancies and forestry, some concentration of agricultural land, water, wildlife and woodlands resources was retained to preserve large-scale, specialised and integrated enterprises, to meet the state's wider development agenda.

Yet, the potential redistributive public benefits from the ARDA estates had, by 2010, not yet materialised, since most of them remained underutilised until 2008, due to various macroeconomic and external constraints. ARDA attempted to expand the area under the production of seeds, wheat and maize, using cheap credit and foreign currency supplied by the RBZ. In 'alliance' with the Nuanetsi Ranch owned by DTZ and Masvingo province ARDA authorities, the GoZ began to clear some DTZ lands for maize production in 2003, through a state-supported contract issued to a Chinese firm. Around 2005, RBZ was contracting locally based food processing and inputs supply agribusinesses (National Foods, INNSCOR, Chemco, Seedco, etc.) to produce seed, wheat and oilseed, but this floundered due to disagreements over product pricing and profit sharing, since agribusinesses invested little of their own cash, but made profits from 'free' state land and financial subsidies (NERC 2006 minutes). The GoZ's attempt to turn around production on ARDA and DTZ estates had not succeeded, as these estates required major repair and construction of the dams and irrigation infrastructure, and the state failed to secure local financing.

Furthermore, Communal Area farmers in Chisumbanje and Chipinge areas of Manicaland alleged that the ARDA sugar plantation was encroaching on their territory and disregarding boundaries, despite protestations from villagers and traditional leaders (Sunday, 30 May 2010), and there was uncertainty over the extent to which peasants in neighbouring villages would gain from the ARDA investments (Moyo and Mujeyi 2010).

The constraints and failures led to a rethink of the land utilisation strategy on hitherto underutilised public estates. The state turned to foreign investments to recover agricultural production on public farming estates, while the export-orientation of the foreign-owned sugar estates was being ramped up, with sugarcane production planned to grow to one million tons per year, based on cropping 30,000 more hectares (on top of the 45,000 ha owned by the estates and outgrowers). To meet Zimbabwe's EU quota and other markets in the context of the Economic Partnership Agreements (EPAs) under the ACP-EU Lomé Convention, the European Commission offered aid towards a National Sugar Adaptation Strategy, which proposed to export 72% of such output. In 2008, 'dollarization' created even more 'incentives' for increased external financing of the foreign estates' sugar export plan, drawing also upon private domestic bank credit and placing greater pressure on scarce national water supplies.

Since 2002, the search for new foreign financing for agriculture had focused on new loans and barter deals. Tentative negotiations ensued on the forward sales of mining concessions, largely to import agricultural inputs and machinery, to expand 'targeted production' (S. Moyo 2011). Foreign investors were by 2004 being encouraged to engage in sub-contractual buying of tobacco and cotton. Substantial From 2006, Chinese state trade credit to import fertiliser, agricultural chemicals, tractors, generators and pumps was realised. From 2007, other foreign investors, including from Russia, Indonesia and Malaysia, were being brokered by white domestic capital to invest in the public estates, with little success until 2011.

By 2009, ARDA had signed a 20-year joint-venture agreement with two private Zimbabwean companies (Rating Investments Ltd. and Macdom Investments Ltd., owned by local whites and blacks), to lease over 50,000 ha of ARDA's Middle Sabi and Chipinge estates, in a Build, Operate and Transfer (BOT) scheme, intended to establish 40,000 ha of sugarcane production and revive the irrigation infrastructure within 8 years, and later to develop 10,000 more hectares (*The Herald*, 15 April 2010). A 2-year rent-free grace period was provided ostensibly to allow the sugarcane to gestate, while some outgrowers were contracted to supply sugarcane. Construction of the USD 600 million sugarcane-to-ethanol distillery plant, with a capacity to produce 35,000–40,000 L per day (Gain 2010) through another foreign investor (Green Fuels Pvt. Limited) was underway. By the end of 2010, over 3,000 new hectares of sugarcane were being reaped for processing at Triangle Ltd. Mills, while ARDA's ethanol processing began in early 2011. No share was provided for the peasants from the adjacent Garahwa Communal Lands, who originally owned the land, while those deemed 'illegal' occupiers of that land were being evicted.

In 2008, the DTZ leased over 140,000 of its land to a joint firm between DTZ and Custa Pvt Ltd., called the Zimbabwe Bio Energy (ZBE) project. Cutsa (Pvt.) Ltd., which is owned by a large white Zimbabwean capitalist (Billy Rautenbach) and foreign investors from Russia and Spain, held 70% of the shares, and had invested USD 15 million. About 100,000 ha were dedicated to sugarcane production towards the production of 500 million L of ethanol per year, while the rest of the land was allocated to increase the cattle stock from 5,000 to 25,000 heads, as well as to increase its 100,000 crocodiles to 300,000 by 2012; over 2,000 workers were being employed by DTZ. This deal led to the non-renewal of the DTZ's grazing leases with black elites and unsuccessful attempts to evict 'illegal' land occupiers, since the central government has pressed the DTZ to allow 263 settlers to retain some land, dissociating itself from dispossessing this constituency.

Unlike the private sugar estates, the government's plan has been to resuscitate and expand ethanol and agro-industrial raw materials production. Triangle Ltd. stopped producing ethanol for the blending of petrol in 1992, but in 2006, the GoZ's National Oil Company of Zimbabwe (NOCZIM) contracted Triangle Ltd. to supply it with 20 million L of ethanol (EU 2007). Thus, in addition to Triangle's Ltd.'s supply of ethanol for industrial, potable and pharmaceutical requirements, and other sugar by-products, such as molasses and bagasse, ingredients for yeast, carbon dioxide, livestock feedstock and fertiliser substitutes from vinesse, the new foreign investments meant to triple these industrial inputs. Sugarcane production for agro-fuel was set to dominate foreign investments in the southeastern region's estate lands, which were expected to produce 90% of Zimbabwe's agro-fuels on over 150,000 ha by 2012.[4]

It is notable that the substantial re-orientation of estate production towards the substitution of domestic transport fuel imports with agro-fuels has run counter to the EU's extroverted strategy. Although the ecological benefits of this are not yet calculated and foreign investment is still relatively low, reducing fuel imports and local agro-industrial capacity and rising agricultural outputs create scope for some national sufficiency.

National Mobilisation for Land, Natural Resources and Mineral Control

The adoption of the Indigenisation Policy and the reality of the emerging opportunities led to a relative increase in the popular mobilisation for broader based redistribution of resources (conservancies and mining) by a wider range of individuals from the petty bourgeoisie as well as through 'Community Trusts', many of which are led by chiefs and urban-based petty bourgeois elements who hail from such areas.

As already noted, before the state had conceded to a policy agenda for popular access to and exploitation of mining resources, 'illegal' and 'informal' mining activities on a small-scale basis had become widespread. Once the Indigenisation Policy regulations were gazetted, and the concept of Community Trusts given legal

---

[4]The National Biodiesel Production Programme promotes agro-fuel production from Jatropha for the remaining annual agro-fuel requirements, on 120,000 ha of small producers' land. 60,000 ha have been planted (interview with E. Mushaka, Noczim 2010).

form, new broad-based movements for access to resources emerged in various localities, such as around platinum in the Mhondoro Ngezi area, the new diamond fields in Marange, and the black granite mining areas of Mutoko. Such movements entailed the creation of Trusts driven by chiefs and their urban-based relatives, usually of middle-class origin. Others were promoted by government and MPs as area-based Trusts. The latter also raised questions about the degree to which local inclusion in sharing the benefits of mining would exclude others from less endowed areas, as well as the adequacy of the national budget.

On the other hand, a range of Indigenisation associations emerged advocating for the access to mining concessions and share equity in mining establishments. This has involved various social categories of people, such as women's and youth associations, as well as sector-specific interest groups (the small-scale miners). Some professional groups, such as engineers, also emerged, seeking to gain access to the procurement contracts of value chain services and technical consultancies.

To be sure, a number of NGOs from the mainly donor-funded 'civil society' stepped up their advocacy for greater 'transparency and accountability' in mineral and natural resource extraction, under the tutelage of the Extractive Resources Initiative (ERI). These appeared less concerned with ensuring greater national ownership of the mineral resources and/or the equitable distribution of shares arising from the proposed transfer of 51% of the mining establishments to indigenous people. The most notable of these was the Zimbabwe Environmental Law Association (ZELA), focusing on the Marange diamonds. Notably, these NGOs have hardly focused their attention on existing Western mining and diamonds ventures, despite their lack of accountability in declaring the value of exports and profits.

In one of the cases of platinum mining related to ZIMPLATS, locally rooted advocacy around the Indigenisation Policy saw a Community Trust demanding greater local access to employment and the shares of procurement contracts for the ZIMPLATS mines, as well as control of the 10% shares to be transferred through the Community Trust. Indigenization discourses and practices became increasingly shaped by local activism to leverage access to local resources, through the agency of chiefs, 'ordinary people', and state agents. As found by AIAS research associates in the Mhondoro Ngezi, where land reform and indigenization discourses were popularised by the Zimbabwean government, local natural resource activism at the South African-owned ZIMPLATS intensified (Mkodzongi 2013). Local chiefs who claim to be the custodians of the land where the mine is located (Interview with chief Benhura 5 June 2010), sought to control a 10% stake for local communities and to control the USD 10 million provided to the newly created Royal Mhondoro Ngezi Trust. This initially led to a conflict between local actors and the state, as gleefully reported in the foreign media, highlighting pitfalls of the Indigenisation Policy. These struggles eventually forced politicians to concede to demands by agreeing that the chairmanship of the trust rotate among all the four chiefs in Mhondoro Ngezi (chiefs Mushava, Benhura, Nyikaand, and Murambwa) on an annual basis.

This demonstrates how local chiefs actively resist state control and forced the state to co-opt them as the legitimate authorities, bypassing influential political elites. Furthermore, local chiefs have directly lobbied mining capital to employ local youths, award some contacts to local suppliers as a way of paying back to local communities, and structure the corporate social responsibility agenda. Pressures from below have thus proved to be critical to the implementation of the Indigenization Policy and have had the effect of strengthening local mobilisation for control over natural resources.

A key implication of these examples of chiefs challenging the political elites to gain access to proceeds of mineral resources and over rural resource administration is that it legitimises the Indigenisation Policy *vis-à-vis* capital. It also demonstrates how the FTLRP strengthened local militancy in general and how this has been carried over to wider resource struggles. Furthermore, it demonstrates how indigenization and local ownership of natural resources have gained some salience in Zimbabwean political discourse and in practice, compelling foreign-owned mining companies to pay much more for the extraction of natural resources, and giving much more to local communities. The Mhondoro Ngezi case study illustrates, finally, how local actors can instrumentalize discourses of indigenization as a way of claiming authority over local resources. Despite claims of corruption and other political challenges with the Indigenisation Policy, it has provided local communities with a platform to challenge unjust resource distribution and environmental injustices associated with mining.

The shift in the minerals policy reflects a response to more general criticisms of class bias to broaden the benefits of indigenisation, as well as the continued need of all the political elites to respond to the reaction by capital in meeting popular demands. Overall, these policies reflect the persistence of a specifically *nationalist* accumulation strategy promoted by black capitalists, with connections to the state, as they remain vulnerable to both monopolistic forces and the need to maintain legitimacy *vis-à-vis* popular forces. In other words, black capital continues to seek to consolidate its position by recourse to a proactive state, against its main obstacle, Western monopoly capital.

Altogether, however, the signing of new contracts in the mining industry with Western, Eastern, or South African firms has been slow. The realities of Zimbabwe's isolation and sanctions, combined with serial droughts and irregular rainfall, has challenged Zimbabwe's heterodox policy over mineral resources control. Moreover, regional partners did not go far enough to provide economic support, limiting Zimbabwe's potential to pursue a fully autonomous policy, to avoid the danger of re-subordination through parasitic international financiers. Since the mining sector continues to be crucial to the earning of foreign exchange and public revenue, and thus to shape development, it requires regulation to ensure that the mines are not sold to the highest briber and that the revenues are reinvested locally, as well as to prevent the corrupt extraction of rents by powerful individuals in and outside government. Ironically, Zimbabwe retains an element of sovereignty by avoiding a wholesale return to the Bretton Woods institutions policy conditions, and has improved the conditions for non-Western capital investments and some domestic capitalists. Nonetheless, the current policy is hardly socially just, as it continues to shut out the poor from the highly iniquitous markets.

Towards a New Policy of Non-alignment and Regionalism

The internal dynamics, including the class character of the indigenisation strategy and the ongoing resistances, will determine the ability of the Zimbabwean state to sustain an inward-looking accumulation process and its legitimacy (Moyo and Yeros 2011, 2013). The foreign policy of the state has, since 2004, been crucial in circumventing Western sanctions and creating external conditions in favour of an inward-looking development strategy. Zimbabwe's radicalisation was accompanied by its Look East Policy, which, in practice, has amounted to a vanguard leadership role proposing a 'positive non-alignment' posture in the post-Cold War period.

External relations heated up again in the late 1990s, soon after the end of apartheid in South Africa, when Zimbabwe not only abandoned structural adjustment in 1996 and initiated extensive compulsory land acquisition in 1997, but also mobilised Angola and Namibia in 1998 to intervene against the US-sponsored invasion of the DRC by Rwanda and Uganda. This initiated a major shift in the correlation of forces in the region and led to a new round of destabilssation and sanctions. The combination of economic isolation and political penetration, as the FTLRP ensued, led to extreme shortages of foreign exchange, production inputs and basic goods, and then to hyperinflation and under-investment in social infrastructure.

Zimbabwe became a laboratory for the combined use of 'soft power', via NGOs and support to opposition parties, and direct economic pressure through sanctions. But it escaped Western military intervention (as in the several cases in North, West, East, and Central Africa) largely because of the new SADC security framework which emerged from 1989 into a mutual defence pact (Moyo and Yeros 2011, 2013). Since 1994, the security context of the SADC region was changing to the detriment of the US geo-strategy (Moyo and Yeros 2011, 2013). Despite the controlled nature of the political transitions, especially in neighbouring South Africa, the new security framework deprived NATO of a staunch ally in Southern Africa, as it previously had, while at the same time the state fracture and war in the DRC shook the main US security pillar in Central Africa, thus unsettling the prior Cold War security arrangements within a span of a few years. Thus, despite Zimbabwe's relative geopolitical insignificance, the re-radicalisation of its liberation movement challenged the controlled character of the transitions to majority rule. The subsequent establishment of the US Africa Command (AFRICOM), whose principal external target is China, reflected the loss of the firm control that the United States enjoyed over the continent.

It is clear that a critical aspect of Zimbabwe's national strategy is the ongoing scramble for natural resources and the systemic transition underway on a world scale. But just as critical is the construction of a strategically and economically autonomous region in Southern Africa. However, SADC regionalism has remained deeply contradictory. On the one hand, the SADC free-trade agreement and its long-term plans to create a common currency rely on market power and a functionalist logic, which reinforces unequal development in the region and harms solidarity. On the other hand, SADC has obtained a mutual defence pact, a rare if not unique achievement in the South, whose strategic posture is based on the principles of equality and solidarity, rather than the functionalist logic of its economic integration project. The West's recent destabilisation campaign put pressure on SADC member-states (particularly South Africa, Botswana, Zambia and Tanzania) to undermine this solidarity, but SADC successfully curtailed the West's direct involvement in Zimbabwe's 2008 political negotiations. SADC member-states realised that they share something very valuable: a common sovereignty regime, conquered collectively by sacrifices and struggles against imperialism; as well as a common security threat in the strategy of the West and NATO, whose objective is the total dismantling of black nationalism and the total defeat of the regional security framework that has proved strategically impervious. Although the engrained contradictions of the region and of nationalism will continue to threaten the advances made, it is also true that Southern Africa has withstood a painful test in Zimbabwe's radicalization and has stood out among other regional integration experiences on the continent.

Conclusion

Substantial areas of large-scale foreign-owned agricultural estates conservancies and mining concessions have been retained in Zimbabwe, despite the extensive fast-track land redistribution process and the Indigenisation Policy. In the context of economic decline and currency shortages, the concessions to capital were justified by the state in terms of a renewed developmentalist strategy. The state gradually stepped up its direct engagement in production and marketing in agriculture, tourism, and mining, while efforts to initiate further local beneficiation of raw materials returned to the agenda. The overall goal was to shore up the state's relative autonomy from the Bretton Woods institutions, to pursue a vision of internal accumulation led by domestic capitalists, and to circumvent sanctions by the West.

The strategy of nurturing a 'national bourgeoisie', along foreign capital, is, however, pitted against popular demands for the further redistribution of land, access to natural resources, and mineral concessions. Provincially based contestations involving chiefs, local political, and business leaders who seek to control sub-national accumulation processes *vis-à-vis* the central state have forced the state to elaborate further the land, mining and indigenisation policies towards a more redistributive stance, including towards increasing state control of resources and participation in the economy. This emerging accumulation outcome, however, continues to be underwritten by exploitative labour relations (Chambati 2011) and unequal trade relations, reinforcing the neoliberal tendency of the Zimbabwean economy, despite the marginal room manoeuvre that state intervention has gained in domestic markets and against foreign capital.

The dynamics of the Indigenisation Policy continues to reflect unequal class, gender, and race relations and ethno-regional cleavages, while playing the East (especially China) against the West in the brokering of foreign investments and resource concessions. Pervasive pressures placed on the state by domestic capital (new black and white capitalists) favour their own strategies of accumulation and become the 'secure' route to foreign investment; however, they provoke wider inter-class and intra-class struggles among blacks over the control of land, minerals, and natural resources, especially in those localities with rich endowments. The ethno-regional character of these competing elites struggles are often instigated by foreign capital. Not surprisingly, the dominant media and NGO discourses continue to be narrowly concerned with transparency and accountability issues around the new investment deals facilitated by the state-owned enterprises rather than on the redistribution of existing large-scale foreign-owned lands and mines, let alone on the strategies to enhance inward-looking development and autonomy from mono-poly capital. In a wider historical perspective, this outcome, despite its contradic-tions, has placed the brakes on foreign-led land and resource grabbing, offering some room to re-negotiate Zimbabwe integration into world markets and providing scope for further popular struggles towards overcoming the legacies of settler colonialism.

References

Abu-Basutu, K. N. (2010). Forestry and the land reform in Zimbabwe: Challenges and the way forward. *SALARN Newsletter, 1*(2), 11.

AFRODAD (2008). *Mapping Chinese development assistance in Africa: An analysis of Angola, Mozambique, Zambia and Zimbabwe*. Harare: AFRODAD.

Amin, S. (1972). Underdevelment and dependence in black Africa: Origins and contemporary forms. *Journal of Modern African Studies, 10*(4), 503–524.

AAPPG [Africa All Party Parliamentary Group] (2009). *Land in Zimbabwe: Past mistakes, future prospects*. London: House of Commons.

Borras, S. M., Jr. (2005). Can redistributive reform be achieved via market-based land transfer schemes? Lessons and evidence from the Philippines. *Journal of Development Studies, 41*(1), 90–134.

Bradley, P. N., & McNamara, K. (Eds.) (1993). *Living with trees: Policies for forestry management in Zimbabwe*. World Bank Technical Paper No. 210. Washington, DC: World Bank.

Chambati, W. (2011). Restructuring of Agrarian Labour Relations after Fast Track Land Reform in Zimbabwe. *Journal of Peasant Studies, 38*(5), 1047–1068.

EU [European Union] (2007, February). *Zimbabwean adaptation strategy to the European union: Sugar regime reform* (Final Report).

FAO [Food and Agriculture Organisation] (2001). *Forestry outgrower schemes: A global overview* (Report based on the work of D. Race and H. Desmond). Forest Plantation Thematic Papers,

Working Paper 11. Forest Resources Development Service, Forest Resources Division. Rome: FAO (unpublished).

GAIN (2010). *Zimbabwe: Sugar annual*. Global Agricultural Information Network (GAIN). Washington, DC: USDA Foreign Agriculture Service.

GoZ [Government of Zimbabwe] (1998a). *Zimbabwe: Programme for economic and social transformation*. Harare: Government Printers.

GoZ [Government of Zimbabwe] (1998b). *The inception phase framework plan of the second phase of land reform and resettlement programme*. Harare: Ministry of Land and Agriculture.

GoZ [Government of Zimbabwe] (2004). *Wildlife-based land reform policy* (revised draft). April 2, 2004.

GoZ [Government of Zimbabwe] (2009a). GPA between the Zimbabwe African National Union-Patriotic Front (ZANU-PF) and the two movement for democratic change (MDC) formations on resolving the challenges facing Zimbabwe, September.

GoZ [Government of Zimbabwe] (2009b, September). *Memorandum to cabinet by the minister of lands and rural resettlement Hon. H. M. Murerwa (M.P) on the update on land reform and resettlement programme*. Ministry Of Lands And Rural Resettlement.

GRAIN (2009, January). Grabbing land for food. In *Grain seedling*.

Hammar, H., Raftopoulos, B., & Jensen, S. (Eds.). (2003). *Zimbabwe's unfinished business: Rethinking land, state and nation in the context of crisis*. Harare: Weaver Press.

Hellum, A., & Derman, B. (2004). Re-negotiating water and land rights in Zimbabwe: Some reflections on legal pluralism, identity and power. In J. Murison, A. Griffiths & K. King (Eds.), *Remaking law in Africa*. Edinburgh: Centre for African Studies, University of Edinburgh.

Hughes, D. M. (2001). Rezoned for business: How eco-tourism unlocked black farmland in eastern Zimbabwe. *Journal of Agrarian Change, 1*(4), 575–599.

Mkodzongi, G. (2013). *Fast Tracking Land Reform and Rural Livelihoods in Mashonaland West Province of Zimbabwe: Opporutnities and Constraints*. PhD Thesis, University of Edinburgh.

MoF [Ministry of Finance] (2010). *Ministry of finance budget speech 2010*. Available from http://www.zimtreasury.org/downloads/834.pdf. Retrieved December 22, 2010.

Moyana, H. V. (2002). *The political economy of land in Zimbabwe*. Gweru: Mambo Press.

Moyo, S. (1995). *The land question in Zimbabwe*. Harare: SAPES Books.

Moyo, S. (1999). The political economy of land acquisition in Zimbabwe, 1990–1999. *Journal of Southern African Studies, 26*(1), 5–28.

Moyo, S. (2000). *Land reform under structural adjustment in Zimbabwe: Land use change in Mashonaland provinces*. Uppsala: Nordiska Afrika Institutet.

Moyo, S. (2008). African land questions, Agrarian transitions and the state: Contradictions of neoliberal land reforms. In *CODESRIA green book series*. Dakar: CODESRIA.

Moyo, J. (2011). Zimbabwe politicians scramble for trusts control. *Mail and Guardian Online*. Available from http://mg.co.za/article/2011-10-24-zim-politicians-scramble-for-trust-control. Retrieved October 2011.

Moyo, S. (2011). Three decades of Agrarian reform in Zimbabwe: Changing Agrarian relations. *Journal of Peasant Studies*.

Moyo, S., & Mujeyi, K. (2010). *Land and bio-fuels industry development in Zimbabwe*. AIAS Monograph. Harare: AIAS.

Moyo, S., & Yeros, P. (2005). The resurgence of rural movements under neoliberalism. In S. Moyo & P. Yeros (Eds.), *Reclaiming the land: The resurgence of rural movements in Africa, Asia and Latin America*. London: Zed Books.

Moyo, S., & Yeros, P. (2007). The radicalised state: Zimbabwe's interrupted revolution. *Review of African Political Economy, 111*, 103–121.

Moyo, S., & Yeros, P. (2009). Zimbabwe ten years on: Results and prospects. Available from http://www.pambazuka.org/en/category/features/54037. Retrieved February 2009.

Moyo, S., & Yeros, P. (2011). After Zimbabwe: State, Nation and Region in Africa. In S. Moyo & P. Yeros (Eds.), *Reclaiming the Nation: The Return of the National Question in Africa, Asia and Latin America* (pp. 78–102). London: Pluto Press.

Moyo, S., & Yeros, P. (2013). The Zimbabwe Model: Radicalisation, Reform and Resistance. In S. Moyo & W. Chambati (Eds.), *Land and Agrarian Reform in Zimbabwe: Beyond White-Settler Capitalism* (pp. 331–357). Dakar: CODESRIA.

Murombedzi, J. (1994). *The dynamics of conflict in environmental management policy in the context of CAMPFIRE* (Ph.D. thesis). Harare: University of Zimbabwe.

NEDPP [National Economic Development Priority Programme] (2006). *A public/private sector partnership*. Prepared by the National Economic Consultative Forum (NECF), Harare.

NERC [National Economic Recovery Council] (2006). National economic recovery council minutes of meeting held on May 8, 2006, Munhumutapa Building, Harare.

Palmer, R. (1977). *Land and racial denomination in Rhodesia*. Heinemann Educational.

RBZ (2011). Reserve Bank of Zimbabwe.

Shivji, I. G., Moyo, S., Ncube, W., & Gunby. D. (1998). *National land policy draft*. A draft discussion paper prepared for the Government of Zimbabwe. Harare: FAO and Ministry of Lands and Agriculture.

SIPRI (2011). *SIPRI Yearbook 2011*. Oxford: Oxford University Press.

Stoneman, C. (Ed.). (1988). *Zimbabwe's prospects: Issues of race, class, state and capital in southern Africa*. London and Basingstoke: Macmillan Publishers Ltd.

Timber Producers Federation (2009). Zimbabwe timber industry statistics for the year ended 31 March 2009.

USAID (2010). *Zimbabwe agricultural sector market study*. Weidemann Associates, Inc.

Utete (2003). *Report of the presidential land review committee*. Under the chairmanship of Dr. Charles M. B. Utete, (Vols. 1 and 2). Main Report to his Excellency The President of The Republic of Zimbabwe. Harare: Presidential Land Review Committee (PLRC).

Wolmer, W. (2003). Transboundary conservation: The politics of ecological integrity in the Great Limpopo Transfrontier Park. *Journal of Southern African Studies, 29*(1), 261–278.

Wolmer, W., Chaumba, J., & Scoones, I. (2004). Wildlife management and land reform in southeastern Zimbabwe: A compatible pairing or a contradiction in terms? *Geoforum, 35*, 87–98.

Yeros, P. (2002). *The political economy of civilization: Peasant-workers in Zimbabwe and the neocolonial world* (PhD thesis). London School of Economics, University of London.

Part IV
Conclusion

Whither Africa in the Global South? Lessons of Bandung and Pan-Africanism

Issa G. Shivji

Africa in the Global South: The Basics[1]

The North–South divide is statistically well documented. I need not repeat it. It is necessary, however, to refresh our knowledge of Africa's geopolitical space in the Global South. The total population of the Global South is roughly 6.2 billion, of which Africa is only one-fifth, or 1.2 billion. The most populous country in Africa, Nigeria, has less population than Brazil. South Africa, one of the partners in BRICS, has only a quarter of the population of Brazil. Just in population alone, leaving aside the size of the economy, Africa as a whole does not reach the size of India or China, the so-called 'locomotives of the South', to use Manmohan Singh's phraseology (quoted in Prashad 2012: 144). But Africa in the Global South, or in the world for that matter, does not speak as Africa, as a Pan-Africa. On the train of the Global South pulled by the locomotives of the South like China, India, and Brazil, individual African countries would be more like cabins, not even wagons. And this, in my view, is true not only in terms of geographical space, but also political and economic space. However, as I would argue, the Global South is not a *political* construct, or at least, not a political construct of the people of the South.

The second point I would like to make is that the Global South exists and makes sense only in relation to the Global North (Amin 2011). The relation between the two has determined the movement of the history of the world over the last five centuries. What constitutes the global whole today? The Global North and the

---

[1]This paper was presented as the Keynote Address to the International Seminar on *The Global South: From Bandung to the XXI Century*, held at the Federal University of ABC, São Paulo, Brazil, 28–30 September 2015.

I. G. Shivji (✉)
Nyerere Resource Centre, Tanzania Commission for Science and Technology,
P.O. Box 953, Dar es Salaam, Tanzania
e-mail: issashivji@gmail.com

© Springer Nature Singapore Pte Ltd. 2019
S. Moyo et al. (eds.), *Reclaiming Africa*, Advances in African Economic,
Social and Political Development, https://doi.org/10.1007/978-981-10-5840-0_12

Global South are linked together in the global capitalist system. What is the motive force of this system? What is it that makes the system tick? A detour into the political economy of global capitalism is, therefore, necessary for us to answer these questions and to understand better and more systematically the trajectories of Pan-Africanism and African Nationalism and its neo-liberal progeny NEPAD, on the one hand, and Bandung and its progeny BRICS, on the other. In the next section, I suggest in a skeleton, and in a somewhat abstract and oversimplified manner, that at the heart of the global capitalist system is the process of worldwide accumulation, or what Amin (1974) in his pioneering work called, 'Accumulation on a World Scale'.

The Global Capitalist System

Capitalism from its birth has been a global system. It continues to be so. The socialist breaches in the system in terms of historical time have been episodic. In Samir Amin's model, the global capitalist system divides into the Centre, roughly the Global North, and the Periphery, roughly the Global South. The heart of the capitalist system is accumulation. 'Accumulate, accumulate!' Marx said, is the 'Moses and the prophets' (Marx 1887: 558). The process of accumulation is worldwide. It is characterized by two tendencies. I call it capitalistic accumulation, CA, and primitive accumulation, or PA. Marx's economic model was based on a closed system of capitalist accumulation. One of the fundamental assumptions of his model of production and reproduction of capital is an equivalent exchange of commodities, including labour power. Appropriation of surplus value by capital created in the very process of production is called exploitation. Exploitation is not stealing or cheating at the level of sale of commodities. In real life, there may be stealing and cheating, but it is not inherent in the system. Exploitation is an appropriation of surplus value that is created in the process of production.

In Marx, primitive accumulation appears as original accumulation to account for the pre-existence of capital before he could work out the production formulae (ibid.: Part VIII). Marx posits two types of primitive accumulation, one internal and another external. The internal refers to the driving out of the peasantry from the countryside to be thrown on the labour market, that is, the enclosure movement. External refers to the looting of ivory, minerals, and slaves from non-European countries, or, what we once called the Third World, and now call the Global South. Marx calls this looting robbery, as distinguished from stealing and cheating.[2] In ordinary language, and even bourgeois law, robbery is distinguished from stealing and cheating by the use of force. Force was inherent and central to the process of primitive accumulation in Marx's sense. In Marx's model of capitalistic accumulation, there is no force involved. But in Marx's model, the process of primitive

---

[2]'The treasures captured outside Europe by undisguised looting, enslavement and murder, floated back to the mother-country and were there turned into capital' (ibid.: 705).

accumulation ceases as the capitalistic accumulation becomes generalized. Primitive accumulation, for Marx, 'forms the pre-historic stage of capital …' (ibid.: 668).

As we know, Luxemburg (1963[1913]) modified Marx and argued that for capitalist accumulation to function and ward off crisis, it has to have non-capitalist sectors on which to feed. Such non-capitalist sectors are found in non-European societies. Using the other tendency of capitalism, concentration and centralization of capital, Lenin (1963[1916]) developed his theory of imperialism. Imperialism invades non-European societies and establishes the rule of the financial oligarchy in which imperialism extracts rent from these societies. In more recent times, Harvey (2005) has revisited Rosa Luxemburg's theory of primitive accumulation to show that in the neo-liberal phase, primitive accumulation resurfaces and takes on different forms, which he calls 'accumulation by dispossession'.[3] Synthesizing these arguments, and developing them further, I argue that throughout its existence, both tendencies, (i.e. capitalistic and primitive) exist side by side in tension. Broadly speaking, hitherto, CA dominated the centres while PA the periphery. Socially, capitalistic accumulation manifests itself in the bourgeois tendency and primitive accumulation in the comprador tendency. From the side of the periphery, we may call the bourgeois tendency *national* bourgeois to distinguish it from the comprador bourgeois. The tension between the two tendencies translates into historically determined social struggles, with class alliances, ruling blocs, and resistances, which allows us to historicise and periodise class struggles.[4]

Extreme forms of primitive accumulation mark the history of the struggles of the Global South, or the periphery. I call them three great robberies. The first great robbery, augmented by the Spanish pirate Christopher Columbus in 1492, is that of the people *of* their lands. In the Americas, the land was robbed from the people by exterminating them, by design or disease. This was the first holocaust in the history of humankind. The second great robbery, augmented by the Portuguese pirate Vasco da Gama in 1498, is that of robbing people *from* their lands. In Africa, people were robbed *from* their lands by being enslaved and shipped *en masse* to work other lands. As history would have it, Brazil found itself at the confluence of these two great robberies, thus boasting today of the biggest African population outside Africa, with an indigenous population reduced to less than half a percent.

The third great robbery is that of people being robbed of their labour. This is central to the colonization process. In the periphery, not only surplus labour is appropriated by capital through the process of capitalistic accumulation, but also the insatiable appetite of monopoly capital usurps a part of necessary labour—that is, labour for survival.[5] This means that the labour power is not exchanged at its

---

[3]One of the problems with Harvey's position is that it abstracts from the relation between imperialist Centres and dominated Peripheries with the potential danger of belittling the national question and, thus its obverse, imperialism.

[4]As Amin (2012) does in broad strokes in his article, 'The South challenges globalization'.

[5]For an example of this in the case of the exploitation of small peasants, see Shivji (1987).

equivalent. I consider the non-equivalent exchange of labour power, which is at the level of production, and not simply at the level of circulation, to be the *defining* characteristic of primitive accumulation in the periphery dominated by monopoly capital. This need not involve the use of force. Primitive accumulation of this type is reproduced by the dominance of monopoly capital both at the level of production and at the level of circulation. It does not matter whether the labour is that of a peasant producer on land, or a craftsman in a workshop, or a proletarian in a factory or a hawker on the street—all labour is pressed to subsidize capital and augment its surplus for further accumulation. In all these cases, primitive accumulation is dominant. Under neo-liberalism, new forms of primitive accumulation are at work based on non-equivalent exchange of labour and on grabbing of resources. The commodification of natural resources, public goods and services; privatization of common and public property, including social wage and public debt; creation and multiplication of *private* money through splitting and splicing of securities—these are the new forms of neo-liberal primitive accumulation which we find both in the Centre and the Periphery. Ultimately, this artificial, intangible economy has to have a base in the real economy in which the primary actor is human labour, whether simple or complex. When the artificial financial economy flies off its anchor in the real economy, you get a crisis of the type the world faced in 2008, resulting in massive destruction of lives and livelihoods of the popular classes. Destruction–construction is another running theme in the narrative of the development of global capitalism (Jha 2006).

It is in the mega-narrative of the development of global capitalism during the last five centuries that we have to locate the Pan-African and Bandung narratives.

Political Milestones in Pan-African and Bandung Trajectories

The Pan-Africanist Trajectory

Pan-Africanism (see generally Soyinka et al. 2016) as an ideology and movement was born in the United States towards the end of the nineteenth and beginning of the twentieth century. Its founders and leading lights were African–Americans and African–Caribbeans like Henry Sylvester Williams, George Padmore, W. E. Du Bois, C. L. R. James, and others (Legum 1965; see also Shivji 2009a). Of course, their conception and perception could only be *African*, because they were snatched from Africa before the continent was sliced into countries by the European imperialist powers at Berlin in 1885. The early Pan-Africanist thought revolved around essentially cultural and racial issues whose main demand was for equality and non-discrimination (Pannikar 1961). This was reflected in the resolutions of various Pan-African congresses before 1945 (Legum 1965: *passim*). The Manifesto of the 1923 Congress, for instance, proclaimed, '[i]n fine, we ask in all the world, that black folk be treated as men' (ibid.: 29).

The turning point was the Second World War. In 1944, some 13 welfare, students', and other organizations based in Britain came together to form the Pan-African Federation, which was to organize the most famous Fifth Pan-African Congress in Manchester, in 1945. The Manchester Congress was most political, with clear demands for independence, and whose rallying cry was 'Africa for Africans'. It was also for the first time attended by young Africans from Africa. Its two organizing secretaries were Kwame Nkrumah from Ghana and Jomo Kenyatta from Kenya. Some 200 delegates attended the Congress; among them were representatives of trade unions, political parties and other organizations. The Pan-Africanist ideology was transformed from a cultural and racial ideology to the ideology of national liberation.

The Manchester resolutions were clearly political, demanding autonomy and independence; sounding warnings that the age-old African patience was wearing out and that 'Africans were unwilling to starve any longer while doing the world's drudgery' (quoted in Legum 1965: 32); condemning and rejecting imperialism while proclaiming in its own language a kind of social democracy. One resolution read: '[w]e condemn the monopoly of capital and the rule of private wealth and industry for private profit alone. We welcome economic democracy as the only real democracy' (ibid.: 155).

The Fifth Pan-Africanist Congress already signaled, in an embryonic form, the idea of African Unity in the following words: '... [t]he artificial divisions and territorial boundaries created by the imperialist Powers are deliberate steps to obstruct the political unity of the West African peoples'. Armed with the Pan-Africanist idea, which rested on two majors pillars, national liberation and Africa unity, Nkrumah returned to Ghana, then the Gold Coast. He organized his people and led them to Ghana's independence in 1957, the first black African country to break off and throw away the shackles of colonialism. This was an earth-shaking event in the annals of the struggle of African people. In the words of that great historian, C. L. R. James, Nkrumah 'led a great revolution' and he 'raised the status of Africa and Africans to a pitch higher than it had ever reached before' (James [1966], in Grimshaw 1992: 356).

Nkrumah passionately pursued his twin objectives of liberation and unity. Between 1958 and 1964, with the help of his friend and mentor George Padmore, Nkrumah organized two sets of conferences: the Conference of Independent African States, and the All Africa People's Conference, pursuing African independence and African unity. Eventually, the conference of African states led to the formation of the Organisation of African Unity (OAU). The OAU charter was a compromise, and as one of the drafters said, 'a far cry from what Nkrumah would have wanted' (Selassie 2016: 131–32). Meanwhile, the All Africa People's Conferences receded to the background and eventually disappeared. Except for the establishment of the liberation committee based in Tanzania, the Pan-Africanist idea on African unity disappeared from the OAU discourse. The new proto-bourgeoisies now in power set to consolidate their states under the ideology of narrow territorial nationalism. Pan-Africanism was drained of its political content and its radical anti-imperialism, which, in the establishment discourse, was reduced to anti-colonialism. African unity became a distant dream to be pursued gradually, rather than a polar star guiding African politics. The gradualist approach to African unity ironically led by another great Pan-Africanist, Julius Nyerere of Tanzania, and Nkrumah's proposal for an immediate African union came to a head in the 1965 Summit of African Heads of State, held in Cairo, in 1965. Nyerere's vitriolic attack on Nkrumah left him a broken man. Nkrumah's militant Pan-Africanism and anti-imperialism cost him his rule. In 1966, he was overthrown in a military coup backed by the Central Intelligence Agency (Shivji 2009b).

For the first 25 years of African independence, the elites in power tried to build their nations, which was essentially a statist project. The political economy of nation-building, whether through the agency of the state or state-aided private bourgeoisies, revolved around domesticating the process of capitalistic accumulation. Imperialist hegemony, however, ensured that whatever national bourgeois elements were born were quickly compradorised, re-imposing primitive accumulation. Even the most radical nationalist elites failed to build popular hegemonic blocks that would spearhead the national project. By the 1980s, when imperialism regained offensive in the form of neo-liberalism, African states were already vulnerable. They quickly capitulated with internal compradors seizing the initiative. Neo-liberalism exposed the limits of the territorial national project. History once again asserted that African nationalism could only be Pan-Africanism.

Pan-Africanism in Africa dies hard. Even compradors have to pay it lip service. Thus was born the African Union (AU). But the AU was born as a neo-liberal project, apparent in its economic programme, the New Partnership for Africa's Development (NEPAD). The North welcomed it. The former Executive Director of the Economic Commission for Africa, Adedeji (2012: 44), in Nyong'o et al. (2012: 35–48) described aptly the partnership between Africa and the North envisaged in NEPAD as a 'feudo-imperial partnership'.

Let me now trace the Bandung trajectory.

The Bandung Trajectory

Twenty-nine nations, five of which were African,[6] some Middle-Eastern and the rest Asian, convened in Bandung, Indonesia, in 18–24 April 1955. The congregation included the most populous Asian nations—People's Republic of China and India—which had attained their self-determination around the same time through different means. The Afro-Asian bloc present at Bandung had just emerged from the colonial phase of imperialism as independent sovereign nations. They were jealous of their political and economic self-determination. Finding themselves in the midst

---

[6]Liberia, Libya, Egypt, Ethiopia and Gold Coast, which at the time had internal self-government and became independent in 1957, as Ghana.

of the bi-polar world divided into military blocs, their only means of survival as sovereign nations was through solidarity among themselves. Amin calls Bandung the first 'Awakening of the South'. I would add 'awakening *and* assertion' of the South on the world stage. In the graphic words of Wright (1956: 12), the great African-American writer who was attending the conference as an observer, this was a meeting of '[t]he despised, the insulted, the hurt, the dispossessed—in short, the underdogs of the human race'.

The Bandung agreement rested on five sets of mutually reinforcing principles (Final Communiqué 1955). Many of them are still relevant and even more pressing in the neo-liberalized world.

1. *Economic, social and cultural co-operation based on mutual interest and respect for national sovereignty.* The accent was particularly on economic co-operation including establishment of joint ventures, national and regional banks and insurance companies, mutual technical assistance, encouragement of inter-regional trade and common policies in matters to do with oil, such as remittances of profits and taxation.
2. *Collective action and unified approach to the stabilization of the prices and demand for primary commodities.* Some countries of the South have graduated to producing and exporting manufactured commodities, but for many African countries, the question of international commodity prices remains a major concern.
3. *Nuclear disarmament and use of nuclear energy for peaceful purposes.* The Conference called for an immediate establishment of the International Atomic Energy Agency. The imperialist countries of the North to this day have retained their monopoly of nuclear arms making exceptions only for their geo-political 'allies', such as Israel and now India.
4. *Independence for remaining colonies and dependent countries.* All those present agreed to struggle together for the freedom of colonised peoples in the councils of the world. In this regard, it is interesting that the Conference declared its support 'of the rights of the Arab people of Palestine and called for the implementation of the United Nations Resolutions' (ibid.: 7). Since then, some leading countries of the South, including India, which was then very strongly against the Zionist state, have broken ranks.
5. *Respect for fundamental human rights generally and in particular the right of nations and peoples to political and economic self-determination.* This was not a blanket endorsement of the Western generated human rights ideology that is characterized by double standards and double-speak. Rather, it was an affirmation of equality of all peoples, races, and nations and made it abundantly clear that the 'rights of peoples and nations to self-determination' includes the right of nations 'freely to choose their own political and economic systems and their own way of life ...' (ibid.: 9). By any standard, this is a powerful statement against the political and ideological hegemony of the North.

The language of the Bandung principles is moralistic, but its content is undoubtedly political and, to an extent, anti-imperialist. The anti-imperialism is that of a proto-national bourgeoisie that had come to power after independence in many Bandung countries. Bandung laid the foundation for the Non-Aligned Movement (NAM) formed in 1961, in Belgrade, Yugoslavia. Notwithstanding its class limitations, Bandung did open space for the maturing of the Third World Project which was preeminently a political project giving voice to the countries of the periphery. In the 1960s and 1970s, non-aligned countries played a vocal role in the UN General Assembly. Responding to the demands and concerns of the developing countries, the UN General Assembly established the United Nations Conference on Trade and Development (UNCTAD). UNCTAD provided both a forum for and a secretariat of the South to investigate and document the unequal international economic relations dominated by the North. Eventually, these analyses resulted in the demand for a New International Economic Order (NIEO). The developed industrialized countries retaliated with the formation of the Group of Seven (G7).

All in all, the movement of the 'Third World' countries set in motion by Bandung exhibited the national bourgeois tendency 'to re-conquer control over the accumulation process' (Amin 2009). Its bourgeois class basis was its limitation. When the crunch came towards the late 1970s and 1980s, when many developing countries found themselves in dire economic crisis, their resistance collapsed. The final nail in the coffin was struck at Cancun in 1981, where the Reagan-Thatcher hegemony triumphed and neo-liberalism was inaugurated in the form of the Washington Consensus. By the time of the 1983 NAM summit, the Third World Project had been effectively defeated by Atlantic powers. The South Project in the form of the South Commission (1987–90), headed by Julius Nyerere of Tanzania, was born in the womb of neo-liberalism. It was not a re-incarnation of NIEO, let alone the Bandung spirit. Its report, *The Challenge to the South*, carried all the birthmarks of neo-liberalism, inviting the label 'Neo-liberalism with Southern Characteristics' (Prashad 2012: 12).

Prashad (2012) gives a fascinating account of the debates within Nyerere's South Commission.[7] There were the doves and the hawks, the integrationists and the auto-centrists. Doves wanted a people-centred development, while the hawks pushed for growth-led, market-oriented development. Hawks were driven by '[b]ureaucratic politics and instrumental economics' (ibid.: 106). Doves wanted a development that would benefit the large majority, even if it did not show up in GDP growth figures. The most vocal spokesperson of the hawks was Sony Ramphal, a veteran who had served on several such commissions. Gamani Corea of Sri Lanka and Abdlatif al-Hamad, a son of a wealthy Kuwaiti family whose politics were rabid anti-nationalist and anti-communist, supported him. The doves were a collective of radical Third World activists, such as Devaki Jain, Marie-Angélique Savané, Ismail Abdalla, and a Cuban, Carlos Rafael Rodriguez. Rodriguez attended only one meeting, although he wrote a hard-hitting note on the final draft pointing

---

[7]The account of the South Commission that follows is based on this source.

out that the Report offered no programme of action for the 'Third World'; the concept of imperialism was missing and terms like the New International Economic Order had been avoided. Sure enough, terms like neo-colonialism and imperialism had been expunged at the insistence of Ramphal. Ramphal considered such terms as 'NIEO type of presentation', which, in his opinion, was outdated. That was the critique he made of the first chapter drafted by Nyerere and his assistant Joan Wicken. Manmohan Singh, the Executive Secretary to the Commission, was an in-between, although leaning more in favour of the hawks. Nyerere played a mediator, resulting in a report that was not only turgid but also disembodied of people's politics.

The Challenge to the South was neither challenging nor exciting, as perhaps Nyerere would have liked it to be.[8] It was certainly not a rallying cry for, much less a call to arms to, the Third World peoples that the Bandung spirit had been. Instead, the Report provided a justification for the 'locomotives of the South' (Manmohan Singh's terminology) to bargain their entry into the G-group under the guise of South–South co-operation which gave birth to BRICS. As neo-liberalism speedily enveloped the Global South in the 1990s, including Nyerere's own country, the Commission's report was forgotten. No one reads or refers to it today.

Bandung and its offspring the 'Third World' were political projects driven by nationalist, albeit bourgeois, social forces. The Global South, and its progeny, BRICS, presents itself as an economic project, innocent of politics, driven by compradorial forces all out to integrate themselves in the G-club. What is BRICS to the Global South, NEPAD is to AU—the neo-liberal outcomes of embattled nationalism.

Neo-Liberalization of Bandung and Pan-Africanism

The end result of the Bandung and Pan-African trajectories is a semi-neo-liberalized Africa and a fully neo-liberalized South, tied to the chariot wheels of the imperialist North. I call this the integrationist path. The path of auto-centric accumulation

---

[8]When Nyerere and Wicken received comments on their draft of the first chapter, Joan Wicken wrote to Manmohan Singh (quoted in Prashad 2012: 117, fn):

> The Chairman, in talking to me said he couldn't put his finger on what it was that was worrying him about the draft now, but somehow has the feeling that the tone has been changed so that it no longer gives leadership, or makes people want to *do* something. He is not sure whether this is still because he doesn't like pretending that there is no neo-colonialism or need for liberation, or whether it is more than leaving out those words. If you could 'beef it up' a bit, and make it more exciting and challenging it would be good. But I don't know whether that is possible while still leaving it acceptable to the 'opposition' [namely, Ramphal and Correa].

offered by the original Bandung and Pan-Africanism has been successfully defeated and subverted, at least for the time being.

In the neo-liberal world, the locomotive and engine of the worldwide capitalist accumulation are located in the North, making nonsense of the so-called 'loco-motives of the South'. If anything, the 'locomotives of the South' are sub-stations pulling the Southern wagons behind them on an onward journey of integration with the North. The surpluses of the South produced by the super-human effort of its working people are sucked into the belly of the *Global Minotaur* servicing the twin deficits of the United States, leaving the people in sub-human conditions.[9] This is primitive accumulation on a global scale.

BRICS and NEPAD are symptomatic of the integrationist path based on hubs and hinterland.[10] Presumably, Brazil would be a Latin American hub, India the South East Asian, and South Africa the African. Brazil's status as the Latin American hub is not uncontested given the ALBA initiative (Bolivarian Alternative for the Peoples of Our America), which has an auto-centric orientation.[11] Whether ALBA can provide a more auto-centric hub is doubtful. The ALBA for-mation is shaky and enfeebled by the day by the concerted and calculated attack from the North, literally and figuratively. China and Russia fall into a category of their own with the potential to provide an alternative centre, or pole, to the North. But this is only a potential. Its actualization can go either way, auto-centric or integrationist. Its development in an auto-centric direction will depend on two conditions. The first condition is the extent to which popular classes are included in their respective ruling blocs on the basis of a genuine social-democratic agenda. The second is the extent to which they are able to resist from being drawn into an arms race. China may well be on the auto-centric path if it is not derailed. Russia, on the other, is quickly losing course. India is firmly on the integrationist path.

Things stand differently for Africa. The continent is marked by two distinct tendencies, external integration and internal disintegration, the social agency being its big and middle compradorial bourgeoisies. The illusion of a 'middle class' Africa is exactly that: an illusion. The three potential hubs—Egypt in North Africa, Nigeria in West Africa, South Africa in Southern, Central and East Africa—are being quickly militarized. Ethiopia, too, is vying for the status of a hub. Its mili-tarization is legendary. They are all bedevilled by their internal social problems, including extreme inequalities and internal conflicts. The dominant tendency is that of primitive accumulation, as the multinational capital of the North plunders and pillages Africa's natural and bio-resources. In spite of the Arab Springs, in the short

---

[9]See, generally, Varoufakis (2015) for the innovative theory of recycling of surplus in the capitalist world.

[10]Whatever the illusions of these locomotives of the South may be, they will only be 'reactors', not 'full actors' in the world economic system, to use Nyerere's phraseology (quoted in Prashad 2012: 166).

[11]ALBA consists of relatively small Latin and Central American countries: Venezuela, Cuba, Bolivia, Nicaragua, Dominica, Antigua and Barbuda, Ecuador and Saint Vincent and the Granadines.

run, alternatives are difficult to discern. Africa's comprador ruling classes, and educated middle class, is so compromised by imperialism, that it is incapable of providing leadership. The only possible alternative bloc is that of the working people made up of popular classes—workers, peasants, small producers, urban and rural poor, the so-called slum-dwellers and informal workers or the 'precariat',[12] small bourgeoisie with nationalist tendencies, and other strata of the rural petty bourgeoisie. They need an ideology, organization and leadership to constitute an alternative political bloc. Can a refurbished Pan-Africanism, integrating the agendas of both national liberation and social emancipation, provide such an ideology?

Lessons of Bandung and Pan-African Spirit

There are five lessons that we can draw from the Bandung and Pan-African spirit to guide the post-neo-liberal phase of the struggles of the peoples and nations of the periphery.

First, both Bandung and Pan-Africanism and their respective derivatives Third World and African nationalism were *political* projects. Economics followed, and was governed by politics, not the other way round. They were ideological rallying points providing vision, hope and dignity to the struggling peoples of the periphery. They were the kind of projects which, to paraphrase Nyerere, would make people want to *do* something.

Second, both Bandung and Pan-Africanism were anti-imperialist in their conception and development. They did not seek accommodation within the imperialist system; rather they sought to provide an alternative to the dominant hegemony. They were in that sense anti-hegemonic, not yet counter-hegemonic.

Third, the Bandung and Pan-African spirit inspired unity and solidarity of the people beyond selective and self-serving 'co-operation' and 'partnership' of the states.

Fourth, as the trajectories of Bandung and Pan-Africanism show, they were led by the bourgeois tendency that sought to install an auto-centric capitalist accumulation within their countries and nations. This proved to be its failure as peoples' projects. The bourgeoisies in Asia and the proto-bourgeoisies—private or state—in Africa were eventually compradorised, thus yielding BRICS and NEPAD—integrationist projects *par excellence*. The auto-centric tendency of accumulation was subverted. *Fifth*, and this is the most important lesson to draw, nations still want liberation and people still want a revolution. The national question in Africa remains unresolved. The agrarian and social questions in much of the periphery remain unresolved. History teaches us that the bourgeoisies in the periphery are incapable of resolving

---

[12]These are casual and unemployed working people who have no guarantee of jobs or livelihood, since much of the proletariat was literally decimated as a result of deindustrialisation dictated by the neo-liberal structural adjustment programmes.

these questions. Their discourses of BRICS and NEPAD and the Global South are, at the end of the day, ideologies of integration with the North, not auto-centric strategies to de-link. They may provide conjunctural spaces for anti-imperialist discourses, but only that and no more. The leadership and the agency of the post-neo-liberal phase of struggle in the periphery have to be reclaimed by the working people[13] and popular classes. What ideologies, organizations and visions would lead such struggles are, of course, concrete questions to be resolved concretely by struggles themselves. Among African intellectuals, at least, there is a resurrection of the ideology of Pan-Africanism, perhaps refurbished to address both the question of national liberation and social emancipation, but definitely anti-imperialist. For the periphery as a whole, we can certainly say that history has once again put back the anti-imperialist and anti-capitalist socialist agenda on the world stage.

History thus beckons the working people and nations of the South to the rendezvous of revolution on the long road to socialism.

References

Adedeji, A. (2012). From the Lagos plan of action to the new partnership for Africa's development and from the final act of Lagos to the constitutive act: Wither Africa? In P. A. Nyong'o, A. Ghirmazion & D. Lamba (Eds.), *NEPAD (New partnership for Africa's development): A new path?* (pp. 35–48). Nairobi: Heinrich Böll Foundation.

Amin, S. (1974). *Accumulation on a world scale: A critique of the theory of underdevelopment* (Vol. 2). New York, NY: Monthly Review Press.

Amin, S. (2009). Beyond Bandung: Awakening of the south. *Pambazuka News, 455*, October 29. http://www.pambazuka.org/governance/beyond-bandung-awakening-south. Retrieved June 26, 2017.

Amin, S. (2011). *Global history: A view from the south.* Dakar: CODESRIA.

Amin, S. (2012). The south challenges globalization. *Pambazuka News*, April 5. https://www.pambazuka.org/global-south/south-challenges-globalization. Retrieved June 26, 2017.

Final Communiqué of the Asian-African Conference (1955). http://www.bandungspirit.org/IMG/pdf/anri-bandung_conference-final_communique.pdf. Retrieved June 26, 2017.

Grimshaw, A. (Ed.). (1992). *The C. L. R. James reader.* Oxford: Blackwell.

Harvey, D. (2005). *A brief history of neoliberalism.* Oxford: Oxford University Press.

Jha, P. S. (2006). *The twilight of the nation state: Globalisation, chaos and war.* New Delhi: Vistaar Publications.

Legum, C. (1965). *Pan-Africanism: A short political guide* (revised edition). London: Pall Mall Press.

Lenin, V. I. (1963[1916]). Imperialism: The highest stage of capitalism. In V. I. Lenin (Ed.), *Selected works* (Vol. 1, pp. 667–766). Moscow: Progress Publishers.

Luxemburg, R. (1963[1913]). *The accumulation of capital.* London: Routledge.

---

[13]I develop my position on why I consider 'working people' as the agency of the next phase of revolutionary struggles in my 2009 lecture, https://soundcloud.com/issashivji/shivji-keynote-speech-accumulation-and-neo-liberalism, accessed 26 June 2017.

Marx, K. (1887). *Capital: A critical analysis of capitalist production* (Vol. 1). Moscow: Progress Publishers.

Nyong'o, P. A., Ghirmazion, A., & Lamba, D. (Eds.) (2012). *NEPAD (new partnership for Africa's development): A new path?* Nairobi: Heinrich Böll Foundation.

Pannikar, K. M. (1961). *Revolution in Africa.* Bombay: Asia Publishing House.

Prashad, V. (2012). *The poorer nations: A possible history of the global south.* London: Verso.

Selassie, B. H. (2016). From colonial borders to African unity. In W. Soyinka, S. A. Amin, B. H. Selassie, M. G. Mũgo & T. Mkandawire (Eds.), *Re-imagining Pan-Africanism: Distinguished Mwalimu Nyerere lecture series, 2009–13* (pp. 113–160). Dar es Salaam: Mkuki na Nyota.

Shivji, I. G. (1987). The roots of agrarian crisis in Tanzania: A theoretical perspective. *Eastern Africa Social Science Review, 3*(1), 111–134.

Shivji, I. G. (2009a). Pan-Africanism or imperialism? Unity and struggle towards a new democratic Africa. In I. G. Shivji, *Where is Uhuru? Reflections on the struggle for democracy in Africa,* G. R. Murunga (Ed.). London: Fahamu Books.

Shivji, I. G. (2009b). Pan-Africanism in Mwalimu Nyerere's thought. *Chemchemi, 1.*

Soyinka, W., Amin, S. A., Selassie, B. H., Mũgo, M. G., & Mkandawire, T. (2016). *Re-imagining Pan-Africanism: Distinguished Mwalimu Nyerere lecture series, 2009–13.* Dar es Salaam: Mkuki na Nyota.

Varoufakis, Y. (2015[2011]). *The global Minotaur: America, Europe and the future of the global economy.* London: Zed Press.

Wright, R. (1956). *The color curtain: Report on the Bandung conference.* Jackson, MS: Banner Books.